South Africa in Africa

To my mother
and to the memory of my father
nawo onke ama-Afrika amahle

South Africa in Africa

A study in ideology and foreign policy

Sam C. Nolutshungu

AFRICANA PUBLISHING COMPANY

A Division of Holmes & Meier Publishers Inc
New York

© 1975 Sam C. Nolutshungu

Published in the United States of America 1975
by Africana Publishing Co.
A Division of Holmes & Meier Publishers Inc
101 Fifth Avenue
New York, N.Y. 10003

Library of Congress Cataloging in Publication Data

Nolutshungu, Sam C.
  South Africa in Africa

  Bibliography: p.
  Includes index.
  1. Africa, South—Foreign relations. 2. Africa,
South—Politics and government, 1948– . I. Title.
DT779.7.N64   327.68'06   74–31011
US ISBN 0 8419 0194 5

Printed in Great Britain

Contents

Tables and maps

Preface

This book gives an account of South Africa's policies towards the rest of the African continent in the period since the second world war, which, with the aid of relevant theoretical writings in international relations and associated studies, it attempts to explain and interpret.

The work for the thesis on which the book is based was commenced in September 1969 and completed in March 1972. The thesis was examined at Manchester in May of the same year. A paper, which was a study for the first part of the work, was read in January 1971 to the Societies of Southern Africa seminar at the University of London Institute of Commonwealth Studies; members of that group made valuable comments which helped in the shaping of the larger study. The revision of the thesis during June–August 1973, prior to going to press, was restricted solely to questions of style and to incorporating material covering the period since 1971 and archival material which was previously not accessible.

In the nature of things, any contemporary study of South African politics, external as well as domestic, is bound to reflect the attitude of its author towards *apartheid*. However, it has not been the aim merely to traduce the white South African State, to pass judgements, or even to vindicate the inevitable preconceptions with which the book was undertaken. Rather, while not claiming ethical and intellectual neutrality, the book does aim to ensure that its findings, however contentious (both in themselves and in their implications for action), are open conclusions, openly arrived at.

The disadvantages of contemporaneity have also been felt in the singular absence of archival materials. Reliance had to be placed on publicly available sources, primary and secondary. Much use has, accordingly, been made of published State papers—parliamentary debates, commission reports, policy statements, United Nations documents—and such sources as *Keesing's Contemporary Archives*, *Africa Research Bulletin* and a wide variety of South African (Afrikaans and English), British and African newspapers. Use has also been made of the BBC *Summary of World Broadcasts*. Memoirs and biographies of politicians, in spite of discretion and official secrecy, have provided useful insights into the thinking of policy-makers. Although it was not possible to interview any South African policy-makers, several persons from other countries who possessed information relevant to South African policy were confidentially interviewed, some formally, others by way of conversation and discussion. A few of the interviews were conducted in England, but most were undertaken during a four-month visit to parts of eastern and southern Africa. While confidentiality precludes mention of some of those interviewed, I am glad to be able to state my profound debt to the following persons. In Kenya, Mr John Gatu, Secretary General, Presbyterian Church of East Africa; Dr I. Makonnen, Advisor, Ministry of Tourism. In Tanzania, Mr O. Adesola, Asst. Executive and Financial Secretary of the O.A.U. Liberation Committee; Dr Agostinho Neto, MPLA; Mr J. Chisano, Frelimo; Mr M. Piliso, ANC of South Africa. In Zambia, Mr W. P. Nyirenda, MP, Minister of Education; Mr A. Nzo, Secretary General, ANC of South Africa; Mr B. Kabwe, Secretary General, Zambian Congress of Trades Unions; Dr I. De Beer, Director, Anglo-American Ltd, Zambia. In Botswana, Dr Q. Masire, MP, Vice-president, Finance Minister; Mr D. Kwelagobe, MP, Minister of Trade and Industry; Mr F. Mogae, Director of Economic Affairs; Mr M. Mpho, MP, leader of the Botswana Independent Party; Mr P. Matante, MP. leader of the Botswana People's Party; ex-Chief Bathoen Gaseitsiwe, MP, leader of the Botswana National Front; Mr D. MacCrum, Director, De Beers, Botswana. In the UK, General Sir William Oliver, formerly Vice-Chief of the Imperial General Staff; Lord Selkirk; Lord Mancroft; Peter Katjavivi, representative of SWAPO; Colin Legum.

Many other people have given me valuable help during the preparation of this book. It is not possible to mention them all by name. I do, however, owe a very particular debt of gratitude to Dennis Austin, who supervised the research on which the book is based, and to the following persons: Bill Tordoff, Ralph Young, Morris Szeftel, Rob Molteno, Motseta Mosoabi, Gunther Adolphsen, Gideon Mutiso, David Martin, Mandla Tshabalala, Victor Hunt, Randolph Vigne, Leloba Young, Eve Hall, Ruth Weiss, Merle Lipton, Cherry Gertzel, Vellie Simela, and the Hayter Committee of the University of Manchester and the UN Southern African Refugee Fund. This book is, however, my own, and I alone bear full responsibility for all its faults.

University of Lancaster, 1974   S.C.N.

Abbreviations used in the text

ANC	African National Congress of South Africa
A.R.B.	*African Research Bulletin*
Ass. Deb.	*Union (later, Republic) of South Africa Parliamentary Debates, House of Assembly*
BBC	British Broadcasting Corporation
BCP	Basutoland Congress Party
BNP	Basutoland National Party
BDP	Botswana Democratic Party
CCTA	Commission for Technical Co-operation in Africa South of the Sahara
CSA	Commission for Scientific Co-operation in Africa South of the Sahara
C.O.	Colonial Office documents
D.O.	Dominions Office documents
ECA	United Nations Economic Commission for Africa
FAMA	Fund for Mutual Assistance in Africa South of the Sahara
Frelimo	Front for the Liberation of Mozambique
HNP	Herstigte Nasionale Party
IDC	Industrial Development Corporation
K.C.A.	*Keesing's Contemporary Archives*
MCP	Malawi Congress Party
MFP	Marematlou-Freedom Party
MPLA	Popular Movement for the Liberation of Angola
NP	National Party
OCAM	Organisation Commune Africaine et Malgache
PAC	Pan-African Congress
PP	Progressive Party
SABRA	South Africa Bureau of Racial Affairs
SAIRR	South African Institute of Race Relations
SOEKOR	South African Oil Exploration Corporation
SWAPO	South West African People's Organisation
UNGAOR	*United Nations General Assembly Official Records*
UNIP	United National Independence Party
UP	United Party
UPP	United Progressive Party
ZANU	Zimbabwe African National Union
ZAPU	Zimbabwe African People's Union

Introduction

With increasing international opposition to their domestic policies, South African governments became apprehensive of the change which the post-war policies of the imperial powers initiated in Africa. It was the object of South African policy to secure an optimal organisational and ideological milieu in Africa. To that end South Africa sought to gain influence among the colonial powers and to persuade them to retain their empires. Even when they withdrew it was hoped that their remaining influence would be exercised to advance South African objectives in Africa. When African States did eventually emerge, they were hostile to *apartheid* and secured the isolation of the republic from the rest of the continent while working for the overthrow of *apartheid*. South African policy consisted in attempts to terminate that isolation, mainly by offering trade and aid to African governments. Economic expansion in South Africa underlined the need for markets in Africa while it enabled the republic to exercise some influence, especially in southern Africa.

The relationship between South Africa and Africa can be viewed as one of ideological conflict, involving on the one hand the South African ideology and, on the other, the anti-colonial attitudes which prevailed in post-war Africa. As such, the relationship was intimately connected with the social structure of South Africa which the white ideology defends. The process of ideological conflict did not adduce major changes in South Africa, and such changes as did occur—as in the structure of the white community—tended to favour South African policies toward Africa. Yet although South Africa was able to stave off the pressures for radical change, it did not achieve its ends in Africa. It failed to gain leadership in the continent or to overcome hostility to *apartheid*. Africa was not made safe for white-dominated South Africa. If the quest for influence in the continent arose out of a desire to facilitate the retention of white privilege within South Africa, white minority rule itself was the principal obstacle to South African policy. There was thus a fundamental contradiction in South Africa's situation in Africa. That contradiction was reflected in the structure of successive South African policies, which were, necessarily, internally contradictory.

For whereas South Africa sought to maintain a racial situation, and champion a racial ideology of a distinctly colonial kind, decolonisation was proceeding in Africa in response to the growth of anti-colonial attitudes and ideologies, to which in turn it gave considerable impetus. African decolonisation had two distinct aspects, which were, nevertheless, complementary. Firstly, there was the once-for-all transfer of sovereignty by the imperial powers to their former colonial dependencies. Secondly, and more broadly, decolonisation involved the transformation of real political, social and economic relationships both within former colonial territories and between them and other societies, including, most particularly, the former imperial powers. This latter process would continue long after the transfer of juridical sovereignty. It was in that situation of societal change away from colonial forms that post-second world war ideologies which were hostile to *apartheid* had their real basis.

In the absence of any real direct material linkages between South Africa and the majority of African States, the contradiction in South Africa's situation in Africa tended to be expressed in an ideological conflict between South Africa and black Africa. That conflict was ideological in three main senses: it was about ideology; it was conducted in an ideological, declaratory fashion, with considerable emphasis being laid on symbolic defeats and victories; most important, foreign policy attitudes arose from wider, more general and more fundamental concerns (which were often more closely focused on domestic problems than on those of foreign policy). Certainly the policies of African States towards South Africa as well as South African policy in Africa tended, during most of the period, not to show great concern with concrete material interests in the urgent manner of classical statecraft.

Yet the issues were real enough. For not only did ideology in each case involve the distinct concepts of material interests and claims on the part of recognisable social groups, but ideological conflict was also by its general and fundamental nature more intractable than any discrete, concrete disputes might have been. The racial ideology of South Africa was basic to the very nature of that society and not merely an ephemeral aberration. The ideologies of black Africans with which it entered into conflict called into question the very right of that kind of society to exist.

If *apartheid* as a colonial remnant was in contradiction[1] with emergent societal forms and ideas in Africa, its policy towards Africa also had its contradictions. The aim of that policy was to gain influence that would make Africa a favourable environment for continued white minority rule in South Africa. Yet *apartheid* itself was the main obstacle to South Africa's gaining in the pre-independence period that 'leadership' in Africa which was thought desirable to secure its 'peaceful development', and, in the latter period, white minority rule was precisely what the African governments objected to most. Minor concessions by South Africa on racial policy—as in relation to black diplomats—contributed to ideological conflicts among South African whites while they went nowhere near to meeting African demands. Similarly, it was always much easier to stimulate South African white popular feeling in favour of supporting racial settler and colonial rule in southern Africa than it was to gain real sympathy at all levels of the white community for a policy of 'dialogue' and social intercourse with black diplomats. Thus even the attempts to gain support for an outward policy in Africa ended by strengthening those very racialist and colonial tendencies of South African policy which were a real impediment to the successful integration of the republic into the comity of African nations as '*n Afrika-horende volk*, a nation that belongs to Africa.

Ideological conflict is therefore the dominant theme. The continuing process of African decolonisation, involving, as it did, the continued vitality of African nationalism—tending now towards the reactionary right, now to the revolutionary left, but always finding legitimacy in repudiating the more obvious forms and remnants of colonial domination—constitutes the secondary theme of this work.

The discussion falls into two parts. The first focuses strictly on South African designs for, and initiatives in, colonial Africa, with the other 'African' powers having a fairly passive role in relation to South Africa. In the second part more attention is devoted to the

---

[1] I use the term 'contradiction' to emphasise the basic character of the anomalies and conflicts in South Africa's situation in Africa. These anomalies and conflicts constitute a contradiction in the sense familiar in European (and Marxist) social science—namely that they are incapable of resolution within the given 'system'. The term implies that the system is capable of theorisation and has a theoretical correlative in which the conflicts and anomalies feature as a contradiction.

reactions of African States to South Africa, for although it was in this period that South African policy became particularly active in Africa, that was in itself a reaction to a more diverse environment which was actively hostile. To explain the opportunities and limitations in the light of which South African policy was conceived in this more complicated context, the nature of African responses and the circumstances leading to them are discussed in some detail. However, this being a work on *South African* policy, these discussions had to be conducted with ruthless economy.

While this study sees foreign policy and domestic politics as being almost inextricably intertwined—both in South Africa and in the other African countries—discussion of domestic politics has in every case been restricted to those aspects of it which bear upon foreign policy in a clearly distinguishable way. Often, too, this relationship is mentioned in the analysis of relations between States rather than dealt with separately. Chapters VI and VII, however, deal with these linkages specifically. Here too the aim has been to distill only what has an important, fairly specific bearing on foreign relations, and to avoid padding the discussion with duplication of what has already been amply dealt with in the substantial body of literature which exists on South African internal politics.

Finally, although this book deals mainly with the period 1945–71, the discussion is often brought up to mid-1973, especially where relevant developments during the intervening period cast particular light on the main issues under review.

PART ONE　*South Africa in colonial Africa*

1 *The context of policy*

The most striking aspect of South African political life in the post-war period has been *apartheid*. The single most recurrent theme of its international relations has been the mobilisation of opposition internationally against *apartheid*, and the countervailing attempts of successive South African governments to neutralise such opposition. South African policy towards the rest of the world has mainly consisted in attempts, by various means and with varying degrees of urgency, to withstand the pressures for internal change and to reduce at the same time the disabling effects for South Africa of hostility to *apartheid*; it has also sought to maintain existing, or to create new, gainful international transactions without white minority rule in South Africa being abandoned. In a sense, then, South African international activity has been little more than the extension of its internal conflict—a struggle to make the world safe for *apartheid*. This fundamental linkage between domestic and external politics has nowhere been more evident than in South Africa's relations with the rest of Africa.

For obvious geographical reasons Africa was destined to play an important part in the working out of the contradictions between South Africa's racialist domestic policies and the universalist, non-racial views that gained currency in the post-war world. It was, however, a distinctive set of historical, rather than geopolitical, conditions which determined the particular relationship which emerged between South Africa and Africa. The official attitude of white South Africa, first to the decolonisation of the African continent and, later, to the emergent African States was influenced by their colonial experience. Essentially a settler community, white South Africa was apprehensive of, and opposed to, the liquidation of the African empires. The attitudes of the rest of African States towards South Africa were in their turn also conditioned by Africans' experience of imperialism and their reaction to that experience. The most militantly anti-imperialist States were also the most vehement opponents of *apartheid*, and, in general, the converse was also true.

During most of the period under discussion, Africa, or most of it, was under colonial rule and could play only a minor role in international affairs and in the campaigns against *apartheid*. Yet the post-war period soon saw that beginning of the devolution of power from imperial metropoles to African centres which was to culminate in the concession of sovereign statehood to most of the colonies. Although in the early period independence for African colonies might have seemed remote indeed, there was always the expectation that black Africans would play an increasingly important part in the politics of the continent. It was against the background of such expectations, and the anxieties to which they gave rise in South Africa, that the early post-war Africa policies were developed.

Because of their domestic social policies South African governments were apprehensive of political rights being granted to Africans in the colonies to the north of the Union. They feared that such concessions would give encouragement to African nationalists within South Africa itself. They also expected that the African governments which came into being as a result of such concessions would be hostile to white South Africa, all the more so because they would be susceptible to non-Western influences—Asian and communist—which were unfriendly to white South Africa. Thus South Africa openly opposed decolonisation until it became clear, in the late 1950s, that the process was irreversible. It continued, however, to support every enclave of colonial and settler influence and control which survived. South African governments gave material assistance to Rhodesia and to Portugal in Mozambique and Angola from the mid-1960s onward. South Africa had earlier also supported the short-lived, settler-backed Tshombe regime in secessionist Katanga. In Namibia (the former mandated territory of South West Africa), and within the republic itself, decolonisation, especially in regard to race relations, was resolutely resisted. Indeed, the general sentiment which pervaded policy—domestic as well as foreign—in the period reviewed was Pretoria's consistent antagonism to decolonisation and the radical forces it seemed to generate. The main aim behind the Africa policies of South Africa was to create in Africa an ideological and organisational milieu which would be favourable to white minority rule in South Africa itself. Continued imperial rule in Africa had the potentiality of providing just such a context. What was envisaged was an overall political arrangement characterised by two distinctive features. Firstly, a colonial order of race relations would be retained within South Africa itself. Before decolonisation was fully under way, and especially during Malan's premiership, it was an important aim of South Africa policy to encourage similar racial policies in other colonial African societies as well. Secondly, an imperial, or inter-imperial, order would be established to regulate relations *among* African societies and territories. It was hoped that South Africa would play a very large part in the ordering and maintenance of such an inter-territorial system.

South Africa's policies towards the African imperial powers, and, later, the African States, are the subject of the chapters that follow and which there is no need to anticipate at this point. It is not necessary either, nor indeed feasible, to discuss in detail the 'colonial' social order in South Africa which external policy was meant to support. Nevertheless, it is desirable, as a general definition of the context of the policies towards the rest of the continent, first, to outline the basic characteristics of the domestic order these policies were meant to help uphold, and, secondly, to identify the main features of the African situation which confronted South African policy-makers as a result of decolonisation. To these themes, respectively, we now turn.

The domestic colonial situation

Political works on South Africa generally emphasise the pervasive nature of racial segregation and discrimination in South Africa. The segregationist outlook is rightly singled out as the most distinctive feature of the orientation to life and politics of the white community in South Africa.[1] It is often identified with *apartheid*, or with Afrikaner nationalism, or even with one of the rival traditions within Afrikaner nationalism. The historical fact that racial segregation and discrimination were practised in South Africa under regimes which were not Afrikaner nationalist as well as under those which were, although it is generally acknowledged, is seldom taken fully into account. Equally, it is often forgotten that the segregation of whites from blacks, advocated with unique pertinacity by Afrikaner

---

[1] See, for example, G. M. Carter, *The Politics of Inequality: South Africa Since 1948*, 1958; Leo Marquard, *The Peoples and Policies of South Africa*, 1960; A. Hepple, *South Africa: a Political History*, 1966; H. J. and R. E. Simons, *Class and Colour in South Africa, 1850–1950*, 1969.

nationalists, has historically been only one of the components of Afrikaner nationalism, the detailed ideological stipulations of which related more to relations among white groups in South Africa— specifically between Boers and Britons—than to blacks.[2] It was taken for granted that blacks were social inferiors whose fate would be disposed of within the framework of white domination. In advocating segregation, Afrikaner nationalists have always done so within a specific historical context, one in which hostility to black people was by no means restricted to Afrikaners, and one in which the relationship of forces was such that, although the mammoth social engineering implied in segregationism might be impracticable, it was not generally regarded by the white community as absurd or immoral: it was seen as politically, if not practically, possible.

Clearly, racial segregation and discrimination are deeply rooted in the historical consciousness of the white community in South Africa, so much so that we can talk meaningfully of the white South African racial ideology as something more—or less—than Afrikaner nationalism as reflected in *apartheid*. This ideology amounts to no more than the self-approbation of South African society as it emerged in the late nineteenth century and as it has been in the twentieth century, and *apartheid* is only one detailed elaboration of the key features of that social order, stressing some of its features and understating others. The question as to what is the South African ideology is best answered, therefore, by reference to the salient features of the South African social order.

To begin with, that social order owes much to the colonial period, in which its key features emerged. South Africa is, in large measure, still in what was identified by George Balandier as a 'colonial situation', although, of course, the republic is not a colony of any power.[3] The 'colonial situation' is invariably characterised by marked social stratification of a dual kind; racial and economic occupational. This means not only that social inequality takes the familiar form of social classes reflecting economic relationships, but that there is a hierarchy of racial groups headed by the settler population. Classes are unequal and so are races in a typical colonial society. That society is most stable when there is complementarity between the class and the racial position of the various groups.

---

[2] Cf. Carter, *op. cit.,* chapter 11.

[3] 'La Situation coloniale: approche théorique', in *Cahiers Internationaux de Sociologie,* 1951.

Incongruity between these, reflected, say, in persons of a 'lower' race controlling more wealth than persons of a 'higher' race, is potentially a source of instability (and is very often a cause of conflict within and between groups). The problem, however, is that it is impossible to determine just how much race–class incongruity is compatible with the stability of a colonial system. Evidently, there is room for a fair degree of it at the individual (or micro) level. In every colonial society, not least South Africa, there are numerous individuals whose social position manifests such and similar anomalies. It is certain, however, that for whole races to reverse economic positions, say, without their social status being thus affected is impossible. Nor can the social and political status of any group deteriorate without a correlative deterioration of their economic position.

The stratification of society along these lines reflects both the superior political power of the settler (in this case, white) population, which is preserved largely because the system, typically, operates to exclude blacks from attaining, even by means of gradual encroachment, to the commanding positions of both the economic and the political systems.

Within each race there are, naturally, social and economic inequalities and resultant conflicts of interests, but the primacy of racial identifications in colonial society indicates that these are— at any rate, in regard to the ruling race—subordinate to an overriding common interest in the maintenance of a colonial order. The dominant class is part of the ruling race, and so are the white lower classes, who, although they occupy a subordinate position, enjoy nevertheless material advantages of such magnitude, and a status so exalted *vis-à-vis* otherwise comparable sections of other communities within the mixed society, that they recognise no community of interest and no unity of destiny between themselves and those groups. Thus, for instance, there is no solidarity at all between white and black working men in South Africa. This is not surprising, since the privileges of the settler lower classes are not paid for by the rest of their congeners with whom they share those privileges; rather, they are met through innumerable exactions on the non-settler communities—mainly the natives—and by deliberate economic and political suppression of those communities.

Conflicts among the different strata of the ruling race are managed by a combination of measures that have become fairly orthodox in other stratified societies also and devices peculiar to colonial systems.

Methods of the first kind include welfare schemes and policies of economic growth which ensure, first, that the economic position of lower-class whites does not fall below a certain level and, secondly, that the increments of absolute lower-class incomes made possible by economic growth assuage the resentments caused by inequality among whites themselves. There is, of course, very little social welfare for blacks, and in many instances their earnings have often actually fallen in spite of overall growth in the economy.[4] The specifically colonial modes of conflict management include the institutionalisation of racially discriminatory practices favouring the less privileged whites. Thus certain types of jobs are reserved for white workers to protect them from otherwise certain competition from blacks. Not only does this create artificial labour shortages which push white wages up but, reinforced by racial prejudice, it helps to establish a high norm for white wages. This, in turn, is institutionalised through para-statal and statal wage determinations (which in South Africa include the Wages Boards set up under the series of racially discriminatory Industrial Conciliation Acts) which in general favour huge income differences between black and white workers. In exchange for economic protection against blacks the white workers (and lower middle class) give support to the economic and political regime which obtains. The rest of the settler community also benefits materially from the low wages and the generally depressed condition of the indigenous working population.

If the 'colonial situation' is mainly characterised by mutually complementary class and race distinctions, then a further condition of its stability, and even survival, is the existence of modes and levels of economic activity which are compatible with dual stratification. Political stability also depends on two related conditions. Firstly, the settler community should not only continue to have a common economic interest, but must recognise this as the basis of its political action. The second condition is that political structures, including institutions, should continue to be preponderantly exclusive of the subject community. The economic and the political systems should be mutually complementary and both functional to white domination —both at the level of ideology and at the level of practical action.

[4] This is manifestly the case with South African blacks in agriculture; Dr F. Wilson has argued that this is likely to have happened in mining from the beginning of the century to 1970. See his *Labour in the South African Gold Mines*, 1971. These, of course, have traditionally been, and still are, important areas of employment for black South Africans.

Thus settlers develop a distinctive racist political consciousness—and the political instrumentalities (usually repressive of the natives) appropriate to that outlook.

Economic change in South Africa, particularly the growth of secondary industry, has led to considerable speculation as to whether the political arrangements of that society continue to correspond with the needs of its economic system. Economic development has undoubtedly brought about some impressive social changes, especially in the living standards and occupational structure of the two main white ethnic groups. The last quarter of a century has seen the virtual elimination of white poverty. There has also been a narrowing of socio-economic differences between Afrikaners and English-speakers. All this has led to a good deal of speculation that cleavages among whites will soon cease to be politically significant. More important, there has also been a deal of prophecy that even the relationship between blacks and whites might, as a result, be deracialised.

The view has often been expressed that economic development in South Africa must result in black people being accorded the same economic and political rights and opportunities as whites. This notion is attractive, if only because *something* must improve the condition of black people in South Africa. Various arguments have been put forward in support of this view, but one deserves serious attention. It holds that as the economy expands the demand for manpower and the need for a larger domestic market will so increase that they can be met only by relaxing the restrictions on blacks in the economy (and thus undermining the colonial character of the economy). Blacks would thus gain greater economic power, which must, in turn, inevitably lead to political power. On the face of it, this analysis is unexceptionable. There are, however, at least two distinct and even opposed views about the course of change that may be envisaged in this general prognosis. One is that blacks—Africans in particular—will be conceded, on an incremental basis, occupations and incomes previously reserved for whites. A few violent popular eruptions may occur, but, basically, the process by which the society will be transformed will be peaceful. Although much truncated, this rendition does not materially distort the core of the argument (popular with some South African and other liberals), which is that *apartheid* interferes with the 'rational' (some say 'optimal') operation of a developing capitalist economy.

It is not difficult to see that *apartheid* interferes with the costs of production in industry by creating artificial shortages in the job categories reserved for whites, or that by its depressive effect on African incomes it retards the growth of a large domestic market for the ever-increasing volume of domestic industrial produce. However, to argue that these bottlenecks will lead to a reform of the system is misleading. The objections to this view are indeed legion but there is no need to discuss all of them here.[5] There are, however, a few observations immediately relevant to present themes which need to be made.

The liberal argument (as I shall, for brevity, call it) fails to give any indication of what will be happening to relations among whites while the system of white privilege is being dismantled. Certainly the changes envisaged would so profoundly affect the nature of the white community and its position in the mixed economy that it is difficult to see how they could be brought about without intense conflicts, including violence, among whites. It is very hard to envisage the circumstances in which it would be in the interests of any white government, or of investors, to create such a situation within the ruling race.

What is apparently envisaged in the liberal theory is a species of 'realisation crises' through which the South African elite would gradually come to recognise the basic requirements of economic 'rationality' and would itself become 'rational'. Behind this belief is clearly evident a rather effete Victorian conception of the free market as the matrix of rationality in social action. This notion was always more ideological than scientific. It is, of course, a complete mystery why anyone should assume that the white elite will behave in the most 'rational' way possible by meeting the requirements of economic rationality with liberal concessions. Surely the crises envisaged could just as easily lead to reactionary (e.g. fascist) as to liberal responses. Finally, the liberal model assumes, with very little justification, that blacks will, by and large, passively accept the concessions, and the pace at which they are made, by white rulers who will consistently have the initiative.

The basic question raised by these speculations is whether the economic system in South Africa is progressive, and is essentially a liberating force in that society. The alternative view that may be

[5] See, for example, E. Johnstone, 'White prosperity and white supremacy in South Africa today', in *African Affairs*, 1970.

proposed differs from the liberal thesis exactly on this question. The problem is too large to be discussed fully here. It must suffice, therefore, to outline, in the broadest terms, the essential features of an alternative theory of social change in South Africa.

In terms of this theory, change in South Africa would neither be incremental, nor the result of largely voluntary concessions, nor, indeed, peaceful. It would be revolutionary not so much in its violence or suddenness as in the complete incommensurability of the order it would inaugurate with the one that went before. The argument which supports this view is basically that—to use a Laskian formulation—the forces of production will enter into conflict so profound with the relations of production that no piecemeal concessions will be able to prevent the revolutionary transformation of society through which alone the conflict can be resolved or transcended. The issue, therefore, is not how to remove 'irrationalities' from an otherwise 'rational' system. The 'colonial situation' has a mode of production appropriate to it which, while it initially makes possible the rapid development of some capitalism in a primitive environment, nevertheless inhibits the full development of that system by restricting the forces of production (e.g. African labour and the African bourgeoisie *manqué*). This is, however, not an irrationality to be expunged by a few, or even several, judicious concessions; it is, on the contrary, a fundamental contradiction in the nature of 'colonial' capitalism. Productive forces are liberated by nationalist revolutions rather than settler reforms.

The most interesting implication of this line of reasoning is that the colonial situation is fundamentally illiberal. Indeed, such liberality as it has is usually the result of external—often metropolitan—intrusions.[6] Part of the reason lies in the fact that the level of exploitation which makes colonialism worth while, and the particular system of inequality which characterises colonial society, can be realised only by deliberate restraint on productive forces (as, for example, on the upward mobility of indigenous labour, on landholding and capital accumulation by natives), and through the suppression of native political dissent. A liberal democratic colony, a free-trading colony, a colonial economy governed by market forces unhampered by racialist restrictive practices, has never existed. It is difficult to see how it could. Post-colonial societies do often retain

[6] Hence Afrikaner nationalists' feeling that it was alien and injurious to their nation (*volkskadelik*).

colonial societal arrangements, in all their illiberality, long after they have ceased to be attached to an empire. They conserve salient aspects of a 'colonial situation' for so long as they continue to be governed by a privileged settler minority ready and able to defend its advantages.

In South Africa over half a century of economic growth—it is now sixty-three years since union—has failed to remove the barriers between blacks and whites, while every year has seen the addition of new measures to prevent black people from attaining equality with whites. It may be safely assumed that in the foreseeable future economic growth is unlikely to undermine the system of white domination. Nor will it corrode the ideological support, among whites, for that system.

In South Africa there has emerged, since union, an effective pact or covenant among the various strata of the white community to maintain the existing social order. It is true that at the margin there has been friction, even violent conflict, among whites, but it has always been only at the margin and has generally been resolved in favour of the maintenance of the existing system.[7] The South African ideology amounts to the commitment to maintain the 'colonial situation', at least with respect to race relations.

The notion of a 'colonial situation' should, however, not be pushed too far. Both its economy and its political system are far more complex than the elementary structures that obtain in colonies. In addition, unlike typical colonial economies, South Africa's political and economic life is largely determined by forces within it, and this is increasingly the case. Like all trading countries, South Africa is, of course, subject to external influences and pressures but in no way to the extent of a typical colony or even what have come to be known as neo-colonial States.

It should not be imagined, either, that the illiberality of South Africa can be wholly attributed to the productive relations of a colonial economy. While anti-liberalism in South Africa is certainly colonial in origin, the growth of State power and repressiveness since the war reflects both the movement of South Africa outside the orbit of British (comparatively liberal) imperial influence and, more fundamentally, its responses to problems arising from the transformation of South Africa from a colonial economy to an industrial national economy. Thus *apartheid* as distinct from mere segregation has been

[7] For example, in the industrial field; see H. J. and R. E. Simons, *op. cit.*

seen, with some justice, as a reaction to the problems (for white South Africa) of urbanisation and industrialisation.[8] What liberties exist in South Africa did not derive from its transformation from a colonial society—indeed, most liberties have withered away during that process—but to earlier developments and influences, particularly the influence of Victorian 'liberalism' during the time of the confrontations with British capitalists and liberal (some not so liberal) imperialists which culminated in the Anglo-Boer war. British power ensured subsequently, and for as long as it endured, the predominance of British ideas and practices, which, relatively, were liberal. In the light of all this, too mechanical a view of the 'colonial situation' should be avoided. Nevertheless, it is the case that the situation obtaining in South Africa is nowhere approximated except in colonies and that in South Africa itself it is comprehensible only in terms of South Africa's colonial past.

The commitment of white South Africans to maintain the 'colonial situation' is the most important aspect of what can be called the South African ideology. All other aspects of the South African ideology are secondary features. Their importance has not been, generally, a matter on which all whites agreed. (How many white South Africans would, for example, insist on 'petty *apartheid*', or on the biblical derivations of the racial ideology, has always been an uncertain matter, varying with time.) About the centrality of the system of stratification there has never been any important disagreement (within the mainstream of white politics)—only about the optimal way in which it might be reformed or developed.

Hostility to black people has been implicit in the social order and functional to the maintenance of the system of stratification. Aversion on the part of whites to social intercourse with blacks has also played a similar role. Expounding, defending and implementing the ideology, Afrikaner nationalists have been the bearers of the ark of the South African covenant for most of the period since the war.

There is, admittedly, a problem in referring to *the* South African ideology: it is that such a presentation begs the question whether, in this case, Afrikaner nationalist ideology is merely a variant of the ideas, beliefs and values held by other whites in South Africa, and not something altogether different (within the framework of the 'South African ideology' as I have outlined it). This is clearly not an easy

[8] See H. Wolpe, 'From segregation to *apartheid*', in *Economy and Society*, 1972, and N. J. Rhoodie and H. J. Venter, *Apartheid*, 1969.

question. To answer it affirmatively would seem to trivialise the passionate and often acrimonious ideological contests that have gone on among whites since union, and before. However ineffectual the wranglings within the white polity may have been with regard to the major contradictions of South African society, they did nonetheless occur and were taken seriously by the participants. By trivialising them one lays oneself open to the accusation of deliberately mis-understanding history to facilitate one's own judgements. That is a position I would wish to avoid. Yet there is no doubt that since union the South African polity has operated on an effective consensus so persistent as to suggest a deeper commitment than mere consensus, and that it is precisely this which trivialises the differences among most white political groupings.

Decolonisation and the post-colonial situation in Africa

The period of the second world war saw a gradual but definite transformation of the political attitudes of the major powers towards international relations generally, and among the imperial powers, France and Britain, a reassessment of colonialism. The war, bringing with it the diminution of the international power status of Britain and France—France more than Britain—dramatised the ascendancy of Russia and America and the relative decline of Western Europe. The climate of ideas which was already beginning to emerge before the outbreak of war now reflected the attitudes of non-colonial powers much more than before. The growth of Asian nationalism, resulting in the emergence of independent Asian States, was also a factor in the formation of world opinion. The creation of the United Nations Organisation, with a built-in tendency towards public diplo-macy, provided an organisational framework for the exchange of international political ideas, while it presented a forum for the dis-semination of ideas of considerable diversity in both content and origin. The ever-increasing network of international communication favoured the development of a concept of 'world opinion' which to some degree influenced the policy attitudes of the powers. The con-clusion of the war, bringing as it did clear divisions among the allied powers about the nature of the peace which was to follow, led to the emergence in the world of two predominant blocs, the communist bloc, centring on Russia, and the capitalist bloc, centring on the United States of America. Military technology, and particularly the development of nuclear weapons, gave relevance to this global cleavage while encouraging the development of global military strategies which in turn encouraged global political strategies.

In the competition which ensued Africa was to gain increasing relevance, while the struggle for global influence and control was to affect the reassessment of imperial roles in an important way. It is essential, therefore, in the discussion which follows, to bear in mind as vividly as possible the shifts in this global competition and its effects on African policies. Although we shall refer to the Cold War from time to time, its importance is much greater than the references that we can pertinently and economically make in this limited study would suggest.

It was the change in the global status of the European imperial powers, alongside the development of the ideas on colonialism, which led to the 'liquidation' of the European empires in Africa.

The British political class saw their role in the colonies as one of preparing the local inhabitants for internal self-government, and, in time, for independence, it being hoped that the independent States would remain friendly if not allied to the metropolitan country and to the West. Together with political preparation for self-government, but of greater priority in the earlier years of our period, was the felt need to develop the economies of the British African possessions to the mutual benefit of Britain and those territories. The expressive term chosen to describe this relationship was 'partnership'.[9]

The French, who had obtained considerable solace and support from tropical Africa during the war against Germany, intended to develop their territories also, but the ideal of self-government, it was hoped, would be realised by direct participation of the colonial peoples, through their representatives, in the government of France. The idea of partnership was paralleled by the ideas of *mise en valeur* and of a multi-continental State *une et indivisible*.[10]

The need to democratise the African empires in the light of the new attitudes towards colonialism shared by the super-powers, Russia and the USA, was perhaps more acutely felt by the French,

[9] Cf. J. M. Lee, *Colonial Development and Good Government: a Study of the Ideas expressed by the British Official Classes in planning Decolonisation, 1939–64*, 1967, pp. 1–77.

[10] E. Mortimer, *France and the Africans, 1944–60: a Political History*, 1969, p. 30 *et passim*. Also R. L. Delavignette, 'French colonial policy in black Africa, 1945–60', in L. H. Gann and P. Duignan, *Colonialism in Africa, 1879–1960*, pp. 251–79.

'whose status as a great power was much less certain' than that of Britain, and whose colonial policy 'had never been devolutionary even in theory'.[11] Nevertheless, both powers in their different ways set out to inaugurate a new era in colonial Africa, not wholly planned, but informed generally by a distinctive ideology or ethos of decolonisation. This ideology of decolonisation arose from different sources and traditions and was addressed to differing objectives and ultimate purposes, but ideas nonetheless converged on a number of important points: the removal of barriers to the self-'advancement' of colonial peoples, their increasing participation in the conduct of the affairs of their territories, and their inclusion as participants in the international organisations created after the war. Altruism and idealism encouraged decolonisation, but international power realities and the competition for global support in the ideological war were the decisive factors behind it.

Design there was, therefore, for post-war Africa, but it would be wrong to see the emergent political pattern in Africa after the war as merely the realisation of elaborate ideological plans. The specific policies of decolonisation emerged out of responses to events and the situations they created, so that, although those policies were informed by a generalised civic ethic, the process of transforming Africa took the shape of a 'disjointed incrementalism'.[12] For this reason there was always room, in the quarter of a century or so after the war, for debate upon the practical implications of decolonisation and the time span within which the ultimate ends might be achieved. It was only in the mid-1950s and later that the direction of change became explicit and apparently irrevocable. Yet even then it was not clear to what extent the French and British governments intended the policy to apply to all of Africa, including the territories with white settler communities, such as Algeria, Kenya and the Rhodesias.

Furthermore, the structural changes which the decolonisation process initiated were different and evoked differing responses as the policy unfolded. South African governments regarded the policy of the Fourth Republic and the policy of the UK government (and that of Belgium) in the period 1945–51 as very much the same because the official attitudes to 'native policy', which was the main point of attention at the time, were similar.[13] After 1951, however, came

[11] Cf. Mortimer, *loc. cit.*
[12] Cf. R. E. Jones, *Analysing Foreign Policy*, 1970, pp. 19–22.
[13] The pace was not the same everywhere, but all the colonial powers were tending, ideologically at least, towards the goal of racial integration.

the particular problem of self-government within Africa, which threatened to introduce changes in the structure of African inter-territorial relations, over and above the relations of white and black *within* territories. In 1957–68 the creation of independent States at *that*, rather than a later time, introduced a new conflict topic. The self-government 'stage' of decolonisation exhibited differences between Britain and France, illustrated, for example, by their responses to claims for self-government and to the position of white settler communities. The attitude of President de Gaulle towards Algeria after 1958 changed the image of France as the one more eager to defend settlers than Britain seemed to be—in South African official eyes, at least—in respect to central Africa. And yet, even at that stage, France seemed less bent on the extension of local autonomy in its colonies.[14] It was in 1959–60 that the positions of the imperial powers, bar Spain and Portugal, seemed to be identical: all seemed to be scuttling their African empires and 'appeasing'[15] the blacks.

South African policy towards Africa had until then either presupposed (as in the decade immediately after the war) or sought the continuation of the imperial order in Africa more or less as it had been in 1945–46. Even when independence came—and after—the residual influence of the former imperial powers remained important for the Africa policies of South Africa.

The African States created by decolonisation came into existence in a Cold War context in which there was intense competition between the Russian and American blocs for global influence. The fact that most of the new States opted for non-alignment, thus reserving their choice of alignment, and the fact that they were new contributed to some uncertainty as to the place they might come to occupy in international affairs. Their tendency to work together, first in the Afro-Asian groupings, and later in the African group at the UN, also tended to encourage a continental evaluation of African States in international affairs, rather than an evaluation on the basis of single nation States. All these factors tended to favour the ascription to African States of a prestige in excess of their physical capabilities. The prestige of African States was all the more important

---

[14] Cf. Paul Sauer's speech reported in *Pretoria News,* 30 April 1958, and the Minister of External Affairs .in *Union of South Africa: Parliamentary Debates: House of Assembly* (hereafter *Ass. Deb.*), vol. 100, cols. 5563–7.

[15] *Ass. Deb.*, vol. 3, col. 4151.

because they lacked the physical means to enforce their will at an international level and had to rely on a pressure-group role to achieve their ends.

The Cold War soon receded, giving way to an uncertain multi-polarity in which the competition for allies all over the globe, and the containment policies to which it had given rise, seemed to diminish. As might be expected, the responsiveness of the super-powers to the demands of African States tended to decrease. The failure of the latter to establish close unity among themselves and the tendency towards narrower nationalism also meant that African States could be regarded and treated as individuals rather than as a group, and as individuals they were considerably weaker than the continental evaluations had tended to suggest. The weakness of the new States in military and economic terms, their failure to overcome at least some of this weakness by collective action, seen against the decline of the Cold War, drew attention to aspects of the world context of the new States which had tended to be ignored in the Cold War. Underdevelopment was the condition of African States in an international order that was markedly stratified.[16] As Professor Galtung has put it, 'two of the most glaring facts about this world' are:

the tremendous inequality, within and between nations, in almost all aspects of human living conditions, including the power to decide over those living conditions; and the resistance of this inequality to change.[17]

Several scholars have tried to work out the implications of the sort of position occupied by these States. The common point of focus among most writers is the tendency towards persistent dependence on the part of African (and similarly placed) regimes on aid, investment and personnel from the advanced countries, particularly the former colonial powers, and the implications of this dependence both for their ability to determine their own domestic politics and for their options of alignment in international relations. Following Myrdal,[18] Galtung stresses the tendency of existing patterns of 'co-operation' to increase the relative deprivation of such States and

[16] Cf. G. Lagos, *International Stratification and the Underdeveloped Countries*, 1953.
[17] J. Galtung, 'A structural theory of imperialism', in *Peace Research*, 1970, p. 81.
[18] G. Myrdal, *Economic Theory and the Underdeveloped Countries*, especially the notion of 'circular and cumulative causation'.

their absolute dependence.[19] Lagos has drawn attention to the
priority of status improvement among the international orientations
of developing regimes as a response to what he calls the 'atimic process'.[20] Writers in the Marxist tradition tend, in general, to reaffirm
Lenin's identification of imperialism with monopoly capitalism[21]
and to argue that the dependence–underdevelopment condition is
simply a necessary consequence of capitalist development at the
international level.[22] It has been objected that while such studies do
give some guidance to Western economic imperialism, they seldom
account for non-capitalist modes of domination of weak States by
strong ones.[23] The authors might, of course, reply that they are concerned to explain the condition of the majority of underdeveloped
countries, which historically have been dominated by capitalist States.
Arrighi and Saul are very much in this tradition when, in assessing
the potential for revolution in Africa, they draw attention to the collaboration among international capitalist concerns and their governments in maintaining the dependence of African States in what they
call the 'second phase' of capitalist imperialism.[24] Arrighi and Saul
see Africa as confronted by a 'rationalising international capitalism',
which has, in Africa, a hierarchy of economic satellites, among which
those in southern Africa are the most highly placed. This contingency
has two implications for inter-African relations. Firstly, by an inter-
locking system of pressures and influences on African governments,
'International Capitalism' exercises itself in favour of the maintenance of the *status quo* in Africa and South Africa. Secondly, the
collaboration of African regimes with 'International Capitalism'
provides an entry point into the continent for South African power
and influence, which are part of 'International Capitalism'.[25] By

[19] Galtung, *op. cit.*

[20] Lagos, p. 24 *et passim*. 'Atimia' signifies the loss or deterioration of
status: 'the evolution of social change that ends in a state of atimia' is the
'atimic process'.

[21] V. I. Lenin, 'Imperialism, the highest stage of capitalism—a popular
outline', in *Collected Works*, vol. 22, Moscow, 1964.

[22] Cf. C. Frank, *Capitalism and Underdevelopment in Latin America*,
1967. See also H. Alavi, 'Imperialism, old and new', in *The Socialist Register*,
1964, which provides a good review of some of the more important literature
till then. See also R. Sutcliffe and R. Owen (eds.), *Studies in the Theory of
Imperialism*, 1972.

[23] For a critique of some of these theories see G. Lichtheim, 'Imperialism,
II', in *Commentary*, 1970.

[24] G. Arrighi and J. S. Saul, 'Nationalism and revolution in sub-Saharan
Africa', in *The Socialist Register*, 1969.   [25] *Ibid.*

virtue of its higher development South Africa can hope to play on an increasing scale the benefactor roles which are the prerogative of major powers, and which, many writers believe, merely intensify the patterns of dependence.

There is in all these writings an unstated but nonetheless obvious view that we share—namely, that there is an imperial tendency in foreign policy—a tendency to influence and, where possible, even to control the behaviour of other States. In this regard it is difficult not to endorse the view that whether asymmetrical co-operation between States or collectivities materialises in 'imperialism' or not is a function of opportunity, defined primarily by the degree of resistance to imperial designs among candidate 'imperialists' and at the periphery of empires.[26] It is a secondary matter whether 'capitalist imperialism' or 'socialist imperialism' have other distinctive structural character-istics beyond these, or what motives are operative in most or all cases of imperialism. There was no once-for-all termination of dependence when African States gained independence, but rather the condition of underdevelopment tended to generate forces in favour of the re-tention of existing patterns of domination and subordination, or the establishment of new ones. It is clearly as a consequence of these features of the African situation that South Africa is enabled to play 'benefactor' roles despite the international opprobrium suffered by the *apartheid* regime. In this regard it must be conceded that there is a *prima facie* plausibility in the Arrighi and Saul argument.[27] If it is not a proven statement of what has occurred, then it is a reasonable statement of what might be expected to occur—subject, of course, to the uncertainties of international politics.

If the case is made that the post-independence situation, or, as Nettl and Robertson have referred to it, the 'inheritance situation',[28] generates associative forces between the new States and advanced —in large part, former imperial—powers, it should not be forgotten that decolonisation itself, seen as more than the simple single act of transferring the instruments of sovereignty, was a *dissociative* process. Nettl and Roberston have indeed drawn attention to the dissociative

[26] D. S. Landes, 'Some thoughts on the nature of economic imperialism', in *Journal of Economic History*, 1961.

[27] Despite its wholly unconvincing treatment of the implications of uneven development for 'rationalisation', it points to a real tendency at this particu-lar juncture.

[28] J. P. Nettl and R. Robertson, *International Systems and the Moderni-sation of Societies*, 1968, Part II, especially p. 66.

aspect of decolonisation as definitive of a 'total situation', and therefore relevant to all 'social levels', i.e. the goals, values and norms of
the new societies.[29] This insight draws attention to the fact that
the international orientations, and therefore alignments, of the new
States will be affected by how dissociation proceeds *within societies.*
The attitude which groups in a society adopt towards the inherited
colonial order may be expected to influence their foreign policies also.
Internal conflicts can be seen as having an external dimension, since
they will mostly affect the attitude that should be adopted towards
the 'inheritance', and what any political group thinks of the 'inheritance' may be expected to affect its attitude to the 'testator', and
conversely. The 'situation of dissociation' explains the primacy of
'self-determination' in the preoccupations of political groups in developing societies, to which P. G. Casanova has convincingly drawn
attention.[30] It also explains the place occupied by 'neo-colonialism'
in the demonology of the new States.

Despite the growing wealth of theoretical writings of the kind we
have cited, there is still little certainty about the future of Africa in
the world, or about the likelihood of far-reaching social, economic
and political changes in Africa. Fanon saw a radical dynamism at
work, favouring an African revolution which would rid the continent
of imperialism and racism;[31] Arrighi and Saul see a comparative lack
of dynamism, favouring, in the practical future, a continuation of the
status quo.[32] Yet these writings are rich in the range of variables to
which they draw attention, and they do temper the tendency to see
African politics from the point of view of political institutions exclusively.

The African situation which confronted South Africa after 1960
must, therefore, be seen as one characterised by an ambiguity expressed in the tension between the associative (and, generally, conservative) tendencies encouraged by underdevelopment, and the
'dissociative' tendencies implicit in decolonisation. Within this dia-
lectic is comprehended a universe of social and political relationships,
within and between societies, which were relevant to South African
policy, with which the second part of this book will deal.

[29] *Ibid.*

[30] P. G. Casanova, 'Internal and external politics of underdeveloped
countries', in R. B. Farrel (ed.), *Approaches to Comparative and International
Politics,* 1966.

[31] F. Fanon, especially 'The pitfalls of national consciousness', in his *The
Wretched of the Earth,* n.d.   [32] *Loc. cit.*

11 *1945-48: the last years of Smuts*

South Africa entered the post-second world war period under the premiership of Field Marshal Smuts, who had led the country throughout the war period. Smuts directed foreign policy personally, and although his views seem to have been widely shared by members of his party, he was, through his definite ideas on the subject as well as on account of his copious experience in international affairs,[1] able to make an authentically personal imprint on the Africa policy of the Union of South Africa.

Smuts had already been in high political office for some time when he became Prime Minister, so that although he adjusted himself to the new conditions, his general outlook on world affairs, and, therefore, on South Africa's relations with Africa, had been formed; so also were his intentions for South Africa in Africa.

Principally, he held the view that white settlers and the imperial powers in Africa had a civilising mission to fulfil there; because of that view he did not question either the justice or the permanence of the colonial presence in Africa. Having thus accepted the 'imperial factor' in Africa, he developed a view of South Africa's political status and future role within that established imperial order. Smuts had entered the national politics of the Union of South Africa as a Minister in the 'conciliationist' Ministry of General Botha.[2] The policy of conciliation can be characterised as one of reconciling the two formerly contending British and Boer sections of the white population of South Africa, and of reconciling the Boers to the British Empire. It was these two features of the conciliationist policy which guided Smuts throughout his career and which were particularly pertinent to his policies toward the African continent.

Smuts considered that the development of the British Commonwealth of Nations meant that the dominions were partners rather than subordinates of the imperial government, and therefore that

---

[1] W. K. Hancock, *Smuts*, vol. I: *The Sanguine Years*, 1962, and vol. II: *The Fields of Force*, 1968.

[2] Hancock, *The Sanguine Years*, pp. 269 *ad. fin.*

the dominions could exert influence on the policies of the imperial government. He convinced himself that the British connection which had been responsible for a 'century of wrong'[3] had become an altogether different thing: it now meant membership of a powerful association, with the promise of increasing freedom and influence for the dominions within the British imperial system particularly and in the whole international system generally.

Having reconciled himself to the permanence of the imperial connection, Smuts championed the British Commonwealth idea and saw the identification of South Africa's interests with those of the Empire and Commonwealth as a matter of honour, obligation and self-interest. The two world wars and the rise of Afrikaner nationalism, with its republican campaigns, adduced from Smuts a legal interpretation of this obligation by which he hoped to enjoin his white countrymen against separatism: a legal claim that was hotly disputed by Afrikaner nationalists. Esssentially the claim was that South Africa did not have the right of secession from the Empire and Commonwealth and that it could not be neutral in the event of Britain's being at war with any power.[4]

Within this framework Smuts hoped to complete the process of territorial unification in southern Africa begun at the time of the Union. The granting to South Africa of a mandate over South West Africa at the Paris peace conference can be accounted his greatest achievement in this regard. It was also proof of what could be achieved for South Africa by working through the British Empire. Smuts attempted, though without success, to unify Southern Rhodesia and South Africa in 1923,[5] but although he expressed enthusiasm when the question was raised again by Southern Rhodesians in 1943,[6] he did not pursue the policy of incorporation with any great vigour.[7]

Various reasons led to this. The areas which might have been

[3] Title of a book written by Smuts, *Een eeuw van onrecht*.

[4] N. Mansergh, *Documents and Speeches on British Commonwealth Affairs, 1931–52*, vol. I, pp. 500–6, for Smuts' speech on the outbreak of war in 1939.

[5] C. Palley, *The Constitutional History of Southern Rhodesia, 1888–1965*, 1966, p. 211.

[6] *Rhodesia Herald*, 7 May 1943; *Keesing's Contemporary Archives* (hereafter *K.C.A.*), 6043A.

[7] One of the reasons might have been that the Southern Rhodesian government clearly saw union with Northern Rhodesia to be a matter of greater priority. See, for example, *Rhodesia Herald*, 9 October 1943.

incorporated included territories of greatly differing constitutional status, and the reasons varied according to the territory. There were the High Commission Territories—Bechuanaland, Basutoland and Swaziland—the incorporation of which had been provided for in the Union of South Africa Act; their incorporation depended largely on the imperial government in Britain.[8] There was the self-governing colony of Southern Rhodesia (after 1923), the mandated territory of South West Africa, and—at a further remove—Northern Rhodesia and the rest of central Africa.[9]

The incorporation of Southern Rhodesia depended on the willingness of the white colonists in Southern Rhodesia, which, for various reasons, was not forthcoming.[10] The annexation of the mandated territory of South West Africa would have depended on the assent of the League of Nations, which would have been more easily obtained —if obtained at all—with British co-operation.[11] The incorporation of Northern Rhodesia into the Union does not seem to have been seriously pursued by any Union government: it was in any case rejected outright by the imperial government, since—like the High Commission Territories—it was a 'native' territory, and as such raised problems because of South Africa's racial policies.[12] After the failure of the Union convention in 1908 to produce a 'liberal' 'native policy' imperial policy was to shelve the question of incorporation until such time as the Union government did provide a 'native policy' which British governments could accept.[13]

In relation to the incorporation of South West Africa such considerations were, however, not decisive, probably because it was not

[8] See L. M. Thompson, *The Unification of South Africa*, pp. 49–60 and 269–84.

[9] Palley, *op. cit.*, p. 195.

[10] L. H. Gann and M. Gelfand, *Huggins of Rhodesia*, 1964, pp. 59–62; G. Murray, *The Governmental System of Southern Rhodesia*, 1970, p. 29; Palley, *op. cit.*, p. 151.

[11] See J. H. Wellington, *South West Africa and its Human Issues*, 1967, pp. 255–317, on the League and the mandate.

[12] Cf. Palley, *op. cit.*, pp. 195 ff.

[13] Thompson, *op. cit.*, pp. 261–84 and D.O. 35/395/11007/70; Hailey, *op. cit.*, and D. Austin, *Britain and South Africa*, *passim*. The question of native policy need, however, not have been decisive. United Kingdom governments have on occasion been quite insensitive to the rights of Africans, as Chamberlain was when he thought to buy off Hitler with concessions in Africa (see L. S. Amery, *My Political Life*, vol. III: *The Unforgiving Years*, 1953, pp. 247–8). The creation of the Central African Federation in the teeth of resolute African opposition is also a case in point. The literature on this is extensive. Some of it is cited in Palley, *op. cit.*, p. 2.

a territory in which British rule had definitely been established. Smuts had been encouraged in his ambitions during the Paris peace conference and he had indicated on more than one occasion his determination to incorporate the territory. The British government reasoned that he could not now be brushed aside without considerable offence being caused to a tested ally. As soon as the first rumblings were heard on this question at the end of the war, the imperial government conceded, in advance, even, of any approach from the Union government. An official in the Dominions Office, J. P[?arker], expressed the opinion which prevailed when he wrote to his colleagues:

I do not think that we can strongly oppose the incorporation of South West Africa as a fifth Province if the Union Government press the matter.[14]

The questions of South Africa's territorial expansion were interrelated and it was, therefore, observed that the fact that 'we intend to resist pressure from the Union to incorporate the Commission Territories [sic]' would 'make it all the more difficult for us to resist the desire to incorporate South West Africa'. The same official made a proposal concerning South West African frontiers which, if it had been adopted, would in time have made an immense difference to the economics and geopolitics of the entire subcontinent:

If . . . the frontier of Bechuanaland is raised and some minor alterations . . . are under consideration, then I would suggest that the transfer of the strip stretching out from South West Africa to the Zambezi should also be considered. This projection of South West Africa was, I believe, administered by Bechuanaland for a period immediately after the war of 1914–18. It obviously could be administered much more easily by Bechuanaland than by the Government of South West Africa.[15]

However, all that this indicated at the time was that there was some uneasiness in British government circles over the transfer, a feeling rather pusillanimously reflected in the Cabinet decision of 13 May 1946, which was that:

The United Kingdom Government would support the incorporation of South West Africa in the Union if the consent of the natives as well as the European inhabitants had been sought and obtained by methods agreeable to the United Nations.[16]

[14] D.O. 35/1119, 5 December 1945, followed a report by Evelyn Baring, then British High Commissioner in South Africa.
[15] *Ibid.*   [16] D.O. 35/1214.

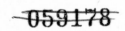

Strong opposition to the incorporation of South West Africa came from one 'native' source outside the territory in question. It emanated from Bechuanaland, from the Regent of the Bamangwato, Tshekedi Khama, who was in close touch with Chief Hosea Kutako of the Hereros in South West Africa, who had strongly opposed incorporation. It was through Tshekedi that the Rev. Michael Scott became involved, and through him as a petitioner the UN itself was kept aware of the opposition to incorporation among South West Africans. Khama drew up a memorandum with the support of six Tswana chiefs, opposing incorporation, requesting that the mandate be transferred to the UK government, or to the UN, and that Bechuanaland be given a free and open route to a free west coast port. In the view of the Dominions Office, this last was based on 'a belief that there is considerable undeveloped mineral wealth in the Protectorate and that unfettered access to the West Coast is therefore necessary'. The chiefs' memorandum also urged that consideration be given to the case of 'certain displaced persons' in Bechuanaland (Hereros who had fled the German terror of 1905 and, according to the memorandum, others who had fled since the Union obtained control).[17] Tshekedi planned to visit England to make propaganda for his cause, but was firmly advised against doing so as it might have stimulated demands in South Africa for the incorporation of the High Commission Territories themselves (of which Bechuanaland was one)—or so Whitehall reasoned upon representations from Pretoria. The reply of the Secretary of State to the memorandum showed little patience with Tshekedi's importunity. He was told:

The United Kingdom Government have no reason to suppose that the native administration of South West Africa by the Union Government as a Mandatory Power has been open to criticism and there can be no question of their supporting a suggestion that the administration of South West Africa should be transferred to some other Government than the Union Government.[18]

Moreover, the British government firmly suggested to Tshekedi that the economic destiny of Bechuanaland, of which he evidently took too sanguine a view, would likely be discovered to be less promising and, in any case, inseparable from that of the Union, whose goodwill would have to be maintained. The British High Commissioner was authorised to tell Tshekedi:

[17] *Ibid.*   [18] *Ibid.*

There is no definate [sic] information that such coal and iron deposits as may have been discovered in the Bechuanaland Protectorate are of sufficient importance to justify a new railway across the Protectorate to connect with a port in South West Africa. Such a railway could only be constructed with the co-operation of the Union Government, and its construction, if financially practicable, would not be affected by the question whether South West Africa was under the Union Government's Mandate or incorporated in the Union. If such a railway were constructed there is no reason to suppose that the Union Government would seek to restrict exports from the Protectorate through South West Africa. If and when the question of such a route seemed to be a practicable proposition, the United Kingdom Government would be prepared to discuss the matter with the Union Government.[19]

In regard to South West African refugees in Bechuanaland, the imperial government was no less self-assured and aloof in its attitude:

As regards 'displaced persons', if in the future any of them should wish to return to South West Africa, any representations from them would be considered by the High Commissioner in consultation with the Union Government.[20]

The Dominions Office was outrightly behind Smuts, choosing to be quite uncritical when he reported that South West African chiefs he had consulted favoured incorporation. It was the Colonial Office which, as late as September 1946, tried to introduce some ambivalence to the British posture, and to recover some of the freedom of action intended, albeit rather palely, in the Cabinet decision. An Assistant Secretary at the Colonial Office, A. H. Poynton, noted that the Africans had been presented with the alternatives either of British (South African) protection by incorporation or full-scale international administration. That was not a correct presentation of the alternatives. Poynton wrote:

We have been at pains to make clear that trusteeship, as in Tanganyika, is entirely consistent with sole British administration and British protected status for the inhabitants. We therefore cannot help having some doubt about the conduct and the results of the consultation, and we foresee that the Assembly, before it is convinced, will probably raise some awkward questions on this point.[21]

Poynton was to the point, and the UN General Assembly bore out his forebodings, sharing his reservations about the method and results of consultation. À propos of the brief for the UK delegation to the

[19] *Ibid.*   [20] *Ibid.*   [21] *Ibid.*

UN in discussion of which these points were raised, Poynton recalled that the Cabinet had decided that UK support of Smuts would depend on opinion in the territory having been surveyed in a manner acceptable to the UN. He therefore suggested:

In the absence of any formal resolution by the United Nations defining what is agreeable, it appears to us that, on our Cabinet instructions, the only practicable course for the UK delegation is to wait and see whether, from the general trend of the debate, it appears that the methods used by South Africa are 'acceptable'; and when that point is reached the delegation can then decide how to vote on the major question.[22]

Although the Dominions Office wrote to the Foreign Office that they were urgently considering these suggestions, the policy that won the day was that of outright support of Smuts. Certainly, Poynton's suggestion about voting would only have led to a negative British vote, a conclusion which HMG wished to avoid, as it sought, in any event, to adopt a position which the Union could accept as friendly. Thus not for the first time, and, assuredly, not for the last either, Britain supported the Pretoria regime on a major question of foreign policy involving race relations.

Smuts, eager for co-operation with the imperial government, was aware of their qualms about the Union's 'native policy' and, accordingly, did not in general press his government's claims to the other territories.[23]

The obvious way of overcoming these objections was to devise a 'native policy' which imperial governments would accept. But this Smuts signally failed to do. And since the 'native question' remained, even after Smuts, the most crippling problem for South African foreign policy, it is necessary to examine some of the more important reasons why Smuts failed.

At the time of the unification of South Africa Smuts had expressed himself against the retention of the 'non-racial' franchise in the Cape after union, and he was resolutely opposed to its extension to the rest of South Africa where black people were completely without franchise rights. Presenting the draft constitution of the Union to the Legislative Council of the Transvaal Colony in 1909, Smuts deeply regretted that the Cape franchise had been retained. 'What was to be feared,' he argued, 'and what was already developing in South Africa' was not the 'native question' itself 'but the division of the

[22] *Ibid.*, Poynton to Dixon, 18 September 1946.
[23] Cf. D.O. 35/395/11007/70.

white people in this country on the Native question.'[24] The 'native'
franchise was 'an apple of discord placed before South Africa';

Sir, on this question . . . we could only take up an attitude of trust—trust
in the future, trust in the wisdom and foresight and experience of the
coming generations. It [the apple of discord] is not of our creation. It is
embedded in the structure of South Africa. All that we could do was to
admit our inability to remove it. We have to admit that, and that it is for
the future South Africa to remove.[25]

The desire to leave a final solution of the question of political rights
for Africans to the future remained with Smuts to the end of his
career, and with it went his unwillingness to give the franchise to
Africans.

In the years after union, especially after World War I, Smuts
tentatively adopted the policy of territorial and political segregation,
with power decisively in white hands; yet although he argued with
much rhetoric for this view he did little to implement it. He hoped
the High Commission Territories might form the basis of such a
division of South Africa into African and white areas,[26] but it also
appears that, within a short while after expressing these views in
1919, he veered to some sort of 'multi-racial' solution, namely a
council on which Europeans and Africans would deliberate, although
this was hardly a solution, since, while it would have given Africans
a platform from which to air their views, it would have had no
political power.[27] Smuts repeated his belief in segregation after the
second world war did not exclude the possibility in the future of
equality among the races, but clearly saw that to be a distant
future.[28]

Aware of the changing attitudes to the colour question in the
British Empire and Commonwealth with which he so closely wished
to associate South Africa, and in the inter-governmental organisations he had helped to form—the League of Nations and the United
Nations Organisation—Smuts preferred caution on the question of
the rights of black people, a caution he expressed with clarity after
the first session of the UN:

[24] W. K. Hancock and J. van der Poel, *The Smuts Papers*, vol. 2, No. 340.
[25] *Ibid*.
[26] *Greater South Africa: Plans for a Better World: the Speeches of the
Rt. Hon. J. C. Smuts*, 1940, pp. 22–30.
[27] D.O. 35/395/11007/90, extract from a letter to Sir E. Harding dated
21 January 1935.
[28] Hancock, *op. cit.*, vol. II, pp. 473–91, and chapter 28, *passim*.

The whole world is being hit by a storm [he warned] and that storm is hitting us in this country too, and in these circumstances, with the small European community we have today and the mass of world opinion against us, we must be very cautious. Do not let us deprive people of rights which have been granted to them. Let us try to come out of the storm unscathed.[29]

Throughout his career Smuts had been ready to deal with the administrative aspects of the 'native question', but he had never been and was not now ready to accept it as the basis of an alternative political order in South Africa. Nor did Smuts ever seriously contemplate deviating from a policy of segregation of the races. Although the Asiatic Land Tenure Bill (1946) was intended as a positive response to external as well as internal criticism, he still defended it in South Africa on segregationist lines. And in doing so he expressed his view of what was possible in the matter of race relations in South Africa:

I think we have decided, I think South Africa has decided once and for all, that our complex society will be dealt with on separate lines. We have done it in the case of the natives, and we are going to do it in the case of the Indians. Any other system I think will lead to endless friction. You will never get it through Parliament in this country, you are simply attempting an impossible solution. It will never be accepted by the people of South Africa [sic]...[30]

It is not intended here to question whether Smuts' representation of the racial feelings of his countrymen was correct or not; suffice it to observe that statements of the sort just quoted could only encourage those who opposed integration. To that extent, therefore, Smuts was in part responsible for the difficulties he faced on the racial question, a difficulty which made unattainable his aim of South African leadership in Africa and the aim of a larger South Africa—enlarged in part by the incorporation of 'native' territories.

Both the Empire and the Commonwealth and the rest of the international system were becoming multi-racial in outlook, and certainly in southern Africa both by now had become quite unwilling to encourage the sort of policies which were being pursued in South Africa. To some extent Smuts realised this, for by the end of World War II he was no longer agitating against the arming and training of native armies as he had done in 1917.[31]

[29] *Ass. Deb.,* vol. 59, col. 10918.
[30] *Ass. Deb.,* vol. 56, col. 4173.
[31] *Greater South Africa,* pp. 22–30; also Hancock, *op. cit.,* pp. 111–27.

The 'native problem' also deprived Smuts' unification policy of some domestic white support. Afrikaner nationalists disliked the idea of the unification of British African possessions near South Africa (as suggested by Smuts on so many occasions) on the grounds that it would result in a State with an even larger black majority than the Union: a 'Kafir State', as it was indelicately called.[32]

For all these reasons Smuts pursued his Africa policy with circumspection. Although South Africa co-operated with other white communities in Africa, close integration of services and constitutional unification were not pursued with any great immediacy, so much so that one is tempted to conclude that Smuts, although he thought these things desirable, was prepared to leave them to the 'abler minds' of the future which would also 'solve' the most disabling anomaly—the 'native question'.

So long as such views persisted among a huge section of the white population it is doubtful whether Smuts' post-war plans would have enjoyed much credibility with the imperial government.

Yet for all the drawbacks of which Smuts seems to have been aware, his Africa policy in the period 1945–48 seemed still to be informed by the same principles. He restated his belief that small powers (like South Africa) could not do much on their own, and he was eager to maintain the British connection, while participating in the United Nations. He placed much store by the friendship of powerful countries, and in spite of the reverses that South Africa had suffered at the first session of the UN he was confident of its future:[33]

On a count of votes, on numbers, it may seem as though we have suffered defeat, but I know—and I know what I am talking about—that we have friends, and if it comes to the worst, we shall find that we are not standing alone.[34]

So long as their support was assured on the 'important questions' Smuts was prepared to be accommodating on 'lesser matters'.[35] As a result, he was not insistent on South Africa's putative legal rights, whether over South West Africa or 'non-interference' by

[32] Cf. *Die Transvaler*, 22 November 1944; *Die Burger*, 11 August, 1942; *Die Transvaler*, 8 May 1943.

[33] The UN turned down his request for the incorporation of South West Africa, and for his pains admitted India's right to bring to discussion the question of the treatment of Indians in South Africa.

[34] *Ass. Deb.*, vol. 59, cols. 10915–16.

[35] *Ibid.*, col. 10918.

India.[36] Moreover, Smuts reaffirmed his belief in the unification of the British territories in southern Africa:

... the whole of my striving has been to ensure the knitting together of the parts of Africa, the parts of southern Africa which belong to each other; parts that must work together for a stable future on the continent of Africa.[37]

If incorporation was not in prospect in 1945–48, there was still considerable room for functional co-operation between South Africa and the British possessions in Africa. Plans, which will be discussed below, were accordingly hatched for co-operation on a variety of technical and economic matters.

Almost everyone in the white polity could agree with the view that South Africa should co-operate closely with the rest of Africa. Africa was South Africa's hinterland, a natural market for its products and a source of cheap native labour;[38] it was also of strategic importance in a world in which Western Europe had 'shrunk' and a hostile communism was rising.[39] It is certain, however, that the Herenigde Nasionale of Volksparty, later to become simply the National Party, and kindred organisations would not have much truck with any attempts to keep South Africa within a British imperial kraal; nor could they endorse Dr Friedman's eloquent restatement of Smuts' principal foreign policy doctrine:

... the attitude of progressive-minded people towards the Commonwealth should be governed by this consideration. The Empire, whatever its defects, still represents a unified system; and in the present anarchy of international relations we should cling steadfastly to any unity we have already achieved ... surely both honour and self interest dictate that we should co-operate with the rest of the Commonwealth and take a full share in its privileges and responsibilities.[40]

[36] *Ibid., passim.*

[37] *Ass. Deb.*, vol. 52, col. 3719, and Hancock, *op. cit.*, p. 223.

[38] On markets in Africa, see, for example, *Die Burger*, leader, 11 August 1943, and the debate on Africa policy in *Ass. Deb.*, vol. 52. One speaker, Native Representative D. Molteno, QC, expressed himself against an Africa policy of: 'regarding the Northern territories as fields from which the Union may draw cheap labour ... in very much the same way as our native reserves have traditionally been regarded' (col. 3958).

[39] Malan, in *Pretoria News*, 20 April 1949, and in Mansergh, *op. cit.*, vol. II, p. 1153; see also P. Maritz, 'Engeland uit, ons in?', in *Die Brandwag*, 11 July 1947; G. S. Labuschagne, *Suid-Afrika en Afrika: die Staatkundige verhouding in die tydperk, 1945–66*, 1969, pp. 5–14.

[40] *Ass. Deb.*, vol. 52, col. 3700.

In the three years after the war, Smuts' Africa policy suffered severe reverses, chief among which was the refusal by the United Nations of his request for the incorporation of South West Africa. But British colonial trade policy in 1948 (the raising of tariffs) was also a setback to the hopes for markets in Africa and could even be taken to prove that the imperial government was not quite as responsive to South Africa's wishes in Africa as Smuts' policy necessitated.[41] As far as closer union with Rhodesia was concerned, by 1948 the subject had become so unpopular that it was not mentioned at all in the electoral campaigns of that year.[42] Finally, as Smuts should have been aware, the imperial government was contemplating a different kind of post-war reorganisation from that which he would have wished.[43] Such changes as were now becoming apparent in the policy of the imperial government would have made his African aims difficult to realise at the best of times; but when Smuts went in 1948, after an electoral defeat, there was no one among his successors who was ready and willing to continue where he had left off. In some measure, therefore, the electoral defeat of 1948 was the defeat of his foreign and Africa policy as well as of his domestic policy. He had failed to create a domestic environment propitious to his external ambitions, while his external environment could not be made compatible with his aims. The decisive problem which he failed to solve was how to develop the white political system in such a way that it would initiate within itself the sort of structural mutations which would be compatible with the emergent structure of race relations in Africa, in the British Empire and Commonwealth, and in the international system as a whole.

Various factors led Smuts to champion his distinctive policy towards southern Africa, Africa and even the world. Some of these were personal—his long association with international politics from the days when he was Colonial Secretary of the Transvaal Colony to the end of the second world war; his interest in 'high politics', which led him to participate in a variety of international and imperial conferences. A personal intellectual tendency to unify and simplify, of which there is evidence in his philosophical speculations,[44] may

[41] *Die Burger*, 23 January 1948, 28 February 1948, 16 February 1948, 1 March 1948.

[42] *Die Transvaler*, 13 September 1948.   [43] See above, pp. 17–19.

[44] Smuts' purpose in *Holism and Evolution* was 'to devise some simpler scheme to explain the unitary character of time, space, matter and all physical appearances and activities': Hancock, *op. cit.*, pp. 176 and 169–7.

have encouraged him to annex contiguous territories and thereby unify and simplify South Africa's immediate political environment. It has even been suggested that Smuts' philosophy of Holism lay at the root of his Africa policy. That view, as it has been stated by Labuschagne in his *Suid-Afrika en Afrika*, is certainly far-fetched; for, as Hancock has shown, there was no political reference in the work on Holism, so that the philosophy of Holism was open to a variety of political interpretations and was indeed variously interpreted.[45]

There were clearly far more immediate political considerations behind the Africa policy which predate the work on Holism. Such were the 'conciliationist' creda: that the Empire was an evolving democratic inter-State system from which South Africa had benefited much and would benefit more in the future, that the future welfare of South Africa depended on the reconciliation of Boer and Briton, which meant that the most powerful British–South African sentiments—such as preserving the British connection—should be respected. That view was strengthened by Smuts' belief—expressed towards the end of his political career—that small powers on their own could do little to secure peace in the world; and, therefore, by implication, they should work in concert with great powers.[46] Having thus accepted the immanence and desirability of the British imperial order in southern Africa, Smuts could naturally look to that connection to achieve for 'his country' a political context in Africa compatible with its internal political, social and economic aspirations. Add to this the same fervour for unity and simplicity which underlay the agitation for union after the Boer war, and Smuts' Africa policy becomes comprehensible as an extension of the sentiments of the earlier conciliation to the external African context. These fragments of an ideology were conceived within a specific imperial order which they needed for their fulfilment, and there is to that extent justice in the Afrikaner nationalists' view that Smuts was an imperialist. Yet while all his laborious conceptions and plans may be reducible to 'expansionism and greed', in the view of its authors the Africa policy of conciliationism was based pre-eminently on their felt need to create for white South Africa an optimal external political context.

---

[45] Labuschagne, *op. cit.*, p. 15, says Smuts was influenced by 'his Holistic views' (*Holistiese beskouinge*). See Hancock, *op. cit.*, vol. II pp. 193, 218 *et passim*.

[46] *Ass. Deb.*, vol. 52, col. 3720.

Thus Botha (and Smuts)[47] argued when they pleaded for the annexation of German South West Africa at the end of the first world war:

It is the firm conviction of the European population of the Union that if South West Africa were restored to the Germans, the permanent security and peace of the Union, and indeed of the whole of British South Africa would be gravely imperilled ... they want to be secured in the peaceful possession and development of their own territory and secured from intrigue. This state of affairs cannot be obtained with Germany as their neighbour.[48]

Now it is possible that the structure of Smuts' thought on 'Holism' may cast light on the structure of his thought on foreign policy, and that the former must be studied for a full understanding of Smuts' foreign policy. This, however, is a more sophisticated view than that to which Labuschagne commits himself. It is in principle a plausible view, although it would be hard to demonstrate in practice. At any rate, it is a view that has to be established by argument rather than merely asserted. For our purposes, while not discounting ultimately the usefulness of such an analysis, the considerations already essayed in this chapter are quite adequate.

If 'conciliationism' was the basis of the African policy of Smuts, that policy suffered from an irreconcilable internal contradiction which was its undoing: for while it envisaged working through an Empire and Commonwealth which was becoming increasingly 'multi-racial', within South Africa it sought to avoid a division of white people on the 'native question' by placing white unity before the rights of the black majority. Certainly, in the post-war world such a policy could hardly have formed the basis of large-scale territorial reorganisation in east, central and southern Africa.

---

[47] There is reason to think that Smuts was much more keen on incorporation than was Botha; cf. Wellington, *op. cit.*, pp. 267–9.

[48] Memorandum to the British government, D.O. 35/395/6408/117.

III *Malan and the 'African Charter', 1948-54*

When the National Party of Malan and Havenga won the South African general election on 26 May 1948[1] it was widely believed outside South Africa that Malan, now Prime Minister, would introduce changes in South African foreign policy.[2] The differences in political thinking between the National Party and Smuts' United Party had been dramatised by the unremitting opposition of the Nationalists to South Africa's involvement in the war with Germany and her allies, and by the collusion between the National Party and such South African pro-Nazi groups as, for example, the Ossewa-brandwag and the Nuwe Orde.[3] It was expected that they would seek to modify the relationship with Britain, to which the more radical Nationalists greatly objected. In short, Malan's electoral victory was an Afrikaner nationalist triumph; his government's policy was therefore expected to reflect the distinctive ideology of that movement.

Malan's Africa policy did not, however, merely reflect an abstract ideology. It represented the aspirations and interests of a distinct section of the white population of South Africa. It is a matter of regret that there are hardly any works on interest groups on which one can draw to substantiate the last remark. Nevertheless, a number of tentative statements can be made about the social groups that might be expected to support each policy—on the basis of a general understanding of South African white politics.

Smuts' view of a united Africa, within the British Empire and Commonwealth, received the support of three kinds of white people in South Africa and outside: big business, imperialists (or Empire

[1] Malan's Reunited Party and C. M. Havenga's Afrikaner Party formed an electoral pact in 1943 and merged completely in 1953 when the name Nasionale Party was readopted.

[2] *Die Transvaler*, 31 May 1948.

[3] On the various Afrikaner nationalist groups, see D. F. Malan, *Afrikaner volkseenheid en my ervarings op die pad daarheen*, 1959, pp. 45–219; J. A. Coetzee, *Nasieskap en politieke groepering in Suid-Afrika*, 1969, pp. 248–90; M. Roberts and A. E. Trollip, *The South African Opposition, 1939–45*, 1947; J. Kruger, *President C. R. Swart*, pp. 77–131.

loyalists) and those liberals who wished to avoid the isolation of South
Africa, all traditionally from the middle and upper classes of the
urban English-speaking white community,[4] of whom the United
Party was the traditional representative. Particular industrialists—
like the mining magnates—could support the policy for a variety of
reasons: it would mean easier access to 'foreign native labour', on
which they were so dependent;[5] they could expect that a 'rationalisation' of the economic and commercial infrastructure would
ensue from union; and, since they were also the principal investors in
the Rhodesian mining industries, they could only benefit from the
harmonisation of the administration of the territories. At any rate,
they did not stand to lose.

For manufacturing industry, union would be beneficial because of
the expansion of the South African market which would follow the
removal of tariff barriers. The Rhodesias were also their major
market in Africa. They too were unlikely to oppose the policy, and
even if they did not actively work for it, their activities were, func-
tionally, in support of it. Even trade unionists saw no harm in supporting the policy, since it was not contrary to their internationalism
and would, it was hoped, facilitate the co-ordination of their efforts
to establish 'socialism' in South Africa.[6]

English-speaking South Africans could, in so far as they were keen
to preserve the British connection, socially as well as politically, look
forward to joining with other British territories, and it was even
suggested that they sought union as a means of preventing the
numerical dominance of Afrikaners,[7] which the faster rate of increase of the Afrikaner population seemed otherwise likely to ensure.[8]

For the rest of the English-speaking South African town-dwellers,
where they might not have had any particular reason to desire union
with Rhodesia, or to interest themselves in Smuts' policy, there was
no reason to oppose him. After all, Smuts' policy represented an

[4] On the occupational structure of white South Africa see S. van Wyk,
Die Afrikaner in die Beroepslewe van die Stad, 1968, pp. 188–219.
[5] Cf. 'Foreign Bantu', in *Standard Encyclopaedia of Southern Africa*,
1970, p. 100.
[6] *Rhodesia Herald*, 16 July 1943; *K.C.A.* 6043A; *The Star*, 19 July 1943.
This is true only of a section of the South African white trade union movement, which, as is well known, is very divided. On some of these divisions
see Muriel Horrell, *South Africa's Workers: their Organisation and Patterns
of Employment*, 1969, pp. 1–25.
[7] Cf. *Die Transvaler*, leader, 22 November 1944.
[8] *Ibid.*

alternative kind of patriotism to that of Afrikaner nationalists, which gave English-speaking South African whites, in prospect, at least, a significance in international affairs which they could approve.[9]

These groups comprised, however, only one part of the divided white polity. There was another part comprising the clients and supporters of the National Party. These included rural interests, the urban poor whites, and groups representing Afrikaner cultural and economic institutions that might expect to flourish in an Afrikaner nationalist-dominated State.[10] To such groups the advantages of politically unifying British Africa were by no means self-evident, while from their point of view the disadvantages were clear. There is reason to suppose, for example, that cattle farmers and tobacco growers would have viewed unification with concern, since they had been among the major opponents in the past of any liberalisation of trading policies.[11]

For the rest, the elite of the Afrikaner nationalist movement was not responsible to the mining companies, and in the light of their political aims, which included converting the Union into an Afrikaner republic, incorporation of the Rhodesias would have been inconvenient. It would increase the number of English voters, while culturally and socially it would favour the predominance of British institutions and ideas.

Yet, when all is said, none of the considerations of the Smutsians need have led to the idea of politically unifying the British territories, while none of the fears of Afrikaner groups need have led to the rejection even of a contingent policy of unification. Clearly, other factors came into play as well. Of these the most important was the symbolic effect of the policy of unification. It was associated with one policy, one outlook which the Afrikaner nationalists regarded as inimical to their own outlook and the interests and aspirations which it represented.

Ideology thus performed the function of enabling political actors to identify their friends and enemies, first by forming a means of aggregating, organising and articulating interests; secondly, by providing symbolic associations which enabled supporters of the political actors to fit situations, events and policies into ideological categories

[9] Although Smuts' followers were not only the English-speaking white but did include large numbers of Afrikaners, it is nonetheless true that the United Party was, by and large, the English-speakers' party.

[10] Cf. Carter, *op. cit.*, pp. 250–81.

[11] Cf. C.O. 767/3 (Southern Rhodesia, 1924, vol. 2), *passim*.

and so decide whether or not to support policies which were not directly or even logically relevant to their own particular preoccupations. It is perhaps redundant to make the point that not all interest groups interested themselves even indirectly in foreign political matters. The study of interest groups in South Africa will have to reveal just which particular groups did; and when and why.

The National Party represented primarily a web of social groups within the white community, and it espoused a specific ideology which among other things was expressive of the aspirations of those groups while providing what seemed the optimal political and social order for the realisation of those aspirations. *Mutatis mutandis*, the same was true of the United Party, although the ideology of the United Party was less explicit. Although, then, we shall concentrate on Malan's policy (as on Smuts') as an aspect of ideology, and with ideological conflict in mind, it should be borne in mind also that its social significance and relevance derived from its identification with real human groups within the Union of South Africa.

The political ideology of Afrikaner nationalism developed over a long period, and those elements of it which were most pertinent to Malan's foreign policy and Africa policy had certainly been established long before his rise to the premiership in 1948. Those elements were republicanism, racial segregation and white supremacy—intended primarily as domestic policies for South Africa, although the last two were meant to apply to the rest of Africa as well.[12]

Republicanism, or the slogan of 'South Africa first',[13] meant that a very narrow interpretation of South Africa's obligations to the British Empire would be accepted, while grave disablements were thought to follow from the imperial connection.[14] The Nationalist movement expressed nationalist values, such as claims to a distinctive fatherland, a specific language and culture, and the right to complete self-government. The existing social order of 1948 was considered to be inimical to those values; therefore the existing order must be changed: South Africa must establish its right of secession (if only by repeated affirmation), it must become a republic —although Nationalists differed in the urgency with which they wished to accomplish this task.[15]

The claim to a fatherland of the Afrikaners' own was interpreted

---

[12] See works cited in n. 3.   [13] *Ibid.*
[14] *Ibid.*, especially Malan, *op. cit.*
[15] *Ibid.*, especially Malan, *op. cit.*

in the context of their hostility to blacks in general and Africans in particular, and their wish to maintain white supremacy. Complete territorial segregation of whites and blacks was to be carried out. The blacks would be excluded from the white 'territories', while in 'their own' territories they should remain under the 'guidance' of white people, not in perpetuity but for a very long time.[16] Certainly there should be no social and political equality, and it is almost correct to say that the formula for race relations was an inversion of Lord Passfield's doctrine:[17] where white and black interests conflict, white interests must be paramount. And this policy Malan intended for the whole of Africa.[18]

Republicanism and *apartheid* so dogmatically formulated were alien to the Smutsian 'system'. Yet one strand of Smuts' web was maintained: the 'rounding off' of South Africa's territory by the annexation of the High Commission Territories which had been promised to South Africa in the Union of South Africa Act of 1909.[19] Later the reason for desiring annexation was to be stated almost exactly in the terms of Smuts' 1919 speech: that the territories should form the basis for the territorial separation of Africans from whites —a domestic colonial solution to the 'native problem'. Before and immediately after his rise to the premiership Malan desired the annexation for slightly different reasons: to ensure uniformity of native policy in South Africa and the High Commission Territories and to complete the liquidation of imperial control in South Africa.[20] It seemed to him important that the 'native policy' pursued in these territories should be the same as that pursued in South Africa, to avoid a dangerous example being set for South Africa's natives by developments in the High Commission Territories.[21] Moreover, so long as Britain withheld its assent to incorporation of territories which were South African, South Africa's autonomy was not complete.[22] It was also alien to Nationalist thought that a white power such as Britain should resist the constitutionally sound claims

[16] The principle of local 'native' self-government was included in all the National Party's *Programmes of Principles*. See D. W. Kruger, *South African Political Parties and Policies, 1910–60*, 1960, pp. 71 and 97.

[17] Cmd. 3573, *Memorandum on Native Policy in East Africa*, 1929–30.

[18] That, at any rate, is what the proposed African Charter would have amounted to.

[19] See above, pp. 27 ff.

[20] *K.C.A.*, 11438A; *Ass. Deb.*, vol. 52, cols. 3946–8.

[21] *Ass. Deb.*, vol. 52; cf. also vol. 75, cols, 6818–21.

[22] *K.C.A.*, 11438A; *Ass. Deb.*, vol. 52, col. 3946–8.

of white people on account of the feelings of black people. Worse, the refusal ruffled the *amour-propre* of Afrikaner nationalist leaders, who felt slighted that their competence to govern 'natives' should seem to be in doubt.[23] Finally, it is also possible that Malan used the topic of incorporation as a convenient distraction for more militant republicans whose aims he had for the present no intention of achieving.[24]

Beyond the question of incorporating the High Commission Territories, Afrikaner nationalists had no interest in annexations, at least not until after World War II. They had been opposed to Smuts' Rhodesian plan for the reasons already mentioned—primarily because the consequent State would be a British State in political inclination. When in 1943 the question of union was raised, *Die Transvaler*, then under the editorship of Dr H. F. Verwoerd, set out the conditions under which Afrikaners would accept union. Rhodesia would have exactly the same status in the parliamentary system as any other province of the Union, with no special privileges as far as seats in parliament were concerned; article 137 of the constitution of the Union would have to be applied as thoroughly in Southern Rhodesia as it should be in the Union: every public servant would, accordingly, have to be thoroughly bilingual, and where there were Afrikaner communities Afrikaans medium schools would have to be established, while every child would have to learn Afrikaans as a subject.[25] The Cape daily *Die Burger*, which Dr Malan had once edited and which was the mouthpiece of the National Party in the Cape province, took pains to show that it favoured closer economic co-operation with the Rhodesians, but made quite clear its opposition to any political merger between South Africa and the Rhodesias.[26]

Even the granting to South Africa of the mandate over South West Africa after World War I had hardly delighted Dr Malan and General Hertzog, who considered the mandate and the rest of the Paris peace conference's work utterly reprehensible. The mandate was the reward for South Africa's participation in 'Britain's war'— a participation which had cost some Afrikaner nationalists dearly.[27] They had never had any grievance against Germany, and Hertzog particularly resented the grounds on which Germany had been expropriated: the allegation that Germany had been cruel to the

[23] *Ibid.*   [24] Cf. *Round Table*, June 1949, pp. 205–6.
[25] 8 May 1943.   [26] 11 August 1943.
[27] Cf. Malan, *op. cit., passim.*

'natives'.[28] To such Afrikaner nationalists the South African mandate over South West Africa was part of the imperialist skullduggery with which they associated Smuts, and to which they objected so much.

In the inter-war period consideration for the feelings of the Weimar politicians, and later for the Third Reich, whose friendship they sought, might have made an Afrikaner nationalist government (which by then would have regarded the transfer as irrevocable) unwilling to seek the incorporation of South West Africa into the Union.[29] At one stage General Hertzog actually suggested that he might contemplate handing South West Africa back to the Germans.[30] And when he had withdrawn from that position Hertzog's party continued to be very sympathetic to German colonial ambitions.[31]

When the second world war ended with the decisive defeat of the German empire, the Nationalists must have realised that there were only Britain and South Africa as decisive powers in South West Africa and that fear of German opposition need no longer influence the question of incorporation.[32] Above all, the possibility of an international organisation like the UN busying itself with the affairs of South West Africa must have clinched the argument for incorporation.[33] There was the concern too for uniformity of 'native policy' in southern Africa. Thus by different routes, but from the same point of departure, namely the desire to establish an African political milieu or context compatible with white domination within South Africa, the policies of Smuts and Malan on South West Africa converged. The same desire was behind the 'African Charter' for which Malan began agitating while still in opposition at the end of the war,[34] and which during his Ministry he tried to implement.

[28] On Hertzog's views on German colonial aspirations see D.O. 35/173/6408/157.

[29] Cf. Z. Ngavirue, 'The German section versus the Union section in South West Africa, 1920–39', unpublished seminar paper, Institute of Commonwealth Studies, University of London, ssa/70/5.

[30] See D.O. 35/173/6408/157.

[31] *Ibid.* They considered that Germany would be satisfied with concessions in Togo and Cameroon.

[32] Cf. Ngavirue, *op. cit.*

[33] Cf. Malan, in *Ass. Deb.*, vol. 52, cols. 3946–8 *et passim*.

[34] *Ass. Deb.*, vol. 52, col. 3956.

The aims of the charter

The African Charter, which Malan wished the powers to adopt, would have preserved Africa for Western European Christian civilisation. Accordingly it proposed to keep out of Africa both Asiatics and communists, and to forbid the arming of 'natives' and their use in white wars:

> ...we shall have to get together all the powers that have interests in Africa and that have territory and possessions here in Africa—it being still at the beginning of its development, and the native population in Africa still under the trusteeship of the Europeans, and having to remain under that for years still—we must have a pronouncement that Africa must be preserved in its development for the Western European Christian civilisation ... For example, the powers that have interests in Africa can agree that the native population should no longer be used in the battlefields of the world, and that they will not be given military training or be armed, so that they will not constitute a danger to each other and to other nations in Africa. I think that is a matter of extreme and tremendous importance.[35]

Dr Malan also wanted the powers to:

> Close the doors of Africa as much as possible for the influx of elements from outside that have already caused the greatest trouble in the territories in the north, and which have already occasioned serious difficulties in South Africa.[36]

By 'elements' he meant, simply, Indians. Apart from altruistic consideration for the underdeveloped natives of Africa, it was in the vital interests of white South Africa to keep Africa for 'Western European civilisation'. Thus Malan asked rhetorically:

> If Africa is not preserved for the Western European civilization and if Russia obtains the ascendancy in Europe, as it may obtain it, and if the whole African continent is thrown open for communist propaganda and South Africa is the magnet for the natives from the north, then I ask what the future of South Africa is going to be.[37]

In 1949 Dr Malan argued that Africa needed economic development, but not quite so much as it needed protection and guidance.[38]

During the years he was Prime Minister Dr Malan was to repeat the demands of the 'African Charter' many times,[39] and the ideas which he had so clearly formulated were to influence South African

---

[35] *Ibid.*   [36] *Ibid.*   [37] *Ibid.*   [38] *Ibid.*
[39] *Ass. Deb.*, vol 64, cols. 1323–44. See also *The Foreign Policy of the Union of South Africa, passim.*

foreign policy long after his retirement, as we shall presently see. The charter was Malan's reply to the Atlantic Charter, and to the emergent, though as yet inchoate, ideology of decolonisation. The leader of the National Party was marking off Africa—sub-Saharan Africa, at least—as one area in which the Atlantic Charter should not apply; while at the same time he accepted—nay, championed— the idea of regional co-operation (suggested by pan-Americanism) in Africa, so long as it could be informed by the Afrikaner nationalist principles of *his* charter.

Yet although the African Charter was addressed to the post-second world war situation, nothing that was in it was new; its sentiments were as old, almost, as the National Party itself. The opposition to Africans being trained in warfare and used in white men's wars had been expressed by Pirow in Hertzog's Ministry in the 1930s and, before him, by Smuts.[40] Nor was the idea that the Union government should exert itself to obtain an inter-imperial agreement to prevent such developments. The matter had been raised several times, as, for example, during discussion with other dominions' representatives of the crisis caused by Italy's invasion of Ethiopia in 1935. Then the Union government, which maintained a militant stance in regard to Il Duce's adventure, would have been quite prepared to abandon sanctions if Mussolini could agree to holding a mandate over Ethiopia which would stipulate that 'natives' should not be armed. Malcolm MacDonald, the British Secretary of State for Dominion Affairs, reported the South African ambassador as having said:

Recognising that Abyssinia was really a barbarous country which ought never to have been admitted to membership of the League, we should agree to Italy's having a mandate over the whole country, on condition that she observed the mandatory principles. The most important of these, in Mr te Water's eyes, is of course that concerning the non-arming of the natives.[41]

Oswald Pirow also argued along the same lines at a meeting with MacDonald a few weeks later. In Hertzog's divided Cabinet this was probably the majority view. Of course, the Union delegate to the League, reflecting Smuts' and Hertzog's particular views, denounced the abandonment of economic sanctions with a show of rectitude:

[40] See J. C. Smuts, *Greater South Africa.*
[41] D.O. 114/68/9, 22 May 1936.

... we know that the Covenant [of the League] is falling to pieces in our hands [Te Water declared]. Fifty nations, led by three of the most powerful in the world, are about to declare their powerlessness to protect the weakest in their midst from destruction. The authority of the League of Nations is about to come to nought [*sic*].[42]

Malan's African Charter did not go as far as Pirow had done in promising to set up a defence arrangement whereby South Africa would defend white interests everywhere on the African continent; nor did he quite as openly advocate the adoption of South Africa's own brand of racial discrimination in the rest of Africa. Yet he too was opposed to what he considered to be dangerous haste in the granting of political rights to Africans.[43]

The defence of whites in Africa was, however, incorporated in the 'African Charter' (and later the Simonstown agreement)[44] under a new description: the preservation of Africa for European civilisation and the defence of Africa, from Simonstown to Suez, against communism.

The 'defence of Africa' was in large measure an extension of the defence of South Africa, as far as Union politicians were concerned. The desire to prevent African armies went with a desire to be *au fait* with military developments on the continent. In addition to both considerations was the strategic doctrine—widely accepted within white South Africa—that in the event of war the enemy must be met as far away from South Africa's borders as possible.[45] From this doctrine arose the willingness to involve South Africa in defending the Middle East and North Africa, 'the gateway to Africa'. In the context of the ideas current in South Africa after the second world war these contingent commitments were appropriate. It was generally believed that Africa would be the prize in a future war because of its raw materials. The shrinking of Western Europe as a result of, among other causes, the Potsdam dispositions would in future place a

[42] D.O. 114/67, 1 July 1936. Pirow was probably nearer to the feeling of the majority of whites, and especially Nationalists. According to MacDonald, 'he did not himself think that this attitude truly represented South African opinion [meaning white South African]. There were other matters which interested South Africans more. In fact South Africans [*sic*] were so little interested in the sanctions issue that it was a case of their taking the line of least resistance and allowing themselves to follow Generals Hertzog and Smuts on the issue.' (D.O. 114/67, 19 June 1936.)

[43] *Ass. Deb.*, vol. 84, col. 4496. See also vol. 75, cols. 6818–21.

[44] Cmd. 9520, *Exchange of Letters . . .* , 1955.

[45] Minister of Defence, *Ass. Deb.*, vol. 72, *passim*.

premium on land bases to supply forces defending the Middle East.[46] South Africa itself would be the workshop of the world, and by its geographic position on the route to the East would be strategically attractive to any power.[47] A new heartland theory was evolving in which the pivot of the world's politics was shifting from McKinder's Europe to northern and eastern Africa.[48]

Perceiving the future world strategies along these lines, Nationalists wanted to be fully prepared for the future. The white population of South Africa was, however, small, and any contribution its small white army could make would have to be subject to the need to keep a sufficient number of men at home to safeguard internal security.[49] In the circumstances the defence of Africa had to be a co-operative effort among African powers. Thus emerged the South African idea of forming an African Defence Organisation[50] to defend Africa from communists, but also, by necessary consequence, to implicate the powers in the defence of white South Africa.

In the Cold War division Malan and his Nationalist followers had firmly taken sides with the West. Already, in the war years, Afrikaner nationalists had been quick to point out that Germany was being broken while communist Russia was being allowed to construct an empire.[51] At the end of the war they deplored the Potsdam agreements.[52] With the increasing disaffection of the West with its communist ally, Afrikaner nationalists could now have their own back against those who had decried their ambivalence towards, if not sympathy with, Nazi Germany. Smuts' United Party, they alleged, was party to this international blunder; what was more, within South Africa, they said, the United Party harboured or gave succour

[46] This was the theme of the Nairobi conference (1951), which the Union Government helped to convene, and of the subsequent Dakar conference (1954), at which it was represented. See Minister of Defence in *Ass. Deb.*, vol. 85, col. 5082.

[47] This was one of the arguments of Union governments in favour of extending the Simonstown agreements to include other powers. See below, 'The defence of Africa'.

[48] McKinder's theory, otherwise known as the heartland theory, was first propounded in a lecture by its author to the Royal Geographical Society in 1904.

[49] Almost immediately he took office Erasmus disbanded the 'native corps' which had served in the second world war: *Die Transvaler*, 28 June 1948.

[50] *Pretoria News*, 9 June 1951; Minister of Defence in *Ass. Deb.*, vol. 87, cols. 1261–2.

[51] Strydom, reported in *Pretoria News*, 27 April 1949. See also *Ass. Deb.*, vol. 52, *passim*.

[52] Eric Louw and Dr Malan, in *Ass. Deb.*, vol. 52, *passim*.

to communists.[53] Afrikaner nationalists might also hope to regain international respectability, particularly in America, by eagerly joining the anti-communist chorus of execration. Anti-communism and its pastime of finding 'the communists in our midst' were, respectively, a cause which Afrikaner nationalists might be expected to champion and a task they might perform with much diligence. In their long campaign for the 1948 general election[54] they had harped on the danger of communism in South Africa, and it would have been very inconsistent not to take a similar stand on international communism. After all, communism's whole aim in South Africa was their main objection, namely, a non-racial republic.

It was against communists, then, that Africa had to be preserved for European Christian civilisation. But it was also against Asiatics. Anti-Indian feeling had a long history in South Africa,[55] only exacerbated among Afrikaner nationalists by India's strictures against South Africa, and by Indians making common cause with Africans. Asians were seen as a potential source of trouble and unwholesome agitation among blacks.[56] Against them too—for the good of Africa as well as South Africa—the continent should be preserved.

Communism meant Russia in this period. Russia was, at least in part, Asian. China, which turned communist within a year of Malan's accession, was wholly Asian. A tendency on that account to equate the East with communism, and to treat both as inimical to white people everywhere, might seem too obvious to credit. Yet, very much on the basis of Malan's views, entrenched as policy, just such a tendency would in time exhibit itself in Afrikaner nationalist intellectual circles, and would yield a convenient view of the world in which peacefulness was the prerogative of the white Western powers, because all other peoples were hostile: Asians because they were communists or nearly so; Africans because they were still savage and susceptible to communist agitation—against which the white men in Africa had to guard them.[57] It is almost completely true to say that this was a major part of the climate of foreign policy

[53] Hancock, op. cit., chapter 28.
[54] The pages of Die Transvaler and Die Burger of 1943–48 bear this out.
[55] G. H. Calpin, Indians in South Africa, 1949.
[56] On some attitudes on Indians see Die Transvaler, 23 October, 1944 ('Baasspeel uit Indië'); Die Burger, 28 February 1948 ('Asiatisme en Kommunisme'); Die Vaderland, 22 March 1949 ('Oos-Afrika vir Indië?'); and, of course Malan's African Charter speeches.
[57] Cf. 'Asiatisme en Kommunisme', in Die Burger, 28 February, 1948. See also G. D. Scholtz, Die gevaar uit die Ooste, 1960, pp. 10, 114, 196.

ideas among Afrikaner nationalists from the rise of Malan and into the early 1960s. The functional significance of such a world picture within their idea and value system was to exalt the Afrikaner nationalists' own racial policies into a major service for mankind, and to magnify the activities of such Asians as Nehru into menaces of millenial significance for white South Africa and the world: in both ways the domestic racial conflict situation was simplified and redescribed in universal terms.[58] It was a desperate attempt, at the intellectual level at least, to argue out a place of importance for South Africa in the emergent international system and to associate the West with the defence of the South African political system.

Malan believed in a white civilising mission in Africa and in the need for trusteeship over Africans—but the expiry of the white man's mandate seemed to him many decades away yet. The idea of a mission in Africa, in the peculiar Calvinist world picture of the Afrikaner nationalist movement, was quite mystically construed, and thus a suprarational justification of the Afrikaner presence in Africa was provided.[59]

On the conduct of 'native affairs' in Africa Malan clearly wished to be consulted. Consequently he complained when changes in the political status of Africans in Kenya and the Gold Coast were initiated.[60] In so doing he was articulating long-standing Nationalist sentiments, and their concern that developments of this sort in Africa might arouse the aspirations of Africans within South Africa as well.[61]

Conceptions of heavenly mandates, the fear of Indians and communists, together with the desire to influence native policy, meant that South Africa had to co-operate closely with the powers which had possessions in Africa. For all their dislike of British imperialism, and for all their desire to liquidate its influence in South Africa, after the war Afrikaner nationalists were constrained to co-operate with Britain, then the strongest African power and an important

[58] There was, of course, always the realisation that 'the West' did not share this view. See, for example, *Die Transvaler*, 26 January 1948.

[59] Cf. *Die Transvaler*, 5 September 1948; J. A. Coetzee's letter to *Die Burger*, 13 September 1948; and the Rev. G. C. Oosthuyzen of Bulawayo: 'The ideal is not Africa for the Afrikaner but the Afrikaner for Africa, which means that Africa needs the services of the Afrikaner. That service is based on a Christian foundation' (*Pretoria News*, 24 January 1951).

[60] E. A. Walker, *A History of Southern Africa*, 1957, p. 825; *Die Burger*, 24 February 1951; *K.C.A.*, 1143A, 8516C, 10023A, 9448A.

[61] *Ibid.*

member of the Western alliance.[62] Thus Malan's desire to maintain good relations between the two sections of the white population of South Africa by not leaving the Commonwealth converged with considerations arising out of his Africa policy to keep South Africa within the association.[63] Thus he affirmed:

We readily acknowledge the uniquely friendly relations existing between our country and the United Kingdom and other members of the British Commonwealth of Nations. It is the desire of the government that those friendly relations shall be continued.[64]

Given, however, the tensions between India and South Africa, and the outlook on racial affairs for which Dr Malan stood, he had reservations about the structure of Commonwealth consultation now that it was no longer a white organisation:

It will be generally conceded that, with the recent accession to the Commonwealth of new members having equal rights, the danger of interference cannot be regarded as imaginary, especially if South Africa's experience at Lake Success are borne in mind. This inevitably leads to the question whether this universally desired friendly co-operation would not be more effectively achieved by means of separate contacts between the individual members of the Commonwealth rather than through discussions at joint and inclusive conferences.[65]

Malan's apprehensions about 'interference' may, however, have been allayed by Nehru's decision not to treat the Commonwealth consultative machinery as a forum of conflict and to reserve confrontations for the UN's meetings.[66] Furthermore, it appeared to Malan that on one very important matter India and the West were *ad idem*—at least for the while:

I am glad to be able to say, in spite of the dissension between us and India, that so far as one can judge today, and according to public statements that have been made, India is also strongly on the anti-communist side. That will mean quite a lot in the future, and we hope that they will stand by it.[67]

[62] Cf. *Round Table*, March 1949, p. 186.   [63] *Ibid.*
[64] Malan, 4 June 1948, in *The Foreign Policy of the Union of South Africa*, p. 5.   [65] *Ibid.*
[66] *Round Table*, September 1951, pp. 359–63.
[67] *The Foreign Policy of the Union of South Africa*, p. 11. See also Mansergh, *op. cit.*, vol. II, pp. 860–71. Note that Malan may have been trying to explain away to the rest of Afrikanerdom why he had not taken a militantly anti-Indian stand and opposed India's admission to the Commonwealth.

Within the Commonwealth framework Malan hoped to implement the African Charter. In addition to the principles of the
charter Africa was South Africa's 'hinterland', a natural market for
its manufactures, and southern Africa was also a source of important
primary commodities, as well as of labour for the mines and farms
of the Union.[68] Furthermore, much economic development was expected to take place in post-war Africa, and South Africa did not
wish to lose any benefits which might accrue. But Malan had long
been opposed to being hemmed in within the British imperial 'kraal'
and he hoped to diversify South Africa's international associations.
As he had put it in 1920:

General Smuts has called on us to leave the ant-heap of isolation and to
rise higher so that we can have a broader view [of things]. We are more
than prepared to heed [*gehoor te gee*] his call. But then we say in our turn,
to General Smuts: do not leave the ant-heap of isolation to go and sit on
the walls of the British imperial kraal [*kraalmuur van die Britse Ryk*] with
nothing in prospect except 'the British Commonwealth, whereto, we will
also soon belong'. Let us leave both kraal and ant-heap behind us, and let
us climb to the mountain-top, with its fresh, healthy air and panorama
[*vergesig*]; let us not only see ourselves and the British Empire, but the
whole of mankind, of which we are a part. And let us take our righful
place among the nations of the world.[69]

In the African context of the post-second world war period this
meant working with Belgium, France and Portugal as well as Britain.

*Implementing the charter: the diplomacy
of Afrikæner nationalism*

South West Africa and the United Nations. The National Party
government of Malan was in favour of a 'firm' line over South
West Africa. Mr Eric Louw, Minister of Economic Affairs, who
represented South Africa at the United Nations in 1949, had long
denied that the UN had any rightful say over South West Africa; he
considered that the UN was not the legal heir to the League of
Nations to which South Africa had been answerable for South
West Africa. The League, he maintained, had died intestate and (as a
colleague added—irrelevantly) insolvent into the bargain.[70] The

---

[68] Cf. 'Foreign Bantu', in *Standard Encyclopaedia*, p. 100.
[69] D. F. Malan, *Wat ons Het . . .*, concluding paragraph.
[70] *Ass. Deb.*, vol. 55, cols. 2382–428; vol. 56, cols. 3654–700.

National Party government therefore chose to disregard the UN and to proceed with the incorporation of the mandated territory.[71] In opposition they had viewed with grave concern the fact that Smuts agreed to send reports to the UN on South West Africa, arguing that this would merely encourage interference in the domestic affairs of South West Africa and South Africa.[72] Their support for the United Nations had, in any case, never been enthusiastic, and in the two years after its first session National Party leaders had expressed themselves strongly against the 'deficiencies' of the UN as an international organisation.[73] In government the National Party therefore adopted an attitude of defiance: the practice of sending reports on South West Africa was discontinued and Mr Eric Louw assumed a belligerent attitude when he led the South African delegation to the UN.[74] The Malan government introduced the South West Africa Representation Bill of 1949, which could be—and was— construed as an attempt to incorporate South West Africa.[75] And when the International Court of Justice advised in 1950 that South Africa should report to the UN on South West Africa, although the Union was not obliged to place South West Africa under the Trusteeship Council,[76] Malan rejected that opinion.[77] It was, he thought, contradictory, while at the same time it would lead to the crudest (grofte) intervention in South Africa's domestic affairs.[78] When the Trusteeship Council decided to hear the Rev. Michael Scott the South African delegation boycotted that meeting of the council.[79]

Britain's decision to place Tanganyika under the Trusteeship Council was, in the light of this, unwelcome in National Party circles, although no official comment was publicly made by the Union government.[80]

Relations with the UN deteriorated during Malan's term of office, so that by 1954, Malan complained:[81]

[71] *Ibid.*
[72] *Pretoria News,* 13 December 1951.
[73] Malan, in *The Foreign Policy of the Union of South Africa, passim.*
[74] See below, pp. 61 ff, and chapter v.
[75] *Die Vaderland,* 9 April 1949. The effect of the Bill was also to increase the number of National Party voters.
[76] See Carter, *The Politics of Inequality,* pp. 388–9.
[77] *Ibid.*   [78] *Die Transvaler,* 14 July 1950.
[79] Carter, *op. cit.,* p. 388.
[80] *Die Vaderland,* 22 March 1949.
[81] See G. M. Carter, *op. cit.,* chapter 15.

UNO is interfering with Africa. It does so directly, but it also does so indirectly ... by simply regarding all people as equal and all nations, whether they are ripe for it or not, must have certain human rights, as they call it, including the franchise; and the inference which these races, the immature and in many cases barbaric races of Africa, draw from it is that they are oppressed, and if they are an oppressed people they must use all possible measures to obtain freedom. That is why one has this unrest in Africa ... because people were brought under the impression by UNO that they were oppressed.[82]

The United Nations Organisation, which might have provided South Africa with an institutional framework for international co-operation wider than the British Empire and Commonwealth, was thus disqualified by its racial outlook.

The British connection and 'native policy'. The assertive attitude towards South West Africa was paralleled by the Union government's desire to annex the High Commission Territories. In 1949 Malan curtly reproached the Southern Rhodesian Minister of Justice and Internal Affairs for asserting that Southern Rhodesia had a right to be consulted in any future disposal of the Bechuanaland protectorate.[83] Malan also reproved the British Secretary of State for Commonwealth Relations for apparently having encouraged such views on the part of the Southern Rhodesian Minister.[84] Malan's indignation was all the more appropriate in view of the controversy which earlier in the same year had surrounded the Bamangwato succession as a result of the heir designate, Seretse Khama, having married an English woman.[85]

Developments in British Africa, where Africans were increasingly being accorded political rights, also made the question of the future of the High Commission Territories more urgent. So long as the territories were not under South African administration the 'native policies' being pursued by Britain elsewhere in Africa might be pursued in these territories also. The opportunity for an assertion of South Africa's claims to the High Commission Territories was provided by Mr Patrick Gordon Walker's visit to South Africa in 1950.[86] The South African Premier then made clear his resentment of

[82] *Ass. Deb.*, vol. 84, col. 4493.
[83] *Pretoria News*, 22 December 1949.   [84] *Ibid.*
[85] Cf. Carter, *op. cit.*, pp. 78–9; M. Goldsworthy, *Colonial Issues in British Politics*, pp. 114–64; J. Redfern, *Ruth and Seretse: 'A Very Disreputable Transaction'*, 1955.
[86] See *K.C.A.*, 11438A.

the condemnation of South Africa's native policies implied in Britain's refusal to transfer the territories.[87]

Moreover, Malan made no secret of the fact that his government considered the British policy of advancing Africans towards self-government misconceived. He regretted the speed of events in west Africa, where Kwame Nkrumah was elevated to the position of Leader of Government Business in the Gold Coast.[88] But as the Union was continually complaining of the interference of others in its domestic affairs, Malan later denied that in criticising Mr Griffiths he had intended to interfere in the internal affairs of Britain and her colonies. He considered, nevertheless, that:

England in Africa is indispensable as a civilising influence; England's leadership and guardianship cannot in the interest of the white man living higher up in Africa, cannot in the interest of the natives themselves be spared. It will take years and generations before the natives will be able to stand on their own feet so that they will no longer require the leadership and control of the white man . . . I had to express myself on that issue.[89]

Malan took pleasure in the fact that there had been favourable reaction to his statement on British policy among the white communities in east Africa.[90] Although he had earlier received a deputation of Kenya settlers, he would not now hold consultations with the settlers over 'native policy', as that would amount to interference in the affairs of another country. Nevertheless, he invited them to 'associate themselves with the statement which I have made'.[91]

South African influence on the conduct of affairs in the British African territories was not welcome in London. One of the reasons for creating the Central African Federation, according to Lord Chandos, was to restrict the infiltration of 'Afrikaner elements' into Southern Rhodesia:

Afrikaaner [sic] elements had begun to penetrate deeply into Southern, and to a lesser extent, into Northern Rhodesia. The Broederbond was the active instrument in this invasion. It was calculated that Afrikaaners would certainly hold political power in Southern Rhodesia within a decade and might within that time force a federation of Southern Rhodesia with the Union.

It is quite unnecessary to enter into any controversy, or here [in Chandos's memoirs] to condemn Afrikaner policy towards the native races;

[87] *K.C.A.*, 11438A.
[88] See n. 71 above.
[89] *Ass. Deb.*, vol. 75, cols. 6818–20.
[90] *Ibid.*   [91] *Ibid.*

it is enough to say that it ran counter to British conceptions of our responsibilities and our mission.[92]

To this Afrikaner nationalists objected.[93]

Malan was apprehensive also about the changes in the United Nations Organisation and especially in the British Commonwealth, both of which were already too multi-racial for his liking, which he feared would follow from the creation of black States and their admission into these organisations. As far as the Commonwealth was concerned, 'My attitude was that this would render the Commonwealth's position impossible. It is difficult even now because there are three countries in the Commonwealth with an Asiatic outlook, and not that of Western civilisation.'[94]

While he was willing to accept India's 'disappointing' neutrality in the Cold War, he much resented Nehru's intervention in African affairs, exemplified by Nehru's call upon Indians and Africans to work together against colonialism. By 1954 not even common membership of the Commonwealth could stop Malan from pointedly blaming Nehru for his share in difficulties like those created for the whites by the Mau Mau: 'I say deliberately,' he declaimed to Parliament, 'that Nehru is the enemy of the white man.'[95] He also dubbed Nehru a communist. With all the difficulties which were being created, Malan wondered, as he castigated Nehru, 'whether it has not become time for the whole world to think a little more about the position of the white man in the world'.[96]

The United Nations, some members of the British Commonwealth, and the British government itself were pursuing policies diametrically opposed to the African Charter; and towards the end of his political career Malan subjectively presented the ideological conflict in these terms:

There will have to be a psychological revolution. One finds in the world today, and especially in England, that there is a sickly sentimentality in regard to the black man. Someone in authority told me in England . . . that one can say with truth that they venerate a black skin . . . The position is that, under these circumstances, I fear that the people of Europe, the white nations of Europe, are becoming decadent.[97]

[92] Oliver Lyttleton, Viscount Chandos, *The Memoirs of Lord Chandos*, 1962, p. 387.

[93] Cf. Dr A. Hertzog, in *Ass. Deb.*, vol. 84, col. 4431.

[94] Malan, in Mansergh, *loc. cit.*

[95] *Ass. Deb.*, vol. 84, col. 4494.   [96] *Ass. Deb.*, vol. 84, col. 4495.

[97] *Ass. Deb.*, vol. 84, col. 4496. See also vol. 75, cols. 6818–21.

Organisations for co-operation in Africa. The Union's difficulties with the United Nations encouraged the government to look for other organisational arrangements for the successful implementation of the African Charter. It participated in the formation of the Commission for Technical Co-operation in Africa South of the Sahara (known by its French initials CCTA) in 1950, an inter-imperial venture intended, according to one analyst, to pre-empt the setting up of a United Nations agency which might have led to United Nations interference in Africa.[98] The CCTA, meeting at least once a year, initially restricted its activities to technical matters rather than social and economic affairs. Several conferences were held, in which the Union government participated fully.[99]

In 1949 the Union government was host to a conference of scientists from all over Africa representing the various powers with possessions in Africa. Such a regional conference had been called for by the Commonwealth Scientific Council in 1945, but it was the Union government which took the initiative in holding one which was not limited to the Commonwealth African powers only.[100] The conference unanimously agreed to recommend to their governments the setting up of a standing scientific organisation with regular meetings. The result was the formation two years later of the CSA (French initials for the Commission for Scientific Co-operation in Africa South of the Sahara.)[101] These commissions and their subordinate bodies provided the main institutions for co-operation in Africa (apart from the usual diplomatic channels). They suited the Nationalist government well, since they were not restricted to British Africa only.

It was some similar form of organisational co-operation that the Union government envisaged for the defence of Africa, but it was not in fact achieved.

Throughout Malan's period of office the idea of a pan-African organisation which might knit together the various co-operative efforts lingered in white South African politics. No explicit plan for the creation of such an organisation was presented, and by 1954 it was felt by some that the dream of pan-African co-operation should be rid of such ambitions. Until a means was found of emerging from

[98] McKay, *loc. cit.*
[99] *Ibid.*; also CCTA–CSA, *Inter-African Scientific and Technical Co-operation*, n.d., *passim.*
[100] *Pretoria News,* 11 August 1949.
[101] *Ibid.*

the impasse which the 'native question' created, talk of pan-African organisations could only raise (as the member of parliament for Groblersdal put it) 'the same trouble which we are now having in connection with UNO'.[102]

When Malan retired at the end of 1954 the trend of events in Africa was contrary to what he had wished. The question of race relations had been fundamental to his Africa policy; but the racial practices of the Union government were, for Malan as for Smuts, a disabling factor in his attempts to influence policy in Africa.

[102] Mr Abraham, in *Ass. Deb.*, vol. 84, col. 4466.

The Union as an 'African' power: the diplomacy of Eric Louw

Eric Louw was already richly experienced in international affairs when he became Minister of External Affairs in the Cabinet formed by Strydom after the retirement of the octogenarian Malan.[1] Both were trained as lawyers, so that both could readily insist on a rigid interpretation of South Africa's rights in international law in respect of non-interference by others in her domestic affairs and in respect of South West Africa—an interpretation upon which Eric Louw had long insisted with aggressive tenacity.[2] As External Affairs Minister, Louw then adopted, towards the UN in particular and toward all other critics, an attitude of truculent defiance.[3]

Strydom, for his part, was the champion of white mastery (*baasskap*) within South Africa, a Transvaler of ardent republican conviction and a very good friend of the reputedly extreme Minister of Native Affairs, Dr H. F. Verwoerd.[4] Strydom was therefore regarded as more 'extremist' and 'right-wing' than his predecessor, and he might therefore be expected to yield to external pressure even less than Malan had done.[5]

The revival of republicanism under Strydom tended to isolate the South African government from the rest of British Africa, and the anti-Afrikaner sentiments which had earlier been expressed by Huggins in Southern Rhodesia gained a new relevance.[6] Issues were

[1] Appointed in 1925 as first Trade Commissioner of South Africa in the United States and Canada, High Commissioner for South Africa in London 1929, Envoy Extraordinary and Plenipotentiary to the United States of America in 1929, etc. Also represented the Union at UN in 1948 and 1949. See *Who's Who of Southern Africa, 1967*, p. 563.

[2] *Pretoria News*, leader, 3 January 1949; cf. E. H. Louw, 'South Africa will not appear before UN as defendant but as plaintiff', *Die Transvaler*, 30 August 1948; *Ass. Deb.*, vol. 55, cols. 2382–428; *ibid.*, vol. 56, cols. 3654–700; E. H. Louw in *The Case for South Africa*, ed. H. H. Biermann, 1963, pp. 19–48. [3] *Ibid.*

[4] In 1948 Verwoerd 'prophesied' in public that Strydom would be the next Prime Minister of South Africa (after Malan): *Die Transvaler*, 30 June 1948. [5] Cf. Walker, *op. cit.*, p. 923.

[6] Cf. *K.C.A.*, 10409A and 11748A, for Huggins's views. See also *Pretoria News*, 31 January 1951; *Die Burger*, leader, 9 November 1951.

mixed, federation and its ideology of 'partnership', republicanism (of the Afrikaner nationalist sort) and its ideology of *apartheid* seeming to represent quite different worlds, and in addition the underlying hostility within the white communities between Boers and and Britons finding expression now and again.

Neither Louw nor Strydom ever fully—at least, not openly—rejected the African Charter and its principal aim that South Africa should play a role of influence in Africa comparable to that of the imperial powers, or that South Africa should hold a position of leadership in Africa. Events progressively made it clear, however, that the African Charter would not be adopted by the powers, and the Union government had to adjust its Africa policy to the changing conditions in Africa.

Louw sought to increase South African participation in the conduct of affairs in Africa principally through the existing organisations, the CCTA and CSA; he accordingly increased South African participation in the work of both organisations.[7] But the principle of co-operation through inter-imperial organisations was nowhere more diligently pursued than in the attempts which began during Malan's term, and continued to the end of Strydom's Ministry, to set up an African Defence Organisation in which South Africa would play a leading part. To the development and implementation of this idea we now turn.

The defence of Africa

Although General Smuts might have had differences with the imperial governments on the organisation of African defence, he always saw Africa as a part of imperial defence and therefore did not seek a defence plan or organisation outside that framework.

Afrikaner nationalists, of whom the government which succeeded his were constituted, had different conceptions about their role in Africa, for although (as we have seen) they were eager that imperial powers should maintain their position in Africa, they nonetheless resented being drawn into Britain's wars. Their 'defence of Africa' policy was quite different, inspired by principles particularly associated with their general ideological outlook.

Where Smuts had concentrated on the Empire, they emphasised 'the white man in Africa'. Where Smuts saw the threats to colonial

[7] Minister of External Affairs, in *Ass. Deb.*, vol. 95, col. 7639.

settler communities as issuing from the overall international situation, Afrikaner nationalists tended to focus on the dangers of the indigenous population—as well, of course, as on the communist threat and the Indian peril. The defence of (white settlement in) Africa against the communist menace was a post-war phenomenon, while the ideas concerning the defence of 'the white man in Africa' antedated World War II and were not eclipsed by the more global preoccupations of the post-war period. Instead, they were integrated, and generally informed by the peculiar racial preoccupation and attitudes of Afrikaner nationalists.

These latter preoccupations received their clearest expression before the war at about the time when Lord Passfield's memorandum on the primacy of native interests in east Africa was exercising the minds and exciting the passions of white settlers everywhere in Africa.[8] It came in a speech by Oswald Pirow, then Minister of Defence in the Union. As the first reaction to decolonisation it deserves careful attention; as the first declaration of an Afrikaner nationalist African defence policy it is of considerable interest.

Pirow made his speech at a dinner in Johannesburg.[9] He noted that vast changes had occurred in Africa in recent years, with tropical Africa acquiring a permanent white population. The white communities so created had almost immediately found themselves quartered with the 'native problem' and had 'almost without exception' taken to the views that were held in the Union on colour policy. Adjoining the territories of white settlement, however, were 'vast areas' where a policy 'diametrically opposed to our policy of differentiation between black and white' was being applied: 'where hundreds of thousands of black men [were] being trained into some of the finest fighting material in the world'. Pirow observed that the 'conflict of policy' might lead to an armed clash, but it was also conceivable that the time might come 'when white men, women and children [would] have to be protected against black invaders'. Should that day come,

I know that we need not ask ourselves what the attitude of the Union should be. At the same time, an ounce of preparation is worth more than a pound of sympathy. The contingency, no matter how remote it may

[8] Cmd. 3573, *Memorandum on Native Policy in East Africa*, 1929–30; cf. G. Bennet, 'British settlers north of the Zambezi, 1920–60', in Gann and Duignan, *op. cit.*, pp. 58–89, especially p. 67; *Swaziland Times*, 13 April 1933; see also D.O. 35/395/11007/52 (Stanley to Thomas, 19 April 1933).

[9] On 22 November 1933; extracts in D.O. 35/395/11007/64.

appear to be, is one that should be considered in any general scheme of defence in the Union.[10]

Pirow did not indicate how this contingency would be 'considered', but went on rather enigmatically to show what South African leadership in Africa meant to him and like-minded white South Africans:

We have asserted our right as regards British Africa that our advice in connection with native policy should not be wholly disregarded. We have contended that we are entitled, if not to be consulted, at least to point out that any policy applied in the northern territories will undoubtedly have repercussions in the Union. If our advice is to be accepted, wholly or in part, and if the result of that is going to be that there may be a clash of policy between black and white, it stands to reason that we may have to assume certain consequential obligations.[11]

The mood of anxiety over native policy in the northern territories was not at the time as acute in the Union as Pirow's speech suggested. But concern there was, evidenced by *Die Vaderland*'s objections to the creation of a black civil service in Northern Rhodesia and its opinion of development in Africa:

Tanganyika Territory and even Kenya are now considered by the British Government as a sphere where in all things the interests of the Natives must have precedence. That they propose to pursue such a policy in Northern Rhodesia is rather disquieting, and this should accelerate a more resolute attitude in our Union.[12]

Already these utterances struck resonant chords in the white population, and there was a climate of ideas, therefore, favourable to the Africa policy of Pirow and *Die Vaderland*. As the British High Commissioner in South Africa observed:

Foolish and short-sighted in the extremity of its illiberalism as the attitude may seem to an unbiased reader in Europe, it reflects, I fear, the opinion of a very far from inconsiderable portion of the white population of South Africa, not only in the Transvaal and Orange Free State, not only among the uneducated and not confined to those whose mother tongue is Afrikaans.[13]

What, then, did Pirow's post-prandial lucubrations amount to? Firstly, they constituted the first explicit statement by a member of the Union government of an Africa policy based on the racial doctrine of Afrikaner nationalism. Secondly, they illustrated the preoccupation of Afrikaner nationalists with intra-territorial racial

[10] D.O. 35/395/11007/64. [11] *Ibid.*
[12] *Ibid.* [13] D.O. 35/395/11007/52.

conflict rather than with external threats to Africa, or even inter-territorial conflict among white communities. Thirdly, they interpreted in military terms the anxieties of the Afrikaner nationalists concerning the process of decolonisation just beginning. For us the interest of Pirow's speech lies in the fact that, although later Afrikaner nationalist governments were more cautious, themes from Pirow's speech recurred in their own utterances. Equally interesting is the generalised fear that the policies of the African powers could in any number of unclearly understood ways result in conflicts between whites and blacks in Africa, and that since the imperial powers did not share the South African outlook on race relations the Union should make its own preparation to defend the settlers. As *defensor fidei* (the faith of segregation and white supremacy) the Union envisaged in Africa a South African peace.

It is worth noting that every Afrikaner nationalist who held high office believed that racial integration would inevitably lead to race conflict. Like Pirow they too believed in the view stated by Smuts in 1917 that 'natives' should not be armed if they were not to be a danger to others and to themselves. Along with these fears went a definite belief that Africa must remain under white colonial rule, a desire which persisted long after Pirow had disappeared from the political scene. The advocacy of European imperialism in Africa by Afrikaner *nationalists* was a part of the political outlook of Union governments ever since, until independence made it unreal; but then the 'influence' of the former colonial powers remained important, as we shall later see.

As a statement of intentions rather than sentiments Pirow's speech was vague, but it did at the very least envisage, as the British High Commissioner realised,

two contingencies, admittedly remote, in which armed intervention by the Union might be necessary. On the one hand, he [Pirow] thinks the pursuit of assimilation, in defiance of Union advice, might necessitate the protection of Europeans against native insurrection and invasion; on the other hand, if the advice of the Union as to the policy of 'white supremacy' were followed, there might be a consequential obligation upon the Union to assist in the enforcement of a policy of repression.[14]

In either case, *in animo habebat ibi aliquid audere.*

It might be considered that a statement made fifteen to twenty years before the period of the African Defence Organisation scheme,

[14] D.O. 35/395/11007/64.

by a politician who had in the meantime become discredited, would be at best only tenuously related to the policy of our period. At the risk of repetition, however, it must be emphasised that the conception of South African capacities and entitlements in Africa which Pirow's policy presupposed were very similar to those embodied in Nationalist policies which succeeded it, in the conditions of 1945 —conditions which were thought, in spite of decolonisation, to be to South Africa's strategic advantage. It was the subjective evaluation of South African capabilities in the post-war period which suggested the particular form of defence co-operation which Union governments (after 1948) desired,[15] on the unaltered principles they shared with the erstwhile comrade and contemporary of many of their members, Oswald Pirow. Those principles were now reinforced by the Cold War obsession with communism.

If the changes following from the war encouraged great expectations on the part of South Africans, and if Afrikaner nationalists eagerly embraced the anti-communism of their Western capitalist friends, they also accepted the regionalism which became a major complement of international organisation. Africa was their region.

The undertaking to contribute to the defence of the West which anti-communism implied would have been a little dicordant with the Nationalists' unwillingness to be embroiled in foreign wars. But Africa was different, and so long as the defence of the West could be convincingly related to making Africa safe for 'the white man' it could be accepted. And so indeed was the defence of the West in the post-war period continually related to the defence of 'Africa'. The Union government interested itself in the Middle East, which was 'the gateway to Africa', while its contribution to the Western war effort in Korea was a unique event which did not lead to a 'defence of Asia' policy.[16]

The occasion for sounding the ideas of the powers concerned about a defence organisation for Africa was probably provided by the Commonwealth Defence Ministers' Conference of 21–26 June 1951, at which it was decided that the Union government and the United Kingdom government should take the initiative in convening a conference of the African powers to discuss the defence of Africa.[17]

[15] See above, p. 35, n. 39.

[16] It seems that the notion of defending the 'gateway to Africa' was accepted in consequence of British pressure. Cf. *Pretoria News*, 9 January 1951, and *K.C.A.*, 11773A, 11701A; the phrase occurs also in *K.C.A.* 13913, and in *Ass. Deb.*, vol. 75, col. 7021.   [17] *K.C.A.*, 11701A.

To this would be invited as observers other Commonwealth and Western powers.

At the time of the Defence Ministers' conference the British government was concerned about the situation in the Middle East, and the conference tended to focus on that issue rather than on sub-Saharan Africa. It was stated that the conference delegates had recognised the importance of the Middle East and agreed that the defence problems of the area 'and the related problems' of south-east Asian defence had been considered in the context of the world strategic situation. Ministers would report to their various govern-ments, which would decide the best defence contributions they could make, and on the size, composition and timing of the development of Commonwealth forces that could be made available.[18] In the first week of July discussions were also held in the Suez Canal zone between General Sir Brian Robertson, Commander-in-Chief of the British Middle East land forces, and a South African military delega-tion including Brigadier Klopper.[19]

While discussions and plans were still formless, they did tend to envisage close co-operation on Commonwealth defence. When Churchill became Prime Minister the Cape Nationalist daily *Die Burger* warned that the idea 'current among many Conservatives' that the Empire must be more closely integrated, and that a common general staff and imperial conference to integrate policy should be set up, would not be acceptable to South Africa, and was not accept-able to Canada:

Our advice to the British Government is that they should forget about all the plans for central economic and military organs [which are intended] to bring the Commonwealth back to that imperial unity on which the Con-servative heart is so set [*waarop die Konserwatiewe hart so gesteld is*].[20]

The Union government shared these sentiments, sending the South African airmen to the Middle East only on the strict condition that they would be under South African command.[21]

The attitude towards the 'gateway to Africa' was ambivalent. There seems to have been the nagging feeling that this was essentially a private British preoccupation, although in general it affected the West. Referring to Egyptian hostility to the United Kingdom

---

[18] *Ibid.*; *Pretoria News*, 9 January 1951, 2 January 1951, 5 October 1951.
[19] *K.C.A.*, 11701A.
[20] *Die Burger*, 29 October 1951.
[21] *Ass. Deb.*, vol. 77, col. 295.

in 1951, *Die Burger* claimed to understand the feelings of the Egyptians. South Africa too had questions still outstanding with Britain which the latter had handled with 'a provocative policy of postponement [*tergende sloerbeleid*]'.

Such postponement and broken undertakings have contributed to the deterioration of British–Egyptian relations to the point that they have become a matter of general concern for the West.[22]

The ambivalent policy towards Egypt in its relations with Britain persisted for some time. Afrikaners had long been doubtful of British Egyptian policies; Malan, for example, had exultantly remarked on the granting of independence to Egypt that there was proof that 'the world is sick of imperialism'.[23] On the Suez crisis which led to the invasion of Egypt by France, Israel and the United Kingdom, the Union government could not easily form an opinion, Eric Louw first deciding that South Africa's good relations with Egypt would determine the Union government's reaction and later deciding to fall in line with the West.[24] Although Louw's reticence was understandable, being not unlike the embarrassment felt by other Western powers, including the United States of America, the Suez crisis was the gravest at 'the gateway to Africa' since the war, and had there been much substance to the notion of defence co-operation among African powers the Union should at least not have been caught quite so unawares.

Conferences on African defence were held at Nairobi and Dakar, but although a large number of matters were discussed no defence plans were drawn up and no undertakings were made.[25] A succession of meetings also took place between the United Kingdom defence department and the South African Defence Minister, Mr Erasmus,

[22] *Die Burger*, 15 October 1951; cf. External Affairs Department statement, 13 October 1951; *K.C.A.*, 11773A.

[23] Malan, *Wat ons het* ...

[24] J. Eayrs, *The Commonwealth and Suez: a Documentary Survey*, 1964, pp. 245–7. Louw is reported as having said, 'The ultimatum had come as a surprise ... This would seem to indicate a major change in policy, for in the past stress has been laid on consultations with the Commonwealth countries on matters of importance. The action of the British government has relieved South Africa of responsibility in the present crisis.' See also *Ass. Deb.*, vol. 95, cols. 578–82.

[25] The Nairobi conference opened on 21 August 1951, the Dakar conference on 11 March 1951. *K.C.A.*, 11781A, and Minister of Defence, *Ass. Deb.*, vol. 85, cols. 5082 ff. There was an excessively strong Union team at each.

and his advisers.[26] There is no doubt that the meetings were mostly at Erasmus' initiative and were aimed at bringing about the African Defence Organisation.

Erasmus' task was not easy. First, he was not an ideal diplomat; too many people found him overbearing, obdurate, or at any rate difficult.[27] Secondly, and more important, his mandate was impossible: to persuade the powers to see a communist threat to Africa while they were busy seeing it in other areas where his government seemed unwilling to look; to persuade, in spite of this, the NATO powers to set up yet another defence organisation, for Africa, which seemed to be enjoying a seven sleepers' rest; to persuade the imperial powers against the use of native armies (where then would the ADO obtain its men?); to persuade them to accept South African leadership or at least chairmanship in such an organisation when South Africa's military contribution could, on account of the exclusion of black people from its armed forces, be only small.[28]

Yet Erasmus pursued the policy with considerable assiduity for the best part of eight years. His *coup de maître*, which helped to keep the negotiations alive, was the decision to link with the 'defence of Africa' the quite distinct problem of the use of the naval base at Simonstown.[29] In this way he could hope to convince Afrikaner nationalists that the 'British connection' was being eroded while at the same time he could convince everyone else that the defence alliance project was being pursued with the co-operation of the United Kingdom.[30] The negotiations over the transfer of the naval base at Simonstown from British to South African sovereignty created the occasion for the discussion of a wide range of subjects— of defence and of other kinds.

[26] 21–6 June 1951, 8 July 1951, 31 August 1951, 11 August 1954, 1–10 September 1954, August–September 1957, and then again in 1958, to mention but a few of the discussions. Cf. *Cape Times* and *Pretoria News* for these periods.

[27] Personal communication from confidential source, 8 December 1970 and 19 January 1971.

[28] The mere fact that South Africa should be chairman of the proposed organisation would perhaps not have been a disincentive in itself, but in the circumstances it illustrated the unreality of the whole idea.

[29] When this decision was taken is unclear. Negotiations over Simonstown began towards the end of 1954. It is probably truer to say that Erasmus appended the defence of Africa to Simonstown negotiations which he might have initiated in any case on other grounds. Cf. *Daily Telegraph*, 13 September 1954.

[30] Cf. Strydom, in *K.C.A.*, 14294A; Erasmus, in *Pretoria News*, 13 September 1954.

Of the latter the most important were the completion of South Africa's progress towards independence, which included the removal of British enclaves within the Union's boundaries; in this connection Simonstown was in some respects like the High Commission Territories, which excited Afrikaner nationalist passions at the time.[31] Erasmus contrived to gain certain over-flying rights in the High Commission Territories and agreement to the UG setting up warning systems there.[32]

The Union government wished the United Kingdom government to link the strategic area of which the Simonstown station was the headquarters to a wider defence area; it was agreed that the United Kingdom and South Africa would defend southern Africa, while internal security remained the responsibility of the governments concerned.[33] From a nationalist point of view it was necessary, however, to establish that there had been a change in the status of Simonstown. For that reason, in addition to any others, the Union government hoped other Western powers would join in the arrangements which it also hoped would form the basis of a wider defence plan.[34]

Many South African politicians thought that Simonstown was very important and could therefore be optimistic about the amount of interest that the base and a defence agreement to cover it would excite. In deference to Nationalist sentiment the Union government desired that a defence organisation set up on these lines should be chaired by the Union.[35]

The United Kingdom government, for its part, agreed to the invitation of the powers to join, but on condition that the Union government would support the United Kingdom to obtain command of all naval forces put in the area consequent to such an agreement among the Western powers. To this the Union government agreed.[36]

Further, it was agreed that the base should be maintained at least at the level of efficiency it had attained at the time of transfer; it

[31] *Pretoria News*, 13 April 1954; Lord Hailey, *op. cit., passim.*
[32] Cmd. 9520, *Exchange of Letters on Defence Matters between the Governments of the United Kingdom and the Union of South Africa*, 1955. See also D. Austin, *Britain and South Africa*, 1966, pp. 121–45.
[33] Cmd. 9520, para. 2, p. 2.
[34] *Ibid.*, pp. 2–3 and 5.
[35] *Daily Telegraph*, 13 September 1954.
[36] Cmd. 9520, p. 5, para. 16.

was also agreed that the United Kingdom should supply the Union with naval equipment to build up its own naval defence forces. The Union government also agreed to provide the commander-in-chief of the British South Atlantic strategic zone with a variety of facilities in peace and war (even in a war in which the Union was non-belligerent).[37]

As far as the defence of Africa was concerned, the agreements were limited. The United Kingdom government preferred to maintain the earlier designation 'South Atlantic zone' to the 'South African strategic zone' preferred by the Union government; the boundaries of the zone approximated those of the South Atlantic station and included the Mozambique channel.[38]

Nevertheless a 'South African area' was, for no clear practical reason, acknowledged. The area would be bounded 'by the coast of South Africa and a line drawn from the northern boundary of South West Africa' through the following positions:[39]

Latitude	Longitude
20°s	0°
50°s	0°
50°s	55°E
30°s	55°E

The agreements were published in 1955, but several supplementary discussions occurred which did not alter the substance of the agreements.

The discussions of 1957 touched particularly on the question of the High Commission Territories, and although transfer of the territories to the Union government was not mentioned, the controversial nature of the topic was obviously fully taken into account, as the statement issued after the discussions showed:

On behalf of the United Kingdom government, Lord Mancroft accepted in principle a proposal by the Union government for the grant of certain overflying rights in the High Commission Territories. He also undertook to give careful consideration to further proposals made by the Union government for facilities in the territories in relation to planning the defence of South Africa, while making it clear that the responsibility for the security of the territories themselves rested exclusively with the United Kingdom.[40]

[37] *Ibid.*, pp. 3–7 *et passim*.
[38] *Ibid.*, p. 4, paras. 5–7.
[39] *Ibid.*, p. 4, para. 7.
[40] Official British statement, *K.C.A.*, 15792A.

The statement was vague, but so also were the discussions. It was not clear to some of the participants why they should have occurred. A participant recalls that Erasmus was obsessed with the possibility of a Russian nuclear attack on Simonstown and wished to be secured against such an eventuality. 'He had a bee in his bonnet and we spent the whole week trying to get it out.'[41]

The fear of an imminent nuclear attack by the Soviet Union does not seem to have been shared by Erasmus' more staid military advisers. Highly placed United Kingdom defence personnel considered that the Russian threat, which was of a different sort from that imagined by Erasmus and which was not in any case immediate, could be countered by a well co-ordinated African intelligence network. By the latter 1950s such an arrangement between the emergent black States and the white southern regimes could not be secured. The alternatives would have been for the colonial powers and the Union and Federation to form a white espionage club, but at the time most of the colonial powers would have little truck with such schemes.[42] The Simonstown agreements were conceived in a situation of unclear objectives, unshared expectations and ultimately unsharable anxieties.

Certainly the West was interested in Africa, which was relevant and could potentially be decisive in the economic, strategic and political competition within and among nations and between the blocs of nations which dominated the Cold War period. But to translate such interest into specific military undertakings was quite another matter. Preoccupied with matters of greater urgency, the United Kingdom government was unable or unwilling to understand, let alone accept, what must have seemed a tedious argument of insidious intent.

From the Union government's point of view, was anything ever done? Erasmus certainly tried to achieve the main aim of the Union government: to implicate the West through Britain in the defence of 'Africa'; if that were achieved, the Union government, with its small and relatively inexpansible military forces, would have

[41] Personal communication; confidential source.
[42] The Federal Prime Minister, Sir Roy Welensky, did envisage a 'multi-racial' organisation like CENTO, but this never got off the ground. See Sir Roy Welensky, *Welensky's 4,000 Days: the Life and Death of the Federation of Rhodesia and Nyasaland*, 1964, pp. 112–13. African leaders, however, had no wish to work with the white regimes: personal communication from confidential source, 19 January 1971.

been free to concentrate on the internal 'communist' threat[43]—
which, after all, had been Erasmus' initial preoccupation[44] and was
still at this time the one most exacting problem facing the National
Party governments of the Union.[45] The rebuff confirmed the impression already gained by some Afrikaners that the West would not
guarantee the safety of the exclusively white political system or the
continuance of the white regimes of southern Africa.[46] The Union
therefore concentrated on building up its defences on the basis of
more self-reliance than before.[47]

Erasmus achieved at least the making of a document which
friendly British governments could invoke in defence of military
collaboration with the South African government in the face of
widespread disapproval.

The rest of the Africa policy of Louw and Strydom

The period of Strydom's Ministry was characterised by ever-increasing international interest in Africa, issuing both from the changes
taking place in the status of dependent territories and from changes
in the international situation. Within the Union, too, interest in
Africa increased. At the unofficial level the Suid Afrikaanse Akademie
decided to form an Africa Institute to study the continent, an aim
which the government welcomed.[48] At governmental level assessment of the South African position in the light of the imminent
creation of new independent black States occurred; Eric Louw reorganised his department and took pains to keep the Cabinet
regularly informed of the international situation.[49]

The main problem, however, was how to take up some sort of

[43] I.e. African nationalist and other liberal opposition.
[44] Carter, *op. cit., passim. Pretoria News*, 5 October 1951, 6 October
1951; *Round Table*, 1948–49, *passim*; Walker, *op. cit.*, pp. 775 ff.; *Pretoria
News*, 14 May 1949, etc.
[45] During most of Strydom's Ministry the Union government was conduct-
ing the spectacular treason trial. See A. Sampson, *The Treason Cage: the
Opposition on Trial in South Africa*, 1958; M. Benson: *South Africa: the
Struggle for a Birthright*, 1966, pp. 93 ff.
[46] Cf. *Die Transvaler*, 16 December 1953; *Die Burger*, 22 October 1951;
cf. E. H. Louw, 'The Union and the emergent States', in *South Africa in the
African Continent*, 1959, p. 19.
[47] See A. S. Minty, *South Africa's Defence Strategy,* 1969, pp. 1–4 and
appendix 1.
[48] *Pretoria News*, 1 July 1955; see also Dr Luttig in *Ass. Deb.,* vol. 91,
col. 4494.
[49] Minister of External Affairs, in *Ass. Deb.*, vol. 87, cols. 5072–3.

convincing position on the movement towards self-government. The Union government had a twofold difficulty in this regard: its own policies towards coloured people within the Union were under increasingly severe criticism outside, suspicions even developing as to its intentions in Africa; the developments in Africa had been denounced by members of Union governments and their supporters only recently. What, in these circumstances, could be salvaged of the African Charter? The Union government 'accepted' that there were to be black States in Africa and was ready to offer a hand of friendship to them on certain conditions. There was, it was considered, room for both white and black peoples in Africa.[50] The position of *white* people was, however, an urgent preoccupation, the Union government wishing to forge co-operation among whites in 'southern' Africa.[51]

Ideas were not completely formed as to where the decolonisation process should end, the Prime Minister taking the view that 'Rhodesia', by which he probably meant Northern and Southern Rhodesia (but not Nyasaland?), should remain white,[52] and the Internal Affairs Minister, Dr Dönges, refusing to 'delineate boundaries'.[53] The Prime Minister thought that Rhodesia and South Africa should co-operate closely in their common interest and for their common security. However, so long as there was tension between Boer and Briton within South Africa this could not be achieved, for as *Die Burger* observed, 'The white racial conflict in the Union is continually being exported to Rhodesia, directly, over the Limpopo, or indirectly via London'.[54] Nor did the Prime Minister make any bones about his belief that the policy of 'partnership' in the Central African Federation would eventually—even if only eventually—lead to black domination.

Therefore I repeat with emphasis [he told parliament] that the only hope the white man has to maintain himself and at the same time to allow justice to be done to non-whites, is to have this *apartheid* or separation . . . We will have to convince the neighbouring States in southern Africa in order to see whether in any case we cannot approach nearer to each other in our viewpoints as to the future of Africa and of the white man in Africa.[55]

[50] T. E. Dönges in *Die Burger*, 3 October 1955; Prime Minister, in *Ass. Deb.*, vol. 91, col. 4129.
[51] Prime Minister, in *Ass. Deb.*, vol. 88, col. 4113.
[52] *Pretoria News* 4 February 1955.   [53] *Die Burger*, 3 October 1955.
[54] *Die Burger,* leader, 11 October 1955.
[55] *Ass. Deb.*, vol. 88, col. 4026.

Support for the Prime Minister's view was not lacking in unofficial Afrikaner circles. The South African Mineworkers' Union decided to involve itself in the defence of the 'rights' of white mineworkers in Northern Rhodesia. The South African and the Northern Rhodesian Mineworkers' Unions sent delegates to meet in Salisbury, Southern Rhodesia, in January 1955, there to resolve that any 'inroads into jobs normally performed by Europeans' in the Northern Rhodesian Copperbelt would be 'resisted to the utmost'. The South Africans agreed to recommend to their general council that 'the fullest moral, financial and other support' be given to the Northern Rhodesian union to 'maintain European standards on the copper mines'.[56]

When later that year a Rhodesian Afrikaner won an election at Kafue on an *apartheid* ticket enthusiasm was excited among Afrikaner nationalists in South Africa. *Die Burger* reflected that 'the final contest between an integration policy and a segregation policy has still to be waged [*Die finale beslissing tussen . . . moet nog gevel word*]'.[57] The Kafue election result gave the cue to the Nationalist member of parliament Dr A. H. Jonker to suggest that like-minded whites should join hands on the native question and that discussions should be initiated by members of the public first, since the governmental positions were so far apart. He had no doubt that the policy of segregation would triumph in Rhodesia in spite of the Federation unless 'Great Britain inundated [*toeploeg*] the Rhodesians with selected, ideologically indoctrinated immigrants'. Co-operation with Rhodesia (and South West Africa) would, he thought, make the 'solution' of the 'native problem' infinitely easier.[58]

Eric Louw was more cautious not to seem to interfere in the internal affairs of other countries. He converted his concern into efforts to obtain closer co-operation among the white African powers. He had had discussions in Paris, Brussels and Lisbon in this connection, but there was 'a hitch as regards the United Kingdom and the Rhodesians'. He hoped to have further discussions with the Lords Home and Malvern. There was, however,

no question of the establishment of any organisation such as the Pan-American Union, for example, nor is there any idea that there should necessarily be regular discussions. All I proposed, and still propose, is that the interested powers in Africa, that is to say England, France, Belgium, Portugal, the Federation and South Africa, should from time to time have

[56] *Pretoria News*, 24 January 1955.
[57] *Die Burger*, 11 October 1955.   [58] *Ibid.*

ad hoc discussions—and these are the key words—on matters of 'common interest'.[59]

One of the 'matters of common interest' was the Soviet penetration of Africa.[60]

The conditions of co-operation with the black States that were to emerge were clearly stated by *Die Burger* and by Dr Dönges and repeated in various versions by others many times afterwards. *Die Burger* exhorted Nationalists to prepare the whites in South Africa for their role in the changing Africa, while 'Nationalism' should keep itself

inwardly unshakeably [*onwrikbaar*] strong to resist every demand from outside for concessions that will cost it its life. Every relaxation of our resolve for freedom [will be to be free] and to have a separate existence will be an invitation to the black nationalisms of Africa to exercise a black imperialism at South Africa's expense.[61]

Dönges insisted that the 'native States' would have to accept that South Africa would become the permanent home of the white man in Africa. Another condition of co-operation was that those States should recognise the 'common dangers', such as communism and Indian imperialism. Further, 'the basic differences between the States must not be rationalised away, but should be recognised'. The most important condition was that there should be no 'interference' in the internal affairs of other States.[62]

There was no lack, then, of reactions to decolonisation and the imminent emergence of 'native States'. The opinions were unclear and somewhat contradictory, a contradiction no less apparent in the Union's attitude to the United States' role in Africa.

In 1955–57 the United States government and many groups within the United States took an increased interest in Africa. We saw that Erasmus hoped to involve the United States government in the defence of 'Africa' by persuading it to join in the Simonstown arrangement. Yet Louw did not like the idea of America 'muscling in' on the work of the colonial powers in Africa, deciding that the idea of the United States having bases in Africa should be approached 'with reserve and caution'.[63]

[59] *Ass. Deb.*, vol. 91, col. 4505: Strydom had long been sceptical of the idea of a Pan-African Union; see *Ass. Deb.*, vol. 52, col. 3961.

[60] *Ass. Deb.*, vol. 91, col. 4505.

[61] 3 October 1955.   [62] *Ibid.*

[63] *Ass. Deb.*, vol. 95, col. 7637.

The attitude towards the United Nations and its agencies was less ambiguous. South Africa left UNESCO because it was 'interfering',[64] and Louw looked with thinly veiled disapproval at the creation of the United Nations Economic Commission for Africa (ECA), which would not restrict itself to 'technical' and 'scientific' questions only but would also deal with the more contentious political and economic issues facing Africa.[65] Nevertheless the Union decided to join the ECA. In the period of this Ministry the CCTA and the CSA too were modernised by the admission of black States and by the extension of their deliberations to social and economic spheres as well.[66] The Cold War idea of aid to emergent States was incorporated into the still largely inter-imperial pattern of co-operation in Africa. A Fund for Mutual Assistance in Africa South of the Sahara (FAMA) was added to the CCTA and the CSA. The fund would not provide financial aid but would co-ordinate the communication of technical information and advice among its members.[67]

Meanwhile, Louw persevered in the efforts to counter Indian activities in Africa, deciding to that end to reopen the South African mission in Madagascar, which had earlier been closed for lack of work.[68] Preliminary to the reopening of the mission the South African Governor General visited the island and was received with a *feu de joie*, marred perhaps only by his having to inspect a 'native' guard of honour.[69] In 1956 the consulate was reopened. For white South Africa the collusion of 'Asianism' and African nationalism which Bandung seemed to augur was ominous. The succession of Afro-Asian meetings and the co-operation of Africans and Asians in the United Nations against South Africa, together with the extravagant rhetoric of anti-colonialism, were viewed in South Africa with concern.[70] South African indignation was directed particularly at India, the Asian State which had been the first to create difficulties for the Union in the United Nations and which had, in Louw's words, 'pursued a vendetta' against South Africa.

On the African continent Louw tried to win the goodwill of

---

[64] *K.C.A.*, 14294A.
[65] *Ass. Deb.*, vol. 97, col. 2483; 2485 *et passim*. See also vol. 95, col. 7633.
[66] V. P. MacKay, *Africa in World Politics*, 1963, pp. 150–66.
[67] *Ibid.*
[68] *Ass. Deb.*, vol. 87, cols. 5072–3.
[69] Reports of the visit in *Pretoria News*, 22 July 1955 and 26 July 1955.
[70] *Dagbreek en Sondagnuus*, 30 December 1956; in *Ass. Deb.*, vol. 88, col. 4112.

African States as they emerged. He took pride in his government's achievement in being the first to congratulate Sudan on its independence. To Ghana's independence celebrations he sent the head of the Africa division of his department, Mr R. Jones, to represent the Union there, with the status of Minister. Louw met one or two African leaders, including Nkrumah, to whom he explained South Africa's racial problems.[71] It was considered, however, by members of the Union government that exchange of diplomats was premature. There were long-standing conventions in South Africa which could not be changed overnight, Louw considered. By which he meant that *apartheid* in South Africa would cause embarrassment for all.[72] Moreover, it would be better if friendship were to develop first and diplomatic representation to be established later—after a sort of probationary period. For if the African States were to be hostile to South Africa their embassies would create the same problems of subversion of which the Russians had earlier been 'guilty'.[73]

Such contacts as a *baasskap*-oriented regime did, informally, establish with black leaders were bound to provoke cynical comments within the Union. Such cynicism was exemplified by the opposition member of parliament Mrs van Nickerk's remarks during the 1958 election campaign, when, according to Louw, 'she made much play of the fact that I had had tea with the Sultan of Zanzibar'.[74]

In the uncertainties of the period 1954–58 the Union government looked to the colonial powers and white regimes in Africa, hoping that they might close their ranks against intruders. Although Louw enjoined the African leaders to fight communism and not to accept economic aid from that quarter on the principle *Timeo Danaos et dona ferentes*,[75] he nonetheless hoped that 'communism' would be fought through the colonial powers in the black world. Thus the Union government stood by the European powers in their difficulties, supporting the governments of Portugal over Goa, of France over Algeria and, to some extent, of England over Suez.

---

[71] *Ass. Deb.*, vol. 96, cols. 838–43; see also vol. 99, cols. 5527–8.

[72] *Die Vaderland*, 25 February 1959; Louw, 'The Union and the emergent States', *passim*, and W. van Heerden in SABRA, *op. cit.*, p. 135.

[73] *Ibid*. On Louw and the Russian consulate see *Pretoria News*, 3 March 1949.

[74] *Ass. Deb.*, vol. 97, col. 2441.

[75] Louw, 'The Union and the emergent States', p. 19.

v *Verwoerd and Eric Louw*

The campaign against South Africa at the United Nations which India initiated in 1945–46 had grown over the years, particularly with the increase in the number of non-Western European States in that organisation. The conflict in the United Nations irked Union governments considerably, so that in November 1956 Louw announced that the Union would reduce its participation in the United Nations to 'token representation'[1]

until such time as the United Nations shows that it is prepared to act in accordance with the spirit of the San Francisco Conference of 1945 and to conform to the principles laid down by the founders of the Organisation in Article 2, paragraph 7 of the Charter . . .[2]

In 1958, however, the Union returned to full representation without it being agreed that the UN was to refrain from further 'interference'. The Union, perhaps realising that most of the changes in the world were irreversible, was to try a policy of apparent conciliation, i.e. of less defiance, but there was to be no less rigid adherence to the earlier positions.[3] Thus Louw explained the decision to invite the 'Good Offices Committee' of the UN General Assembly as an attempt to meet the other parties half-way.[4]

This new approach did not stem the tide of criticism and vituperation, either in the unofficial meetings of Afro-Asians in Cairo or Accra or in the United Nations:

'We did everything possible,' Louw remarked, 'in the face of allegations and accusations made by Ceylon, Liberia and Ghana; I turned the other cheek and gave the soft answer that is supposed to turn away wrath. It did not do so in this case.'

At the unofficial level, too, adverse publicity was being given to the Union in many parts of the world and hostility was increasing,[5] but the principal villains seemed to be the Afro-Asians—and, of

[1] H. H. Biermann (ed.), *The Case for South Africa*, 1963, pp. 37–8.
[2] *Ibid.*   [3] *Ass. Deb.*, vol. 100, cols. 5563–7.   [4] *Ibid.*
[5] Cf. Paul Sauer's (Minister of Lands) address to SABRA: *Pretoria News*, 30 April 1958.

course, the communists. It was in such circumstances that Dr H. F. Verwoerd took office as Prime Minister upon the death of Strydom at the end of 1958.

Verwoerd, who had hardly ever participated in public foreign policy debates, retained Eric Louw as Minister of External Affairs for a while,[6] but he also had definite ideas of his own. His *tour d'horizon* was made in his New Year message, replete with effective if jejune metaphors. Africa, Verwoerd noted, was a 'restless giant' which although it was awakening was 'still heavy-lidded with sleep'. Thanks to white colonialism,

Black States are coming into being although they do not appreciate those who freed them from the bonds of their own past and ignorance.[7]

Ingratitude, impatience, arrogance—all the results of immaturity —characterised these black States. However, 'maturity' would come, and with it 'better mental balance' and a 'more modest estimate of their own capabilities' and recognition of the entitlements of others.

Verwoerd's defiant attitude was reflected in the Union's decision not to participate in the inaugural meeting of UNECA.[8] But defiance was not a policy to win friends and influence people. It was discordant with Louw's policy of conciliation and playing down the conflict, which was signified by the restoration of full representation in the UN, the increased participation in the work of CCTA, CSA, and FAMA—in spite of what must have seemed African ingratitude; and of course, the visit to Ghana which he and Nkrumah had agreed to—in spite of the latter's hostility in the UN. If Louw, however ineptly and however reluctantly, had been prepared to ride so rough a wind, Verwoerd for his part was prepared to sow a wind.

The shape of things to come was shown by Jamaica when, following another Indian lead,[9] its government decided in early July 1959 to stop its trade with South Africa. It is interesting that Louw's response was to approach the colonial power—the United Kingdom— to protest. According to Louw's statement of 3 July, Sir John Maud, the United Kingdom High Commissioner in the Union, argued that although the West Indies Federation was not yet independent, the regulation of trade was exclusively within the competence of the Jamaican Council of Ministers. Louw disagreed:

[6] Eric H. Louw retired on 31 December 1963.
[7] *Pretoria News*, 2 January 1959.
[8] *Ibid.*, 7 January 1959.
[9] India was the first country to boycott South African goods in 1946.

I told the High Commissioner that the Union government could not but regard this matter in a very serious light, particularly in view of the fact that the West Indies Federation is not yet an independent State, and that sovereign power still rests with the British government. I pointed out that the proposed action was obviously not for the regulation of trade, but for the purpose of protesting against South Africa's policy of *apartheid*: that it constituted interference by another government in South Africa's domestic affairs.[10]

Within days of this particular incident it was reported that the Ghanian Trades Union Council wanted South African goods to be banned from Ghana.[11]

For a while, however, the government party in South Africa could take comfort in the fact that in spite of all the criticism of South Africa abroad, the boycott movement was limited to relatively un-influential groups in the African countries in 1959 and early 1960.[12] *Governments* were still co-operating; Dr Luttig was led to conclude:

That being so I think we should consider this aspect: that there is no hostile climate in Africa that we cannot seriously consider achieving the object of 'African peace through African trade'.[13]

Dr Hilgard Muller, too, shared this mercantile theory of 'peace' and its optimism:

the governments of the independent States have not as yet officially boy-cotted the Union in spite of the pressure which has been exerted on them by the trade unions, and in spite of the threats that they should do so.[14]

Both men looked to the Union's industrialists to do the job, and Luttig hoped that the Union would succeed in spite of competition from the Chinese and the Japanese because it was the 'industrial giant of Africa' and a 'white sovereign State'. Such reassuring comments were perhaps desirable in view of the disquiet felt by some businessmen about the sluggishness of the Union government in creating favourable conditions for trade expansion into Africa. The time had not yet come, however, for an export-led diplomatic advance into Africa, for, as events were to show conclusively, political questions had primacy in Africa at this time.

1960 was the year of independence, as seventeen African States were scheduled to 'emerge' in that year. Certainly the structure of inter-governmental relations in Africa was bound to change markedly

[10] *Pretoria News.*   [11] *Ibid.,* 6 July 1959.
[12] See *K.C.A.*   [13] *Ass. Deb.,* vol. 103, cols. 703 ff.
[14] *Ass. Deb.,* vol. 105, cols. 5537 ff. Muller later became Foreign Minister, while Luttig was subsequently accredited ambassador to the court of St James's.

too. And so too, it was feared, would the United Nations. Echoing Dr Malan's prophecies of doom,[15] Louw noted that by 1970 the composition of the Organisation would have changed so considerably that in consequence of the accretion of new, independent States which were hostile, or at any rate unsympathetic, to the West, the latter would be forced to rely on intra-Western organisations. It would extend alliances like NATO and create new ones like a South Atlantic treaty organisation.[16] In the altered conditions in Africa, with Western influence declining, the West should all the more close ranks with South Africa, taking advantage of South Africa's position as the only African power with an unambiguously pro-Western policy.[17]

The creation of new States in Africa could not fail to give rise to such apprehensions, for it had a radicalising effect on the views of the leaders of black States. Certainly in the new competition for leadership in Africa it might be expected that Africans would outdo each other in their attacks on colonialism and what seemed its vestigial remains—the white regimes of southern Africa. But more important was the fact that independence could hardly fail to bring into sharp focus the disabilities that Africans had suffered under white rule. Pan-Africanism and independence encouraged a feeling of solidarity that reached across colonial boundaries even to embrace, however inadequately, the cause of black South Africans. At the Accra conference of 1958, which such opponents of the South African government as Michael Scott (representing Chief Hosea of the Hereros), Patrick Duncan of the Liberal Party and Louise Hooper of the African National Congress attended, Nkrumah declared that 'the independence of Ghana will be meaningless unless it is linked with the total liberation of Africa.'[18] The PAC and the ANC in South Africa identified themselves with the sentiments expressed in Accra. Subsequent African conferences incorporated this commitment to liberating southern Africa, and the objective was to feature importantly at the Addis Ababa conference which set up the OAU in 1963. The OAU itself set up an African Liberation Council to help fulfil this commitment. At the UN too, African States, operating

---

[15] In April 1949 Malan observed that 'unless it [the UN] is reformed, its end may ultimately be more inglorious than that of its predecessor, the League of Nations'; see Mansergh, *op. cit.*, vol. II, p. 1153.

[16] *Ass. Deb.*, vol. 105, col. 5625. [17] *Ibid.*

[18] C. Legum, *Pan-Africanism: a Short Political Guide*, 1962, p. 44. Cf. also J. Woronoff, *Organising African Unity*, 1970, pp. 31–79.

first within the 'Afro-Asian group' but later increasingly as the 'African group', were the foremost critics of the South African regime.[19] If independence inaugurated a season of black indulgence, it also brought, if only for a while, a period of compassionate re-collection.[20]

Black South African political organisations such as the African National Congress, the Congress Alliance and the Pan-African Congress were intensifying, within their modest capabilities, their activities against the South African regime. And the sensitised atmosphere of 1960 was heavy with imponderable contingencies.

In government circles in South Africa it was hoped that, in the new Africa, South Africa, the 'tough' Portuguese and Southern Rhodesia would remain as a white redoubt.[21] But with respect to Southern Rhodesia that was not a view shared by the United Kingdom government, which at the time was preoccupied with finding a 'liberal' reconciliation of African nationalist aspirations and white settler attitudes in the disintegrating Central African Federation.[22] It was with such views that Macmillan undertook the African tour which ended in the South African parliament, where he warned politicians of the 'wind of change'.[23] Macmillan's speech in Cape Town showed how widely South Africa's and Britain's views on Africa had come to diverge. It marked the failure of the grand idea of an enduring imperial order in Africa which South Africa would shape with the aid of the imperial powers.

There was irony and even bathos in Macmillan's reminding South Africans that they could not ask to be left alone; he recalled, appro-

[19] See Legum, *op. cit.*; Woronoff, *op. cit.*; V. B. Thompson, *Africa and Unity*, 1964; V. P. McKay, *Africa in World Politics*, 1963; Wallerstein, *Africa and Unity*.

[20] See I. Wallerstein, *Africa: the Politics of Unity—an Analysis of a Contemporary Social Movement,* 1967, pp. 18–22. On differences among Africans, however, see also G. de Lusignan, *French-speaking Africa*, 1969, pp. 268–317; D. Austin, 'Pan-Africanism, 1957–63' in D. Austin and H. W. Weiler (eds), *Interstate Relations in Africa*, part I, 1965; also C. Hoskyns, 'The part played by the independent States in the Congo crisis, July 1960– December 1961', in Austin and Weiler, *op. cit.*, pp. 30–50.

[21] *Ass. Deb.*, vol. 105, cols. 5665 ff.

[22] Welensky, *op. cit.*, *passim*. See also R. Gray, *The Two Nations*, 1960; P. Keatley, *The Politics of Partnership,* 1963; H. Franklin, *Unholy Wedlock*, 1963; T. Franck, *Race and Nationalism*, 1960.

[23] *K.C.A.*, 17267A. (February 1960). Welensky writes that when Butler visited Rhodesia in 1958 he meant to go to South Africa to give a similar speech but was prevented by the death of Mr Strydom: see Welensky, *op. cit.*, p. 101.

priately, the famous injunction from John Donne's *Devotions*: '. . . and therefore never send to know for whom the bell tolls; it tolls for thee'. It was indeed a speech at the graveside of the pan-African policy.

Soon after Macmillan's controversial visit occurred the Sharpville massacre, which brought the South African political system under considerable external criticism. To an expectant world it seemed indeed that Verwoerd had begun to 'reap the whirlwind'. Sharpeville had an enormous impact on the Union's external relations. What co-operation there had been between the Union and black African States came abruptly to a halt, and the boycott campaign was under way.[24]

The republic which Verwoerd proclaimed as the culmination of the Afrikaner nationalist constitutional campaigns was born into a hostile internal and external atmosphere; when Verwoerd attended the Commonwealth Prime Ministers' Conference in 1961 with a view to applying for continued South African membership, he met with such universal criticism that he withdrew the application.

It is difficult to say that it mattered much to Verwoerd that the British Commonwealth connection, which incidentally was also an African link, was severed. But no such uncertainty attaches to the nature of his differences, as he saw them, with Macmillan. For when the latter asserted that, if the South African Prime Minister had been prepared to make concessions, however small, rather than adhere steadfastly to dogma, South Africa would still be in the Commonwealth,[25] Verwoerd's embittered rejoinder clarified the conflict of policies:

I see as a result of his [Macmillan's] policy the white man disappearing from Kenya in the course of time or being submerged . . . I fear for the position in the Central African Federation as long as this theory of the British government [of making small concessions] remains the policy for that country . . . the policy that Britain is following in Africa does not do justice to the white man, and ultimately will not be best for the black man either.[26]

[24] *K.C.A.*, 17266A, 17528A, 17554A, 17576A.
[25] Macmillan told the British House of Commons on 22 March 1961, 'I am convinced of this. Had Dr Verwoerd shown the smallest move towards understanding the mood of his Commonwealth colleagues or made any concession, or given us anything to hold on to, any ground for hope, I still think the conference would have looked beyond the immediate difficulties to the possibilities of the future.' (*K.C.A.*, 18135A.)
[26] *Ass. Deb.*, vol. 107, col. 3507.

Verwoerd explained that he did not object to Britain's policy with regard to countries 'like Nigeria and Ghana', which were 'undoubtedly wholly black man's countries' and should have become free. He wished to do the same 'for the Native areas of my country as it becomes possible'.[27]

The old question of the High Commission Territories came up again but, like Anouilh's Antigone, Verwoerd was not crying for any good it might do him; his argument was gratuitous, it was kingly. He pointed out that the multi-racial policy was being applied to the High Commission Territories whereas South Africa would have made those territories black man's countries, whites having no political rights at all.[28] Yet Verwoerd knew that his remark might appeal to some African nationalists in those territories.

From 1961 onward, as all the colonial powers, except Portugal, 'abdicated', South Africa would have to find new partners in Africa. The hostility of African States and the boycotts and walk-outs were thought to be a transitory feature of the political scene; yet ever since Bandung, but increasingly in the late 'fifties and early 'sixties, Afrikaner intellectuals and politicians had felt that the solution to the race problem must be found so that relations with black States could improve.[29] The official response was to hasten the implementation of the Tomlinson report to the extent of granting a degree of local self-government in the reserves,[30] and to introduce the slogan 'separate but equal', the positive side of the 'total *apartheid*' that Verwoerd was introducing. On that policy and on its success would be based any future African policy.

Even Western powers such as America and France joined in the criticism of South Africa in the UN, though they were cautious so to juggle with words that they did not commit themselves to action against the government of South Africa.[31] Within the UN the two-pronged attack against South African administration of the South West Africa mandate, and against race policies within South Africa

[27] *Ibid.*   [28] *Ibid.*

[29] See, for example, *Die Burger*, 17 January 1957; W. van Heerden (editor of *Dagbreek*), in *Die Burger*, 23 April 1957; Professor L. J. du Plessis, in *Dagbreek*, 23 December 1958; *Die Transvaler*, 12 November 1958.

[30] *Report of the Commission of Inquiry into the Socio-economic Development of the Bantu Areas within the Union of South Africa* (official summary), U.G. 61/1955.

[31] Austin, *op. cit.*, p. 103; P. Calvocoressi, *South Africa and World Opinion*, 1961, *passim*; Legum, *South Africa: Crisis for the West*, 1964, pp 235–42.

itself, was being intensified, and the decision of the International Court of Justice in 1962 to hear contentious litigation by Ethiopia and Liberia against South Africa marked a new phase. In fourteen years the United Nations had achieved little in its attempts to persuade the Union to change its policies, and the measures hitherto suggested had proved inadequate.[32] Nor did the visit to the Union in 1958 of a delegation of the Good Offices Committee fructify in a narrowing of the gap between the republic and its opponents in the General Assembly.[33] But the decision to seek a binding judgement of the World Court was a serious innovation with likely difficult consequences for the republic should the judgement favour the plaintiffs.

It was perhaps awareness of such implications which led Verwoerd's government to accept UN 'meddling' by inviting yet another delegation to visit the Union and South West Africa in 1962.[34] This mission, which consisted of Drs Carpio and de Alva,[35] ended in farcical recriminations between the republican government and the delegates, particularly Dr Carpio, after what had seemed a triumph for the republic.[36] Clearly, no solution of the South African problem would follow from such initiatives, and the hostility towards the republic continued unabated.

If no South African government renounced the African Charter idea after Malan's demise, it was now clear that the situation out of which it had arisen, and the situation it hoped to create, were no longer possible. Indeed, almost the reverse situation was now occurring. Whereas the Union had hoped to influence 'native policy' in the rest of Africa, the new African powers now wanted to influence 'native policy' in South Africa. From a position of importance

---

[32] Cf. *Exchanges of Correspondence between the Governments of India, Pakistan and the Union of South Africa, in regard to a Round Table Conference to discuss a solution to the Indian Question, July 1949 to June 1950,* 1950. See also G. M. Carter, *The Politics of Inequality: South Africa since 1948,* 1958, chapter 15, and J. E. Spence, 'South Africa in the modern world', in M. Wilson and L. Thompson, *Oxford History of South Africa,* vol. II, 1971.

[33] *Pretoria News,* 2 June 1958, 12 June 1958, 13 June 1958.

[34] Announced in parliament on 13 April 1962. See *Ass. Deb.,* vol. 3, col. 3899.

[35] Dr Carpio was chairman of the UN Special Committee on South West Africa.

[36] This episode was well reported in South African newspapers from July to August. See Institute of Race Relations (London) *Newsletter,* May 1962, June 1962, July 1962, August 1962, September 1962.

in imperial post-war Africa, South Africa had been reduced to ignominy and increasing economic and political isolation. Black leaders to the north considered that their revolutions were not complete so long as white domination persisted in southern Africa.[37]

There was probably little that need be feared, in the short and medium run, as regards isolation from black States, which was in any case thought to be temporary. These States were not thought to possess the coercive power which would be necessary should the republican government fail to comply.[38] African leaders, too, were divided in their interpretation of pan-Africanism and in the militancy of their objections to colonialism and white domination—although the extent of this division was not immediately apparent at the time. South African politicians could, and did, come to believe that in time African leaders would become 'realistic', accepting white-ruled South Africa as a permanent and even desirable part of the African political scene.[39]

As far as the West was concerned, South Africa was prepared—or Verwoerd thought it should be prepared—to accept ideological isolation:

Our strength lies in isolating ourselves from those policies in which we do not believe, and which we believe will lead to the disappearance of the white man's rule in South Africa . . . But that does not mean that we shall be isolated as a State from all those other States.[40]

But ideological isolation would not mean political and economic isolation, Verwoerd considered.[41]

On the African continent South African diplomatic activity was focused mainly on Africa south of the equator, and principally upon countries neighbouring on South Africa itself. But there was one spectacular involvement in African politics away from South African borders—in the Katanga crisis of 1960. Sympathy was lavished on the secessionist State and the white settler minority. Mercenaries for Katanga were recruited in South Africa, and the South African government cultivated good relations with M. Tshombe, some of whose Ministers even visited South Africa.[42] Together with the

---

[37] Cf. J. A. Gbedemah, Ghanaian Finance Minister, reported in *Pretoria News*, 26 June 1958, and Ben Bella's famous speech, quoted in Wallerstein, *Africa: the Politics of Unity*, p. 67.
[38] Cf. J. J. Fouche, in *Ass. Deb.*, vol. 8, col. 8626.
[39] Cf. Verwoerd's New Year message of 1959.
[40] *Ass. Deb.*, vol. 3, cols. 3761–2.   [41] *Ibid.*
[42] C. C. O'Brien, *To Katanga and Back: a UN Case History*, 1962, p. 193.

Central African Federation, Ruanda–Urundi and Angola, the republic became the object of Katangese attempts to find sources of food and other supplies. According to Catherine Hoskyns, although no details are available, 'it seems likely that trade agreements of one kind or another were made with all these countries'.[43] O'Brien has disclosed also that black South Africans were at one time also thought likely, by the Katangese, to come to their aid (and thereby aid South African diplomacy?):

> There did exist—among *gendarmerie* papers captured by the UN forces—a curious project for recruiting Zulu warriors from South Africa, with the co-operation of the South African government, but it does not appear that anything came of this particular 'phenomenon of African nationalism'.[44]

That such speculations did not materialise is hardly surprising. The South African government had always opposed the training of its 'natives', and would have been violating long-established policy which had the force of an article of faith had it given blacks in South Africa the opportunity to learn the use of firearms and the carefully preserved secrets of the art of modern warfare.

Verwoerd was cautious not to be seen to be meddling in the domestic affairs of another country. When, for example, press reports appeared announcing the departure of a number of South African mercenaries for Katanga, he disowned knowledge of the object of their journeys. The South Africans concerned had obtained their passports on the pretext that they were bound for Rhodesia:

> If the statement that they were going to Katanga to join the Foreign Legion was correct, then the Union government wishes to state explicitly that this did not happen with its approval and that the government is not prepared to extend passport facilities for this purpose.[45]

This denial was disingenuous. Apart from the fact that a former mercenary has given accounts of far greater involvement, at the official level[46] a South African diplomatist, E. M. Rhoodie, in a hysterically pro-South African work, has stated the matter succinctly:

The Ministers concerned were Mr Kibwe, Vice-premier of the State of Katanga, and Mr Kitenge, Minister of Public Works, cf. also C. P. Mulder in *Ass. Deb.*, vol. 28, col. 318.

[43] C. Hoskyns, *The Congo since Independence: January 1960–December 1960*, 1965, p. 285.

[44] O'Brien, *op. cit.*, p. 197.   [45] *Ass. Deb.*, vol. 106, cols, 2574–5.

[46] Personal communication from British editor of an underground political journal, October 1970.

It is said that these were 'soldiers of fortune', drifters, etc., who would fight anywhere for money.[47] This may be so but the fact is that Tshombe's government advertised for hiretroops [*sic*] in South African newspapers and the recruiting offices were set up openly in public buildings. Had the government of South Africa [and Rhodesia] wanted to, they could have put a stop to the recruiting immediately . . . M. Tshombe therefore knew very well at the time that without official blessing the White mercenaries would never have materialised.[48]

And thus a spectacle never dreamed of by Malan in his African Charter, of white South Africans fighting side by side with black Africans under a black government, materialised. In like manner, the Union government played host to Tshombe's already mentioned Ministers; and in giving support to Katanga the Union government acted less than honestly, as Verwoerd's dissembling statement showed. Having supported the recognition of Katanga, the Union refused to come out openly and was not there to be counted, for instance, among Portugal, Angola and the Federation at the Elizabethville International Fair, which was held to coincide with Katanga independence day on 11 July, and whereby 'it was hoped, apparently, to draw foreign exhibitors into some sort of implicit recognition of the State of Katanga'.[49] The fact of the matter is that, as Malan's continued collaboration with the multi-racial Commonwealth and the United Nations and Eric Louw's lunches and teas with Nkrumah and the Sultan of Zanzibar had shown, the ethical and racial simplicities of *apartheid* theory could yield to a prospect of advantage. Under Verwoerd, and in the troubled times he had helped to create, *apartheid* continued—at the international level, at any rate —to be tempered by the considerations of *raison d'état*.[50] In accep-

[47] Cf. O'Brien, *op. cit.*, p. 197: 'Motives given for enlistment, according to the UN report, "ranged from financial reasons, domestic troubles and lust for adventure to serve what they [the mercenaries] considered a good cause". My own recollection, from reading the interrogatories in New York, is that, in about twenty-five of the thirty cases, the motives given ranged from financial reasons to financial reasons.'

[48] E. M. Rhoodie, *The Third Africa*, 1969, pp. 64–5.

[49] O'Brien, *op. cit.*, p. 140.

[50] It might be objected that 'whatever the circumstances, the business of ruling is . . . always carried out in accordance with the principles of *raison d'état*', as Professor Meinecke has observed, but, to quote the same author: 'It [*raison d'état*] is not realised, however, as a principle and an idea until a particular stage of development has been reached; namely when the State has become strong enough to break down [the] obstacles and to lay down its own unqualified right to existence in the face of all other vital forces.' It would be good to bear this remark in mind in reading the ensuing chapters

ting eventual diplomatic intercourse with all willing black States the Union Ministers foreshadowed the extension of those considerations. On the question of diplomatic relations, racial fastidiousness, a hallowed principle of internal political control, would, as we shall see, be locked in a fight to the knives with the principle of *raison d'état*, the element of necessity in the life of the State.[51]

TABLE I   *South African expenditure on diplomatic representation in African capitals, selected years, 1946–61 (£)**

	1946	1949	1952	1955	1958	1961
Cairo	4,900	9,940	10,845	16,139	16,747	23,015
Elizabethville	3,710	4,636	11,199	12,136	17,190	21,192
Leopoldville	5,940	5,844	9,028	12,926	13,543	19,347
Lourenco Marques	4,380	6,159	9,323	11,440	12,180	16,132
Luanda					1,089	16,943
Nairobi	6,900	8,550	6,696	11,899	15,472	20,115
Salisbury			11,556	13,150	17,078	38,756
Tananarive	4,160	3,915	3,718			

*Allocation of estimated total provision for the year ending 31 March.

Note: South Africa's diplomatic relations with Cairo were discontinued in 1961. Except for Salisbury others terminated relations on accession to independence. Although there was no diplomatic representation at Tananarive after independence, in 1971 an agreement was reached between the Malagasy Republic and South Africa for the setting up of a joint commission to deal with matters of common interest. At the time of writing Malawi and Lesotho are the only States to exchange diplomats after independence. No figures are available for expenditure on representation in Africa in the post independence period.

Source. Estimates of Expenditure to be Defrayed from Public Revenue, published by the *Cape Times* for the Government Printer, various issues.

Barring the Congolese imbroglio, there was not much involvement on the part of the South African government in the politics of black-ruled Africa. Apart from Cairo, the 'gateway to Africa', South African diplomats' activity had hitherto been focused on southern Africa and the areas of white settlement, as expenditure on diplomatic representation indicated (see table 1). Much of the diplomatic

---

of this work. Meinecke is quoted from his *Machiavellism: the Doctrine of Raison d'État and its Place in Modern History* (tr. D. Scott), 1957, p. 25.

[51] As in the *verligte–verkrampte* split in the National Party between 1965 and 1970.

TABLE 2 *South African trade with Africa: exports for selected years since 1938* (R *millions*)

	1938	1950	1957	1964
All Africa	5 (8%)	69 (16%)	153 (19%)	114 (12%)
Southern Rhodesia ⎫				51 ⎫
Zambia ⎬	4 (7%)	40 (9%)	114 (14%)	29 ⎬ (8%)
Malawi ⎭				0.8 ⎭

Source. D. H. Houghton, *The South African Economy*, 1967, p. 170.
Note. R = £0·5 before sterling devaluation of 1967.

business was conducted, of course, through the metropolitan capitals, so that the allocations for representation in African capitals probably understate the degree of interest in 'Africa' which South African governments had. The pattern of trade, as can be seen from table 2, also reflected the emphasis on southern Africa, especially what used to be called British South Africa, so that, of the relatively small amount of trading that South Africans did in Africa (see table 3) well over 60 per cent on average went on in British South Africa. South African direct investment in Africa revealed a similar

TABLE 3 *Imports and exports, 1957–62* (R *millions*)

	1957	1958	1959	1960	1961	1962
Imports						
Africa	75·4	75·6	69·8	76·9	68·8	72·9
Europe	596·3	639·4	539·0	597·4	557·9	570·4
Asia	157·9	143·8	139·8	156·6	139·9	154·5
Oceania	6·8	8·3	11·5	13·9	16·5	15·4
Misc.					1·5	2·7
Total	836·4	867·1	760·1	844·8	784·6	815·9
Exports						
Africa	155·6	135·6	147·9	141·6	129·7	120·5
Europe	425·3	357·8	373·2	390·4	453·2	457·6
Asia	40·7	34·8	58·9	71·2	86·5	105·8
America	63·6	61·6	82·2	66·4	81·0	91·9
Oceania	9·2	9·8	10·7	14·1	14·7	10·7
Misc.	108·6	115·2	114·3	114·1	86·2	81·7
Total	803·0	714·0	787·2	797·8	851·3	868·2

Sources Republic of South Africa, Bureau of Statistics, *Special Report* No. 260.

pattern, centring on the Federation, while the mining sector in the Federation was deeply penetrated, at both the entrepreneurial and the skilled-labour levels, by white South Africans. Of importance, too, by their proximity to the Union were the High Commission Territories and the Portuguese-occupied territories.

TABLE 4   *Foreign and South African labour* in the associated mines, selected years since 1945*

Year	South African	Foreign	Total
1945	143,370	159,004	302,374
1950	121,609	173,086	294,695
1960	141,806	233,813	375,619
1961	146,605	241,742	388,347

*Black Africans only.

Source. *Standard Encyclopaedia of Southern Africa*, 1970, p. 100.

Sanctions and isolation came at a time when the eyes of South African businessmen were increasingly being focused on Africa. Secondary industry had grown a good deal since the war and, with the notorious difficulty of penetrating markets for secondary industrial produce, Africa seemed to promise a future to South African producers. Southern and central Africa held out prospects not only for trade but also for investment and construction. The South African Federated Chamber of Industries and the South African Foreign Trade Organisation had long sought to draw attention, and to facilitate access, to African markets.[52] Now other organisations were also beginning to show interest.[53] Furthermore, South African

[52] Cf. South African Federated Chamber of Industries pamphlet *African Markets for Union Exporters*, 1942, and SAFCI, 'South African Export Trade Goodwill Mission, 1946' (mimeo): 'It is considered that the [colonial] development already contemplated, and the immense potentials [sic] generally of the [African] territories fully warrants [sic] South African manufacturers taking a lively and permanent interest in them ... South Africa must endeavour to get in on the ground floor.' In 1957 a new South African Exporters' Association was formed. See editorial comment in *The Manufacturer*, November 1951.

[53] During a conference of the International Road Federation held at Salisbury in 1957 'strong representations were made' for one major road from Cape Town to Nairobi. The administrator of South West Africa felt that it was of 'cardinal importance' to have a road from South West Africa to Rhodesia. It would be of great strategic significance and would stimulate the marketing of South West African products. This proposal was supported

mining had long been and still was dependent on cheap 'foreign native labour' from the surrounding African territories, as can be seen from table 4. Agriculture also used 'foreign natives', although the extent of its use of this labour can only be guessed.[54] It was estimated in 1961 that there were some million foreign Africans in the republic, and although the government appointed a committee 'to investigate the question of sending them away in large numbers',[55] it was only unwanted Africans who were sent away, and the inter-territorial labour migration was maintained intact, to remain at one and the same time a pillar of the African labour system in South Africa and, as we shall show later, an important aid to South African diplomacy.[56] From an economic point of view alone, isolation from southern Africa could not be, and was not, accepted complacently.

The intensification of political conflict within South Africa itself gave a new importance to relations with neighbouring States. Opponents of the South African regime required for interrogation or imprisonment under the plethora of political laws of the republic could escape to neighbouring territories and seek asylum, or even continue their political activities and thus precipitate 'incidents'.

There was little enough likelihood of the Portuguese-controlled territories being used for these purposes, so long, at any rate, as they remained under the unyielding control of metropolitan Portugal. But there were uncertainties with regard to the British colonies, subject as these were to constitutional changes which might or might not favour South African aims, and, pending constitutional change, they remained subject to a different code of conscience. For, in spite of all the collaboration between British southern Africa, Britain and South Africa, the republic's conceptions of legality differed from the British and the political laws of the republic (like the Suppression of Communism Act) were regarded with qualified sympathy in official British southern African circles at the time. And indeed, as politics became more conflictual in the republic, relations with the High Commission Territories in particular were

---

in principle by the organisations represented, which included the Suid-Afrikaanse Handelsinstituut and the South African Road Federation. See *Agenda en Jaarverslag van die Uniale Vereniging van Afrikaanse Sake-kamers, 23–5 September 1958.*

[54] South African Institute of Race Relations (SAIRR), *A Survey of Race Relations,* ed. M. Horrel, 1961, pp. 131–2.

[55] *Ibid.* See below, chapters VI and VII.

[56] See Part II below.

sullied by a number of incidents involving the South African police. Among such incidents the more outstanding included the kidnapping on 26 August 1961 of Anderson Ganyile, a South African student who had taken refuge in Basutoland;[57] the arrest on 30 December 1961 of Dr Ambrose Zwane, secretary of the Swazi People's Party, on the Bechuanaland border, for failing to produce a reference book (pass book);[58] and the arrest of Mr Ntsu Mokhehle, president of the Basutoland Congress Party, together with five companions, for a similar offence on 27 January 1961.[59]

There was good reason for apprehension on the part of the South African government, for many of the politicians of the High Commission Territories had friendships among black South African politicians, with whom they had either grown up, or studied or worked in the republic and with whose people they often had close ties of consanguinity and affinity. But the real harm which the High Commission Territories could do to the Union, without external aid, was small. Certainly, there was no likelihood in 1956–64, say, of these territories being used as bases in an armed invasion of South Africa or infiltration of the republic for that purpose. Apart from anything else, they were still under British rule and the British government was unlikely to countenance such behaviour towards a friendly (to the British) government. And had there been any attempt so to use the High Commission Territories they would have been severely constrained by their great vulnerability to the wide range of retaliatory measures the South African government might apply.[60] Finally, arms and other war materials would in any case have to be secured from outside, and there was little likelihood of a significant flow of arms to Basutoland—which was completely surrounded by the republic, to Swaziland—hemmed in between South Africa and Portuguese-controlled Mozambique, to Bechuanaland—surrounded by the republic, the Federation and South African-controlled South West Africa. It is even anachronistic to consider the High Commission Territories as a source of concern for their probable part in

[57] International Commission of Jurists, *South African Incident: the Ganyile Case*, 1962. Ganyile was detained from 30 March to 3 August 1960.
[58] *Rand Daily Mail*, 1 January 1962 and 30 January 1962. Dr Zwane was detained for three days.
[59] Institute of Race Relations (London) *Newsletter*, 26 August 1961.
[60] On the independence of the High Commission Territories see, for example, J. Halpern, *Basutoland, Bechuanaland and Swaziland: South Africa's Hostages*, 1965; D. Austin, *Britain and South Africa*, 1966, pp. 58–91

guerrilla warfare at this stage. The idea of guerrilla warfare had not yet emerged as a probable strategy against the republic. The South African political organisations which resorted to force restricted their activity at this time to selective sabotage and had not yet—by all indications—thought to launch a war of liberation in the style which was later to become familiar.[61]

Next to the High Commission Territories in importance, from the point of view of internal security, was Southern Rhodesia. It was important that the co-operation of this territory should be secured. Verwoerd told the South African parliament on 23 April 1963 that, concerned to maintain good relations with the Rhodesias, he had restrained himself from criticising their internal race policies even when the politicians of the Federation took the liberty to say of South Africa what they pleased: 'I always sought to avoid comment on what I regarded as their business . . . in order to retain their friendship.'[62] Also in the spirit of friendship Sir Roy Welensky, the Federal Prime Minister, visited the republic in May to meet Verwoerd. 'Great friendship' between the Federation and South Africa was affirmed, and while the two leaders would not 'interfere in each other's domestic affairs' they would, it was said, co-operate on economic and other matters of common interest.[63]

The Welensky visit could not fail to be associated with the mood of the African statesmen meeting in Addis Ababa at about the same time, where they were to decide to set up the African Liberation Council, with the object of liberating the remaining colonies and South Africa.[64] Welensky had long been defence-minded, and had previously submitted proposals to the United Kingdom for regional defence in Africa.[65] It was therefore thought at the time that a united front, comprising the republic, the Federation and the Portuguese-controlled territories, might yet emerge.[66] Again the question of a new rail link between the republic and the Federation was broached, though it is unclear to what effect.[67]

[61] Cf. M. Benson, *South Africa: the Struggle for a Birthright*, 1966, p. 234 ff.; L. Kuper, 'African nationalism in South Africa, 1910–64', *passim*, in Wilson and Thompson, *op. cit.*

[62] *Ass. Deb.*, vol. 6, col. 4599.   [63] IRR *Newsletter*, May 1963.

[64] *Africa, 1963*, No. 11, 31 May 1963. Cf. Z. Cervenk, *The Organisation of African Unity and its Charter*, 1968.

[65] See his *Welensky's 4,000 Days: the Life and Death of the Federation of Rhodesia and Nyasaland*, *passim*.

[66] *Rand Daily Mail*, 4 August 1964.

[67] *Newsletter*, May 1963.

The Federation, however, was disintegrating, and of the emergent units Southern Rhodesia was from the South African point of view clearly the most salient, and as it turned out, the most dependable, prospective ally. The rise of Ian Smith to the premiership, at the head of the Rhodesian Front, put South African–Rhodesian relations on a new footing. In July 1964 Smith visited the republic and conversed with Verwoerd. He told journalists that Rhodesia was now looking more towards the south than it had done since federation. He had mentioned, 'just in passing', the question of a unilateral declaration of independence of Britain, which he said would not occur without consultation with the electorate[68] (thus recalling the National Party of South Africa's promise—never fulfilled—that a republic in South Africa would be established only upon 'the broad basis of the national will' (die breë grondslag van die volkswil).[69] It is not known how much discussion of UDI did in fact occur on this occasion of Smith's abject pilgrimage to the heart of whiteness.

By this time the South African government's hopes with regard to the High Commission Territories were higher than they had been in 1960–62, as it began to appear that sections of the black leadership in those territories might, after all, turn out to be accommodating towards the republic.[70] This had, of course, been expected by some leaders of Nationalist opinion in South Africa; in 1958 Die Transvaler had written:

Britain can lead them towards self-government . . . but she can never give them economic self-sufficiency. When she has 'brought them up' and then granted them full independence, as has happened with other formerly independent territories in Africa, they will, like it or not, fall into the lap of the Union only because they cannot exist either together or separately.[71]

Sobered by international hostility, which had since 1958 gathered pace, Verwoerd was more cautious in his utterances. He remarked à propos of the High Commission Territories:

I sometimes wonder whether our troubles are not greater while Britain remains guardian, because by taking into consideration her international

[68] *Rand Daily Mail*, 4 August 1964.
[69] The republic was, in the event, agreed to by only some 52 per cent of the white electorate. The quoted phrase occurs in D. F. Malan, *Afrikaner volkseenheid my ervarings op die pad daarheen*. It became the slogan of 'moderate' republicans.
[70] Cf. J. J. Fouche in *Ass. Deb.*, vol. 15, col. 101.
[71] 12 November 1958; see SAIRR, *Thought*, vol. 3, No. 4.

interests, she may perhaps act differently from the course that would be followed by a local government which has only to take its more restricted interests into consideration.[72]

The withdrawal of the colonial powers from Africa had two complementary effects of which South African governments could not wholly disapprove: it removed the organisational framework for opposing South African pan-Africanism, while at the same time it removed an apple of discord in the otherwise friendly relations of South Africa and the West. Just as South African governments could no longer hope to achieve their ends mainly by using the white colonial powers, they could, by the same token, proceed with such of their plans as were still relevant without fear of opposition that really mattered, and without jeopardising their relations with the Western powers which seemed so eager to 'appease' the Afro-Asians.[73]

By such considerations Verwoerd was led to contemplate a multiracial political and economic commonwealth to which the High Commission Territories and parts of the disintegrating Central African Federation might belong.[74] It was as if the *Walpurgisnacht* of Sharpeville had turned the African Charter on its head, although it was only the strategies and intermediate objectives which changed; the main aim of the African Charter and of all the Africa policies, which was to create in Africa a context ideologically and organisationally favourable to the maintenance of white minority rule in South Africa, remained the same.

In the period which followed, southern and central Africa were to become more clearly focal to South African policy. Policy itself became more and more concerned with warding off the liberalising influence of decolonisation from South Africa itself. In that respect the domestic and external conflicts in which the republican governments were involved became more closely related. It is appropriate, therefore, that we conclude this part of our enquiry with a review of the interrelations of domestic and external conflicts in the period of transition—the high years of decolonisation. To this theme we now turn.

---

[72] *Ass. Deb.* vol. 6, col. 4599.
[73] Cf. Minister of Foreign Affairs, in *Ass. Deb.*, vol. 3, col. 4161.
[74] See J. E. Spence, *The Republic Under Pressure*, 1965, p. 95.

VI *The changing domestic political setting in the high years of decolonisation*

Internal conflict and internal change

The agitation in the international arena against the race policies of South African governments gained encouragement from the concessions which some colonial powers were making towards anti-colonialism and was spurred on by developments within South Africa itself. There Africans, Indians and, to to a lesser extent, coloureds were increasing their efforts to secure themselves inclusion in the South African polity.[1] These campaigns in their turn were greatly encouraged by the changes that were taking place outside South Africa, in colonial Africa and in the international community generally. In the late 1950s and early 1960s the leaders of black political organisations in South Africa forged links with nationalist and radical movements in the rest of Africa, thus reducing further the effective boundaries between the two conflict arenas, the national and the international.

South African governments had long made clear their views on the political aspirations of black people and their resolve to adhere to those positions. To the National Party increased pressure in favour of the enfranchisement of the blacks seemed to make all the more

---

[1] Following Parsons, we may regard the vote as 'a unit or quantum of authority' (in our case the basic unit) to participate in the work of the political system. (See T. Parsons, 'The political aspect of social structure and process', in D. Easton (ed.), *Varieties of Political Theory*, 1966, pp. 76–8). Unlike Parsons and others, however, we use the term *polity* to denote those who are authorised to participate rather than as a synonym of 'political system'. (See Parsons, *loc. cit.*, and W. C. Mitchell, *Sociological Analysis and Politics: the Theories of Talcott Parsons*, 1967, pp. 99–123; see also H. V. Wiseman, *Political Systems: Some Sociological Approaches*, 1966, chapters IV and V.) Those who are not authorised to participate may be referred to as the *non-polity*. When they are mobilised to alter the framework of political interaction with a view to creating an alternative order in which they will participate, or decide the norms, they become a *counter-polity*. Although it is graphic and therefore useful for our immediate purposes, the idea of 'units of authority' is in principle, quite unsatisfactory.

urgent the need to implement their own policy. *Apartheid* or 'separate development' was progressively implemented through a series of Acts designed to insulate the various races from each other, politically and physically, to abolish for ever the representation of blacks in the national parliament at Cape Town and thus to ensure in perpetuity white political supremacy. Of these laws the most outstanding as well as the most controversial were the Group Areas Act and the series of Bantu laws;[2] constitutional amendments early secured the termination of native representation in the white parliament[3] and, eventually, of coloured representation also.[4] Different ethnic 'home-lands' having been declared by the Tomlinson Commission,[5] the late 1950s and the 1960s saw attempts by the government to create political institutions in those homelands in order to give substance to its claim that blacks and whites belonged to different political communities.[6] To enforce separate political development the government brought legislation to prevent what it called 'improper political interference', i.e. the participation of members of one group in the designated politics of another group.[7]

A number of preparatory measures adopted by the post-1948 Nationalist governments facilitated these exclusions. These measures had the dual function of defining the boundaries of the polity and of defining the area and the terms of legitimate political action more rigorously than before. Concomitantly measures were adopted to increase the dominance of the political system over other sub-systems and to increase the dominance of the executive over the judicial institutions of the political system, all with a view to facilitating the suppression of opposition. Among the legislative instru-ments devised for these purposes the Suppression of Communism Act and the General Law Amendment Act are the most notable. The first created a statutory definition of communism and gave the

---

[2] The Group Areas Act, 1950; of the 'native' laws the more important in-clude the Bantu Laws Amendment Act, 1961, as subsequently amended. See also Carter, *op. cit.*, Benson, *op. cit.*, Marquard, *op. cit.*, and Hepple, *op. cit.*

[3] See M. Ballinger, *From Union to Apartheid: the Trek into Isolation, 1969.*

[4] Hepple, *op. cit.*, pp. 122 ff.

[5] *Report of the Commission of Inquiry into the Socio-economic Develop-ment of The Bantu Areas,* 1955.

[6] The Promotion of Bantu Self-government Act, 1958, and the proclama-tion of Transkei 'self-government' in 1963 are instances of this.

[7] Prohibition of Political Interference Act, 1968. See also 'Death of the Liberals' in *Africa Digest*, June 1968.

government extraordinarily wide restrictive powers over persons it chose to name 'communists'; the second created a system of indefinite detention without trial of persons suspected of 'sabotage' at the Attorney General's pleasure. Against government action taken under these laws there could be no effective recourse to the courts. To that not inconsiderable extent the capacity of judicial institutions to implement justice was reduced.[8]

If the judiciary was reduced in power, the scope of executive action was enlarged, thus creating a need for new organisational facilities to perform the extended functions. The special (political) branch of the police was enlarged and reorganised, and later a Bureau of State Security, answerable only to the Prime Minister, was formed.[9] At the same time extra-governmental support for the performance of intelligence functions was sought, with extensive use being made of informers and *agents provocateurs*.[10] It emerged during the 1970 election campaign, for example, that the Africa Institute, founded nominally as a non-governmental, quasi-academic research organisation, had, through its director, Professor Weiss, been implicated in military intelligence work.[11] Further attempts to maximise the viability of the political system included the expansion of para-military organisations and attempts to keep the white polity physically and psychologically in a state of maximum preparedness for armed conflict—short of battle-readiness. Critics of the regime might justifiably conclude that the sun State of Afrikaner nationalist expectation was beginning to assume the character of a garrison State. By its intolerance of 'liberalism' and 'communism', by its racist doctrines, and by the accretion of statal power it began to resemble the Third Reich.[12]

There was definitely self-closure of the political system against communists, liberals and blacks, within South Africa and outside.

[8] E. H. Brookes and J. B. Macaulay, *Civil Liberty in South Africa*, 1960; International Commission of Jurists on the Rule of Law in South Africa, *South Africa and the Rule of Law*, 1960; F. Mathews, *Law, Order and Liberty in South Africa*, 1970.

[9] Created under clause 29 of the General Law Amendment Act, 1969.

[10] This has been amply borne out by the testimony of State witnesses in political trials in South Africa.

[11] The *Cape Times*, 21 April 1970, reported the Prime Minister as having said that a confidential intelligence document on 'eavesdropping' (or telephone tapping) had reached Mr Jaap Marais (one of the leaders of the breakaway right-wing Herstigte Nasionale Party) through Professor Weiss, to whom it had been sent, as he was (then) Director of the Africa Institute.

[12] B. Bunting, *The Rise of the South African Reich*, 2nd edition, 1970.

The movement of Africans outside South Africa was severely restricted by the refusal of the government to grant passports to Africans as a general rule (and when passports were granted prohibitive deposits had to be paid to the State). Movement of Africans from other countries into South Africa was extremely limited, not least by the government's decision that the time was not ripe for diplomatic relations between South African and African governments. To a lesser extent, constraints were placed upon the movements of white, coloured and Indian persons in and out of South Africa. Several foreigners were declared prohibited immigrants because of their opposition to *apartheid*. Propaganda was intensified, the State-controlled radio network being the main medium in this regard. To prevent contrary influences, censorship of written material and of the arts was intensified.[13]

Around 1960 internal conflict in South Africa came to a head and the black franchise movement came to an abrupt conclusion. With the banning of the African National Congress and the Pan-African Congress, and the restriction of members of allied political organisations of all races, an era of non-violent protest by constitutional means on behalf of black people came to an end. From then on the PAC and the ANC, the largest mass organisations for blacks in South Africa, would either go under or would reassess their goals and strategies. They chose the latter course. No longer would they merely seek admission into the polity but they would explicitly seek to supplant the existing political system and replace it with another. They declared themselves the vanguard of a counter-polity. Faced with the coercive power of the State and its habits of coercion, they resolved to meet the violence of the State with revolutionary force. In short, they raised the standard of armed revolt.[14]

In such circumstances 'system maintenance' became an ever more pressing preoccupation of government, and political repression escalated. System maintenance required more than just legislation and executive control of political life. It made necessary the consolidation of the polity. The Nationalist government, which had

[13] Cf. the discussion of 'Ideological conflict', in K. Boulding, *Conflict and Defence*, 1962, and 'The self-closure of political systems', in K. W. Deutsch, *The Nerves of Government*, 1963.

[14] See, for example, E. Feit, *African Opposition in South Africa: Dynamics of the African National Congress*, 1962; Benson, *op. cit.*, p. 220 *ad fin.*; L. Kuper, 'African nationalism in South Africa, 1910–64', in Wilson and Thompson, *Oxford History of South Africa*, p. 468.

traditionally relied on Afrikaner support mobilised through a plethora of nationalist cultural, religious and economic organisations, had to seek support outside the *volk*.[15] White unity, to which all South African governments claimed to be committed, but about which little was effectively done, became an urgent preoccupation in the 1960s. But white unity might be expected—and came, indeed, to be expected—to lead to a decline in the responsiveness between government and some of its traditional supporters.[16]

The solidarity of the governing party was further tried when the government construed system maintenance to require an expansion of the polity through immigration (of whites). Immigration threatened to introduce competition for whites in the market place, but it was also thought likely to affect their ideological purity.[17] Thus, although there was widespread eagerness to receive into South Africa white settlers who were fleeing from the northern colonies that were gaining independence, there were also hesitant voices, later to become more hostile, among their hosts.

Tensions developed among supporters of the National Party in response to subtler changes in the form of white society. Gradually the effects of urbanisation and industrialisation came to be felt as threats to the quality of the core membership of the ideological population, the Afrikaners. It was, however, in the latter 1960s that these changes became central topics in intra-polity debate. As elsewhere, organisation and industrialisation were thought likely to corrode solidarity and to result in a decline of ideological fundamentalism. Such apprehension gained substance from the progressive secularisation of political life, which, in the view of traditionalists, threatened to undermine the ideological foundations of the State. In particular such changes should have facilitated a re-examination of older patterns of political collaboration. It might, indeed, be hoped by some of those who ruled that the exclusive aspects of Afrikaner nationalist ideology would yield to that wider white identity and solidarity thought to be so essential for system mainten-

[15] On relations among Afrikaner groups see Carter, *op. cit.*, chapters 8–10, and Coetzee, *op. cit.*, *passim*.

[16] See S. C. Nolutshungu, 'Issues of the Afrikaner "Enlightenment"', in *African Affairs*, 1970, and 'Party systems, cleavage structure and electoral performance', in *African Review*, 1972.

[17] Cf. Brand and Tomlinson, 'Die Plek van die Landbou in die Suid-Afrikaanse Volkshuishouding', in *South African Journal of Economics*, 1966, and cf. *Report of the Commission of Inquiry into the White Occupancy of the Rural Areas*, 1960.

ance.[18] This would not be easy, as the celebrated *verligte–verkrampte* split was to show.[19]

External and internal pressure and relationships

In assessing the impact of decolonisation on white South Africa it should be remembered that South Africa itself is a product of Western European colonialism, retaining within itself colonial modes of social organisation, such as, for example, the double stratification system to which reference has already been made.[20] The passing of the colonial order in Africa was therefore felt as a traumatic event. It was bound to impinge on the conceptualisation of internal relationships as well. For South African white elites, as for colonial elites everywhere, the European metropolitan elites were the reference groups, so much so that, however deeply decolonisation was deplored by most white South Africans, a domestic emulative homologue of decolonisation was sought.[21] South African governments, particularly from Malan onward, thought to meet African nationalism by means of domestic 'decolonisation' through the concession of 'self-government' and later 'independence' to black tribal 'homelands'. It was, however, left to Verwoerd to declare 'total *apartheid*' and, under the slogan of 'separate but equal' freedoms for whites and blacks, to initiate the process of 'decolonisation' in South Africa. Since, however, there were no unproblematical black colonies in South Africa and there was no unproblematic white metropolitan country, colonies (the 'Bantu homelands') had to be promulgated into existence and —hopefully—progressively promulgated out of existence by a self-styled metropolitan elite.[22]

---

[18] On identity and solidarity functions of ideology see D. Apter, 'Ideology and discontent', in D. Apter (ed.), *Ideology and Discontent*, 1964, and R. A. Scalapino, 'Ideology and modernisation–the Japanese case', in Apter, *op. cit.*
[19] See S. C. Nolutshungu, 'Issues of the Afrikaner "Enlightenment"' and 'Party system, cleavage structure and electoral performance', *locc. citt.*
[20] See chapter 1 above. Cf. also F. Fanon, *A Dying Colonialism*, n.d. and H. J. and R. E. Simons, *Class and Colour in South Africa, 1850–1950*, 1969.
[21] Application of sociological reference group theory has been made in the pioneering work of Gustavo Lagos, *International Stratification and Underdeveloped Countries*, and more explicitly in J. P. Nettl and R. Robertson, *International Systems and the Modernisation of Societies*, 1968, to which I am indebted.
[22] See, for example, Hepple, *op. cit., passim*; Ballinger, *op. cit., passim*. It was announced in June 1971 that the Bantustans would become completely independent by 1979.

The South African governments claimed that they were doing exactly what others were doing, only more gradually, and therefore, in their view, better.[23] There is no doubt that White South Africans *felt* they were conforming at least to this extent and were making important concessions; yet because those concessions did not deviate from any of the official versions of *apartheid* theory and were in no way intended to concede to Africans a share in the control of the government of the whole of South Africa, rather than restricting them to phantom homelands, the South African 'decolonisation' programme was only apparent. The slogan 'separate but equal' was a weapon in the white government's struggle to resist demands made upon it at home and abroad, but at the level of ideology it was a retreat from the doctrine of *baasskap*.

A greater impact upon internal relationships was probably that occasioned by the boycott campaign begun in earnest in 1959 and intensified after Sharpeville. In the light of this campaign, the international reactions to the Sharpeville massacre induced a 'search process' within the polity. Government and business sought areas of co-operation in the face of the common threat. In December 1959 the South African Foundation had been created at the initiative of businessmen as an extra-governmental propaganda organisation to promote foreign investment in, and trade with, South Africa.[24] But it was in the autumn of 1960 that the importance of such collaboration became clear. The Sharpeville incidents were followed by a fall in share values on the Johannesburg stock exchange which indicated a crisis of confidence in the political stability of South Africa.[25] Sharpeville was only part of the fairly widespread African unrest in South Africa, and in this atmosphere of grievance a number of business organisations decided to intervene in politics openly. The South African Federated Chamber of Industries presented on 3 May 1960 a memorandum to five Cabinet Ministers in which it expressed the belief that

the recent wave of lawlessness had a genuine basis of grievance and dissatisfaction which agitators had been able to exploit, and that the only

[23] Cf. p. 7 above and 121 below.

[24] South African Institute of Race Relations, *A Survey of Race Relations, 1959–60*, p. 92.

[25] *The Star*, 14 May 1960. The flight of foreign capital due to adverse share market dealings continued for another four years. The tendency had begun about 1959. See South African Reserve Bank, *Quarterly Bulletin*, several issues, 1960–66.

alternative to a continuance of riotous outbursts was a new approach based on consultation [between whites and blacks] as the key to a peaceful solution.[26]

The Afrikaanse Handelsinstituut, the Association of Chambers of Commerce of South Africa, the South African Federated Chamber of Industries, the Steel and Engineering Industries Federation of South Africa, and the Transvaal and Orange Free State Chamber of Mines handed a joint statement to the Prime Minister making a 'practical suggestion' and reiterating the view of the Federated Chamber of Industries. They specified the causes of grievance as the pass laws, influx control, curfew regulations, and the liquor laws —as if Africans could know no deeper discontent.[27]

The intervention of business in politics in this rather critical manner was not unequivocally welcomed by some of the traditional supporters of the Nationalist government.[28] And while these attempts by the white businessmen to contribute to a solution of the race problems of South Africa might be construed as progress towards 'white unity', that unity was belied by other facts of political life. The republican campaigns already mentioned[29] (a matter of both internal and external politics) were, in 1959–60, approaching their climax. Republicanism necessarily emphasised the distance between the two main language groups in the polity. In the midst of all the disquiet which characterised the period the Afrikaner nationalists themselves began to show signs of internal division, both over the strategies that should be adopted to maintain the overall system and over how far exclusive Afrikaner nationalist ambitions should be pursued.

Nowhere was division more apparent than in the Nationalists' responses to the attempted assassination of Dr H. F. Verwoerd. The division was manifest on two issues—the leadership of the National Party and the uses to which Verwoerd's misfortune should be put.[30]

26 *Rand Daily Mail*, 4 May 1960.

27 *Star*, 3 May 1960. See also *Star*, 2 June 1960; *Die Vaderland*, 11 June 1960; *Cape Argus*, 13 June 1960.

28 On the occasion of the creation of the South African Foundation, *Dagbreek* had written (22 December 1959): 'Perhaps they [businessmen] will also admit one day the extent to which they contributed to the creation of the false picture which has to be repaired with so much trouble and at such a terrible cost.' Cf. J. B. Vorster, in *Die Vaderland*, 24 June 1960.

29 See above.

30 Protracted conversations I had with Mrs Elaine Potter while she was working on the press and politics in South Africa helped to clear my own thoughts on these matters.

Throughout Verwoerd's period of illness and recuperation the National Party failed to appoint a deputy Prime Minister.[31] There was a division also between those who sought to placate international opinion by affecting to accept that in the troubles it was experiencing the government had, as it were, had no end of a lesson which should do it no end of good, and those who thought to emphasise defiantly their steadfastness in the pursuit of their ends as if nothing had happened. For the latter Sharpeville and its aftermath were no turning point, hardly even a set of traffic lights.[32]

The attempt on Verwoerd's life was used by some to attract support for a project close to the ailing Premier's heart—the republic. Contributions were invited to the Republikeinse Strydfonds (Republican Campaign Fund) which, it was said, Verwoerd had set up shortly before his attempted assassination.[33] This, arguably, was a divisive use of tragedy. The *Rand Daily Mail* reported that there was also division between Nationalists who wanted to use the attempted assassination as an occasion to discredit the white opposition and the English-language press[34] and those who thought like Paul Sauer, the Minister of Water Affairs, who 'appealed to everybody "not to say or do anything which can have any effect other than to inspire confidence and respect for our country in the eyes of the outside world" '.[35] The Afrikaans Sunday paper *Dagbreek en Sondagnuus*, for its own part, however, acknowledged no such restraint.[36] Its editor, Mr W. van Heerden, wrote in a militant Afrikaner nationalist vein hardly calculated to overcome divisions among whites or to inspire much 'confidence and respect' among those abroad who thought such conciliation a condition of the survival of the white State:

When I think of the campaign which has been waged now for more than ten years against the present government, and particularly of certain English newspapers' uninterrupted hate campaign with accusations of

[31] *Rand Daily Mail*, 12 April 1960. *Die Transvaler* denied this but went on to say that Mr P. O. Sauer would continue to act as leader of the House of Assembly and 'a senior Cabinet Minister' would take the chair at Cabinet meetings during the Prime Minister's absence.

[32] Cf. Paul Sauer's speech at Humansdorp, reported in *Die Transvaler*, 20 April, 1960, with *Die Vaderland's* report that Sauer had, according to F. Barnard, the Premier's private secretary, not consulted with Verwoerd.

[33] *Die Transvaler*, 13 April 1960.

[34] 12 February 1960.

[35] *Raind Daily Mail*, 12 April 1960.

[36] 17 April 1960.

pride, callousness, meanness, pettiness, dishonesty and every other ignoble motive which can be ascribed to political behaviour, it does not surprise me when there are so many signs of dark, unreasoning passion taking the place in some people of normal political argument.[37]

In short, Van Heerden was placing the blame for the attempted assassination of Verwoerd at the door of the more liberal English-language papers. So did *Die Volksblad* when it observed, 'the opposition and English press may now realise what fire they are playing with when they make unbridled attacks on nationalist leaders.'[38] A voice that was later to grow more shrill was that of Dr Albertus Hertzog, who thought the time had passed 'when we could walk arm-in-arm with our enemies'. And these enemies he named as the British press, the 'mining press' in South Africa, the British Prime Minister, Harold Macmillan, the universities of Cape Town and the Witwatersrand, the African National Congress and the United Party.[39]

Some Afrikaner nationalists there were, also, who doubted the soundness of key features of Verwoerd's policies, such as the Bantustan system. It was suggested that instead of dealing with the chiefs in the native reserves the government should consult directly with the urban-based African nationalist leadership. This view had been stated in 1958 by Professor L. J. du Plessis when he asked:

Why is it that we do not welcome the emancipation of the black people in Africa as we would like to be welcomed as a free nation? Is it because we have a guilty conscience? We ourselves are the oppressors of the non-white peoples.

He urged the government to push ahead with separate development but added that there were capable people in the ANC with whom it would be possible to negotiate. Verwoerd said some of these comments that whites oppressed blacks were irresponsible. He rejected the idea of consultation with the ANC.[40]

But there was a good deal of disquiet among Nationalists. In 1959 Professor J. H. Coetzee told the Africa seminar of the University of Potchefstroom:

[37] *Dagbreek en Sondagnuus,* 17 April 1960. Translation from *South African Press Digest*, vol. 5, No. 3.

[38] 12 April 1960.

[39] *South African Press Digest* (mimeo), 7 May 1960, pp. 182 ff.

[40] See SAIRR, *Thought*, vol. 3, No. 2.

In a country like South Africa the National Party and the African National Congress should have been the greatest allies rather than antagonists . . .

He went on to ask:

Should not the 'spiritually emancipatory' [*geestelikbevrydende*] crisis act be bringing heads together, white and non-white, to set up the plan for the freedom day on a definite year and day not too far in the future?

Although Professor Coetzee thought this was reconcilable with *apartheid*, he clearly had an unfamiliarly permissive conception of *apartheid*.[41] From religious quarters, too, heretical views were expressed:

Apart from the political stupidity and unstatesman-likeness of it, Tom Mboya's words ['the whites who do not want to be under native government must leave the country'] yet contain a profound truth. Those who do not want to live with the others must find refuge elsewhere. It sounds cruel and hard, but how else?[42]

Others suggested that the white polity should be strengthened (against Africans) by the admission of coloureds into the polity.[43] But Verwoerd re-entered political life in no mood for any such concessions. He would continue his Bantustan policy, would not enfranchise coloureds and expected those churchmen who felt uneasy about his native policy to hold their peace if they were not prepared to support him.[44] That little more was heard of these rumblings after 1961 reflected the immense power of Verwoerd— a martyr come back to life within an embattled Afrikanerdom which valued 'heroes'; by his unyielding adherence to his policies he gave assurance in a time of uncertainty.

Verwoerd himself accepted the collaboration of business, and it is certainly the case that, as the boycott movement spread, Verwoerd came to rely more and more on the economic importance of South Africa in the world.[45] This, as we shall see, was to become an important feature of the period of the 'outward-looking' policy.

[41] See SABRA, *Journal of Racial Affairs*, April 1960.

[42] See the Dutch Reformed Church organ *Woord en Daad*, March 1960, quoted in *Press Digest*. Consider also rows among Dutch Reformed churches and between Verwoerd and the 'Delayed Action' group, see SAIRR *Survey,* 1961, pp. 63–70.

[43] See Hepple, *op. cit.*, p. 132.

[44] *Ibid.*, and SAIRR *Survey*, 1961, pp. 63–70.

[45] Cf. his reference to the aid South Africa could give to African States: *Ass. Deb.*, vol. 3, cols. 3763 and 3757, and the suggestion of a southern African common market.

Verwoerd created an organisation to facilitate collaboration on economic matters between government, business and academics.[46]

In spite of the areas of co-operation that were found, however, the critical years 1959–60 were a period of disagreement and confusion within the white polity, and particularly among Afrikaner nationalists. The containment of dissent within Afrikanerdom was attributable not to any inherent features of the polity but to the uniquely powerful position of Verwoerd—especially after the *fortuitous* attempt on his life. Differences came home to roost, however, in the terminal years of his Ministry, and neither the growth of 'terrorism' nor the assassination of Verwoerd, nor, indeed, the troubles experienced by settlers in Southern Rhodesia and in the Portuguese colonies, could prevent the eruption between 1965 and 1970 of some of these differences in their most acriminous form in the whole post-war history of Afrikanerdom. The internal unity of the opposition did not remain intact either. If the entire post-war period may be viewed as one which saw the fragmentation of political consensus within the opposition-supporting section of the polity,[47] the period after 1957 saw the acceleration of that trend. In 1959 the 'left wing' of the United Party broke away to form the Progressive Party, counterbalancing the defection of United Party members to the government.

More ominous for the white polity as a whole, but particularly revealing of the quality of commitment within the English-speaking section of the polity, was the egress of whites from South Africa after Sharpeville. Many of these people were probably fleeing for safety, but some of them left because they could not find a meaningful role within the white polity which they could accept—they had failed to find a political home in the area of 'legitimate' political action in South Africa.

As can be seen from the figures in table 5, 1960 and 1961 saw the greatest number of emigrants from South Africa. The emigration figure for 1960 was less than the recorded 12,879 for 1956, but 9,495 of the 1956 emigrants had gone to the Rhodesias, probably in response to the economic boom there, whereas in 1960 only 4,551 emigrants were bound for the Rhodesias (the 1961 figure was 4,635).[48]

[46] The Economic Advisory Council, established in July 1960.
[47] See, for example, Carter, *op. cit.*, *passim*; Hepple, *op. cit.*, *passim*; Marquard, *op. cit.*, *passim*.   [48] *Statistical Yearbook*, 1968.

This would suggest that the reasons for the egress in 1960–61 have to be sought within South Africa itself. Probably the change in the political status of South Africa, from dominion to republic and out of the Commonwealth, accounts for the increased number of emigrants in 1961; but any account of the high figures for the two years must include, in the absence of more direct evidence, the political troubles as an important cause.[49]

TABLE 5   *White emigration, 1957–64*

Year	Total
1957	10,943
1958	8,807
1959	9,379
1960	12,612
1961	14,894
1962	8,945
1963	7,151
1964	8,092

Source. Statistical Yearbook, Bureau of Statistics, Pretoria, 1968.

Of those who remained, though disenchanted with the 'legitimate' political opposition options, some began to intensify outside the permitted limits their attempts to bring about political change. Some resorted to violence: an African Resistance Movement constituted of white university graduates thought to force change by a series of acts of selective sabotage, the banned Communist Party of South Africa and its affiliates continued to give their full support to the Congress alliance which had now gone underground and was increasingly turning to violent revolutionary means.[50] It would be instructive to know just how many white people were now involved in extra-legal political activity. There is no doubt that there were more people on the 'left' involved in violence than ever before, but by the nature of the case it is impossible at this juncture to know the figures. The numbers involved overall were in any case very small.

We have laboured the divisions and the intensity of feeling among whites in order to discredit the often expressed view that external (and internal) pressure merely consolidates the white polity. Clearly,

[49] Most of the emigrants were probably English-speaking. A fair proportion came from the higher occupational groups.

[50] See Benson, *op. cit.*

this curious theory is not borne out for the period of greatest stress, the high years of decolonisation.

Yet it may be suggested that after the establishment of the republic and the formerly divisive imperial connection was sundered, unity did in fact emerge, at least on questions of foreign policy[51] and internal security. The bi-partisan approach to the Katanga crisis, to the Rhodesian crisis and to relations with Britain over the sale of arms and the Simonstown agreement,[52] the increasing readiness of the United Party through the mid-1960s to affirm its commitment to white supremacy, and its equal readiness to support the government on matters of internal security, might be cited as evidence of 'consolidation'. Indeed security, internal and external, seems to be the paradigm case in support of consolidation theories. Yet while both establishment parties sought to suppress revolutionary opposition (could they be expected to do otherwise?), it can hardly be said that they would at earlier times—of less pressure—have been less willing to do so. The question had simply not arisen as an urgent policy issue before. Secondly, the apparent shift to the 'right' of the United Party was attributable less to 'pressure' from internal and external opponents than to the exodus of liberal and 'left-wing' members from the party as the political positions of English-speaking South Africans, in the wake of Afrikaner nationalism, became polarised.[53] The Katanga crisis (1960) and the unilateral declaration of independence in Southern Rhodesia (1965) stand out as the most spectacular events to which the two parties in South Africa had to respond. It would be far-fetched to suggest that their support for white refugees from Congo and for independent Katanga was bi-partisan in consequence of pressure having 'consolidated' the whites in South Africa. The bi-partisan sympathy with Katanga, with the white Congolese settlers and with Tshombe is more convincingly explained as a consequence of a wider empathy with settlers in Africa and of the traditional policy of both parties to support the colonial powers and the West, who in this case were particularly

[51] The British connection had been a contentious component of foreign policy under Smuts, and under Botha before him.

[52] Cf. J. E. Spence, *The Strategic Significance of Southern Africa*, 1971, pp. 10ff.; G. Cockram, *Vorster's Foreign Policy*, 1970, pp. 63–81.

[53] The two major exoduses were in 1953–54, when the Liberal Party was formed, and in 1959, when the Progressive Party was formed. See J. Robertson, *Liberalism in South Africa, 1948–63, passim*; also Carter, *op. cit.*, chapter 12, and Marquard, *op. cit.*, chapter 7.

sensitive to the hardships of the settlers and seemed deeply moved by the cause of secessionist Katanga.[54]

It is true that, as far as can be judged, there was widespread sympathy among white South Africans with white Rhodesians. It is also true that effectively there were no differences after 1966 between the government and the official opposition on Rhodesian policy. Bearing in mind that the white Rhodesians merely wanted for themselves what white South Africans supporting these parties had always been saying was good for whites, was the birthright of whites in Africa—namely, white supremacy over Africans—it would indeed have been surprising if there were not this sympathy. It should be noted, however, for what it is worth, that for a few months after UDI the United Party (and some splinter parties of the National Party from the 'right') did not scruple to play up for electoral advantage the 'differences' of policy between themselves and the government on the question of UDI. What was of particular interest in the Rhodesia–South Africa situation was that no split occurred in South Africa along the traditional pro- and anti-British cleavage line. This, however, points not so much to consolidation due to pressure but to the fact that the imperial factor ceased, after the severance of the Commonwealth connection, to be a potent issue in South Africa. Any party campaigning on a pro-British ticket would be flogging a dead horse, while the support of many white South Africans with Rhodesian family and business connections would be alienated without advantage.[55]

The foregoing general remarks on white politics in South Africa should suffice to establish our contention that there is little firm evidence for the view that external (and internal) pressure merely consolidates white unity in South Africa, and while it is probably based on the sound theoretical observation that intra-polity conflict may be functional to the emergence of a new consensus, the consolidation thesis over-stretches the point to such an extent that it ignores other important aspects of conflict.

One naturally would avoid the opposite danger of seeming to exaggerate the importance of the disagreements among white South Africans both in terms of their moral import and as to their political

[54] Cf. C. Hoskyns, *The Congo since Independence, January 1960–December 1960*, 1965, pp. 285, 295, 453, etc., and O'Brien, *op. cit., passim.*

[55] This is in addition to any strategic, or foreign-relations advantages which might be expected to ensure from a secure white presence in Rhodesia, i.e. on South Africa's northern frontier.

effects. To be sure, the evidence suggests that compared to the conflicts between the polity and its extra-polity opponents these disagreements seem like the 'non-battles between Tweedledee and Tweedledum'. Our view is simply that they are not more so now than they have ever been—at least on the question of the entitlements of black people. To the extent that they appear to be so—as in the case of foreign policy and internal security—there are more convincing, more immediate explanations related to intra-polity contests within South Africa rather than to pressures brought to bear from without, as the consolidation thesis portentously pretends is the case.

It is against the knowledge of the fissiparousness of the South African polity that the capacity of foreign policy-makers to create an internal environment fully supportive of the Africa policies must be estimated. And while the Africa policies were intended to facilitate system maintenance, what system maintenance meant in practice was and, arguably, always will be a matter of considerable political contestation. And that, ultimately, must reduce the viability of the white polity in conflict. It is, of course, impossible to assign any precise significance to ultimacy in this regard.

PART TWO *South Africa in post-colonial Africa*

The response of South African policy-makers to the further de-colonisation of Africa, and to the forces seeking the isolation of the republic and the overthrow of its *apartheid* regime, developed into what is now commonly referred to as the 'outward-looking' policy. It differed from the earlier pan-African policy in its acceptance of the irreversibility of the transfer of power from European metropoles to African centres, and could be characterised as a more or less systematic and vigorous attempt on the part of successive South African governments to find opportunities of co-operation and friendship with willing African States which would turn a blind eye to *apartheid* and not interfere in what the South African government considered its domestic affairs. Although direct contact with African governments, bilaterally (rather than through organisations), would be sought, South Africa would, and did, use the residual influence of the former colonial powers (notably France) to its purpose; inter-governmental bodies such as the UN General Assembly also provided a platform for the public diplomacy of the outward-looking policy, but the main emphasis was on direct inter-governmental relations.

Characteristic features of the outward-looking policy, which will emerge from the ensuing discussion, included the urgency with which it was executed, its close relation to a wider political strategy, the diversity of support from non-governmental bodies within South Africa, and its clear dependence on the physical factors of South African military and economic power. Above all, the outward-looking policy occurred in a distinctive operational setting, both internally, in South Africa, and externally, in Africa and the world.

Domestic politics

External and domestic opposition forced the Verwoerd government to modify its internal and foreign policies. This process of adjustment continued after Verwoerd's demise and was carried even further. The changes in the character of South African political life which began to emerge had an important bearing on policy towards Africa and deserve, therefore, some discussion here. Since, however, the subject has been copiously dealt with elsewhere, this chapter will be restricted to an outline of only the main distinctive features of South African political life in the period of the outward-looking policy.

The shifts in policy that were introduced in this period were not always—on the surface, at any rate—easy to reconcile with the traditional attitudes of Afrikaner nationalists. They therefore resulted in the *verkrampte–verligte* split within the National Party, with some right-wing dissenters eventually breaking off to form the Herstigte Nasionale Party (HNP)—the Reconstituted National Party. To meet the dangers threatening the republic the government called for white unity. Ever a controversial issue in Afrikaans politics, the white unity policy became positively divisive when Verwoerd's successor carried it so far as to give English-speakers ministerial positions and to play down some of the traditional cultural and ideological preoccupations of the party. Equally controversial was the policy of encouraging (white) immigration, which, it was feared by verkramptes, would merely strengthen the English-speaking group, since immigrants generally found it harder to adjust to the Afrikaner way of life.

In its eagerness to maintain and augment its economic relations with Western and other willing countries Verwoerd's government and, to an even greater extent, that of Vorster after it, was forced to collaborate openly with private financial interests, including 'big business' and multi-national companies, and support such schemes designed to promote 'international goodwill' as the United States–South African Leadership Exchange Programme (USSALEP). In the past this would have been thought dangerously liberal and anti-Afrikaner, and was even now so regarded by traditionalists.

The conflict among Afrikaners which followed from these ideological revisions reflected the tensions in the white community which had always existed between the outward pull of a metropolitan-oriented economy and culture and the inward-looking, self-regarding tendency, the settler nationalism, of those who benefited less than other whites from imperialism. In general, the most economically well-to-do whites tended, comparatively, to be outward-looking, while the less privileged sought refuge from the burdensome demands of the outside world—be it British imperialism or Western investors in general—in an exclusive particularism unhampered by universalist ideologies and the imperatives of international capitalism.

As more Afrikaners became well-to-do more of them could be expected to become outward-looking. What was, however, the main impetus for change was this. In the past the Afrikaner elite saw that every advantage, economic as well as political, lay in gaining control of the State with the use of a nationalist political machine which was exclusivist and inward-looking. Having gained that control, and having done so in a particularly difficult period in which the very idea of white minority rule was being questioned or challenged everywhere, they became preoccupied with the survival of the State itself. That depended on an outward movement on the part of the Afrikaner elite towards potential allies, in South Africa and elsewhere, in the pursuit of power. Strength thus lay in asserting the preeminence of State interest over the particularistic ambitions, illusions and grudges which had been, and would still to some extent continue to be, characteristic of Afrikaner nationalism.[1]

Having successfully suppressed the main opponents of their State —it is the most important political feature of the period that the African nationalists, liberals and communists had been suppressed— the government was willing to seek areas of co-operation with willing non-Afrikaners. At the same time, unnecessary friction was to be avoided while the *apartheid* system and its inevitable instruments of repression were retained. Thus the various white groups were urged to unite, and thus also, within the framework of white domination, political institutional roles were devised for willing blacks. Coloureds were given a parliament (following the end of their indirect representation in the South African parliament), while Africans, said to belong to a variety of nations, were variously accorded 'homelands' in which they would become increasingly 'self-governing'.

The Bantustans (as the system of 'self-governing' African 'homelands' is generally known) were a feature of the period of the outward policy and were, indeed, seen to be closely related to the policy towards the rest of the continent. Members of the government and their supporters associated the Bantustans with their policy of seeking political and economic links with black-ruled African States. Often they saw the contacts involved in each case as similar (which, in racial terms, they were, although, in political terms, the com-

---

[1] That is to say, beyond that degree of division on which the State itself rests and depends for its stability. See Nolutshungu, 'Party system, cleavage structure and electoral performance', for some discussion of the relationship between white cleavages and the stability of the political system.

parison of independent African States with subordinate 'native' reserves was invidious). Sometimes the idealised Bantustans were seen as the corner-stone of a wider system of economic co-operation between South Africa and all the neighbouring black States.[2] Pro-government ideologists offered it as that much sought-after solution of the racial problem of South Africa which should finally end the dispute between black Africa and the republic. The government itself was wiser (given the limitations of the Bantustans) in seldom admitting that the racial issues or any of its proffered settlements, including the Bantustans, was any concern of the African States, these being South Africa's 'domestic affairs'. Nevertheless, the government did look to the success of the Bantustans to help allay international criticism of South Africa.

As early as 1963 Verwoerd had declared the Transkei self-governing and had held out the prospect of more territories approaching that status. This was partly a propaganda move to impress Western powers and partly the implementation of a long-standing National Party policy response to the 'native question'— a matter with which Verwoerd had been closely connected both as the reputedly doctrinaire Minister of Native Affairs and as the Prime Minister who declared himself in favour of 'total *apartheid*'. With more Bantustans being created,[3] there emerged a diversity of Bantu-stan political leaders, some of whom rejected the policy of *apartheid*. This had two distinct, even opposite consequences. On the one hand those who criticised the concept of 'separate development' un-doubtedly gave comfort to other critics of the government in South Africa and abroad. Even those who, like Matanzima, the Chief Minister of the Transkei, accepted *apartheid* principles and those who remained silent on this fundamental issue did, by their frequent demands for more resources, including land, show up the inadequacy of the 'concessions' made to blacks. On the other hand, however the controversy thus aroused gave a certain vitality and reality to the Bantustans which could hardly have been thought possible in the early 1960s. Thus the Bantustans became more credible, especially to well disposed outsiders, both as an earnest of the South African government's desire to meet some of the aspirations of black South

[2] Cf. J. A. Lombard, J. J. Stadler and P. J. van der Merwe, *The Concept of Economic Co-operation in Southern Africa*, 1968; E. M. Rhoodie, The Third Africa, 1969, and also G. J. Labuschagne *et. al.*, *Suid-Afrika en Suider-Afrika*, 1970.

[3] See a concise discussion in *Third World*, June 1973.

Africans and as a worthwhile institutional framework for blacks to seek some amelioration of their condition in South Africa. Some African leaders, like Chief Buthelezi of Kwa-Zulu, opposed *apartheid* and emphasised that Africans were herded into Bantustans only because they had not the power to resist, arguing with unimpeachable sincerity that Africans might as well do the best they could for themselves within the system. At best the effect of such a political stance was ambiguous and, at worst, anyone who took such a view merely ended by contributing, through the diversionary power of his illusions, to the very system which grieved him. In domestic politics the force of the example of anti-*apartheid* leaders working within the system was to confer legitimacy on the collaborative roles for blacks which were being institutionalised.[4] It is, of course, the case that the Bantustan leaders 'working within the system' only managed to do so with any ease in the political circumstances resulting from the destruction of the nationalist mass movements. Bantustans continued to be viewed with suspended incredulity or even downright scepticism by most Africans, and the Bantustan leaders were generally rejected by the student-led Black Power movement which, in Vorster's South Africa, was the nearest spiritual heir of the nationalist movements.

To be sure, some advantages could be derived by Africans from the Bantustans. In addition to obtaining a platform to air their grievances, Africans could gain administrative positions previously denied to them. The government could, it might be hoped, be urged with greater success than before to promote the economic development of the backward regions in which the Bantustans were located.[5] In the event the Vorster government even agreed to allow investment by white enterprises in the Bantustans (an idea which Verwoerd had completely rejected), and later expressed itself not

[4] This is not intended as a judgement on personal political–moral positions. It is merely an assessment of objective effects; it cannot, and is not intended to, impeach the moral validity of the sort of position taken up by, say, Buthelezi. Nor do I wish in any way to understate the enormity of the dilemma the situation poses in ethical terms for black South African intellectuals (the group who do have a choice) living there. *A propos* of Buthelezi it should be noted that he has sought to avoid any condemnation of those who are committed to using more drastic means than he feels he can responsibly do.

[5] Cf. M. Lipton, 'The South African census and the Bantustan policy', in *World Today*, June 1972. For an up-to-date discussion see *Third World*, special issue, 'South Africa's Bantustans', June 1973.

averse to foreign investment in the Bantustans.[6] It did appear, however, that such benefits as might issue from the Bantustans—in so far as they were not wholly speculative—were, and would continue to be, concentrated in a small section of the population of the reserves (which includes the hundreds of African town-dwellers 'repatriated' to the reserves), and that, so very far from that leading to the ultimate relief of Africans in South Africa generally, it was creating a group of Africans fulfilling roles that favoured stability while they themselves developed a material interest in the preservation of the *status quo*. That group would owe its social and economic advantages to the very *apartheid* State it was meant to oppose and undermine by 'working within the system'.

It has been argued that Bantustans would contribute to the radicalisation of the rural populations either by leading to the growth of an assertive black exclusivism[7] or through the effects of industrialisation.[8] However, such developments did not, in the period reviewed, seem likely to outweigh the functions for which the Bantustans were designed and which they performed to the evident satisfaction of their authors.

The concessions concerning white and foreign investments in the Bantustans were of a piece with other policy changes in the economic field which were very contentious among Afrikaner nationalists and which were quite revealing of the nature of the period of the outward-looking movement. *Verkrampte* critics of the government often complained that it was turning a blind eye to infringements of the industrial colour bar. In some industries shortages of skilled white labour necessitated such a policy if economic growth was to be maintained. In the view of one *verkrampte* trade unionist, G. H. Beetge:

The Government delays the implementation of *apartheid* because it has yielded to the pressure of big employers, who for the sake of bigger profits wish to maintain an abnormal growth rate and to rake in great wealth [*groot rykdom inpalm*]. Job reservation is indeed on the statute book but it is not being implemented in practice.[9]

[6] *Today's News*, 1 February 1973.
[7] See M. Szeftel, 'The Transkei: conflict externalisation and black exclusivism', unpublished M.A. thesis, University of Zambia, 1970.
[8] A similar view was put to me by Professor J. Simons of the University of Zambia in April 1973.
[9] *Die Afrikaner*, 13 March 1970. Beetge was Chief Secretary of the white Building Workers' Trade Union.

In the 1970s, following strikes in Namibia and in South Africa itself, the government's attitude towards black workers in industry showed some slight modification. Wage increases were recommended for blacks in a wide range of occupations, while the strikes were treated as industrial disputes rather than as acts of subversion, and in some cases the need for better African wages was recognised. At the same time, however, the strikes were blamed on agitators and the police and army intervened in some of the major strikes. Two issues were involved in these responses to the industrial situation. Firstly, wage levels had to be increased so that the domestic market could expand to meet the increased production.[10] This could be achieved only by increasing the wages of black workers, since those of whites, already very high, contributed to cost inflation without substantially affecting the market for South African produce.[11] The second issue was industrial reform. There were indications that in some industries the wage structures were changing to some very slight degree as more Africans would move into higher work grades for which they would receive training not previously given to them. At the same time the law governing black labour was altered to the extent of conceding black workers the right, upon certain conditions, to go on strike.[12] These reforms had two obvious aims. One was to relieve African discontent and to prevent industrial disputes from developing into political crises by providing machinery with 'safety valves' within the industrial arena. The other, equally important, aim was to allay the criticism to which foreign companies investing in South Africa continued to be subjected in their home countries.

All the developments in the field of industrial and economic policy reflected the Vorster government's commitment to a policy of economic expansion. That policy was attractive because the economy was in fact expanding and the fruits of that expansion were thought desirable not only in economic but also in political terms. At the lowest estimate, prosperity would enable South Africa to meet its defence needs however high their cost might be. More important, however, was the belief, probably justified, that it would be in

[10] See below.

[11] Cf. I. Hume, 'Notes on South African wage movements', in *South African Journal of Economics*, 1970.

[12] It is easy to exaggerate the importance of this 'concession' in a situation where, given the government's wide powers (which have often been used to subdue workers' unions), the right to organise strikes offers the organisers of the strikes little protection.

conditions of economic recession rather than growth that political conflicts would mount to dangerous levels—both among whites in different class positions and between whites and blacks. The South African government had accepted the ideology of growth. Finally, growing economic prosperity would attract even greater investments from major Western countries and seal the commitment of those powers to 'stability' and 'peaceful change' in South Africa and in its economic periphery.

The period since the war, and particularly the phase after Sharpeville, had seen considerable economic expansion. Economic expansion increased the upward mobility of Afrikaners and undoubtedly influenced their political and social outlook as well. The urbanisation of that group also favoured the adoption by its elites of a 'modernising' outlook.[13] Thus whereas in the pre-war years the attitude of that elite towards capitalism vacillated and was at times suspicious, particularly its attitude to oligopolistic capitalism (which they called *die georganiseerde geldmag*), now it readily encouraged capitalist development even, and perhaps particularly, in its monopolistic and internationalist forms. This was, of course, one of the issues in the *verkrampte–verligte* split.[14]

It is basically this general change in outlook, which made possible the concessions that have been described. There is, however, a further factor which explains South Africa's preoccupation with improving its external image. In Vorster's time the danger of isolation was neither as urgent nor as credible as in Verwoerd's time. In general, also, it is impossible to argue with any conviction that the consciences of foreign interests *had* to be assuaged by concessions to blacks— worse forms of oppression have not in recent history materially affected either Western trade with, or investment in, any country. South Africa clearly did not *have* to devote as much attention to its external image as it did. Nor did its adoption of a capitalist 'growth ideology' in itself necessitate this. Why, then, was it so concerned? It seems that these revisions had an international sociological basis, wider than the immediate calculations of profit and loss by the Afrikaner government and those who supported its policy.

Reference has already been made to the emulative character of the Bantustan 'solution'. In industrial policy, too, some of the 'concessions' might not have occurred had there not been a general

<hr/>

[13] Cf. H. Adam, *Modernising Racial Domination*, 1971.
[14] Cf., for example, *Die Afrikaner*, 20 March 1970.

disposition to align economic policy with the usages of the former imperial centres (and by extension the advanced capitalist countries in general)—provided always that it could be done without endangering the State.[15] This tendency can be seen in a wide range of activities; it is most manifest in matters of taste and elite culture, but it is also evident in the economic and social aspirations of those elites. It is partly due to the fact that their basic ideologies are, in any case, derivative, but it is also due to the structure of what (for lack of a better term) may be called international society. That society is a highly stratified one in which national elites compete for status which is determined by prestige as well as material resources (hence the importance of national images).[16] Galtung has noted that the inequalities in that stratified order, including the unequal ability of powers to influence them, are a distinctive feature of a system which is imperialist by its very structure.[17] That imperialism is operative at the level of ideas as well as in the material sphere. Thus once more we are drawn to seeking the springs of social and political action in the syndrome of imperial social and inter-societal conditions which, in a discussion of formerly colonial areas such as this, is appropriate.

In the 1960s South Africa had long ceased to be an imperial dependency; it had even left the Commonwealth. Its external trade was diversified and its economy more complex and more balanced than that of any colonial territory. Yet in many ways it retained or sought to retain for ever the relationships of colonialism. Its external relations with neighbouring black States retained much of their colonial character, and the racial situation in South Africa continued to be colonial (even the contemplated Bantustan 'solution' was a 'domestic colonialism'), and for that reason continued to create problems for that outward policy which both economic expansion and military developments encouraged, and to which we now turn.

External policy

The requirements of economic expansion were vitally important in the shaping of South Africa's policies towards Africa. Firstly they dictated that South Africa should maintain the system of labour

[15] It is strikingly the fact that it is in political organisation that new States show themselves least willing to adopt metropolitan forms.

[16] Lagos, op. cit.

[17] Galtung, op. cit.

migration, dating back to the nineteenth century, whereby neighbouring black territories (Malawi, Lesotho, Botswana, Angola, Mozambique, Zambia and Tanganyika[18]) supplied cheap labour to the mines and white farms. Secondly, South African industrialists and the government, seeking to protect their domestic market from competition coming from neighbouring States, including those in the customs union, clearly preferred the continuation of the relationship between South Africa and these States which colonialism had created. Thirdly, South Africa had to find markets for its industrial produce and, provided it was possible to find them there, Africa was a logical target. It was particularly important to find external markets because the domestic market was not growing rapidly enough. G. J. J. F. Steyn, Secretary for Commerce, reviewing the growth of South Africa's foreign trade, put the matter thus:

Despite the favourable growth factors [high natural population growth rate, constant influx of immigrants, sustained increase in standard of living, higher expenditure by non-whites] the scope of the domestic market still remains relatively limited, by international standards, with the result that South African manufacturers and producers will also have to rely to an increasing extent on enhanced foreign outlets for their products if they wish to reap the benefits of the economies of scale.[19]

A major contributory factor to this need for foreign outlets is undoubtedly the severe inhibition of the earning power of Africans due to *apartheid*, which in turn considerably limits their contribution to a growing domestic market.

Molteno has also pointed out that in the period of the outward-looking policy South Africa was encountering balance-of-payments problems which encouraged it all the more to seek access to African markets.[20] There was also a long-term structural aspect to the problem of the balance of payments. This factor, which because of the upward movement in the price of gold in recent years tended to be ignored, was that the production of that mineral, which had for so long been and still continued to be the main balancing item in South Africa's foreign trade, was showing a downward trend. Steyn concluded:

[18] Zambia and Tanganyika ceased to permit this migration after their independence.

[19] G. J. J. F. Steyn, 'Some aspects of the development of the domestic and foreign trade of the Republic of South Africa during the post-war period', in *Yearbook of Statistics*, 1972.

[20] R. Molteno, *Africa and South Africa*, 1970.

It is obvious, therefore, that a strong and sustained increase in exports is indispensable to South Africa's continued economic welfare. With the [sic] consideration in mind the government has decided to strengthen still further its promotional services and to devote particular attention to the more purposeful promotion of the country's export of manufactures. As part of the efforts in the latter direction, arrangements are now being made in collaboration with the private sector to establish export targets which particular industrial undertakings will try to achieve over a specific number of years.[21]

Collaboration between government and the private sector has, of course, been a particular feature of the period.

Another area in which expansion affecting policy has taken place is that of investment. With growing investment funds South Africa was able over the period to support projects in Angola and Mozambique, thereby encouraging the efforts of Portugal to retain those countries as colonies.

The growth of South Africa's counter-insurgency forces and their dispersal in southern Africa was both a contributory factor to the outward movement and a result of that movement. Pursuing African nationalists and liberals fleeing from South Africa in the early 1960s, South African agents penetrated deep into what were then the High Commission Territories and the Federation. Afterwards, as guerrilla activity spread in the area, South African paramilitary forces became more deeply involved, their commanders continually reminding public opinion of 'terrorist' threats from the north, thus preparing it for the increasingly assertive role they were being assigned throughout the area.

It was the apprehended dangers to South African political and economic security, as well as the increasing requirements of its growing economy for an African hinterland, that ensured that the republic would respond in an active way to the events which decolonisation and resistance to it in white southern Africa brought about. Events in her immediate African environment[22] created for South Africa opportunities for para-military and economic intervention in the affairs of its neighbours by removing some obstacles to

[21] Steyn, loc. cit.
[22] E.g. Rhodesian UDI in 1964, the growth of armed struggles in Angola and Mozambique in the mid-1960s and guerrilla infiltrations in South Africa and Namibia; the grant of independence to neighbouring States, Lesotho, Botswana and Swaziland, and the World Court's ruling on the South West Africa cases. All these, as will be seen in the chapters that follow, were vitally important in the shaping of South African policy after 1963.

such involvement, and by rendering a number of governments (notably those of Portugal, Rhodesia and Malawi) well disposed to such growing implication of South Africa in their affairs. With British imperial power withdrawn, and Portugal engrossed with three colonial wars, South Africa's strength inevitably secured it a position of dominance in the area. That role was supportive of Portuguese colonialism and of settler rule in Rhodesia, while, as we have observed, it sought to retain the patterns of economic collaboration in the area which were inherited from colonialism. And of course, its primal and ultimate task was to maintain the essentially colonial order of racial relations within South Africa itself.[23]

The forces for expansion, in southern Africa at least, were material enough, and the calculations of South African policy-makers evidently practical and precise. Yet South African efforts to improve relations with black States in Africa, which for most of the 1960s was a dominant foreign policy objective, came to centre on a symbolic rather than material objective. That was to establish diplomatic contacts and secure the reversal of the pan-African policy seeking isolation of the regime. This would, of course, carry material advantages, but it is by no means certain that in the way it was pursued it was the only or even the most effective means of securing such advantages.

Although the 'dialogue' campaign came to be accepted by white South Africans, it was firmly rejected by traditionalist Afrikaner nationalists, who believed that the inevitable social contacts with black diplomats would be subversive of *apartheid*. Thus when Dr Banda, President of Malawi, visited South Africa, *Die Afrikaner* opposed the visit and subsequently used photographs of the Prime Minister in social intercourse with his black guests in order to discredit his party. This was subsequently done by the main opposition party, the UP, also. Vorster complained to parliament in 1972:

I find it reprehensible that in the Brakpan by-election the agents of the United Party are walking round with that photograph of myself and the two Malawi women. They are walking from one house to the next in order to make propaganda.[24]

---

[23] That this should have been so should be food for sobering reflections on the part of those who believe in the liberalising effects of economic development in South Africa. Cf. chapter 1 above.

[24] *Ass. Deb.*, vol. 37, col. 396. The picture referred to showed Vorster sitting at dinner between two conspicuous Malawian ladies. It appeared in every copy of *Die Afrikaner* for many months after the visit.

Banda's visit was the climax of the dialogue movement and was clearly intended to be symbolically climactic. It was meant to symbolise the final break with past hesitancy over receiving black diplomats, and it was intended to dramatise the beginning of the end of South Africa's forced isolation in Africa. But above all, like the outward policy in general, it was intended to impress the world—the West in particular—with the continued viability of *apartheid* South Africa in Africa. What it did certainly represent was the growing emphasis on *Realpolitik* in South Africa and the super-session of some Afrikaner racial sensitivities by the ascendant principle of State interest.

Subsequent developments in the 'dialogue' campaign show not only that the Banda visit was a climax not subsequently repeated but that 'dialogue' had reached a climacteric. In the downturn which followed in the fortunes of that policy, even Banda's visit came to be seen by the loyal opposition (which was always friendly to the government's ambitions in Africa) as a monument to failure. Dr G. J. Jacobs, MP, put the matter thus:

We are so famished in this field [of relations with African States] that when a small, impoverished State from the north comes here in order to virtually ask for alms, it is regarded as a major diplomatic breakthrough.[25]

Although the period was dominated by material considerations, symbolic achievements and failures continued, as before, to be important, and so also did the ideological conflicts to which they were closely associated continue to be waged. For that reason it is fitting that we conclude this conspectus of the outward policy with a brief note on ideology and South Africa's policies in Africa.

Ideology and policy

Africans and Afrikaners had radically different experiences of colonialism, especially in the final half-century of formal imperialism (when Afrikaners and the British Empire had made their peace). In each case it is in the historical consciousness which arose out of these experiences that the explanation of the apparently instinctive mutual hostility and suspicion of South Africa is to be sought in addition to any specific dangers (*and* opportunities) the two worlds

[25] *Ass. Deb.*, vol. 37, col. 12.

held out to each other. It is also in the colonial experience that the racialist ideology of South Africa was, and still is, rooted.

This book is informed by the view that the policies of the South African governments towards Africa in the years since the second world war are best comprehended under the category of ideology. The policies were the result of distinctly ideological preoccupations and they were ideological in character. It was the notions that the white South African governments had of their entitlements in Africa which encouraged them, in the pre-independence period, to seek a continental role alongside the imperial powers in order to determine the future of the continent. In the years since the African colonies gained their independence South African policy continued to be motivated largely by a desire to push back unwelcome ideological influences and to give support to ideological affines (Rhodesia and Portugal), quite apart from any definite calculation of material advantage. By and large, ideology did not conflict with material needs in the field of foreign relations. There were, however, subtle shifts of emphasis which tended in the later years to favour *Realpolitik* rather than some more narrowly ideological enthusiasms (such as avoiding multi-racial social contacts). These relatively minor adjustments provoked a good deal of ideological and political conflict among Afrikaner nationalists. Basically, however, South African policy towards Africa remained totally subservient to an ideology of white domination in southern Africa which hardly changed in its key features since the beginning of the period under review despite marked changes both in the international environment and domestically, in the material conditions of domination.

For the period before African independence it is easy enough to demonstrate that general prejudices and vague intimations rather than calculations of gain or loss, or vivid apprehensions of approaching military exigencies, dominated the African policies of South Africa. Those policies lacked a specific material focus. To be sure, a good deal was said about South Africa's trading prospects in Africa and of its need for a hinterland of markets for its industrial output, which was expected to grow. Similarly, the fact that South Africa employed many labourers from neighbouring countries had substantial commercial and investment interests in the Federation, and was exposed to the epizootics and epidemics of the continent were given as reasons why South Africa needed an African policy. Yet none of these could justify the particularly assertive policies South

Africa pursued, especially under Smuts and Malan. Besides, ministerial exhortations and initiatives by the South African foreign trade organisations and chambers of commerce and industry failed to raise South African exports to Africa north of the Federation to any noticeable extent. There was even a plan to establish a shipping line for such trade which came to naught. All this supports the view that these 'practical' and 'material' arguments were attempts to anchor in reality in a specific way, and to rationalise, an essentially ideological posture in foreign policy. The policies tended to be declaimed —again, particularly in Smuts' and Malan's time—in terms of rather grandiose designs. Strydom and Verwoerd took firmly ideological positions, as we have seen, despite the concessions the latter was forced to make. The South African plans for continental defence, which engaged the energies of Erasmus for so long, were vague also. Security threats were often exaggerated and yet, sensibly enough, such apprehensions were not reflected in, say, expansion of the armed forces, weapons, or even in readiness to contribute forces in the series of anti-communist-inspired enterprises in which the West entangled itself (except in Korea and very briefly in the early 1950s in the Middle East).

The single overwhelming fact of the period since independence was the hostility of African States to South Africa and its friends, a hostility leading African States to support armed struggles against them. South African policy in this period was clearly dominated by the need Pretoria felt to defeat the dangers which this hostility involved. Accordingly, the country's military preparedness was increased. As South Africa's industrialisation proceeded the African markets—so much discussed to such little effect in the earlier period —also began to assume a definite significance for policy. In addition South Africa became more of an exporter of capital from the mid-1960s onward and could—*did*—take advantage of emerging investment opportunities in the rest of the continent.[26] Industrialists and financiers gave their support to the policy. The economic power of South Africa enabled it to adopt an active policy—militarily as well as economically—aiding well disposed black governments as well as Rhodesia and Portugal. But all these were supporting factors, supporting a policy which was moulded by anxieties and pretensions

[26] See UN Documents ST/PSCA/Ser A/11, *Foreign Investment in the Republic of South Africa*, 1970.

which in their ultimacy transcended the particular threats facing the republic and its specific economic needs in the continent.

The difference in the material circumstances before and after independence *is* radical and it would, of course, be wrong to understate it in favour of too abstract and idealistic an insistence on the primacy and pervasiveness of ideology. Nevertheless, it does seem much easier to understand the general attitude to *a whole continent* as an essentially ideological thing rather than as merely the sum of discrete, identifiable material concerns and needs. In a few instances, especially in southern Africa, policy did increasingly relate to very specific material issues and was often prudentially executed (rather than conducted in a grand 'ideological' style). Nevertheless during the period covered here such cases were fully conformable with the overall ideological context which, of course, predated them.

In the chapters which follow considerable attention will be devoted to the initiatives of African States against South Africa and their responses to South African initiatives. It will emerge that the policies of African States towards South Africa were themselves largely influenced by their ideological reactions to the post-colonial situation and to the colonial experience which preceded it.

VIII *The customs union area*

Botswana, Lesotho and Swaziland

Although the progress of the High Commission Territories towards self-government and international sovereignty[1] marked the end of South African demands for their incorporation in the republic, it was widely speculated after independence that the South African government might try to gain by stealth what it had failed to obtain by agreement: the effective subjugation of the High Commission Territories and their incorporation into a South African *Ausgleich* in terms of which the tribal 'homelands' of South Africa's Africans would be joined to the three States in a final solution of the 'native problem'.[2] Verwoerd's references to the economic dependence of the territories were also viewed as threats that South Africa might use its economic power to coerce these States into collaborating closely with the republican government.[3]

By an agreement drawn up in 1910 the three emergent States belonged to the Southern African Customs Union, of which South Africa was the fourth member. Since it has been suggested that 'systematic co-operation' could provide a strategy for development and 'co-prosperity' throughout the area,[4] the customs union deserves some attention not only for its importance to the member countries but also for what it suggests concerning the present practicability of grand designs of 'systematic co-operation'.

Under the 1910 agreement Botswana received a fixed share of 0·28 per cent, Lesotho 0·89 per cent, Swaziland 0·15 per cent and South Africa 98·7 per cent of total customs revenue collected. When

[1] As Lesotho, Botswana and Swaziland; the first two in 1966 and Swaziland in 1968.
[2] Cf. D. Austin, *Britain and South Africa*, 1966, pp. 59–61; R. P. Stevens (ed.), *Botswana, Lesotho and Swaziland: the Former High Commission Territories*, 1967, pp. 257 ff.
[3] J. E. Spence, *Lesotho: the Politics of Dependence*, 1968, chapter 5.
[4] Cf. J. A. Lombard *et. al.*, *The Concept of Economic Co-operation in Southern Africa*, 1968.

the smaller territories became self-governing their leaders hoped that the 1910 agreement might be revised to take account of the changes which had taken place in the fifty years since union in the relative shares of the territories in the external trade of the area.[5] In 1965 Botswana, Lesotho and Swaziland agreed to readjust their shares so that they respectively obtained 0·31 per cent, 0·47 per cent and 0·53 per cent. Pending overall revision of the agreement, South Africa retained its former share. As early as 1965 the governments of the three smaller States urged South Africa to enter negotiations for a new agreement, but South Africa stalled, and it was not until 1969 that a new arrangement was concluded.[6]

The 1910 and the 1969 agreements were drawn up under vastly differing operational assumptions. The first one anticipated the eventual unification of the four territories; the second accepted their permanence as sovereign States. From an economic point of view, the assumptions were also radically different. The 1910 assumptions were those of a *laissez-faire* economic regime; those of 1969 reflected the preoccupation with development through State intervention. The earlier agreement was considered unsatisfactory because, while restricting the freedom of action of the under-developed smaller countries (especially as far as fiscal policy inducements to industrialists were concerned) it made no allowance for compensation; the later one accepted that the smaller territories should be enabled to protect infant industries. Moreover, it recognised the need for a dynamic principle of revenue allocation. Finally, it was recognised that the co-operation of underdeveloped countries with an advanced one in a customs union had a 'polarising' effect— with development tending to be concentrated in the more developed area. It was felt that these effects amounted to losses for the smaller countries which had to be compensated. It was also considered that Botswana, Lesotho and Swaziland incurred further loss through the

[5] See P. M. Landell-Mills, 'The 1969 southern African customs union agreement', in *Journal of Modern African Studies*, 1971, and B. Turner, 'A fresh start for the southern African customs union', in *African Affairs*, 1970.

[6] 'Agreement between the Government of the Republic of Botswana, the Government of the Kingdom of Lesotho, the Government of the Republic of South Africa, and the Government of the Kingdom of Swaziland terminating the customs agreement of 1910 and concluding a new customs agreement, together with a memorandum of understanding relating thereto.' One of the urgent reasons for discussion was the unilateral imposition by South Africa of a sales tax which adversely effected BLS. For details see Landell-Mills, *op. cit.*, and B. Turner, *op. cit.*

price-raising effects throughout the Union of trade diversion.[7] Such losses are notoriously difficult to quantify,[8] with the result that there is no sure way of assessing the amount of compensation owed to the disadvantaged partners. The 1969 agreement provided for each country to obtain every year a share of total revenue proportional to its share of the value of total dutiable production consumed, and of imports in that year. To compensate for losses the smaller States' allotment would be adjusted by a factor of 1·42. The revenue of Botswana, Lesotho and Swaziland would then be computed by the formula[9]

$$R = \frac{i+p}{I+P}(C+E+S) \times 1·42$$

where

R = revenue received by Botswana, or Lesotho, or Swaziland;

i = total value c.i.f. at border of all imports into Botswana, or Lesotho, or Swaziland, inclusive of customs, excise and sales duties;

I = total value c.i.f. at border of all imports into the customs area, inclusive of customs and sales duties;

p = total value of dutiable goods produced and consumed in Botswana, or Lesotho, or Swaziland, inclusive of duties;

P = total value of goods produced and consumed in the customs area, inclusive of duties;

C = total collection of customs duties within the customs area;

E = total collection of excise duties within the customs area;

S = total collection of sales duties within the customs area.

By this formula the smaller territories obtained R17,010,000 in 1969–1970 as compared with the R6,430,000 they would have received under the old agreement.[10] The multiplier, or adjustment factor, would have been unnecessary had there been a joint development bank, or joint planning, including redistribution of the gains from

---

[7] Cf. Landell-Mills, *op. cit.*, and B. Turner, *op. cit.*

[8] Cf., for example, the protracted debate in the mid-1960s about gains and losses in the East African Common Market, especially D. Ghai, 'Territorial distribution of the benefits and costs of the East African Common Market', *East African Economic Review*, 1964; A. Hazel, 'The East African Common Market: importance and effects', *Oxford University Institute Economics and Statistics Bulletin*, 1966.

[9] This is reproduced from Landell-Mills, *op. cit.*, pp. 274–5.

[10] Landell-Mills, *op. cit.*, table 4, p. 276.

trade, or if there were a joint plan to counteract the polarising effects
of the union. It is such integration which the Econburo in Pretoria
would presumably have favoured,[11] yet it is agreed among pro-
fessional commentators who participated at the negotiations that
nothing could have been further from the intentions of the parties
concerned.[12] So much, then, for 'systematic co-operation'. The

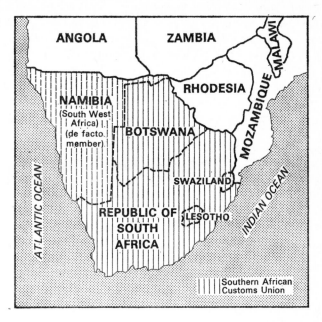

FIG. 1 *The South African Customs Union area*

smaller governments felt that they obtained under the 1969 agreement only what they were entitled to, and even that with considerable difficulty. Indeed, while conceding the need of infant industries
in the smaller countries for protection, the South African government
retained its right to protect its own industry against competition from
those infant industries. The danger of such competition for South
Africa was small and likely to remain so for a long while, yet it was
an old fear of some white South Africans that entrepreneurs might
seek to take advantage of the cheaper labour of Botswana, Lesotho

[11] See Lombard *et al.*, *op. cit.*, *passim*.
[12] See B. Turner, *op. cit.*, and Landell-Mills, *op. cit.* Both writers were
participants in the discussions.

and Swaziland by setting up industry in those countries.[13] Such fears had been behind Verwoerd's enduring opposition to private white capital being 'exported' to the Bantustans.[14] Certainly, the government's 'right-wing' critics could make much propaganda capital of any suggestion that it had laid white enterprise and white jobs in South Africa open to 'ruinous' and 'unfair' competition. The South African government, no doubt in deference to such considerations, also retained its freedom to take unilateral 'fiscal' action.[15] By so reserving its options the South African government retained a stick with which to beat any of the smaller governments should they become refractory in future.

The advantages of the customs union arrangement from the point of view of the smaller States did not lie in their being relieved of the burden of collecting their own duties, as has sometimes been suggested. It is in fact estimated that as development proceeds the cost of revenue collection would become bearable, especially for Botswana and Swaziland.[16] The great advantage lay in access to a large market. Termination of the customs union arrangement would probably occur in an atmosphere of acrimony in which South Africa would be tempted to use its considerable economic strength to drive home the imprudence of breaking away from the Union. It might impose restrictions on the movement of goods through South African territory and it could withdraw from joint agricultural marketing schemes such as those concerning wool. On the other hand, the smaller territory or territories opting out would withdraw labour from South Africa, but this would be a costly measure, especially for Lesotho, and could be taken only in very extreme circumstances by Lesotho.[17] The position of Botswana and, even more, that of Swaziland is slightly different, as will be pointed out later in this chapter. Landell-Mills notes, however, quite correctly, that 'confrontation with BLS on economic matters would hardly assist South Africa's efforts to win wider sympathy overseas'.[18] As for the agreement of

[13] Cf. Landell-Mills, op. cit., p. 269.

[14] Cf. 'Native policy in industry: report of discussions held in Cape Town between Dr H. F. Verwoerd and representative of organised commerce and industry', in The Manufacturer, 1951. This restriction was lifted after Verwoerd's demise.

[15] Landell-Mills, op. cit., and B. Turner, op. cit.

[16] Cf. Landell-Mills, op. cit.

[17] See Austin, Britain and South Africa, chapter III; Landell-Mills, op. cit.; B. Turner, op. cit.

[18] Op. cit., p. 280.

1969 itself, it reflects the inequalities in power. To quote Turner's appraisal:

South Africa's prerogatives under the agreement are considerably greater than those of the other States, but this is no more than a reflection of their great economic disparity . . . Any form of economic union between them must of necessity be subordinated to the overriding interest of the South African economy . . . South Africa could doubtless continue its phenomenal growth without the Customs Union (although not without BLS migratory labour), but BLS would be hard pressed to go it alone. The black States have pushed about as far as South Africa can be expected to go. Further concessions from Pretoria would be charity, and neither side wants their relationship so labelled.'[19]

Landell-Mills, on the other hand, argues a convincing case for the view that the new agreement 'cannot be regarded as adequately tackling the regional differences within the Southern African geographical unit'.[20] On both assessments the agreement falls far short of the grandiloquent notions of 'co-prosperity'.

The weakness of the three new States relative to South Africa, which arose from their poverty,[21] their geographic location[22] and the orientation over the years of their economies towards South Africa,[23] has been thoroughly discussed by several writers and it is not the intention to add another description to the existing ones. Suffice it to say that they are individually and collectively totally non-viable in any full-scale inter-State conflict with South Africa. They could continue a conflict with South Africa only so long as it

[19] *Ibid.*, p. 275.
[20] *Ibid.*, p. 281.
[21] All three countries continued to receive substantial budgetary aid after independence. See also Austin, *Britain and South Africa*, chapter III; J. Halpern, *South Africa's Hostages: Basutoland, Bechuanaland and Swaziland*, 1965, *passim*; Spence, *Lesotho*, chapter IV; Stevens (ed.), *Botswana, Lesotho and Swaziland*, *passim*.
[22] Lesotho is wholly landlocked within South Africa; Botswana is surrounded by South Africa, South West Africa (controlled by South Africa) and Rhodesia, and has only a tiny, disputed common frontier with Zambia. See map.
[23] According to G. M. E. Leistner's estimates, there were 31,000 Botswana, 10,618 MaSwati and 100,934 Basotho working in South Africa in 1964. These figures accord well with census estimates of absentees from Botswana, Swaziland and Lesotho. See Leistner, 'Foreign Bantu workers in South Africa', *South African Journal of Economics*, 1972, table II; *Report of the Census of the Bechuanaland Protectorate, 1964*; *Report on the 1966 Swaziland Population Census*, 1968; *Kingdom of Lesotho, 1966 Population Census Report*, vol. I.

was kept at a level at which South Africa would not wish to eliminate them as parties to the conflict: in the language of conflict theory, they were 'conditionally viable'. All that they could do to maximise their autonomy relative to South Africa would be to maximise the probability that conflicts would take place at the levels where they were viable. As these are notional levels which are not objectively determinable, how far each or all of the States could antagonise South Africa with tolerable consequences for itself or themselves would be a matter of judgement on which experience alone could finally decide. As judgements were bound to be the basis of their actions in foreign policy *ex ante*, certain categories of policy positions had to be eliminated in advance of experience. It was thus readily accepted by all parties in Lesotho, Botswana and Swaziland prior to independence that they would have to play a very minor role in the pan-African campaign of coercing South Africa to abandon *apartheid* by isolation, boycotts and even violence. Experience had also clearly indicated in the run-up to independence that South Africa would never allow them to harbour people suspected of revolutionary political activities in South Africa.[24] It might safely be conjectured, also, that if they gave encouragement at the UN and elsewhere to the more militant opponents not only of the policies but also of the regime in South Africa, the republican government would take a very poor view of their conduct indeed.[25] At its independence each State therefore affirmed its desire to co-operate and to maintain friendly relations with South Africa.

There were, however, areas not unimportant in the ideological conflict between the National Party and the world in which the freedom of action of the three States could be asserted without provoking severe retaliation from South Africa, precisely because those areas were not vital to South Africa's security, despite the fact that they were vital for the security of the governments of Lesotho, Botswana and Swaziland. Such areas of activity included their domestic (political and economic) policies, their external policies towards countries other than South Africa, the treatment of refugees (in so far as they were distinguishable from freedom fighters—a distinction which the South African government did accept, if diffidently) and even the treatment of white settlers and their interests in the three countries. Furthermore, they had some freedom on the

[24] See especially Halpern, *op. cit.*, chapter I; also chapter III above.
[25] Especially if they advocated international intervention in South Africa.

question of how much friendship—how much more than the notional minimum friendship—they should exercise. In fact it could be argued that they were free to do anything, provided it could credibly be presented to South Africa through diplomacy (of their own or that of their friends) either as being consistent with their friendship or as being intimately tied up with the credibility of their own independence.[26] The extent of this freedom of action would, in the last resort, depend on the strength of the domestic support for their policies, the measure of international support from countries influential with Pretoria, the extent of their support in influential circles within white South Africa, and the resolution and the solidarity with which they asserted their freedom of action.[27] On the other hand, they might, of course, not attempt to assert any freedom of action at all. In the event it was all these elements, in varying combinations in each case, which seemed in 1966–71 to shape the attitudes of the four governments to each other.

In all three cases the parties which gained power at independence were conservative, but the degree of conservatism, as reflected in both domestic as well as external policies, varied, and this was to become clearer with the passage of time. The degree of conservatism of each government reflected the social basis of its domestic support, that is to say, the location of its main supporters in the stratified colonial social order. In Lesotho the ruling Basutoland National Party (BNP) owed its power to traditionalist elements—the tribal chiefs, the white settlers (mostly traders), the Roman Catholic Church, and the older generation of semi-literates (as distinct from 'modern' college and university graduates, who tended to support the opposition and to identify themselves with the South African nationalists)[28]—all groups which saw Chief Jonathan as the bulwark

[26] The South African government, after all, continually affirmed its adhesion to the principle of 'non-interference' and could not, in the light of accusations that *apartheid* was a threat to international peace, afford to be seen to be violating the independence of these States (except, of course, in extreme circumstances; otherwise interference would be done *sub rosa*).

[27] Except for the last one, all these sources of strength would be of a conservative nature, tenable only if the regimes adopted conservative foreign policies, though not necessarily more conservative than the policies of most Western or capitalist States.

[28] This is particularly true of the BCP, although its leader, Ntsu Mokhehle himself, was apprehensive of threats to his leadership emanating from ANC influences, deciding as a result to patronise the PAC. See Halpern, *op. cit.*, chapter 8.

against 'communists'. Jonathan's party had virtually been created by the Roman Catholic Church, Jonathan himself having been pushed from virtually complete obscurity to pre-eminence through Church propaganda. Neither communism nor religion had been real political issues among the Basotho, with the result that Jonathan's party could not, especially in the election of 1970, count on either platform to earn him a parliamentary majority. The rise of the BNP indicated how much could be achieved through the manipulation of a semi-literate African petty aristocracy by a vested institutional interest.[29] In 1970, following an electoral defeat, Jonathan forcibly seized power, and, through the actions of some of his chiefly supporters and of the South African-supported Mobile Unit of the police, rapidly led the country to a civil war. Vorster subsequently observed that the *coup* had been necessary to meet a communist threat. Thus the 'nodal clusters' of support of the BNP were constituted of those groups which had a vested interest in maintaining the passing colonial order.[30]

In Swaziland the structural basis of conservatism was more clearly evident, finding expression in two main features: the domination of Swazi political life by the dual monarchy[31] and its courtiers, and the domination of Swazi economic life by a relatively large settler contingent, mainly of South African origin.[32] The fact that about two-fifths of the land area of Swaziland was owned by whites, some resident but many others absentee landlords in South Africa, also meant that a conservative party would receive a considerable amount of sympathy from private as well as official circles in South Africa. A further factor favouring conservatism was that the opponents of Sobhuza's Imbokodo Party and its ally, the conservative, white United Swaziland Association, were themselves relatively conservative,[33] so that the general tone of political opinion in Swaziland was

[29] This passage is based on information contained in B. M. Khaketla, *Lesotho 1970: an African Coup under the Microscope*, 1971. I have compared this account with results of my own interviews with several participants, including the distinguished Mosotho journalist Mr Motseta Mosoabi (on whose reports for *The Friend* Khaketla's book draws heavily).

[30] Cf. Stevens, *Botswana, Lesotho and Swaziland, passim*, Austin, *Britain and South Africa*, chapter III, and Halpern, *op. cit.*, chapter 8.

[31] See Kuper, *The Swazi: a South African Kingdom*, 1963, chapter 3; Halpern, *op. cit.*, chapter 10; Stevens (ed.), *Botswana, Lesotho and Swaziland, passim*.

[32] *Ibid.* Cf. also Leistner, 'Economic problems and prospects', in *Swaziland on the Eve of Independence*, Africa Institute, No. 4, 1969.

[33] Cf. Halpern, *op. cit.*, chapter 10.

conservative. That being so, there was little stimulus on the king to constrain his own greater conservatism. It was a mark of the king's conservatism that even before independence he came to rely on the most conservative Afrikaner nationalists for advice on constitutional matters, all in an attempt to forestall the dangers to traditional rule implicit in modern African nationalism, thus winning golden opinions in South Africa.[34] The conflict between the king and democracy eventually led to a royal *coup d'état* in 1973, the abolition of parliament and the repression of the opposition. The South African Broadcasting Corporation commented favourably.[35]

In Botswana also the ruling party aimed at maintaining relatively intact the colonial social order while bringing about some piecemeal reforms. The BDP had considerable support both among the settlers and the traditional elements. To a large extent it owed its influence to the dominant position of the Bamangwato and of the Khama family in Botswana.[36] Seretse Khama was not, however, simply a traditionalist and enjoyed considerable support in all sections of the community, including the modern elite. He had had a long personal struggle against *apartheid* which meant that of all the leaders in Botswana he could not lightly allow his government to seem to be a puppet of the republic's government.[37] For these reasons, among others, the BDP turned out to be less conservative than the ruling parties of Lesotho and Swaziland.

In the first few years of independence, however, Botswana under Khama and the Democratic Party was cautious. Stern measures were taken against South West African and Rhodesian guerrillas straying into Botswana territory, and firm, well publicised warnings were issued after some of these had been deported to Zambia in

[34] G. Henry, 'The economy of Swaziland', in Stevens (ed.), *Botswana, Lesotho and Swaziland*, especially p. 246; cf. S. van Wyk, *Swaziland*, chapter 4.

[35] *African Research Bulletin (Political Series)*, 2817c.

[36] See, for example, M. Benson, *Tshekedi Khama*, 1960, and J. Redfern, *Ruth and Seretse: 'A Very Disreputable Transaction'*, 1965; both give an insight into the considerable standing of this family in the modern period. Although Seretse Khama's BDP was 'principally' an alliance of individual leaders drawn from [the] nine main tribal areas', (Legum and Drysdale (eds.), *Africa Contemporary Record*, 1968–69, p. 274), it probably owed a lot of its popular appeal to Seretse's own image of modernity.

[37] The quarrel with South Africa was over Seretse's marriage to a white woman in the early 1950s and the consequent crisis over the Bamangwato succession. See Redfern, *Ruth and Seretse*.

1966.[38] There was further police action against guerrillas again in 1967, leading to suggestions, denied by the Botswana government, that the BDP government was collaborating with the South African and Rhodesian governments. In 1967 Botswana entered into negotiations with South Africa for the construction of a road link through Botswana between Windhoek (in the disputed territory of South West Africa) and the Transvaal.[39] In 1967 the President of Botswana paid a visit to Malawi, where in a joint communique with Dr Banda it was stated:

The Presidents feel that in seeking to bring about a change in the thinking of the peoples in the countries of southern Africa, the best hope lies in contact and discussions between the independent African States, on the one hand, and the minority-governed countries on the other.[40]

Yet even at this time there was evidence that within the limits of conservative legality Botswana's president did want to show sympathy with the African nationalist cause in South Africa and Rhodesia. Professor Z. K. Matthews, once a prominent member of the ANC of South Africa, was made Botswana's first ambassador to the UN, and although Matthews took a conservative view of his assignment,[41] the appointment was undoubtedly more daring than anything which the other two governments would have contemplated at that time. Likewise, Botswana, while exempted by the UN from mandatory sanctions against Rhodesia, did try to reduce its trade with Rhodesia.[42] For a time, too, after UDI the Botswana government allowed the BBC to broadcast to Rhodesia from its territory. In 1968 the tone of Khama's foreign policy began to change. Where it had been very conservative it now tended to become cautiously radical. In 1966 there was evidence of a desire to cultivate

[38] See the section on Zambia in chapter IX below.

[39] See *A.R.B.* (*Pol.*), 740C and 845B.

[40] Malawi Ministry of Information, 'Communique issued at the end of the visit to Malawi of HE the President of the Republic of Botswana, Sir Seretse Khama, KBE, 5–7 July 1967'. It should be pointed out, however, that the communique was much more restrained in its approbation of collaboration with the 'White south' than Dr Banda's own statements had by this time become. It is reasonable to assume that the moderating influence was Khama.

[41] Cf. E. M. Rhoodie, who states in his *The Third Africa* that Professor Matthews was a guest at the Republic Day champagne party given by the South African embassy in Washington (p. 45).

[42] See UNGAOR, Fourth Committee, 1631st meeting, 'Note verbale, 11 February, concerning implementation of Security Council Resolution 232 (1966)', Document S/7813.

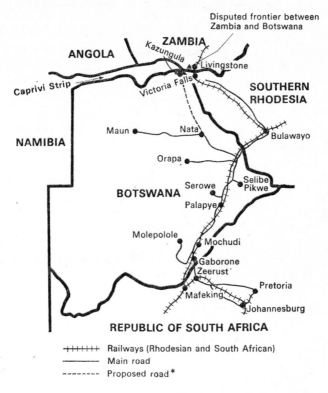

FIG. 2 *Botswana: surface communications.* *Towards the end of June 1973 a contract for US assistance to the tune of $13·5 million for the construction of the Botswana–Zambia road was completed. The road, which was to be built to all-weather gravel standards, would stretch from Nata to Kazungula, approximately 300 km, and would be completed early in 1976. The contractors were to be the American firm Grove International. A 65 km road was also to be built from Kazungula to Ngoma in Zambia, and a short turn-off of 6 km to Pandametenga. Three road maintenance depots would also be established. (Source: *Botswana Daily News,* 27 June 1973)

closer relations with Zambia, which as a result of UDI had become an important market for Botswana beef. The Zambian government was eager to replace Rhodesia as a meat supplier by Botswana and Madagascar, a proposal which the Botswana government readily welcomed.[43] In May 1969 the Botswana government received Dr Kaunda on a four-day state visit. Although Khama's own speeches during this visit were, from a South African point of view, 'correct', Kaunda delivered a speech little short of an incitement of South Africans to breach the republic's 'peace'.[44] What went on between the two heads of state during that period is not known, but it is evident that a friendship was begun and Khama's cautious radicalism received definite encouragement. Certainly there was a marked improvement in the Botswana government's standing among exiled African nationalist politicians from southern Africa.[45]

What seemed to have emboldened the Botswana government more than anything else was the discovery of a wide range of minerals, especially copper, nickel and diamonds, in sufficiently promising quantities to attract the leading mining houses of the West to seek concessions. By late 1968 Roan Selection Trust and De Beers were fully engaged in developing the mining potential of Botswana.[46] At last, it seemed, Botswana could look forward to much greater and much faster economic growth than years of colonial inertia had suggested possible, and it could hope to provide employment for its own population without relying on the South African mines and farms. Furthermore, it could hope to interest the powerful financial houses of the West sufficiently in Botswana to enhance its bargaining power vis-à-vis South Africa.[47] It was, however, the policy of the Botswana government to diversify its sources of funds without seeming to discriminate against South Africa, which, pending the realisation of the promise of mining development, remained important.[48]

---

[43] A.R.B. (Economic Series), 1968, 892A.

[44] See below.

[45] Personal communications with various South African, South West African and Rhodesian nationalist politicians in exile.

[46] A.R.B. (Econ.), 1968, 924B, 955C, 1179A, 1121A.

[47] See Botswana High Commission (London), 'Statement by the President of Botswana, His Excellency Sir Seretse Khama, in the General Debate at the 24th Session of the United Nations General Assembly, 24 September 1969'.

[48] The Botswana government has commissioned large-scale hydrological surveys with a view to developing dependable water supplies (see Africa Contemporary Record, 1968–69, 1970–71. In this connection the development of the Okavango swamps in Botswana in joint major irrigation projects between Angola, South Africa and Botswana has been held out as a 'carrot' for Botswana by pro-South African writers who favour the integration of southern Africa; but not much seems to have come of this idea. See Lombard, et. al., op. cit., pp. 57 ff., and Rhoodie, op. cit., p. 142.

Although the government originally wished to minimise the use of South African companies in developing its mining industry such a policy soon proved impracticable. The main reason was that the alternative candidates turned out to have neither sufficient capital nor all the required competences.[49] By 1970 companies engaged in mineral exploration included the following from South Africa: Johannesburg Consolidated Investment Co. Ltd, International Nickel (S.A.) (Pty) Ltd, South Africa Vendome Co. (Pty) Ltd and Anglo-American through its subsidiaries, De Beers Botswana Mining Co. (Pty) Ltd, Anglo-Transvaal (through its subsidiaries, Theta, Zeta, Jupiter and Neptune Mining and Prospecting Companies (Pty) Ltd and Tuli Exploration (Pty) Ltd).[50]

It was evident also that Botswana would still continue to rely on South African mines to provide employment for nearly half its manpower. Thus while 35,921 Batswana were recruited for the South African mines in 1970, the total number of registered employed (male and female) within Botswana in 1971 was 37,520. Deferred pay and remittances from South Africa amounted to R1,083,951·86, which was slightly more than the total monthly wage bill of the modern sector.[51]

Botswana's new stand was signified by the official endorsement of the Lusaka manifesto[52] by Khama at the UN in 1969 when he also appealed emphatically for the continuation of sanctions against Rhodesia. But by far the most outspoken expression of the resentment of *apartheid* and the frustration at not being able to do anything daring against it was contained in a speech by Khama to the Foreign Policy Society of Copenhagen in 1970. After stating Botswana's vulnerability the President said that, while acknowledging South Africa's realism in abandoning the claim for the incorporation of Botswana, he would never accept the role that Verwoerd had envisaged for his country as a Bantustan:

[49] Interview with the Acting President, Gaborone, May 1973.

[50] Republic of Botswana, *Annual Reports of the Geological Survey and Mines Department for the Years 1969 and 1970*.

[51] Migrant workers enter into an agreement with their South African mining employers that a portion of their wages be deferred and paid out to them on their return home. Sources of figures: Republic of Botswana *Statistical Abstract*, 1971.

[52] Fifth Summit Conference of East and Central African States, *Manifesto on Southern Africa*, Lusaka, 14–16 April 1969. See also 'Statement by the President of Botswana ... in the UN General Assembly ... 24 September 1969'.

Botswana is not a Tribal Homeland, based on ethnic exclusiveness and the separation of races, but a non-racial democracy which rejects all forms of *apartheid* and racial discrimination wherever they are applied.[53]

While Botswana was still largely dependent on South Africa, 'it would not accord either with Botswana's principles or our interests to accept aid from South Africa'.[54] President Khama added:

Doubtless the South African Authorities do not relish our criticisms of *apartheid*, but neither do we care for the arguments they advance in favour of racial separation which cast doubt on the viability of our non-racial society.[55]

The speech was even less restrained in its attack on the Cabora Bassa project (and European support for it), which, Khama said, was 'designed to perpetuate Portuguese colonialism, and threatens further to strengthen the links between South Africa on the one hand and Mozambique and Rhodesia on the other'. While he felt that peaceful change was desirable and preferable to violence in Rhodesia and the Portuguese colonies, he did feel, in line with the Lusaka manifesto, that:

It is unhelpful to condemn the independence movements of Southern Africa for having resorted to violence when all other paths were closed, if no positive alternative strategy is put forward for achieving the self-determination which the world community claims as a common objective for the area.[56]

Finally, Khama condemned Western arms supplies to South Africa.

As an earnest of Botswana's 'northward-looking' policy the Botswana government entered into negotiations early in 1970 with the US government to persuade it to finance a joint Zambia–Botswana project—the construction of a road link between the two countries. The American administration announced in April that it would provide $6 million for the project. The South African government protested that Zambia and Botswana had no common border.[57] The Botswana government insisted that there was a common border,

---

[53] Text of the address to the Foreign Policy Society, Africa Bureau, London, para 5.

[54] *Ibid.*, para 8.   [55] *Ibid.*, para 10.   [56] *Ibid.*, para 12.

[57] *Africa Contemporary Record*, 1970, pp. 8471 ff.; *A.R.B.* (*Econ.*), 1969, 1472c; 1970, 1640c, 1756c. See also J. Craig, 'Zambia–Botswana road link: some border problems', in University of Zambia School of Humanities and Social Science, *Zambia and the World: Essays on problems relating to Zambia's Foreign Policy*, 1970.

although it was not defined. South Africa lifted its objections, noting that Botswana would not be building a bridge at Kazungula which could infringe (as far as the South Africans were concerned) the territorial integrity of South West Africa, which it controlled. Although it maintained that the meeting point between Zambia and Botswana was a point with no magnitude, the South African government conceded that Zambia and Botswana had a right of way across the river, established by usage over the past eighty years.[58] Botswana further asserted its independence, to obvious South African displeasure, by concluding diplomatic relations with the Soviet Union, although no resident representatives were exchanged.

Within Botswana itself, a measure of its moderate radicalism was the fact that the 4,000 or so refugees from Angola, South Africa, South West Africa and Rhodesia were treated well, with only seldom any indication that the ruling party resented the influence they might have on its political opponents. On the other hand, the Botswana government expressed grave concern at the tendency of white employers to practise job reservation in Botswana; the vice-president, Dr Masire, stated in May 1971:

The practice whereby white expatriate staff who have no qualifications or previous experience are employed simply to avoid employing Botswana is widespread. Botswana workers are widely stigmatised by many white employers as dishonest or lazy and are denied promotion on merit or experience, but at the same time we find employers making no effort to screen applicants, or to provide training for their African staff. Too few prospects are held out for the honest and diligent. All over Francistown one can find cases of preference being given to unqualified non-Africans, even for the simplest jobs. Sometimes as a concession to non-white susceptibilities coloureds may be employed as middle-rank supervisors, but rarely African.[59]

Dr Masire had touched on an area which could create even greater difficulties and which could be a radicalising factor in Botswana as mining development proceeded. It remained a problem for policy-makers whether and how far Botswana could or would rely on white South African skilled miners, as Zambia to a large extent did, for the development of its mining. If so, would the miners' racial attitudes not work for the breakdown of race relations in Botswana, unleashing such strong anti-South African feeling among the rank and file as to make good relations with South

[58] *A.R.B.* (*Econ.*), 1970, 1839c.
[59] 'Speech by the Hon. Q. K. Masire, Vice-president of Botswana, at Francistown Residence on 17 May 1971.'

Africa even more difficult than they had been? For South Africa the problem would be how the white workers could be made useful to the outward-looking policy (and be made to benefit by it) as well as the more sophisticated, more exportable technical experts dispensed to collaborating black States. It is on the official positions taken on such questions that the class nature of the outward-looking policy will become evident. What could be seen in the difficulties of African-isation were probably the beginnings in miniature of the intricate racial and labour problems that Zambia at one time acutely experienced.[60] Perhaps in these respects Batswana had a good deal more to learn from Zambians than from South Africans. The end of our period saw the beginning of a new and important phase in the development of Botswana–South Africa relations.

The government of Lesotho early made clear its determination to work closely with the National Party of South Africa. Chief Jonathan appointed as his adviser the Afrikaner millionaire Dr Anton Rupert, and of the fact that he intended to rely on South Africa for the economic development of Lesotho there could be no doubt. Chief Jonathan tried to persuade the South African govern-ment to participate in a hydro-electric project, the Oxbow scheme, which would supply water to part of the Orange Free State and the Transvaal as well as Lesotho. Unless the South African government was willing to buy electric power and water the project would not be economically viable. If it succeeded, the project would not only provide much-needed revenue to Lesotho coffers but would give Lesotho agriculture a much-needed fillip. Negotiations proceeded slowly, not least because of South Africa's disinclination to rely on a foreign State for such an important service as supplying water for a populous area,[61] but perhaps also because of opposition from South African mining interests.[62] Delay was also due to the fact that Lesotho favoured a plan which would make the scheme more service-able to its irrigation needs while South Africa, being concerned mainly that the water be made available to the republic, was not prepared to meet the extra cost, a factor which caused not a little resentment in Lesotho. In the period since independence the Lesotho government readily accepted technical aid from official and private

[60] See, for example, Republic of Zambia, *Report of the Commission of Inquiry into the Mining Industry*, 1966, and chapter IX below, *passim*.
[61] *A.R.B.* (*Econ.*), 1966, 554C.
[62] See n. 17, p. 167.

sources in South Africa, as well as a limited amount of financial aid.[63] The rest of the technical aid was directed at helping Basotho to improve their agriculture. The Lesotho government also sought to attract South African tourists as a further source of income, and decided in 1971 to construct a R10 million luxury hotel and holiday resort in the Maluti mountains.

To attract South African aid, Chief Jonathan became the most outspoken critic, after Dr Hastings Banda, of militant African opposition to the South African regime. He won the approbation of Dr Banda.[64] By 1971 Chief Jonathan was even willing to send an emissary of solidarity to the Ivory Coast to encourage President Houphouet-Boigny in his pleas for a conservative approach to South Africa,[65] and his government used the occasion of Lesotho's fifth independence celebrations for a 'mini-OAU' to consolidate those countries favouring 'dialogue' with South Africa.[66]

Because of his close co-operation with South Africa, Chief Jonathan came to feel unsafe in Lesotho so long as political refugees from South Africa continued to live there and to sympathise with his political opponents, although there were not many more than thirty of them. Chief Jonathan accused them of meddling in the domestic politics of Lesotho. Being committed not to return the refugees to South Africa, he arranged for their deportation to Zambia, persuading the South African government to allow them safe conduct.[67]

Because of the very close ties that Basotho in Lesotho have with those in South Africa in particular, but also with other Africans in South Africa, it was necessary for Chief Jonathan to affirm his

[63] £25,000 was given to the Lesotho government in 1967 for the expansion of the Lesotho Mounted Police, in which South Africa showed particular interest. It is widely believed in Lesotho that during the civil war the government obtained arms supplies from the republic. The Mobile Unit, led by the white South African, Roach, together with Maseribane and the Youth League, played a major intimidatory role during that period. Aid also included a gift of maize from the South African government to relieve famine in Lesotho.

[64] Malawi Ministry of Information, 'Speeches made during the visit of . . . Chief Leabua Jonathan, Prime Minister of Lesotho, 12–17 May 1967'.

[65] Senator Molapo arrived in Ivory Coast on 19 July 1971 with a goodwill message from Chief Jonathan: A.R.B. (Pol.), 2156B.

[66] Cape Times, 5 October 1971.

[67] A.R.B. (Pol.), 697A, 1968, 974A. It was reported in 1967 by South African radio that extradition talks between Lesotho and South Africa had failed when South Africa asked that South West Africa be included in the general extradition agreement.

opposition to *apartheid* from time to time, while maintaining that it was in Lesotho's vital interests to collaborate more closely with South Africa. This was necessary if Lesotho were to be acceptable to other African leaders, and indeed the majority of its fellow members of the UN. This fact introduced a slight element of ambiguity in official Lesotho utterances. At the Singapore Commonwealth Prime Ministers' Conference in 1971, which was dominated by the question of arms sales to South Africa, Chief Jonathan said he was opposed to the international traffic in arms and saw no reason why the West should monopolise the Indian Ocean.[68] On returning to Lesotho the chief said his remarks about arms sales were not directed at the trade in arms between the UK and South Africa but were meant more generally. He favoured the British decision to sell arms to South Africa.[69] Similarly, when, following Banda's visit to South Africa, a conference of 'pro-dialogue' countries was to be (informally) held in Lesotho, Chief Jonathan delivered himself of what appeared to be a tirade against *apartheid*. He expressed his fear of a bitter racial confrontation in South Africa. He said peace would be maintained only in an atmosphere of equality and the acceptance of majority rule irrespective of colour. Violence might come 'next year or in twenty years but it will eventually come'. No African could tolerate *apartheid*, and the Bantustan solution to South Africa's race problem would not work. He advocated dialogue between South Africa and African States to obviate this catastrophic contingency. Dialogue, he said, should take place within the terms of the Lusaka manifesto, but if South Africa wanted a different basis, perhaps that could be used.[70]

It could be argued that the anti-*apartheid* remarks were a mere stratagem intended to attract attention to the 'dialogue' proposal, and to create the impression that States like Lesotho which favoured 'dialogue', so very far from seeking to conserve the *status quo* were really eager to change South Africa. Within South Africa it was congress time for the National Party, a congress in the aftermath of a controversial state visit by Dr Banda. In a world composed so much of odds and ends, of treasons, stratagems and spoils, Chief Jonathan's speech and the 'mini-OAU', as a South African journalist called his informal conference, could—after consultation with Pretoria or even at the initiative of Pretoria—have been aimed at vacillating sup-

[68] *A.R.B.* (*Pol.*), 1971–1976c. [69] *A.R.B.* (*Pol.*), 2027A.
[70] *Cape Times*, 5 October 1971.

porters of Vorster's policy. Another line of reasoning which accounts for both the Singapore speech and the later one is that the speeches were intended to rehabilitate Chief Jonathan in Africa. His policy of maintaining close relations with South Africa had reduced his standing in Africa when it had led him to stage a coup when it seemed that Ntsu Mokhehle and his Basotho Congress Party (which was more openly hostile to the South African regime) might win the 1970 general election—an action which Vorster 'retrospectively' approved as having been necessary to rid Lesotho of 'communists'.[71] Such arguments are impossible to establish; all that can be done is to acknowledge that they point to real probabilities that are not in any case inconsistent with what is otherwise known of the relationship between the Jonathan and Vorster administrations.

Since the civil war following Jonathan's *coup d'état* more critical speeches were made, but these did not seem to have any noticeable effect on relations with South Africa. For in May 1972 Muller announced to the South African Parliament that South Africa and Lesotho had agreed to establish reciprocal consular representation at Consular General level. Jonathan's speeches against South African *apartheid* became particularly strident in 1972–73 as he attempted to reconcile his party with the opponents it had coerced, as he tried to obtain that popular acceptability in Lesotho which had always eluded him (leading to the defeat in 1970 which provoked his government to seize the State), and, finally, in his attempts to regain acceptability in Africa at large.[72] The climax came at the reopening of parliament (which had been closed since the coup and its aftermath), a supposedly climactic event symbolising national reconciliation. Then Jonathan not only condemned 'flagrant contraventions' of sanctions against Rhodesia by Western powers but also attacked those States which sold arms to 'white minority regimes in Southern Africa, to perpetuate oppression and retard political progress'.[73] Evidently, South Africa, recognising the pressures to which he was subjected, was prepared to treat Jonathan's speeches with tolerance and understanding. Certainly they signified no practical change in the state of affairs in the two countries.

---

[71] *Africa Contemporary Record*, p. 3552.
[72] Based on wide-ranging interviews with political participants and various African diplomatic sources.
[73] *A.R.B. (Pol.)*, 1973, 2817.

Yet whatever the immediate short-term objective which Jonathan's speeches were meant to serve, the speeches did reach South Africans of all colours, probably helping to encourage those Africans who felt that *apartheid* had not heard the last of militant African opposition within South Africa, and probably intensifying the sense of insecurity of white South Africans. It is of some interest that none of the States willing to collaborate with South Africa had one good word to say for *apartheid* itself or the Bantustan policy in particular.

The government of Swaziland, like that of Lesotho, readily accepted that its major development projects should be geared to South Africa. Swaziland's relatively higher level of economic development had implications for its government's foreign policy. Firstly, Swaziland was less dependent on South Africa for revenue, aid or employment opportunities for its workers; secondly, Swaziland might and did begin to develop its manufacturing sector in a way that competed with South African manufacturing; thirdly, because of its mineral wealth and its industrial activities Swaziland was attractive to white South African investors who would, if the Zambian experience is anything to go by, continue to invest for sound commercial reasons even if the Swazi government did not conform to the demands of the National Party in South Africa. If Swaziland hoped to develop manufacturing it would need to cultivate African as well as South African markets for its simple manufactured products: thus, for example, when it was decided to establish a tractor assembly plant in Swaziland, the markets of Malawi, Zambia and Tanzania were specifically borne in mind.[74] In a peculiar way, also, the presence of a sizeable white minority with voting rights in South Africa as well as Swaziland, in addition to the close collaboration between the king and prominent Afrikaner nationalists, meant that Swaziland could have powerful advocates in South Africa against South African retaliation for autarchic economic and foreign policies, provided these were broadly reconcilable with a continued commitment to the maintenance of the racial and class *status quo* in both Swaziland and South Africa.

Swaziland's administration did not, however, fully exploit its opportunities of asserting a vigorous independence. Instead, the government went on record in 1968 as having said that if African guerrillas on their way to South Africa traversed Swazi territory, the

[74] *A.R.B.* (*Econ.*), 1971, 2162.

Swaziland government would call in South African help.[75] Further, it entered into agreements with South Africa for the supply of civil servants to Swaziland.[76] On labour remuneration the government of Swaziland also took the view that the depressed wages of AmaSwati and the comparatively inflated wages of white skilled workers (so reminiscent of the labour situation in South Africa) should not be radically altered.[77] Yet the king's Ministers were less conservative than the Ngwenyama.[78] The Ministers were in any case a coalition which included some who had earlier opposed the king from the 'left'.[79] The Swazi government, unlike that of Chief Jonathan of Lesotho, studiously avoided the image of 'South Africa's political megaphone'. It opposed South Africa at the UN over the South West Africa question, and endorsed the Lusaka manifesto in 1970 and took a position on 'dialogue' strictly in line with OAU policy. When Prince Makhosini Dlamini, the Prime Minister, visited South Africa to meet Mr Vorster, there were suggestions that this was part of the 'dialogue' enterprise. The Swaziland government sharply rejected these suggestions, stating that while for concrete historical and geographical reasons the Swazi government had to consult with South Africa from time to time, Swaziland would not take a unilateral stand on dialogue, and that the 'only meaningful basis' for such dialogue would be the Lusaka manifesto, 'which proposes a non-violent solution to southern Africa's problem'.[80]

These bold remarks had to be seen, however, against two important decisions that tied Swaziland even more closely to South Africa: the initiation in 1969 of negotiations for the setting up of a thermal power station that would feed both Swaziland's network and the

[75] Cf. van Wyk, *Swaziland*, chapter 4; *African Contemporary Record*, 1968.

[76] *Today's News*, 7 February, 1969.

[77] Cf. Leistner, 'Economic problems and prospects', who defends the wage system on the grounds that: 'labour that becomes too expensive is replaced by machines. Where the State takes the decisions and thus attempts to avoid such replacement of labour by capital, the country is even more certain to run into a crisis because the necessary adaptations are delayed and are later more painfully enforced by circumstances.' This is the merest stipulation, as simple-minded as it is dogmatic.

[78] Honorific title of the king, meaning 'Lion'.

[79] E.g. Dumisa Dhlamini (trade unionist), Simon Nxumalo and Dr Allen Nxumalo, who joined Imbokodo shortly before independence.

[80] The phrase 'political megaphone' was used by Mr Mpata of the BCP to describe Chief Jonathan: *A.R.B.* (Pol.), 1967, 879c. For Prince Dlamini's statement see *A.R.B.* (Pol.), 1971, 2073c. See also *Africa Contemporary Record*, 1970–71, 8554 ff.

South African national grid, negotiations which were successfully
concluded in September 1970;[81] and the initiation of negotiations in
February 1968 for the construction of a rail link between South Africa
and Swaziland. These negotiations continued throughout 1970.[82]

All the governments of the former High Commission Territories
were cautious in their attitude to South Africa. They all chose to
remain within the South African Customs Union and within the
South African monetary area.[83] In terms of physical capacities
Lesotho was undoubtedly the weakest of all, while Botswana and
Swaziland, because of alternative links with the outside world, and
in the case of Botswana because their mineral wealth promised
to be a source of income independent of South Africa. It might
be argued, justifiably, that Botswana and Swaziland had more
freedom of action; but it would be incorrect to argue that, because
Botswana was linked with Zambia, while Swaziland's alternative
outlet was Mozambique, Botswana was better placed than Swaziland. Botswana's links with Zambia had to be asserted in defiance
of South African objections. Also there was a precedent (in the
case of Zambian diversion of traffic from Rhodesia to Angola)
of Portugal providing services against the interests of another
white southern African regime. Admittedly the precedent was
muddy, and it is also true that, because of South Africa's greater
power, Portugal might be more concerned not to offend the
South African regime than it was the Rhodesian regime. But
none of these things was certain, and had the Swazi government
been so disposed it could have risked disappointment and gone ahead
with a policy of linking Swaziland more with the north through the
Portuguese-controlled outlet if only as a means of reducing its
already considerable dependence for its markets on one country.
For reasons already discussed it was not so disposed. It is not the
purpose of this volume to speculate on the policies which govern-

---

[81] *A.R.B.* (*Econ.*), 1978 and 1969.   [82] *Ibid.*, 1968, 940A and 1970.

[83] On the difficulties of the customs union agreement of 1910, and the
improved position of the three smaller countries under the 1969 agreement,
a result of a joint approach to South Africa on the matter, see B. Turner, 'A
fresh start for the southern African customs union', in *African Affairs*, 1970.
The three governments also subsequently joined in the venture to create a
Southern African Regional Tourism Council, with headquarters in Malawi
and having as its other members Madagascar, Malawi, Mauritius, Portugal,
South Africa and Swaziland. The idea of such a council (which did come
into existence in 1971) came from the Malawi government. See *A.R.B.*
(*Econ.*), 1971, 1851B.

ments might alternatively have followed. Yet it is desirable to discourage the view which holds that geography or economics determined the policies of these governments in their detailed particularity. It is *known* that the governments of Swaziland and Lesotho were conscientiously and aggressively conservative even in areas of internal politics that need not have interested South Africa directly. Those conservative orientations must find a place in any account of their foreign policies. Likewise it should be borne in mind that although less conservative governments, had they gained power, would probably have made little difference to the pattern of interaction at the concrete level between their countries and South Africa in the short term, to conclude on that account that the influence of ideology—conceived in terms of orientations to the dual stratification of post-colonial southern African societies—was null, is not only historically elliptical (in failing to find a place for important variables that *have* been observed) but would also fail to take account of the changeability of the situation which Botswana's case illustrates. Finally, it is a superficial and crude functionalism that considers only the short-term, practical effects of policies. A more radical policy in the case of Swaziland or Lesotho would have had a different impact on the minds of men even if it had to be constrained in practice, and so long as men's minds are relevant to their actions that would affect reactions (of Africans in South Africa and the rest of Africa in particular) differently from the way that a policy of thoroughgoing conservatism would.

It is argued, then, that while physical factors placed abnormally severe constraints on foreign policy options for all three governments concerned, they did not dictate their detailed policies. All three governments could, in a non-trivial sense, have behaved, if only to some slight degree, other than they did. In so far as they did not adopt more radical policies or postures it was not only because of objectives, reasoned assessments of State needs within their geo-economic situation but also because (and to the degree that) they owed their power to definite social groups favouring the social relationships inherited from colonialism and to which the preservation of the political *status quo*, in the wider southern African context, was directly functional. Reciprocally, the internal social relationships within these countries, commensurately with the degree of their conservatism, were functional to the ends of the South African government.

By comparison with the other territories in southern Africa, Botswana, Lesotho and Swaziland did not, in the period of their independence, attract much South African economic activity by the State or by para-statal organisations. Lesotho, because of the very accommodating attitude of its leaders (and also because of the radicalism of the opposition, which was the alternative government, while it existed), received most aid from those sources, the most promising coming from the South African Wool Board and SOEKOR. In 1967 the Wool Commission and the Wool Board of South Africa announced that they were considering the creation of a simple textile industry in Lesotho and a programme of aid, including the supply of good-quality sheep and training facilities for Sotho technical staff.[84] SOEKOR announced in March 1969 that the South African oil hunt would be extended to Lesotho, but it wanted 'the aid of a leading oil exploration company', in other words private money.[85] For the rest, South Africa supplied 'technical experts' in a variety of fields, engaged in—on the whole inconclusive —discussions about development projects that would 'integrate' southern Africa, but made no cash transfers amounting to aid.

There were various reasons why this was so. Firstly, a policy of financial aid would have been controversial among the whites of South Africa themselves. The South African Minister of Information, Social Welfare and Pensions, and Immigration, Dr C. P. Mulder, gave evidence of this when he quoted in parliament a pamphlet by the Hertzog group (with which he disagreed); he then denied that, apart from the 100,000 bags of maize given to Lesotho by Verwoerd, there had been any gifts to African States. The Hertzog group evidently felt that the government was trying 'to gain the favour of neighbouring States by trying to persuade them with gifts of money and cheap loans to enter into relations which have to serve principally commercial interests'.[86] The second reason was that there was no shortage of candidates for 'aid' within South Africa itself—the Bantustans. But perhaps the most important reason was the attitude of the countries themselves, which, Lesotho excepted, were not eager to solicit donations from South Africa.

As far as political policy was concerned, it was difficult to know how far the idea of eventually attaching tribal homelands to

[84] *A.R.B. (Econ.)*, 1967, 710B.
[85] *Today's News*, 5 March 1969.
[86] Quoted by Minister of Information, etc., *Ass. Deb.*, 1970, col. 313.

Botswana, Lesotho and Swaziland still lingered on in South African official minds. In that connection the long-standing claims of Basotho and Maswati to territory across their borders could in the future provide an 'African nationalist' appearance to that tribal territorial redistribution. If such readjustments still remained as ultimate South African objectives, there was no likelihood that they might be implemented soon. For the Bantustan policy—the sole and single 'solution' that the National Party offered to the race problem —stagnated after Verwoerd, with not a single new major policy idea being elaborated,[87] while within white politics the policy remained controversial. With opposition to *apartheid* growing in the Bantustans, as well as in the former High Commission Territories, the grand division would have to wait for better times.

Ironically, had South Africa's relations with the rest of Africa improved, as seemed likely to be the case in the late 1960s and, for a while, the early 1970s, the value of the friendship of the three States, which was always mostly a propaganda value, would have diminished. In pleading for more African collaboration with South Africa Chief Jonathan might well have been reducing his own bargaining power through over-collaboration. In any case, in measurable terms Botswana, Lesotho and Swaziland reaped little reward from the outward-looking policy and seemed to have as uncertain a future in the shadow of South Africa as they had when they came into existence as sovereign States.

Namibia (formerly South West Africa)

The decision in 1966 of the International Court of Justice not to adjudicate on the substantive issues of the South West Africa cases, on the grounds that Ethiopia and Liberia had no standing to bring the action,[88] meant that South Africa's plans for the territory, which had had to be shelved while the case was *sub judice*, could now be implemented. The plans consisted mainly in the implementation of the proposals of the Odendaal Commission, which had been appointed to look into how best the policy of *apartheid* could be applied to South West Africa as it then was.[89] The South African

[87] See, however, chapter VII.

[88] International Court of Justice, *The South West Africa Cases, 1966, Rep. 6.*

[89] *Report of the Commission of Inquiry into South West African Affairs* (Odendaal Commission Report), 1964.

government could thus look to a 'final solution' of the racial problems of South West Africa and thereby, it was hoped, secure collaboration between the various ethnic groups and South Africa, thus strengthening South Africa and its friends in the United Nations. In addition, it was argued that the success of separate development would thwart the aims of such nationalist organisations as SWAPO (South West African People's Organisation) and SWANU (South West African National Union) and so make nonsense of UN demands for the granting of independence to Namibia as a single unit. Finally, should South Africa have to concede independence to the separate ethnic States, their smallness and multiplicity would ensure that South Africa would remain a decisive influence even after 'independence'. Such were the reasons advanced for rejoicing when the World Court's judgement was announced.

The victory at the Hague did not, however, inaugurate a period of passive resignation in the UN or in Namibia itself. Indeed, quite the contrary occurred. Having failed to obtain a favourable judgement at the Hague, African States (excluding Malawi), along with other opponents of the South African regime, proposed successfully that the UN should revoke the mandate given to South Africa, take over control of South West Africa and prepare it for independence in 1968.[90] There was no indication that the United Nations Council for South West Africa, established for these purposes, could establish by force a physical presence in South West Africa, yet the resolution was not without effect. Nationalists could take some comfort in the fact that the public relations war with South Africa was not yet lost, South West Africans could continue to petition the UN against South Africa, and the UN itself was able to initiate a search process for means within its reach to give substance to the revocation resolution. One of the means found was a variant of the sanctions idea. It was later recommended that UN members should dissuade their nationals from investing in South West Africa, or in any way assisting the South African government in its violation of the General Assembly resolution.[91] By 1971 this position was acceptable to the overwhelming majority of UN members,[92] and when an advisory opinion of the International Court of Justice confirmed, in June 1971, the illegality of South Africa's continued administration of

[90] *UNGAOR, 21st Session*, 1966, item 65, Doc. A/C 483 and Add. 1–3.
[91] January 1970. See *Africa Contemporary Record*, 1970–71, p. 8537.
[92] *Ibid.*

Namibia,[93] it seemed that the African group at the UN had at last found a concrete policy around which to rally international opposition to South African control of South West Africa.

The South African government rejected the 1966 resolution revoking the mandate.[94] In 1968 it refused members of the UN Council for Namibia permission to land in Namibia,[95] and when the world Court handed down its opinion in 1971 the South African Prime Minister indicated that his government would ignore the judgement.[96]

The most important consequences of the 1966 World Court verdict were not, however, in New York but in South West Africa itself. Having failed to gain redress through the Ethiopia–Liberia suit, SWAPO decided in August 1966 to launch an armed struggle for the liberation of Namibia.[97] As early as March 1966 some guerrillas had begun to enter Ovamboland from Angola in the north, but it was in August 1966 that the first gun battle with the South African police occurred. During 1966–67 there were several attempts by guerrilla groups to enter the territory via Angola and Botswana, and there were a few confrontations with the police.[98] South African security activity was stepped up, and Portuguese assistance was enlisted—at least one PIDE agent was used in Ovamboland to trap an Ovambo 'gun-runner'.[99] South African security forces had some difficulty with intelligence work, being unfamiliar with the terrain and because the Ovambos (according to the police) were hostile to whites.[100] In the latter part of 1967 there was, as SWAPO put it, a 'slight lull' as new tactics were being developed. Subsequently SWAPO seemed concerned to send men into the territory unarmed for the purpose of politicising the population and establishing an underground resistance network within

[93] A.R.B. (Pol.), 1971, 2142A, B.
[94] For a full report of the reactions of the Prime Minister, the Finance Minister and the Minister of Defence, see UNGAOR, 22nd Session, Annexes, Doc. A/6700/Rev. 1, 'Report of the Special Committee on the Situation with regard to the Implementation of the Declaration on the Granting of Independence to Colonial Countries and Peoples', chapter iv.
[95] Die Burger, 3 April 1968; see also Namibia News, January–March 1969, for some African reactions.
[96] A.R.B. (Pol.), 1971, 2142C, 2143.
[97] Personal interview with Peter Katjavivi, SWAPO representative in London, May 1970.
[98] A.R.B. (Pol.), 1966, 6338; Johannesburg and Salisbury radio broadcasts, BBC Summary of World Broadcasts, ME 2302/3/1.
[99] UNGAOR, 22nd Session, Doc. A/6700/Rev. 1.   [100] Ibid.

Namibia.[101] From time to time attacks on South African defence personnel and on property occurred; it was also established that SWAPO had set up bases within South African-controlled Ovamboland for the purpose of training guerrillas and for the purpose of launching attacks in the territory.[102] The intensification of political activity led to a series of arrests by the South African police,[103] the planting of informers among the Ovambos,[104] and to a lengthy trial under the Terrorism Act[105] at which the Namibians invoked the UN resolution of 1966 in an attempt to deny South African jurisdiction in Namibia.[106]

Armed conflict in South West Africa was probably the single most immediate factor behind the stepping up of South African official concern with counter-insurgency as distinct from sabotage. It marked, as it were, the transition from the era of the General Laws Amendment Act (1960–65) to the era of the Terrorism Act and the Bureau of State Security. It was probably one of the major forces behind the outward-looking policy in that it drew the government of the republic into a more active concern with counter-insurgency throughout the region.

South African policy towards Namibia itself, as has been indicated, was to accelerate the implementation of the proposals of the Odendaal Commission which provided for the creation of six African nations as self-governing, eventually 'independent' nation States. Legislative instruments devised in 1968 and 1969 designated no homelands for the Coloureds and provided for the incorporation of 'white South West Africa' into the republic as a fifth province.[107] In connection with these plans population removals began soon after the World Court verdict, but only Ovamboland, Kavangoland and Damaraland have so far been granted legislative councils and executive governments.[108]

[101] Cf. *Namibia News,* October–December 1968, pp. 7–8; *X-ray,* vol. 1, No. 6, December 1970.

[102] *UNGAOR, 22nd Session,* Doc. A/6700/Rev. 1; South African police raided one of these bases.

[103] *Africa Contemporary Record,* 1968–69, p. 351; ibid., 1970–71, p. 8536 *et passim; Namibia News,* January–March 1970, p. 12.

[104] *Africa Contemporary Record,* 1968–69, p. 351.   [105] *Ibid.*

[106] *Namibia News,* October–December 1968, p. 1; *UNGAOR, 23rd Session,,* Doc. A/7338; *Africa Contemporary Record,* 1968–69, p. 349.

[107] *UNGAOR, 24th Session, Supplement No. 24,* Doc. A/7624/Rev. 1, 'Report of the UN Council for Namibia'.

[108] *Africa Contemporary Record,* 1970–71, p. 349; *A.R.B. (Pol.),* 1971, 1903c.

The economic policy for the 'new South West Africa' was very like the policy towards the rest of southern Africa: to incorporate the territory's economy in that of South Africa even more closely, to encourage foreign investors and prospectors, especially in the mining sector, to search for oil and to develop agriculture by means of improved irrigation through the facilities of the projected Kunene River scheme. SOEKOR and IDC played a leading part in directing investment activity, and a few of the international companies involved with oil in Angola and Mozambique operated also in South West Africa.[109] Discovery of uranium and new copper deposits attracted new participants, like Rio Tinto Zinc Ltd—and new controversy.[110]

Opposition to South African rule among the Namibian Africans grew after 1966, when 'several incidents of mass action by Africans in the Police Zone [the "white" area] of a character not previously noted in the territory' occurred.[111] These incidents included disturbances in May 1966 in the Ovambo migrant workers' compound at the Katutura 'native' location of Windhoek; a stone-throwing episode by Africans after a traffic accident in which an Ovambo was killed, and an attack on police who arrested twenty Ovambos for illegally brewing beer at the compound. A major incident of 'mass action' in the beginning of 1967 was a work-to-rule by migrant Ovambo workers in Walvis Bay following riots at Windhoek railway sheds on 3 January at which sixty-one Ovambos were arrested.[112]

In 1966 the idea of moving Africans from the old location in Windhoek to the new native township at Katatura was revived by the South African government, which now threatened sanctions against those Africans who refused to move and their employers.[113] There was vigorous opposition to this proposal (which in 1959 had caused severe rioting in Windhoek, leading to the appointment of a commission of inquiry)[114] and the chief designate of the Hereros, Clemens Kapuuo, petitioned the UN to establish a presence in South

---

[109] I.e. US Gulf Oil, Chevron Oil, De Beers, Syracuse Oils.

[110] *Africa Contemporary Record,* 1970–71, p. 8542; *X-Ray,* August 1971, December 1970, September 1970.

[111] *UNGAOR, 22nd Session,* Doc. A/6700/Rev. 1.

[112] *Windhoek Advertiser,* 21 January 1969.

[113] *Security Council Official Records, 23rd Year,* Supp. Doc. S/8729. Annex II; *Africa Contemporary Record,* 'South West Africa', *passim.*

[114] Cf. *Report of the Commission of Inquiry into Occurrences in the Windhoek Location on the Night of the 10th to the 11th December 1959, and into the direct causes which led to those occurrences,* 1960.

West Africa to prevent such policies from being implemented.[115]
The South African government had its way, and by the end of 1968
Africans had been moved to Katutura.[116]

The removal of Hereros to Katutura caused anxiety among the
Rooinasie ('red nation') Namas of Hoachanas, whose headman, the
Rev. Markus Kooper (also a representative of the South West
African National Independence Organisation), petitioned the UN to
prevent the dispossession of his people of a reserve to which they had
been told they had an 'inalienable right'.[117] Some opposition to
South African rule was also described in a less militant body, the
Basterraad, the deliberative assembly of the Basters.[118] Opposition
did not deter the South African government, nor did it approach
the dimensions of popular revolt—until the end of 1971, when again
Ovambo migrant workers went on strike. This time some 30,000
workers were involved, and the South African government had to
concede that they had cause for grievance. The strike seemed to have
been aimed mainly at the contract labour system,[119] but it emerged
in the aftermath of the strike that some of the leaders of the workers
were sympathetic to SWAPO, and they were equally aware of continuing opposition to South Africa at the UN.[120] There was also
manifest a considerable amount of anti-white feeling among the
workers (to be precise, resentment of 'Boer' rule); the gravity of the
situation created by the strike can be inferred from the fact that,
following incidents of violence in Ovamboland, the government
decided to send in the Defence Force to assist the police.[121]

How far the workers were encouraged in their doings by the new
circumstance of armed resistance to South Africa and by the UN
revocation of the mandate it is impossible to say. It is certain, however, that their actions could not have been lightly embarked on in
the face of the severe measures which could be taken against them
under the laws of the republic. At any rate, all these activities by
Africans were elements in the qualitatively new situation of post-

[115] *UNGAOR, 22nd Session,* Doc. A/6700/Rev. 1.

[116] *Africa Contemporary Record,* p. 349.

[117] *UNGAOR, 24th Session,* Doc. A/7624/Rev. 1.

[118] *Ibid.*

[119] *Observer,* 2 January 1972; *Guardian,* 21 January 1972, 14 January
1972; also various issues of *The Times* and *Guardian* for December and
January 1971 and 1972 respectively.

[120] Cf. *Observer,* 13 February 1972.

[121] *Guardian,* 27 January 1972; *The Times,* 13 January 1972; *Guardian,*
18 January 1972; *Observer,* 30 January 1972.

1966 Namibia. Subsequent events like the successful boycott in August 1973 of Bantustan elections by the Ovambos, in response to a plea from SWAPO and the newly formed Democratic Co-operation Party confirmed the repudiation of *apartheid* by a substantial section of Namibia's black population. The strikes themselves were followed by strikes in South Africa itself, to which they must have given a lead.

What emerged from these developments, which we have sketchily outlined, was that South West Africa, along with all the other territories of southern Africa began to undergo an important transformation, not only in its international aspect but in the quality of its internal politics. Its strategic importance to South Africa, as well as its economic importance, make it very difficult to imagine that it could ever be willingly relinquished in its present form to black majority rule. And if it were relinquished in truncated form, it would be more than likely that opposition to the chiefs ruling the various homelands would draw South Africa back into closer involvement in the affairs of the 'homelands' and thus make a nonsense of 'independence'. Of the States that were once meant to be incorporated in Greater South Africa, South West Africa seemed to have been the most captive up to the end of the second world war; of all these territories it had gone furthest, at the beginning of the decade, towards the politics of mass protest and guerrilla insurgency.

IX *White-controlled southern Africa*

Portugal's colonies

Unlike Britain, France, Belgium and even Spain, Portugal resisted the anti-colonial movement and showed not the slightest intention of decolonising in the early and mid-1960s. Yet the beginning of the 1960s saw the start of revolutionary opposition to Portugal in Angola, and by 1965 a more effective liberation campaign was launched in Mozambique. There was also a revolution in Portuguese-controlled Guinè-Bissau, which in military terms was still more successful. The Portuguese position in Africa was under severe pressure, and by 1968 Portugal had about 100,000 fighting men committed in Angola and Mozambique alone.[1]

Such pressure made Portugal more disposed to co-operate closely with other white regimes in Africa which were subject to similar international difficulties; the South African government, on the other hand, always opposed to the anti-colonial movement, was predisposed to co-operate with the Portuguese. The strategic location of Angola and Mozambique, as buffer States protecting South Africa and Namibia, meant that the South African government could not be indifferent to the conflict in those territories.[2] With many African markets closed to South African exporters, there was also good reason for cosseting an economic partner which, although it did not account for much of South Africa's African trade, supplied the republic with cheap African labour for the mines and for white farms.[3] South

---

[1] See, among others, United Nations, *A Principle in Torment: the UN and Portuguese-Administered Territories*, 1970; E. Mondlane, *The Struggle for Mozambique*, 1968; B. Davidson, *The Liberation of Guinè: Aspects of an African Revolution*, 1969; J. Marcum, *The Angolan Revolution*, vol. 1, *The Anatomy of an Explosion*, 1969; D. M. Abshire and N. A. Samuels (eds.), *Portuguese Africa: a Handbook*, 1969; A. Cabral, 'A brief report on the situation of the struggle, January–August 1971' (mimeo), 1971.

[2] Cf. D. A. S. Herbst 'Suid-Afrika en die Portuguese gebiede–Angola en Mosambiek', in G. S. Labuschagne *et al.*, *Suid-Afrika en Suider-Afrika*, 1969; G. Cockram, *Vorster's Foreign Policy*, 1970.

[3] The use of Mozambican African labour dated back to the late nineteenth century; at the beginning of this century various understandings were arrived

Africa therefore sought to intensify the ties of friendship with Portugal, to augment existing areas of economic co-operation, and to encourage consultation on military matters of common interest.[4]

A sense of common purpose did not emerge immediately and automatically. In the post-war period the white regimes of southern Africa had different subjective conceptions of their systems of rule, and particularly their 'native policies'. The Portuguese made much of the fact that they did not practise *apartheid* in their territories, and, presumably, did not wish to share the international disapproval suffered by South Africa on account of *apartheid*. The division between the Portuguese and British spheres of influence in Africa also made for divergence in the patterns of co-operation among the regimes of southern Africa. Where, for example, the former British areas had their economies geared to British and, to a lesser extent, other Commonwealth markets, the Portuguese territories were economically oriented to Portugal. In consequence, trade between neighbouring territories was abnormally sluggish, reflecting the exclusivist and competitive tendency of empires.[5] Portugal was notoriously eager to maintain a virtual monopoly of economic (as well as political, social and cultural) influence in its territories by effectively excluding foreign investment, presumably because, being the poorest

---

at with the Portuguese in terms of which South African mines were allowed to recruit in Mozambique in exchange for a promise to use the Mozambique Railway for a certain proportion of their seaborne trade. In 1909 these understandings were formalised into the Mozambique Convention, subsequently renegotiated, the extant agreement being that of 1938. The convention allows for virtually compulsory remissions to be made on behalf of workers to Mozambique. See E. A. Walker, *A History of Southern Africa*, 1957, pp. 501, 614, 754. About 105,590 Mozam-Africans worked in the South African mines in 1964, out of an estimated 500,000 Mozambicans working there. Their earnings in 1964–65 were estimated to be R1,950,000 in cash, R990,000 in kind, in agriculture, and R17,358,000 and R15,900,000. These figures are taken from G. R. E. Leistner, 'Foreign Bantu workers in South Africa; their present position in the economy', in *South African Journal of Economics*, 1967.

[4] Cf. Herbst, *loc. cit.*; Cockram, *op. cit., passim*; Rhoodie, *The Third Africa, passim*. For an official reaction to the outbreak of fighting in Angola in 1961, see African Defence Minister, in *Ass. Deb.*, vol. 186, col. 7393.

[5] It has been argued that the suppression of horizontal trade is a structural feature of imperialism; see J. Galtung, 'A structural theory of imperialism', in *Journal of Peace Research*, 1970. This is mainly a function of the type of production encouraged in colonies, which is usually production (beyond that of goods for the subsistence economy) for the metropolitan markets. Tariff walls and social barriers often stifle trade between territories belonging to different empires.

of imperial powers, Portugal might not otherwise have been able to maintain its predominant position in the colonial economies.[6]

South Africa traded more with Mozambique than with Angola; with the former its export peak did not exceed £7 million in the period 1957–68, and with the latter it hardly reached £2 million.

TABLE 6 *South African imports from and exports to Angola and Mozambique, selected years (£)*

(a) *Selected years, 1957–61*	*1957*		*1959*		*1961*
(i) *Imports*					
Angola	523,904		346,490		246,862
Mozambique	2,713,370		1,447,720		1,131,945
(ii) *Exports*					
Angola	246,209		436,328		363,684
Mozambique	5,164,664		6,494,410		4,909,163

(b) *1964–68*	*1964*	*1965*	*1966*	*1967*	*1968*
(i) *Imports*					
Angola	283,000	442,100	983,300	702,300	109,200
Mozambique	2,667,000	3,540,000	3,541,000	3,634,000	3,673,000
(ii) *Exports*					
Angola	804,800	801,700	794,500	981,400	1,768,000
Mozambique	4,892,000	4,214,000	5,042,000	5,186,000	6,375,000

Notes. Figures in (a) above are derived from South African Department of Customs and Excise, *Annual Statements of Trade and Shipping* (various years). As no South African trade figures are published for trade with individual African countries after 1961, the figures in (a) are derived from the United Nations *Yearbook of International Trade Statistics*, 1966 and 1968, where they are entered under Mozambique and Angola—not under South Africa.

Figures in (a) were given in millions of escudos. Using 1966 values, conversion factors were as follows: new US cents per escudo=3·478; new US cents per £ sterling=280·00. Four-figure logarithmic tables were used for computation, with the result that there may be over-rounding of the figures, which would have the effect, *inter alia*, that values of imports and exports would be slightly depressed, but not consequentially so.

As can be seen from table 6, South Africa was in both cases a net exporter—much more so in the case of Mozambique than in that of Angola. The volume of trade in 1964–68, after the 'emergence' of black Africa, was noticeably greater than in the earlier period 1957–1961. This probably reflected an overall growth and development of the economies involved; the figure may also reflect the diversification of South African markets which followed upon the loosening

[6] Restrictions were, however, relaxed in 1965. See below.

of South Africa's ties with the Commonwealth. But it is reasonable in addition to suppose that the difference between the two sets of figures reflects the deliberate attempts to encourage co-operation. Table 6 illustrates these differences and also the contrast between South African exports and imports.

The relatively small volume of trade between South Africa and its neighbours illustrates the domination of economic activity by imperial political frameworks. The trading advantage which South Africa enjoyed probably reflected that country's higher level of economic and commercial development. The unequal trading relationship with Mozambique exports might become a stumbling block to further expansion of trade unless Mozambique exports were given preferential access to South African markets. In deference to this fact the South African government tried to revive the Mozambique Convention,[7] which had become almost abrogated by disuse. In terms of the convention, Transvaal businessmen had to use the Mozambican port of Lourenco Marques for 45 per cent of their sea-borne imports, but as they were no longer doing so the South African government paid compensation to Mozambique Railways for lost traffic, amounting to R4,385,600 between 1965 and 1968. The Department of Commerce also appealed to businessmen to use the port.[8]

The development of closer co-operation between South Africa and the Portuguese-controlled territories had also been hampered in the past by the fact that the Afrikaner minorities who had settled in Angola exhibited an inability to be assimilated and tended to look to the Union for support. A few Afrikaner nationalists within South Africa affirmed solidarity with these *diaspora* Afrikaners in disregard of Portuguese official susceptibilities.[9] These were, however, minority feelings. Leading National Party opinion had long sought to improve relations with the Portuguese as part of the attempt to wriggle free from what it considered the tight framework of the British Empire. Removal of indigent Afrikaners from Angola was part of the attempts to improve relations. In 1928 the South African government had moved 2,000 Afrikaners from Angola to South West Africa, and in 1957 a further 400 Afrikaners were moved to the republic and

[7] *A.R.B.* (*Econ.*), 1968, 1025.
[8] *A.R.B.* (*Econ.*), 1968, 1025.
[9] Dr J. A. Coetzee's letter to *Die Transvaler*, 13 September 1948, is a case in point: referring to Angola, he wrote, 'If we do not preserve white civilisation in Africa, we shall not preserve it in South Africa.'

to Namibia.[10] Several affirmations of the friendship between the two countries were made after 1957, and Nationalist politicians tended to blame Afrikaner settlers themselves for the hardships they had endured in the Portuguese-controlled territories.[11] By the mid-1960s it was a commonplace of South African international relations that this friendship should be intensified by closer consultation, but the sentiment lacked a concrete focus in action.

The break came when, under increasing political and military pressure, the Portuguese decided upon a policy of colonial development, consisting principally in exploring the territories (for minerals), construction programmes, and a policy of colonial migration, i.e. (white) Portuguese being encouraged to emigrate to the colonies. That South Africa was expected to feature prominently in this programme of colonial development was indicated by the establishment of a Bank of Lisbon and South Africa and by the creation of a Portuguese–South African Economic Institute.[12]

Following discussions with the South African government, the Portuguese government decided in 1965–66 to launch the Cabora Bassa dam project: the dam would provide hydro-electric power to Mozambique and South Africa; it would support an irrigation scheme in Mozambique and, hopefully, hasten the economic development of the colony.[13] Agreement was also reached in principle in 1966 for the construction of another dam in Angola, on the Kunene River, which would be part of an irrigation scheme for Namibia; but this latter project was not finally sanctioned by the Portuguese until almost four years later.[14] Without the agreement of the South African Electricity Supply Commission (ESCOM) agreement to purchase the power the Cabora Bassa hydro-electric scheme would not have been possible; without loans from the Industrial Development Corporation and ESCOM, and export credits from the South African government, the project would certainly have been

[10] *Standard Encyclopaedia of Southern Africa*, vol. 1, pp. 425–6; for some early policy views see Walker, *op. cit.*, p. 685.

[11] Cf. Eric Louw in *Ass. Deb.*, vol. 52, col. 3715; Oost in *Ass. Deb.*, vol. 64, col. 1294. Also P. S. van der Merwe in *Ass. Deb.*, vol. 99, cols. 5468–70.

[12] Cockram, *op. cit., passim*; Rhoodie, *op. cit., passim*.

[13] Africa Bureau, *X-Ray; Fact Sheet No. 1; A.R.B.* (*Econ.*), 1969, pp. 1364B, 1388C, 14508B, 1490B.

[14] South African embassy, Information Division, *Today's News*, 22 November 1968; see also *ibid.*, 31 January 1969.

frustrated.[15] The international consortium, Zambeze Consorcio Hidro-Electrico (ZAMCO), which won the contract to construct the dam included the South African companies Anglo-American, LTA Ltd, Shaft Sinkers Ltd, VPC Ltd and Power Lines Ltd, and five West German and seven French companies. The Portuguese government had paved the way in 1965 by means of investment guarantees for that penetration of its colonial economy which it had studiously avoided in the past, and which the Cabora Bassa scheme now made unavoidable.[16] In South Africa, on the other hand, the exportation of capital in a collaborative venture by the State and by private capitalists was accepted by the political classes without any public objections.[17]

The most striking structural feature of South African policy towards the Portuguese that began to emerge was its domination by relatively coherent economic and strategic factors. In the first place, South African economic power enabled South Africa to participate in the construction projects and to guarantee essential markets for their output. In the second place, development along these lines in the Portuguese colonies was expected to strengthen the South African economy by providing cheap power and water from sources which, so long as the Portuguese remained in control, were dependable. From the point of view of military strategy, economic development would protect the buffer territories by creating a more contented population and by attracting more white settlers to southern Africa. South African participation in the colonial development scheme might also provide the republic with a means of participating also in the political development of the colonies.

Probably more important than the dam construction projects was the development of oil production in Angola, including the search for more and better oil there. Portuguese oil searches were complementary (from the strategic viewpoint of finding strategic raw materials within southern Africa) to, though potentially economically

[15] *X-Ray, Fact Sheet No. 1; A.R.B. (Econ.),* 1969, 1364B, 1388C, 1450B, 1490B; W. A. Hance, 'Cahora Bassa hydro-project', in *Africa Report,* 1970.
[16] *A.R.B. (Econ.),* 1965, 305B.
[17] Contrast with the reservation of the president of the South African Chamber of Mines about the projected Orange River hydro-electric scheme involving Lesotho (see below) that 'it would seem more logical if in this coal and uranium producing country . . . the power potential were developed by means of considerably less expensive capital installations required either for conventional coal-fired stations or for nuclear stations' (*A.R.B. (Econ.),* 1965, vol. 2, No. 9; see also *A.R.B. (Econ.),* 1966, 554C.

competitive with, oil exploration within South Africa, which was stepped up at about the time of Rhodesia's break with Britain and the imposition of sanctions. Within South Africa (and Namibia and Lesotho) the exploration, which was expected to have cost a total of R60 million by 1971, was led by the State corporation SOEKOR (South African Oil Exploration Corporation), and the participants included a South West African subsidiary of Shell, HM Mining and Exploration Ltd, Syracuse Oils and Oceana Petroleums.[18] In January 1971 it was announced that off-shore drilling operations would commence. Working under an agreement with SOEKOR was a group of South African, British, French and American companies: Atlantic Richfield, Chevron Regent, Security Resources Petroleum, Continental Oil, Oil Ventures International, American Pacific and Total.[19] At the end of 1971, however, no oil deposits had been found.

In Angola oil had already been found in commercial quantities by 1965, and Angola was able to export about R4·25 million worth of oil to Rhodesia.[20] A South African company sought a concession to prospect for oil in Angola, but the oil venture was dominated by Portuguese—or nominally Portuguese—concerns, as, for example, the Portuguese Companhia dos Petroleos de Angola (PETRANGOL) in which a number of non-Portuguese companies hold shares and which works in partnership with two South African, two Portuguese and Italian and French companies; the Cabinda Gulf Oil Company (a subsidiary of the US Gulf Oil) is the other main 'Portuguese' company.[21] South African banks were expected to 'figure prominently' in financing the construction of a 220-mile gas pipeline from Mozambique to the Witwatersrand (to be constructed by another Portuguese subsidiary of Gulf Oil).[22] A South African company in partnership with a French one gained a concession in Mozambique.[23]

The biggest mineral prospecting concession to be granted to a

18 On-shore the oil search covered an area of 40,000 square miles, in the northern Orange Free State and the Natal midlands: *Today's News*, 15 March 1969.

19 *Today's News*, 8 January 1971; areas selected for off-shore drilling were Mosselbay, Plettenberg Bay, Durban and Port Elizabeth: *Today's News*, 19 August 1970.

20 *A.R.B.* (*Econ.*), 1965, 380C; see also 381A and 403B.

21 *A.R.B.* (*Econ.*), 1965, 380C; see also Rhoodie, *op. cit.*, p. 181.

22 Rhoodie, *op. cit.*, p. 181.

23 The companies involved were Anglo-American (South African) and SNPA and ERAR–ELF (both French).

South African company in Mozambique was one by the mining company Johannesburg Consolidated. It was announced in December 1969 that a contract was to be signed by the Portuguese government with a company to be formed jointly by Johannesburg Consolidated and a Mr Leones Gomes dos Santos for rights in an area thought to be potentially rich in asbestos, graphite, coal, copper, iron ore, chrome, tin, wolfram and nickel.[24]

The effect of all these developments was to involve the private sector in South Africa increasingly in support of the government's Africa policy, and to create for them a vested interest in 'stability' in the area—or, by another name, the political *status quo*. By the same token, the involvement of influential international corporations in the Portuguese territories as in South Africa was a successful outcome of the Africa policy in so far as it contributed to the development of an influential international lobby favouring the maintenance of the *status quo*, that is to say, a political as well as a socio-economic framework in southern Africa which would be favourable to the retention of white minority rule.

Strategic and economic considerations (of the private as well as the public sector) argued for a deeper and more thorough South African commitment to the defence of 'Portugal overseas'. Several courtesies, exchanges of visits, and consultations between the two governments and military personnel occurred during the period. The South African Defence and Foreign Ministers also received high decorations in Portugal.[25]

Military consultations with Portugal probably helped to keep alive the South African hope for the creation of a southern-hemisphere defence arrangement, analogous to the North Atlantic Treaty Organisation, in which South Africans would play a prominent part. Portugal and South African interests might perhaps warrant a regional defence organisation, but the idea was of a wider South Atlantic community including South America and extending into the Indian and Pacific Oceans. With respect to South America, the Portuguese connection was important, since Portugal maintained fairly close relations with its former colony Brazil. A South Atlantic defence community, if it emerged, would have automatic links with NATO through Portugal and indirectly through Britain (via the Simonstown agreements). Australia and New Zealand were for the

---

[24] *A.R.B.* (*Econ.*), 1969, 1537B.
[25] Cockram, *op. cit.*, ch. 11;

present preoccupied with Asia and the Pacific rather than with either the Atlantic or the Indian Ocean, but there was a marked increase in South African co-operation with South American countries, economically and militarily.[26] It is unlikely that such sentiments favouring co-operation crystallised in any definite organisational plan.[27] Nonetheless a southern-hemisphere treaty agreement would be consistent with the South African preoccupation with communist threats on land, at sea and in the air; it would give an object to South African naval expansion and a justification of the considerable expenditure on the instruments of war.[28] In a militarily and economically stratified international society it would enhance the influence of South Africa on the major powers and the power of South Africa to withstand its challengers.

Foreign policy, however, is often more programmatic in conception than in execution. The absence of a discernible common threat retarded the closing of ranks among the anti-communist powers of the southern hemisphere. Even within southern Africa, Portuguese collaboration was not without its strains, among which were the contradictions of uneven development. Because of its economic superiority to these territories South Africa was able to play an

[26] Cf. A. S. Minty, *South Africa's Defence Strategy*, pp. 19–22; also Cockram, *op. cit.*, ch. 4. On 18 April 1969 *Today's News* announced that South African General Mining and Finance had won a R15 million for the construction of an irrigation tunnel in Peru. Construction would be financed partly by the State-owned Industrial Development Corporation of South Africa, partly by a Peruvian subsidiary of General Mining and Finance, and partly by Roberts Construction Ltd. On 17 June 1970 the conclusion of a credit agreement between South Africa and Bolivia was announced. In September it was reported that a Brazilian trade mission had begun negotiations with businessmen and governments in Angola, Mozambique and South Africa. It was also reported that the Brazilian State bank, the Banco de Estado de São Paulo, would give support to Brazilian busnessmen, who mainly hoped to export automobile parts to southern Africa. (*Today's News*, 4 September 1970). During the same month a seventeen-man Argentinian trade commission led by the Under-Secretary for foreign affairs, Dr Alberto Fraguio, seeking to promote trade and friendship, visited South Africa with the immediate object of promoting the sale of secondary produce to South Africa: *Today's News*, 18 September 1970; see also *ibid.*, 16 April 1969, 17 June 1970, 15 September 1970, 23 September 1970.

[27] Cf. *Today's News*, 23 April 1969.

[28] For a favourable review of this build-up see 'The strategic importance of South Africa' in *International Defence Review*, 1969. This article is obviously promotional rather than analytical—its only value is that it provides a summary of South African defence projects and expenditures. See also Minty, *op. cit.*, and J. E. Spence, *The Strategic Significance of Southern Africa*, 1970, p. 23.

economic role with respect to Angola and Mozambique that tended to resemble that of a metropolis to its colonies (e.g. importing raw materials and minerals, exporting manufactures and capital),[29] a pattern of asymmetrical interdependence beginning to emerge: a South African market for the produce of the Portuguese colonies was likely to be less dispensable to Angola and Mozambique than their markets would be to South Africa.[30] Although Portugal remained the metropolitan country, the South African position could be described as 'sub-imperial' (that of a subordinate imperial partner). From such a conjunction could follow severe role conflicts not only between Portugal and South Africa but also between South Africa and the settler (and indigenous) populations of the territories.[31] Conflicts might also arise from competitive attempts by Portugal and South Africa to maximise their respective areas of influence, which although they were complementary in the period surveyed might not always be so. While Portugal might need all the South African goodwill it could obtain, there would not be much point in the Portuguese expending so much in human and material resources to prepare a bequest for South Africa. Equally, it would be mistaken to suppose that Portugal might never decide to cut its losses by withdrawing from southern Africa,[32] nor, conversely, that South Africa might not at a future date be prepared to trade its

[29] Cf. G. Arrighi and J. S. Saul, 'Nationalism and revolution in sub-Saharan Africa', in *Socialist Register*, 1969.

[30] The produce of these territories might not however be expendable, especially the hydro-electric power. Lombard *et al.*, *op. cit.*, were led to conclude that 'a measure of supra-national control would have to be accepted' if an integrated hydro-electric scheme were to be adopted in southern Africa (p. 60). Needless to say, this is contrary to Rhoodie's rather vacuous slogan for 'southern Africa' which runs 'economic interdependence and political independence'; *The Third Africa, passim*. In the long run South Africa might, however, develop nuclear power, which could reduce the importance of the Mozambican scheme.

[31] The best theoretical analysis of role-taking behaviour and role conflict in the dissociative situation of decolonisation is that by J. P. Nettl and R. Robertson in 'The inheritance situation', in their *International Systems and the Modernisation of Societies*, 1968. It is not difficult to see that although Nettl and Robertson dealt only with situations where there had been a transfer of sovereignty, their conceptual model could be transposed to the kind of intermediate situation, between the colonial and the post-colonial situations.

[32] It was, in fact, widely believed before Dr Caetana's accession that he would decolonise, it being thought that the aging dictator Salazar had been the real obstacle to change. Cf. D. G. Anglin, 'Zambia and Portugal', in *International Journal*, 1970; M. Howe, 'Portugal's colonial wars', in *Africa Report*, 1969.

support of Portuguese colonialism for a sure prospect of diplomatic support elsewhere—especially in Africa—or even support a favourable secessionist movement from metropolitan Portugal. These would be the parameters of assurance in any co-operative relationship between two States placed as Portugal and South Africa are. But they are likely to be of immediate relevance in these imperial–sub-imperial conjunctions because of centrifugal tendencies within empires,[33] because of the proliferation of decisional centres, because Angola and Mozambique might (for geo-political reasons) become more important for South Africa than for Portugal, and because, when all is said and done, colonies are always more expendable to their metropoles[34] than to those powers within whose defence perimeters they may at a particular time fall.[35] Indeed, if one looks at what facilitates the retention of empire, rather than at the real or imagined advantages of empires (for the metropoles), one is constrained to agree with Landes' 'dynamic equilibrium model' of imperialism. Landes sees imperialism as a response to an opportunity consisting in a disparity of power; its dynamics (which is what is of immediate interest) are governed by its 'inner logic':

This inner logic finds expression in two fields: within the context of a given area of imperialistic influence; and in the larger context of the international relations of imperial powers. Concerning the first, the decisive determinant at the working level—as distinguished from the level of plans and intentions—is the instability of any relationship of unequal power. In the long run, the weaker party will never accept his inferiority . . . In return the stronger party must ceaselessly concern itself with the security of its position. Hence this imperialism of the 'turbulent frontier' so well described by John Galbraith;[36] each strong point requires outposts to defend it, and

[33] I.e. the self-decolonising tendencies resulting either from revolutionary severance of imperial bonds or the concentration of decision-making power within the colony rather than the metropolis.

[34] G. Lichtheim has argued interestingly for this view in his 'Imperialism II', in *Commentary*, 1970 (in an attempt to debunk the Leninist argument that imperialism, or, specifically, the new imperialism, was an historical necessity of capitalism at a certain stage of its development).

[35] There are perhaps no better illustrations of this tendency than the growth of US involvement in Indo-China upon the waning of French influence and interest there. The history of US involvement in Latin America, from the Monroe doctrine onward, could be understood in these terms—the supersession of European imperial interests and commitments by the challenge of a more interested and committed power.

[36] J. S. Galbraith, 'The turbulent frontier as a factor in British expansion', in *Comparative Studies in Society and History*, 1960, pp. 150–68.

each outpost calls for new ones beyond it. The spiral of increasing commitments and obligations is limited only by the balance of power.[37]

For the Portuguese the turbulent frontier might be a point of weakness but for South African governments turbulence at the frontiers of the buffer territories might be a powerful imperative for the expansion of the sub-imperial role—the voluntary role of subordinate partnership with Portugal in the maintenance of the colonial order. The inherent instability of the Portuguese position in Africa must be an important factor in the shaping of South African policy. Indeed, South African policy towards Portuguese-controlled Angola and Mozambique can be seen both in terms of an attempt to forestall or postpone Portuguese concessions, to 'frontier turbulence' as it manifests itself in the revolutionary wars, and at the same time as an attempt to create a South African foothold within the territories' settler population against the eventuality of metropolitan Portugal's withdrawal.

After 1965 the South African government involved itself closely in the military affairs of Angola and Mozambique. In addition to the exchange of visits by military and political personnel, South African police were engaged in 1967–68 in counter-insurgency activity in Mozambique: the reason given was that South Africans belonging to the banned Pan-African Congress of South Africa were with the Mozambican guerrillas and had infiltrated into Mozambique.[38] Within South Africa, both from the official opposition and from the ruling National Party's supporters, there were calls for some support to be given to the Portuguese in their colonial wars in southern Africa—support of a 'non-military' kind.[39] However, apart from one operation, the Portuguese, unlike the Rhodesians (see below), did not encourage further South African para-military participation. The common boundary between Angola and South West Africa in the south-east did, as will be seen, create occasion for collaboration there, and South African uniformed men have upon occasion been descried well within Angola, though evidently not in a combatant capacity.[40] Moreover, the limited co-operation on the battlefields of

[37] D. S. Landes, 'Some thoughts on the nature of economic imperialism', in *Journal of Economic History*, 1961, p. 510.

[38] Vorster in parliament, *Ass. Deb.*, vol. 23, col. 4075.

[39] Cockram, *op. cit.*, chapters 10 and 11.

[40] Confidential Angolan and Namibian sources. There have also been persistent reports of a substantial South African military presence in Tete in Mozambique.

Angola and Mozambique probably understates the greater degree of collaboration in espionage in the neighbouring territories and elsewhere.

Were the liberation movements to be more successful it would be difficult for Portugal to resist the tendency to rely more and more on South African collaboration in all fields. By 1971 there seemed to be little scope for a substantial expansion of the Portuguese war effort in southern Africa (unless Portugal decided to abandon Guiné-Bissau). The Portuguese might diversify their fighting methods to include more efficacious psychological warfare tactics than had previously been employed: they might try to win over the non-combatant black population by more generous economic and social administration;[41] or they might increasingly resort to large-scale intimidation of African villages suspected of supporting or harbouring guerrillas;[42] or they might attempt to do both. Such tactics might prolong the wars without reversing the inexorable process of self-decolonisation which constitutes the dialectical antithesis of imperialism, seeming to grow from the very measures that are introduced to contain it.

Rhodesia

The unilateral declaration of independence by the Rhodesian government on 11 November 1965 was probably more catalytic than any other single event to the 'outward movement' of South African foreign policy in southern Africa. It inaugurated a period of closer collaboration by the Rhodesian government with both South Africa and Portugal, collaboration which, for the general reasons already mentioned, had grown sluggishly in the period before the mid-1960s. International sanctions, imposed at the instance of the United Kingdom government, made Rhodesia utterly dependent on South Africa and Portugal for goods and services that could not be supplied within that colony. South African and Portuguese policies on Rhodesia converged and the two powers found themselves in the common international position of providing Rhodesia with the means of evading —in the event, successfully—the sanctions that were imposed upon it. The dangers of assisting Rhodesia—the possibility of sanctions against

[41] D. A. S. Herbst, 'Suid Afrika en die Portuguese Gebiede', and M. Calvert 'Angola's two little wars', in *Spectator*, 1 January 1972.
[42] *Guerrilheiro*, September–October 1971; *Guardian*, 17 December 1971.

South Africa itself—and the opportunities of giving aid to Rhodesia, as well as replacing Rhodesia as a supplier of goods in southern and central Africa, argued for a clearer definition of the South African role in southern Africa while they created the occasion for the execution of that role.

There had been consultations between the Rhodesian government and the governments of Portugal and South Africa prior to UDI. Contingency plans to meet the possibility of an armed attack on the colony had, reportedly, been agreed upon in 1964–65,[43] and the Portuguese made no secret of the fact that they were accelerating oil production in Angola in order to enable Rhodesia to meet its needs from local sources, obviously in anticipation of oil sanctions.[44] It is unclear what counsel Rhodesia received from South Africa and Portugal on the specific question of whether or not it should unilaterally declare itself independent, but there is no reason to suppose that UDI surprised South Africa and Portugal, or that Mr Ian Smith, the Rhodesian Prime Minister, did not take his decision in the light of consultations with those governments and upon an assessment of the extent and quality of support he might expect to receive from them.[45]

Shortly before UDI Verwoerd had advised the Rhodesians to be patient. Before and after UDI he exchanged letters with the prime ministers of Rhodesia and the United Kingdom to try to bring them to a negotiated settlement. Vorster, his successor, subsequently explained to parliament:

In that correspondence there was an appeal to Mr Wilson as well as an appeal to Mr Smith, to see if they could not through mutual discussions solve a problem which he regarded as their domestic problem, but which, if it were to go further, would have far-reaching consequences also for us and the rest of the world.[46]

There was no doubt that he was apprehensive of the possible complications which might follow between Rhodesia and the United Kingdom in a world composed so much of forces which were hostile not only to what Rhodesia stood for, but to what South Africa and Portugal also represented. Such apprehension was shown by the influential Nationalist daily newspaper *Die Burger*, which wrote on

[43] K. Young, *Rhodesia and Independence*, 1969, p. 420.
[44] *A.R.B.* (*Econ.*), 1965, 380, 381A, 403B.
[45] Cf. Young, *op. cit.*, p. 145.
[46] Vorster in *Ass. Deb.*, vol. 17, col. 2546.

the morrow of UDI an editorial headed 'Rhodesia does it' (*Rhodesië doen dit*):

What is . . . clearly predictable is that South Africa (possibly together with Portugal) will have to share the international hostility towards Rhodesia even more. South Africa will be accused of helping to thwart the aims of the economic blockade, and Britain and the other Western countries which participate in it will be urged to extend the measures to the Republic. What is emerging before us is a future of increased pressure and greater vulnerability for the whole of southern Africa.[47]

Understandably, although perversely, the view thus gained currency in England that Verwoerd was *opposed* to UDI and would not assist Rhodesia to bear its consequences. Such views were hard to reconcile with Verwoerd's attitude to decolonisation, with the ideological position on race relations which he so staunchly championed, and with the fact that if not in Verwoerd, then in the ranks of his sup-porters, racial feeling would militate against such a policy. True, South Africa might favour a 'neo-colonial solution', a Tshombe regime in Rhodesia rather than an embattled and probably ulti-mately non-viable settler government. But there was no 'Tshombe' within sight, and in the period under review no alternative 'neo-colonial' government (i.e. one that would ostensibly be popularly representative but would in effect represent only white or capita-list interests, which is presumably what was meant by 'neo-colonial solution' and 'Tshombe regime' in the Rhodesian context)[48] ever seemed even vaguely likely to emerge. The belief that South Africa would not support Rhodesia was, therefore, the product more of fancy than of diligent thought. Admittedly, it may be true that the South African government did not wish to be involved in a major international crisis on behalf of the Rhodesian Front Party, and that Verwoerd was solicitous to bring about an early conclusion to the dispute in order to normalise the relations of white southern Africa with the United Kingdom, which was an otherwise friendly major capitalist power. That is consistent with our view that

[47] *Die Burger*, 12 November 1965.

[48] Leading journalists and academics have expressed such views to the present writer. None of these views is ever backed by reference to a single concrete attempt—in the form of help withheld, for example—to dissuade the Rhodesians from the UDI. Rather these views are based on some notion of what would have been the optimal reaction for the part of South Africa. In that event they were wrong in both their factual premises and their infer-ences. See also Nolutshungu, 'The implications of the Rhodesian settlement proposals for South Africa', in S. E. Wilmer (ed.), *Zimbabwe Now*, 1973.

Verwoerd was committed to helping Smith, but, as with virtually all commitments in international relations, it was a contingent commitment: as long as Smith could hold his own, and so long as South African material interests were not jeopardised by South African collusion with Rhodesia, South Africa would continue to give support, while doing its best not to sully its relations with the UK. Should, on the other hand, Rhodesia be too weak, or the price too high for South Africa to bear in terms of its own economy and security, then the 'white man's cause' in Rhodesia would be abandoned, provided that earlier illusions, as they would then turn out to have been, about the viability of the Smith regime had not irretrievably implicated South Africa by that time. This judgement is consistent with the refusal of the South African government to recognise Rhodesia and its insistence that its policy was one of neutrality.[49]

The carefully balanced ambiguities of diplomacy were soon subverted by developments within South Africa. A general election was in the offing in the republic when UDI was proclaimed, and the Rhodesian crisis became an election issue. The leader of the official South African opposition, Sir de Villiers Graaff, called for an immediate declaration of support for Rhodesia[50] (and later accused the government of dilatoriness in its support for Rhodesia). The Republican Party—the small but vociferous Van der Merwe group —consisting of right-wing opponents of the Verwoerd government, attacked that government for its supposed failure to give support to the 'white man's cause' in Rhodesia.[51] Verwoerd, who had met the declaration of independence with the usual disclaimer that South Africa would not interfere in the domestic affairs of another country, elaborated a definite, if unconscionably complex, policy of 'neutrality' in his New Year message of 1966.[52] South Africa would be neutral, and accordingly would not participate in sanctions. Normal co-operation with Rhodesia and Britain would continue. Verwoerd later expounded on the notion of 'normal trade' on the opening of the National Party's election campaign on 5 March. The expression 'normal trade' had, according to him been wrongly defined by others

[49] See J. A. Coetzee, *Nasiekap en politieke groepering in Suid-Afrika*, 1969, and *id.*, 'Suid-Afrika en Rhodesie' in Labuschagne *et. al.*, *Suid-Afrika en Suider-Afrika*, on the question of recognition and 'neutrality'.
[50] *Die Burger*, 12 November 1965; *Daily Dispatch*, 1965.
[51] *Hoofstadnuus*, 2 September 1966.
[52] *Cape Times*, 1 January 1966.

according to their own wishes: 'Normal trade does not imply that
you can continue selling only the commodities or the quantities you
sold before.'[53] It was precisely that kind of 'neutrality' which the
Rhodesian government needed. Verwoerd's statements made nothing
happen; they only indicated that private initiatives to help Rhodesia
as well as private profiteering on sanctions had his official encouragement.

Verwoerd was not long encumbered with the Rhodesian problem.
On 6 September 1966 he was assassinated. The death of Verwoerd,
who had shown himself cautious to maintain good relations with the
UK in spite of his 'neutrality' and who had unaccountably acquired
a reputation of legalism in Britain, created uncertainty about the
likely policy of the next administration. Mr Harold Wilson, who
was Prime Minister at the time, recalls that at the September Conference of Commonwealth Prime Ministers (which was mostly
about Rhodesia) it was feared that South Africa might more defiantly
support Rhodesia if Vorster—a militant right-winger—were to become Prime Minister.[54] Vorster for his part considered that a warning was due to those Commonwealth leaders who thought that the
uncertainty created by the assassination provided an opportunity
for quick action in Rhodesia:

From the tone [of] some overseas comments it would seem that there exists
an impression that because the South African Prime Minister has been
murdered, the country is bound to be plunged into a period of uncertainty
and confusion, during which she will be vulnerable to increased pressure.
An example of this kind of thinking is the demand made at the Commonwealth Conference that speedy action be taken against Rhodesia whilst
South Africa is otherwise occupied.

The assumption that South Africa is too preoccupied to attend to her
normal affairs is a false one, and a dangerous one if it prompts any hasty
action.[55]

On 21 September Vorster affirmed that he would continue in
Verwoerd's footsteps over the Rhodesian issue. The situation was
changing, however: mandatory sanctions were now being resorted
to, and Verwoerd had articulated no public policy on mandatory
sanctions. A Rhodesian journalist, reporting an interview with

[53] *A.R.B.* (*Econ.*), 1966, 462A.
[54] H. Wilson, *The Labour Government, 1964–70: a Personal Record,* 1970,
p. 278.
[55] *BBC Summary of World Broadcasts,* Part IV, *Africa and the Middle
East* (hereafter, *BBC Summary*), 8 August 1966, ME/2265/B/5.

Vorster, wrote in his despatch, read in the studios of Rhodesian Radio in Salisbury:

. . . should selective mandatory sanctions . . . be adopted by the United Nations, South Africa will ignore them; and should that step be followed in due course by full mandatory sanctions, South Africa will undoubtedly continue to provide Smith with his life-saving oil anyway.[56]

Vorster subsequently stated this view explicitly.[57]

Such a forthright and defiant policy was probably encouraged by the fact that the United Kingdom, in April 1966, had surreptitiously initiated 'talks about talks'[58] with the rebel regime: a sign which was bound to convey in the calculus of diplomacy an impression of weakness or irresolution. South Africans, like the Rhodesians, might be expected to become more intractable as the UK government showed itself more and more eager for a negotiated settlement with the Smith regime.

As the British policy gradually proved to be ineffective and as the UK government continued to seek a negotiated settlement—through the '*Tiger* talks' and the '*Fearless* talks'[59]—the possibility that sanctions or UN intervention might be extended to South Africa receded into a mere chimera—no less because the black African States, which were supposed to spearhead the campaign against Rhodesia, were becoming divided on the methods to be used against Rhodesia —and later (especially from 1968 onward) the South African government was able to play that role of 'honest broker' which Verwoerd had evidently sought.[60] In the meantime, South African intervention in Rhodesian affairs, proceeding *pari passu* with the deterioration of Anglo-South African relations not only over the Rhodesian question but also over quite different matters (e.g. the UK refusal to sell arms to South Africa), increased. In 1967 on the pretext that members of the ANC of South Africa were helping ZAPU (Zimbabwe African People's Union) guerrillas fighting in Rhodesia (which they were), South African police joined the Rhodesians in counter-

---

[56] *BBC Summary*, ME/2272/B/1, 21 September 1966.

[57] Johannesburg Radio; *BBC Summary*, ME/2272/B/8, 21 September 1966.

[58] R. Hall, *The High Price of Principles: Kaunda and the White South*, 1969, p. 149.

[59] See Cmnd. 3171/1966 and 3793/1968.

[60] As the Verwoerd letter, already referred to, indicated.

insurgency activity in Rhodesia.[61] They remained there in spite of British requests for their withdrawal.[62]

'Terrorism' in Rhodesia, following upon guerrilla activity in the Portuguese colonies, and after 1965, to a more limited extent, in Namibia also, exercised the passions and minds of South African Ministers and defence personnel in 1967–68, quite considerably.[63] Vorster, who had himself been interned for suspected pro-Nazi subversion during the second world war, had since made his name in South African politics as the counter-insurgent *par excellence* (as if to confirm the trite psychological principle *Fur furem cognoscit*). He had piloted through parliament the General Laws Amendment Act, which provided for the indefinite detention without trial of political suspects. As Minister of Justice and of Police he had led the reorganisation of the political branch of the South African police. When, after systematic use of these instruments, radical black and white opposition within South Africa was all but contained, at least for a while, or was in disarray, its leadership in gaol or in exile, Vorster turned his attention to what he called 'terrorism'—the infiltration into the republic and South West Africa of armed guerrilla fighters—from 1966 onward. Vorster, the police and the military began to create a new mood of apprehension.[64]

Such a mood of apprehension might be functional to a wide range of policy objectives and ideological revisions within South Africa: Vorster could attempt to forge 'white unity' by drawing attention to the common external threat. Likewise, such controversial policies as the Bantustan policy could be furthered with minimum opposition.[65] That these were motivating factors behind South African policy on Rhodesia and 'terrorism' is a matter of conjecture: yet it is a conjecture that must be seen against the fact that since 1948 white

[61] C. Legum and J. Drysdale (eds.), *Africa Contemporary Record*, 1965–1968, pp. 286–94, 373–4.

[62] Cockram, in a chapter of her book, characteristically headed 'Terrorists —the racehorses of the Apocalypse', quotes a South African Minister as having dismissed British protests as 'sanctimonious'.

[63] Cf. *BBC Summary*, ME/2252/B/4, ME/2254/B/4, ME/2271/B/3, ME/2272/B/4. Also deputy Minister of Police in *Ass. Deb.*, vol. 23, col. 4117–18; 1967, col. 4173; vol. 26, col. 7063; and Prime Minister in *Ass. Deb.*, vol. 26, col. 4579.

[64] Cf. *BBC Summary*, ME/2252/8/4, ME/2271/8/3, ME/2272/8/4; also deputy Minister of Police in *Ass. Deb.*, vol. 23, cols. 4117–18; 1967, col. 4173; vol. 26, col. 7063; and Prime Minister in *Ass. Deb.*, vol. 26, col. 4579.

[65] See above ch. VII.

South African politics has been dominated by the National Party's vision of an apocalypse. By the very nature of such cultural constructs it is, of course, impossible to specify the functions of such a vision uncontroversially.[66]

It was a matter of concern for the South African government that a revolution had been launched against the minority regimes of southern Africa—an armed struggle with the possibilities of complication, including (however remotely) international intervention. However small the scale of fighting within South African-controlled territory, it seemed impossible to rout the guerrillas completely. At the same time, although weakened and disorganised, southern African nationalist organisations, with a few exceptions, had survived exile, showing remarkable resilience (in spite of severe internal divisions). Within South Africa also, the government had failed to put a complete end to radical black and white opposition. The psychological impact of what guerillas symbolised—the irredeemably embattled situation of the *apartheid* regime—probably weighed more heavily upon policy-makers than the actual yardage of mud and blood.[67]

South African policy towards the growing liberation wars in southern Africa was encapsulated in Vorster's statement that South Africa would fight terrorism wherever it occurred if asked to do so.[68] Vorster, so disposed, would not hesitate to disregard or even censure British sentiment on Rhodesia. In marked contrast to Verwoerd, Vorster, referring to mandatory sanctions, spoke in threatening terms about British policy:

Mr Wilson has said on various occasions that he is not seeking a confrontation with South Africa. My reply to that is this: If you do not seek a confrontation, you must not come forward with proposals which, to put it mildly, hold the potential of leading to that.[69]

On the presence of South African police in Rhodesia Vorster was equally dismissive of British susceptibilities. He told the South African parliament:

[66] Cf. C. Geertz, 'Ideology as a cultural system', in Apter (ed.), *Ideology and Discontent.*

[67] A fairly accurate impression of this psychological impact is easily gleaned from speeches in and outside parliament, in laws to combat 'terrorism', and in the amount of police energy and time devoted to 'anti-terrorism', and in military expenditure. See for example, *X-Ray*, September 1970, December 1970, August 1971; Minty, *op. cit.*

[68] *Africa Contemporary Record*, 1968–69, pp. 286–94.

[69] *Ass. Deb.*, vol. 23, col. 4075.

I have been asked by Britain how long the South African police will remain there. My reply was, for as long as it is necessary to safeguard South Africa's interests there.[70]

Vorster added that the reason South African police originally went to fight in Rhodesia was 'to take our own chestnuts out of the fire in that it was PAC and ANC terrorists who were trying to infiltrate there'.[71]

So far from repudiating the implicit South African claim to a right to intervene in 'British' Rhodesia to take its chestnuts out of the fire, the British government continued to seek a negotiated settlement with the Rhodesian government, to which end it continued to rely on the good offices of the South African government. Sir Max Aitken and Lord Goodman, after consultation with Mr Wilson, visited South Africa, according to Wilson, to try to meet Smith, but according to other sources to discuss the Rhodesian question with Vorster also.[72] Again rumours began to circulate in the United Kingdom—suspected to have been inspired at the highest official level[73]—that South Africa would put pressure on Smith to settle with Britain.[74] Expectedly, Vorster sharply repudiated these suggestions during the budget debate on his vote (in April 1969):

. . . the propaganda which is being made in certain circles that the Government, and I in particular, are exerting pressure on the Prime Minister of Rhodesia to negotiate with Britain at all costs, is an infamous lie; it is devoid of all truth. In this connection I have made my standpoint and that of the Government very clear. It is known to Britain what my attitude is . . . I have made it very clear to Britain that I am neither prepared to twist Mr Smith's arm, nor prepared to dictate to him—for the simple reason that if I were to do so, I would be interfering in the domestic affairs of Rhodesia, and that while I do not tolerate anyone interfering in my domestic affairs.[75]

No one had suggested that Vorster wanted Smith to negotiate 'at all costs', but this rhetorical excess on Vorster's part should not be allowed to obscure the fact that what he was saying, in no uncertain terms, was that he was by no means on Britain's side, in sentiment or in practice, on the Rhodesian question.

The South African government had cause to object to mandatory sanctions because they made South African 'neutrality' illegal (and

[70] *Ibid.*   [71] *Ibid.*
[72] H. Wilson, *The Labour Government*, pp. 565–6.
[73] Cf. *Africa Confidential*, 28 October 1968.
[74] *Economist*, 12 October 1968.   [75] *Ass. Deb.*, vol. 26, col. 4580.

the involvement of the UN had to be seen against South African hostility to that organisation). In resorting to mandatory sanctions the UK government was, therefore, in Vorster's eyes seeking a quarrel with his government, and he responded in kind. On the other hand, the apparent weakness of the UK government and its unwillingness to use force probably convinced the South African government that the Smith regime and UDI would triumph. Another, possibly more decisive, factor was the division of the British political elite over the Rhodesian question. Relations had deteriorated between the South African government and the British Labour government (the aggregation implicit in 'Britain' and 'South Africa' is apt to be misleading), but not necessarily with an alternative, Conservative government. A number of Conservative members of Parliament, including such ministerial candidates as Sir Alec Douglas-Home and Mr Selwyn Lloyd, visited South Africa in 1968,[76] and their attitudes to the republic were in sharp contrast to those of the Labour government, as were their views on South Africa's value to the West, and on Rhodesia.[77]

The election of a Conservative government under Edward Heath in Britain in June 1970 marked the beginning of a new and, for South Africa, a more favourable period in Anglo-South African relations. The British Foreign Secretary, Sir Alec Douglas-Home, soon announced that the British government had decided to reopen the question of arms sales to South Africa. After widespread and often acrimonious opposition the government announced its decision to sell only limited categories of arms.[78] On his return from the stormy Commonwealth Prime Ministers' Conference, Heath said that he had told African leaders at Singapore (where the conference was held) that if they feared South Africa might use the arms against them, they should conclude non-aggression pacts with South Africa.[79] Naval co-operation between South Africa and Britain increased, and the new UK government showed itself more willing to co-operate with South Africa than any UK government had done since Macmillan's 'wind of change' speech in Cape Town in 1960.[80]

[76] *Africa Contemporary Record*, 1968–69, pp. 317–19.
[77] Cf. Dennis Healey, former British Defence Minister's speech in Durban in September 1970; *The Times*, 18 September 1970.
[78] Institute of Strategic Studies, *Strategic Survey*, 1970.
[79] BBC Radio 4, interview, 22 January 1971.
[80] *Strategic Survey*, 1970; *Africa Contemporary Record*, 1970–71, pp. A75–A80; C18–C28.

Speculation that South Africa might put pressure on Rhodesia to settle with Britain soon revived, now more credibly than before. Rhodesia's financial problems—principally, a shortage of foreign exchange[81]—inflation, and the beginnings of a recession in South Africa,[82] together with the changed relationship between Britain and the republic gave substance to these reports. If South Africa, in deference to these factors, was willing in 1971 to use its influence or to put pressure on the Rhodesian government, then it might be supposed that it would be expected by the Rhodesians to do the same for them with respect to Britain. At any rate, the UK government did tone down its demands not only by dropping the sixth 'principle' for a settlement but also by accepting a very controversial interpretation, to put it mildly, of the remaining 'five principles', as the terms of the eventual settlement showed.[83] It is, of course, impossible to know in which direction South African pressure, overt (i.e. explicit diplomatic solicitation or threats), or covert (continued support or withdrawal of support for Rhodesian UDI), was most effective. South Africa, it appears, however, did play an important part in the negotiations of 1971;[84] the settlement that was eventually arrived at was acceptable to Vorster, as well as to the British and Rhodesian governments, although it was wholly unacceptable to the political and religious leaders of Africans in Rhodesia.[85]

The single most striking lesson of the Rhodesian imbroglio was the acceptance by both the Labour and the Conservative governments of Britain, albeit not in so many words, of the view expressed by P. Cillié, the editor of *Die Burger*, to the South Africa Club in London in January 1969: 'I suggest not very much can be accomplished in southern Africa without South Africa or against her will and interests.'[86] It is a view which holds—provided that the power concerned 'does not seek a confrontation' with South Africa, but rather looks to South African mediation for the resolution of the problems of racialism and colonialism in southern Africa.

South African economic activity in Rhodesia, apart from extensive interests existing before UDI, was limited mainly to assisting Rhodesian trade, an activity in which both the private and the public sector was involved. This activity being *sub rosa*, very little informa-

[81] *A.R.B.* (*Econ.*), 1971, 1983B.   [82] Cf. *X-Ray*, June 1971.
[83] *The Times* and *Guardian*, 26 November 1971.
[84] *Guardian*, 8 July 1971.
[85] Cf. *Guardian*, 30 November 1971; *Observer*, 28 November 1971.
[86] South Africa House, London, *Report from South Africa*, January 1969.

tion exists about the extent of financial assistance, import credits or other assistance which the State might have given; even the trade figures that exist are highly inferential.[87] No attempt will be made here to analyse the assistance given in this connection. A few general remarks should, however, be made about the difference between trade with Rhodesia and trade with the Portuguese territories, namely, that because of the higher level of industrialisation in Rhodesia,[88] the South Africans and the Rhodesians were competitors; trade-restrictive tendencies to protect developing secondary industries were manifest,[89] and although there were deliberate attempts at trade creation in the run-up to UDI,[90] protectionist tendencies in South Africa soon became evident again[91]—and this in spite of the fact that in 1964 (the last year for which official Rhodesian figures are available) South Africa had been in its trade with Rhodesia, as in its trade with all of Africa south of the equator, a net exporter by a substantial margin.[92]

Further to these contradictions must also be noted the encroach-

[87] *A.R.B. (Econ.)*, 1968, 1222A: 1970, 1787; see also 1966, 831A, and 1968, 934B.

[88] Manufacturing accounted for 18 per cent of gross domestic product, on average, in 1964–68; Rhodesia, *National Accounts and Balance of Payments*, various years, cited in R. B. Sutcliffe unpublished paper 'Stagnation and inequality in Rhodesia, 1946–68', read to the Royal Institute of International Affairs in December 1970.

[89] Economic protectionism is deeply rooted in the South African political tradition, since it has historically been one of the principal supports of the 'civilised labour policy' or job reservation—as an inducement to employers to adhere to the costly policy of reserving skilled jobs as far as possible for whites. There has always been, therefore, more than the familiar infant industry argument—namely a synthetically high cost structure caused by a labour policy which makes *apartheid* possible and which is itself possible because of the racial bifurcation of the South African working class. Cf. M. Kooy and H. M. Robertson, 'The South African Board of Trade and Industries; the South African customs tariff and the development of South African industries', in *South African Journal of Economics*, 1966, pp. 205–33.

[90] A new trade agreement was conduced in November 1965. See Minister of Economic Affairs, in *Ass. Deb.*, vol. 13, cols. 7655 ff. The Minister concluded: 'The new agreement represents an important step in the commercial relations between South Africa and Rhodesia. It will, I feel sure, serve to contribute not only towards the growth of two-way trade between them but also towards a strengthening of their relations in other fields of common interest' (9 June 1965); col. 7657).

[91] See R. B. Sutcliffe, 'The political economy of Rhodesian sanctions', in *Journal of Commonwealth Political Studies*, 1969, especially pp. 124–5.

[92] South African exports to Rhodesia in 1964 amounted to £26,589,441, while imports for the same year were £8,907,155. See *A.R.B. (Econ.)*, 1965, 328B.

ment of South African producers on central African markets, notably
in Zambia, that were previously dominated by Rhodesia.[93] The
economic retardation which sanctions inevitably caused in Rhodesia
probably worked to underline the South African advantage, so much
so that it might persist even after sanctions. It might, therefore, be
expected that as soon as Rhodesia were rehabilitated competition
would be joined between it and South Africa for markets and
economic influence generally in southern Africa. This may have
influenced the readiness of statal corporations in South Africa to
invest in Rhodesia over and above the short-term disincentives of
sanctions, the fewer lucrative investment opportunities (in comparison with Mozambique and Angola) and the fact that South
Africa was probably already doing a lot financially for Rhodesia in
connection with its foreign trade. For apart from a loan of not more
than £2·5 million to enable the Rhodesians to construct a new rail
link with Mozambique, there was no official investment or lending
programme on the scale of aid to the Portuguese. In 1970 an irrigation dam off the Limpopo river was being considered by the two
governments but there were no definite undertakings.[94] In discussing
the railway loan in parliament in 1965 the South African Minister
of Finance explained:

It is exclusively a gesture of goodwill but, having a choice as to the various
projects for which this loan is being made, we accepted those projects
which we thought were also of indirect importance to the exporters of
South Africa. It is, however, first and foremost a gesture of goodwill to a
neighbouring State which, as we know, is finding it difficult to get assistance
in other ways.[95]

The notion that South Africa might take the initiative in a railway
construction project to link Rhodesia with the Namibian port of
Walvis Bay, although it was strongly supported by some of the
government supporters in 1969 on 'economic, international, political
and strategic' grounds, did not gain much official support. Ben
Schoeman, the Minister of Transport, considered, as he had done for
twenty years or more, that the initiative should come from Rhodesia
and not from South Africa.[96] He estimated that the rail link would
cover a distance of about 600 miles and would cost £50 million.

[93] See the section Zambia in chapter x below.
[94] *A.R.B.* (*Econ.*), 1970, 1698A.
[95] *Ass. Deb.*, vol. 13, col. 2264; see also *A.R.B.* (*Econ.*), 1965, 3554A.
[96] *A.R.B.* (*Econ.*), 1969, 1463A.

Schoeman had, however, favoured the construction of another direct rail link from Rhodesia to South Africa—from Rutenga to Beit Bridge,[97] at any rate, to the extent of having intimated that South Africa would be prepared to adjust tariffs to make the project economic.

It would appear from this broad scan of economic co-operation between Rhodesia and South Africa during the period of sanctions that a different pattern might be expected to emerge in this conjunction, different from that emerging in the relationship between South Africa and the underdeveloped, mineral-rich (including oil) Portuguese colonies. In terms of the relationship of dominance and subordination, and the regional political roles which the Rhodesian and South African governments might develop and assume after sanctions, their economic collaboration during the sanctions period was far less conclusive than the more asymmetrical collaboration between the republic and the Portuguese colonies.

Although South Africa was joined to Rhodesia and Portugal by an overriding common interest in the continuation of white domination in their own territories, there were nevertheless important disputes between them, often involving important conflicts of interest. It will illustrate the underlying instability of the unequal alliance if some of the more important disagreements are considered.

As guerrilla activity was intensified in Tete, the area of Mozambique bordering on the north-eastern part of Rhodesia, the Smith government openly expressed concern about what it considered to be the inadequate response of the Portuguese forces. In October 1972 Smith visited Lisbon and there discussed the situation with the Portuguese Prime Minister, who reassured him. Portuguese indignation at the Rhodesian Premier's conduct was evident from a statement made in a radio broadcast by Caetano, who, after claiming that they maintained military supremacy, noted:

But some of our neighbours without experience do not conceal their fears and in this way play the game of the enemy. They have been told more than once that there is no reason for their great apprehension.[98]

As if to confirm Rhodesian apprehensions, ZANU (Zimbabwe Africa National Union) guerrillas did subsequently infiltrate through

[97] *Ibid.*, 1967, 682A.
[98] *K.C.A.*, 25755, 1973.

Mozambique, evidently with the help of Frelimo, making spectacular raids in Rhodesia.

South Africa did not take any public part in this dispute, although it is evident that the government took a serious view of the Mozambique situation, which the Minister of Defence and the commandant general of the defence forces discussed with their Rhodesian counterparts.

There were also conflicts over Portuguese guerilla operations between Portugal and Malawi—the only black State north of the Zambesi willing to collaborate with the white minority regimes.[99] While Malawians resented Portuguese intrusions into their territories, many Portuguese settlers for their part suspected Malawi of harbouring 'terrorists'.[100] In this dispute, too, the South African government remained discreet, although later providing Malawi with weapons to meet the 'terrorist' threats.

Finally, there was one major dispute which was to show very clearly that each power will look to its own interests first. That was the unilateral decision by Rhodesia to close its border with Zambia. The Portuguese were indignant because it meant that their railway line to the port of Beira, which Zambia used, would not only lose revenue but would now be open to bombing from freedom fighters who had previously, on Zambian insistence, scrupulously avoided interference with it. The Portuguese expressed to the Rhodesians their 'profound concern', warning them against further escalation of the conflict. South Africa, for its part, declared itself against interference in the domestic affairs of other States, unwilling either to initiate or reciprocate boycotts, and unconditionally opposed to terrorism, adding: 'Where and when *we are directly threatened* we shall at all times take steps to protect the life and property of our people and our territorial integrity'[101] [italics added].

Smith had consulted neither Caetano nor Vorster over the closure of the border. He 'explained' subsequently that prior consultation would have been a 'diplomatic blunder' on his part and would have caused 'acute embarrassment' to Rhodesia's neighbours. Whatever may have been meant by that—and the meaning is certainly not lucid—it is not difficult to see why he would not have consulted

[99] See chapter XI below.

[100] This rumour was reported in the South African and Rhodesian press and subsequently exploited by opponents of Vorster's outward policy. See *Die Afrikaner,* 4 June 1971.

[101] *K.C.A.*, 25797.

South Africa and Portugal. They would have disagreed—South Africa because of its trade with Zambia (which had expanded as a result of sanctions against Rhodesia), and Portugal for the reasons already outlined. Thus Smith served notice not only on Kaunda but also on South Africa and Portugal that if these powers did not show themselves sufficiently responsive to the interests of Rhodesia his government could at least create difficulties for all and sundry. It was a futile gesture, for while Zambia survived it and Kaunda gained enormous encouragement for his policy of reducing Zambia's links with the south, Rhodesia continued to be abjectly dependent, in counter-insurgency as in so many other fields, on the support of South Africa and Portugal.

With time the Rhodesian regime also became more burdensome to South Africa, while its prestige gradually diminished among some members of the white elite. Following the Pearce Commission's visit to Rhodesia and the repudiation of the settlement proposals by the majority of Africans there was certainly considerable room for doubt whether the Smith government had its domestic situation under control. The fact that it was so dependent on South Africa, while it made Rhodesia dependable as an ally, nevertheless contributed to diminishing its prestige. That being so, it became more evident, as in the case of the blockade, that South Africa had no desire to be politically identified with Rhodesia. Nevertheless, South Africa's extensive involvement in the Rhodesian anti-guerrilla campaign had the effect of drawing the republic closer to that colony. Indeed, statements by senior South African para-military police personnel on the guerrilla threat to Rhodesia were more frequent than statements by their political chiefs, and in general these police statements tended to see the dangers to Rhodesia and South Africa as indivisible (in a way they did not seem to do in relation to Portugal). In addition, at lower levels of the forces there was also an impetuous militancy which did lead to border incidents with such neighbouring black States as Botswana and Zambia which the politicians in Pretoria might not have authorised.[102] Thus there was a distinct

[102] Re. Botswana interview with Vice-president and Minister of Finance, the Rt Hon. Dr Quet Masire. An incident which it would be hard to attribute to government was reported in the *Zambia Police Annual Report for the Year 1971*, p. 4: 'On the 22nd February 1971 thirteen South African soldiers entered Zambia at Katima Mulilo in two army vehicles. They drove to the Zambian Immigration Office at Katima Mulilo, where they shouted, "One Zambia, one fokof", and thereafter they returned over the border.'

likelihood that, whatever South African politicians might feel was politically or even economically prudent, they would be drawn ever more deeply into the Rhodesian war with guerrillas. The same was true in relation to Portugal. If, however, South Africa's involvement would become, more than before, a matter of military necessity, or a response to a military interest group, South Africa's policy might be expected increasingly to reflect the needs of power. That might not always be consistent with its support for the present policies and governments in those areas. In the foreseeable future, however, there were no credible alternative candidates for South African support.

While South Africa became inextricably involved in the defence of white dominance in Rhodesia and in Portugal's colonies, each power within that trigon continued to look to its own very distinctive needs. Often those needs conflicted, contributing to the basic instability of the alliance, which in turn reflected the sharp contrasts among the allies. Portugal had the option of withdrawal—the prerogative of imperial powers; Rhodesia was abjectly weak and on its own probably not viable; South Africa, as yet not subject to guerrilla warfare on a major scale within the territories it controlled, could hold its own for a very long while—if Rhodesia and Portugal did so too. This was a further reason why it was that while South Africa might be eager to encourage Portugal to remain in Africa, in supporting *Rhodesia* it would, more and more, do so on its own terms.

'One Zambia, one nation' is the slogan of the black republic, and 'fokof' is a South African corruption of a well known English obscenity.

x Malawi and Zambia

Zambia and Malawi, the former British territories of Northern Rhodesia and Nyasaland, lie midway between two worlds—white-dominated southern Africa and the rest of the continent. While they share boundaries with Rhodesia and Portuguese-controlled territories, and are thus closer to the area of racial conflict than other African States north of the Zambesi, they do nonetheless have access to the rest of the continent independently of the white regimes through Tanzania and Zaire. It is true, however, that the railway link between Zambia and the Atlantic which runs through Zaire is the Portuguese-controlled Benguela Railway, which also traverses the Portuguese colony of Angola. Previous colonial policies tied the economies of both Zambia and Malawi to the south, and this would create severe difficulties for these States should they seek to identify themselves with the continental policy of opposing and isolating the white minority regimes. In the event the policies of Zambia and Malawi diverged, the one favouring militant opposition to South Africa and the other increasing its political and economic co-operation with the white-ruled countries.

Because of their comparable geographical situation and their common colonial background Malawi and Zambia offer interesting opportunities for comparative foreign policy study, and it is indeed impossible to analyse the relations of either with South Africa without making some mental comparisons. Tempting though it would be to compare at length the policies of these governments, the present chapter avoids such a comparative analysis because its object is to analyse South African policies rather than the policies of these States towards South Africa. A detailed comparison of Zambian and Malawian policies would require more detailed discussion of the politics of those countries than can pertinently and economically be accommodated in the present study.

'Mental' or informal comparisons are, however, unavoidable, and we shall have occasion to draw attention to some of the contrasts. The main comparative analytical point that will be seen to follow from the discussion in this chapter is that the view that the policies of Banda and Kaunda can be stated in terms of 'realism' and 'idealism' is misleading. Neither policy is determined by geographical or economic realities in any automatic sense;[1] rather, geography and economics create the problems which foreign policy, as a more or less reasoned response, seeks to overcome. Geographical and economic circumstances are problematic only in so far as they make difficult the attainment of some consciously selected political objective. Similarly, it should emerge that ideas or ideology and *Realpolitik* are deeply woven into the policies of both governments. It is not that the one is pragmatic and the other ideological; on the contrary, the policy differences are largely attributable to their opposed ideological positions on southern African liberation.

Malawi

Soon after Malawi gained its independence at the beginning of 1964, Dr Hastings Banda, then Prime Minister, outlined to the conference of heads of state and government of the OAU held in Cairo in July 1964 the policy he would pursue towards Portugal, Rhodesia and South Africa. It would be a conservative policy. Because Malawi was economically linked to the white-ruled States and colonies of southern Africa as a result of geography and previous colonial policies, it could not participate in a boycott against those regimes. Banda considered, therefore, that it would be hypocritical for him to support an OAU resolution favouring an African economic and diplomatic boycott of those territories. Although he affirmed his opposition to racialism and colonialism in Africa, he did not indicate how Malawi hoped to contribute to the pan-African struggle against those forces, nor did he intimate that his government might seek to strengthen its position in such a way that it could in time also participate in the African campaign against the minority regimes.[2]

Within weeks of Banda's return from Cairo there was a Cabinet

---

[1] On the weaknesses of geographical determinist approaches, see M. and H. Sprout, 'Man–milieu relationship hypothesis', in *The Context of International Politics*, 1956, and 'Environmental factors in the study of international relations', in *Journal of Conflict Resolution*, 1957.

[2] See J. G. Pike, *Malawi: a Political and Economic History*, 1968, p. 164; H. B. M. Chipembere, 'Malawi's growing links with South Africa—a necessity or a virtue?' in *Africa Today*, 1971.

crisis in which the Prime Minister's southern Africa policy, as well as his overall outlook on international relations,[3] came under severe attack. Six Cabinet Ministers—Chiume, Chirwa, Bwanausi, Chokani, Chisiza and Chipembere (a seventh, Mrs Rose Chibambo, was also involved as an 'accomplice')—took Banda to task on a variety of domestic and external policy matters, including, besides his southern Africa policy, his decision to impose charges for health services and to accept a slower rate of Africanisation of the civil service. This 'left'–'right' polarisation in the Cabinet, with Banda a solitary figure on the right, was exacerbated by the feeling of his colleagues that he was behaving in an arbitrary and dictatorial fashion.[4] Banda's autocratic tendencies were all the more serious as it appeared that he was constructing a personal power base in opposition to the collective power base of the Malawi Congress Party and of the government.[5] To the growing disaffection of his erstwhile political benefactors[6] Banda's southern policy was a catalyst which gave it a wider significance for all concerned.

Banda had been moving, for some time, to a more and more conservative position on foreign policy, to a narrow definition of Malawian responsibilities towards the unliberated territories and South Africa, thus tending to maintain the colonial order largely intact not only within the country but also externally, in Malawi's relations with the southern regimes. Chipembere has traced the earliest signs of this move to 1962, when Banda decided to pay an official visit to Salazar in Lisbon.[7] In 1963, according to Chipembere, Banda unaccountably decided to invite to Malawi Sir Roy Welensky and the leader of the Rhodesian Dominion Party.[8] But the southward movement of Banda's policy was evidently clinched when he failed, against the sentiments of his Ministers, to agree with the presidents

---

[3] Pike, *op. cit.*, chapter 5; Chipembere, *art. cit.*; Ministry of Information, 'Address to the National Assembly by the Prime Minister, Ngwazi, Dr Kamuzu Banda, 8 September 1964'.

[4] See Pike, *op. cit.*, chapter 5; Dr Banda himself said he returned to find 'disunity, disloyalty, indiscipline and disobedience' on the part of his Ministers. See 'Address to the National Assembly, 8 September 1964'.

[5] See A. Ross, 'White Africa's black ally', in *New Left Review,* 1967.

[6] It was the ex-Ministers, and particularly Chipembere, who had urged Banda to return from Ghana to Malawi to lead the nationalist movement, this conceding to him the leadership of an organisation he had, until his return in 1958, had no part in building up.

[7] Chipembere, *art. cit.*; 'Address to the National Assembly, 8 September 1964'.

[8] Cf. Chipembere, *art. cit.*, especially, p. 23.

of Zambia and Tanzania on the details of an alternative outlet through Tanganyika to the sea for Zambian and Malawian merchandise.[9]

The Cabinet crisis was followed by the departure into exile in Zambia and Tanzania of four of the ex-Ministers, while one, Chipembere, took to the hills in defiance of restriction orders placed upon him by the President, there to organise and launch armed resistance to Banda.[10] In February some of his supporters attacked Fort Johnston police station, and there followed engagements between them and the police in the southern part of Malawi. Similar troubles occurred in the Central and Northern Regions, believed to be master-minded by the exiled Ministers. Fighting continued into the following year, by which time the police claimed to have broken the back of the resistance. In 1968 the police were still active in the Fort Johnston area, disposing of the 'remnants' of Chipembere's army.[11] In various parts of the country, especially in 1964–65, there were outbreaks of faction fighting.

This period of grave crisis, 1964–65, was also a period of industrial unrest, in itself a measure of the political instability in the country. In 1964 the largest number of man-days lost owing to industrial disputes since 1960 (the crisis year of colonial Nyasaland) was recorded. Then there were sixty-four disputes and 24,096 man-days were lost; in 1965, although there were only twenty-eight disputes, as many as 20,319 man-days were lost. By contrast, in 1966 only 3,221 days were lost; in 1967, 4,862.[12] Whatever the relationship between industrial unrest and the political crisis in causal terms, one thing was clear: for Banda this was a time of distress and perplexity.

The Banda administration responded to internal insecurity not by revising its policies to conciliate the disaffected elements, mainly the educated Malawians, but by resolute intensification of its collaboration with the white regime. The South African government seized the opportunity created by the departure of the opponents of collaboration by agreeing to finance through its Industrial Develop-

[9] Chipembere writes that the disagreement arose when Banda insisted, against the economic judgement of Nyerere and Kaunda, that the projected TanZam railway should pass through central and northern Malawi. Banda himself has not said anything about the TanZam railway in public.

[10] Pike, *op. cit.*, pp. 154–70; Chipembere was also acting in defiance of a chronic diabetic condition, according to Pike, *op. cit.*, p. 137.

[11] See Malawi Government, *Annual Report of the Malawi Police Force for the Year Ended 31 December*, various issues 1964–69, 1965–70.

[12] Malawi Government, *Ministry of Labour Report, 1963–67*, 1969.

ment Corporation a £3 million project to build a sugar mill at Chikwawa, near Zomba. The condition of this 'aid' (loan) was that 60 per cent of all materials used for the construction of the mill should be South African.[13] Meanwhile at the UN the Malawi government, while still affirming opposition to racialism and colonialism in Africa, expressed itself against violence 'unless in the long run there should prove to be no other alternative'. This was a novelty,

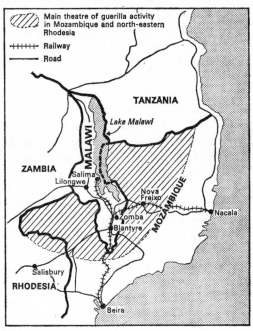

FIG. 3   *Malawi's frontiers*

for in Cairo Banda had stated only that his country could not participate in the OAU programme; he had not opposed it. Banda wanted it to be known that he was opposed to 'interference in the domestic affairs of other countries' and was equally opposed to the tendency of the specialised bodies of the UN to discuss political matters.[14] In 1966 the Malawi government reacted to the verdict of the International Court of Justice in the South West Africa cases.

[13] *A.R.B. (Econ.)*, 1965, vol. 3, No. 2.
[14] Ministry of Information, 'Prime Minister's Address to the General Assembly of the United Nations, read by Mr A. M. Nyasulu, 27 September 1965'.

It expressed regret that the matter had not been resolved, but hoped that litigation would continue and the matter be kept out of the political arena. It was also opposed to the UN resolution revoking the South African mandate on the grounds that it could not be implemented.[15]

By all these means Banda moved to an international position which the South African government could approve. The southward movement of his policy, uninhibited now that the Cabinet had been cleared of militants, was complemented by right-wing movement on other, remoter international issues. Banda openly opposed the recognition by the UN of communist China and was opposed also to the recognition of the German Democratic Republic.[16] Within Africa, the fact that the dissident Ministers had fled to Zambia and Tanzania, which were attempting to pursue policies towards the minority regimes in particular and to the communist countries which were opposed to those of Banda, led to a deterioration of the Malawian government's relations with other African States. Banda believed that the governments of Zambia and Tanzania were giving active support to the insurgency movement against him, and severe recriminations followed.[17] Banda quarrelled with the United Arab Republic also because an Egyptian diplomatist in Malawi was believed to be abetting the campaign of the ex-Ministers. The quarrel with Egypt evinced in Banda a rare hatred of Arabs in general, but in particular those in Africa, whom he believed to have no better claim to being African than the white settlers and their regimes.[18] It later became a reason for Banda's refusal to participate in the OAU that African leaders at the OAU meetings toasted each other along with Arab 'murderers'.[19] Further difficulties arose between

[15] Ministry of Information, 'Malawi and the United Nations: an address to the 21st Session of the General Assembly, 1956, delivered by the Hon. Alec Nyasulu on behalf of the President of Malawi, Ngwazi, Dr H. Kamuzu Banda', 1966.

[16] See Ministry of Information, 'Prime Minister's address to the General Assembly . . . 27 September 1965'.

[17] See, for example, 'The President speaks: Malawi's relations with Tanzania and trade with South Africa, 8 February 1967', Ministry of Information; Malawi *Hansard*, 12 December 1967, p. 124, 4 October 1967; also *Hansard*, 1965, p. 569.

[18] Ministry of Information 'Opening address to 1968 annual convention of the Malawi People's Congress, 16 September 1968'; 'Interview between His Excellency the President, Ngwazi Dr Kamuzu Banda and Dr Hans Germani, Correspondent of *Die Welt*', 16 March 1968.

[19] Ministry of Information, 'Opening address . . . 1960'.

Banda and the neighbouring government of Tanzania when territorial claims were made by Tanzania in 1967 and even bigger ones by Malawi in 1968. Whereas Nyerere laid claim to parts of Lake Malawi, Banda laid claim not only to territory claimed by Tanzania but also to a substantial part of Zambia. Insults were exchanged between the governments of Malawi and Zambia, the latter asserting that Banda was counting on South African and Portuguese support in staking these claims.[20] Enmity developed also between Banda and a number of southern African liberation movements, including the ANC of South Africa.

These quarrels with neighbours and with revolutionary organisations confirmed Banda's view that the security of his regime lay in closer co-operation with the 'White South'. On 11 March 1967 a ministerial mission left Malawi for South Africa to conclude a new trade agreement.[21] In September it was announced that Malawi and South Africa had agreed to exchange diplomatic representatives.

South African economic power and its para-statal organisations once more came to the support of the Foreign Ministry in sealing the developing friendship with Malawi by encouraging a project close to the dictator's heart. Banda had appointed a commission constituted of Britons to investigate among other things the feasibility of his scheme of moving the capital of Malawi from Zomba to Lilongwe in Central Region and of forging a new rail link to Mozambique that would give Malawi access to the port of Nacala as well as Beira. The commission had rejected (in 1965) both projects on grounds of economy.[22] With the increasing co-operation between Banda and South Africa, Banda decided to appoint another commission to investigate his project, this time led by Dr Rautenbach, director of the Resources and Planning Advisory Council of South Africa. Dr Rautenbach reported favourably and, in passing, outlined the principles which, in the South African view, should have guided the earlier commission (which Banda believed had taken too narrow and short-sighted a view of economic development). Rautenbach wrote:

[20] Cf. *Africa Confidential*, 11 October 1968; Ministry of Information, 'Opening Address ... 1968'. Although there were bitter recriminations, attempts were from time to time made to patch up relations through correspondence, discontinued in 1969, with the Tanzanians and through ministerial contacts with Zambia and Malawi. See chapter ix, n. 84.

[21] Malawi *Hansard*, 1967, pp. 294–360.

[22] Dr Banda in parliament, 29 January 1968; *Hansard*, pp. 229 ff.

development as such, praiseworthy as it might be, is *not* a goal in itself, but is the *result* of the pursuance of certain definite goals. Due to the absence of specific and clearly defined goals [presumably at the time of the earlier commission], we felt that most of the project reports could and have not purposefully been evaluated.[23]

Rautenbach's team indicated that (rather than tell governments what projects to implement or reject on grounds of economy) in South Africa planners subserved 'our national aims and policy as laid down by our government'. Without stating the 'definite goals' which 'development' had to subserve in Malawi, Rautenbach based his recommendation not on the 'definite goals' but, with rare vagueness and circularity, upon the need for 'balanced development of the three regions of Malawi, around certain focal points [which] was, for socio-political–economic reasons, one of the goals of the Government of Malawi'.[24]

A loan of R8 million (about £4 million) was provided by the South African government to the Malawi government for the first stage of this project.[25] More aid was given to Malawi in connection with the Nacala rail project, but this time through the Industrial Development Corporation. The corporation gave a series of export credits to pay for Malawian imports from South Africa, amounting to R10,340,336. This indirect loan was repayable after fifteen years at an interest rate of 6 per cent per annum. A condition of the loan was that it should benefit South African exporters, for as the Minister of Economic Affairs (of South Africa) explained, the Industrial Development Corporation's object was to enable a South African consortium (Roberts Construction and Dorman Long) to secure contracts for R10,942,154 the content of which was mainly South African, including materials and labour.[26] There followed technical assistance from South Africa in a wide range of areas, including broadcasting, economic planning, police training and tourism. In planning and in information services several Afrikaners were appointed to very senior positions in Malawi.[27] A certain

[23] Quoted at length by Banda in *Hansard*, 1968, pp. 229 ff. I have been unable to obtain a copy of the Rautenbach report and have therefore relied on Dr Banda's account.

[24] *Hansard*, 1968, pp. 229 ff.

[25] Malawi News Agency, *Daily Bulletin*, 26 June 1968; *Ass. Deb.*, vol. 28, col. 359.   [26] *Ass. Deb.*, vol. 28, col. 360.

[27] In 1969 Dr Banda appointed as Director of Information David van der Spuy, who had served on South African legations in London and New York: see *Africa Confidential*, April 1969.

amount of private investment by South African companies also took place.[28] Private groups of white South Africans, ranging from students of the Afrikaans university of Stellenbosch to the Friesland Cattle Breeders of South Africa, made gestures of goodwill and declared their willingness to aid the Malawi government.[29] Indeed, the Africa policy began to acquire in 1967–68 the character of a crusade, or a popular movement, reminiscent of some historic periods in the policies of other major powers—the Cold War policies of the US, for example; indeed, barring the conspicuous absence of any involvement of the white working class in the ranks of its private supporters, the outward-looking policy, based upon a distinctive power advantage and distinguishable material needs, was also constituted of those very missionary intentions—to 'convert', to 'civilise' and to 'help'—which once characterised the new imperialism.[30]

As between governments, co-operation took its most decisive form in the attacks, Banda now made on the OAU policy he had earlier suggested he was being deterred from supporting only by the 'realities' of geography and economic history. Dr Banda (1968–69) abused the opponents of co-operation and explained that, far from being a concession to weakness, his policy was nothing less than an elaborate moral essay. By co-operating with South Africa he hoped to convert white South Africans to the obvious view that *apartheid* was wrong; by inviting them to Malawi he would enable them to see that not all Africans were uncivilised (presumably there were not enough 'civilised' Africans among the 14 million in South Africa.)[31] Banda became the foremost advocate of 'dialogue' with South Africa as the most practical and most moral weapon against *apartheid*. He was also one of a few African heads of state who publicly supported the British policy of selling arms to South Africa.[32]

[28] Cf. Molteno, *South Africa and Africa*, *passim*; Rhoodie, *The Third Africa*, *passim*.

[29] See *Daily Bulletin*, various issues, especially 24 June 1968, 23 August 1968; *Today's News*, especially 4 December 1968. See also Cockram, *Vorster's Foreign Policy*, and Rhoodie, *op. cit.*

[30] Cf. Landes, 'Some thoughts on the nature of economic imperialism', also J. A. Schumpeter, 'Imperialism and capitalism', in P. M. Sweezy (ed.), *Imperialism and Social Classes*, 1951.

[31] *Daily Bulletin*, 29 August 1968, upon the occasion of the visit of South African Foreign Minister, Dr Muller, to Malawi.

[32] *Africa Contemporary Record*, 1970–71, pp. 8138–49.

On Rhodesia, South African and Malawian policies had converged from the start.[33] During the sanctions period Malawi became
the 'country of origin' for a number of Rhodesian exports,[34] and in
1969 South African exporters of maize imported Rhodesian maize
via Malawi. Malawi, like South Africa, though not, of course, to the
same extent, increased its exports of those commodities which
Rhodesia used to export.[35] Indeed, the period was one of relative
prosperity for Malawi.[36]

The strains of sanctions, curiously enough, led to an amelioration
of Zambian–Malawi relations, since, increasingly after 1968, Zambia
had to import maize from 'Malawi'. When, however, Zambia's
relations with South Africa reached their lowest point over the arms
issue,[37] and when the Portuguese were imposing sanctions on Zambia
at the beginning of 1971,[38] Zambia experienced an acute shortage of
maize, and the 'Malawi' sources proved inadequate. Zambia had
to import directly from Rhodesia, and admit publicly that it was
doing so; in addition it was seen to have deprived its people of their
staple food for some months because of the sanctions policy, and to

[33] Ministry of Information, 'Malawi and the UN . . .'.
[34] Personal communication from several sources; see, however, n. 35.
[35] Although officially Zambia was supposed to be obtaining maize from
South Africa and Malawi, rather than from Rhodesia, at this time, in fact
in 1969 South Africa itself suffered a maize shortage (*A.R.B.* (*Econ.*), 1969,
passim) and the Malawi maize crop for 1970 also failed (see *Monthly Bulletin of Key Economic Indicators* (Malawi), December 1970). The commentary on the indicators added that in 1970 Malawian imports of maize from
Rhodesia increased markedly, 'largely due to the purchase of maize, which
was actually procured by South African suppliers in Rhodesia'. At the time
of the Portuguese blockade of Zambia (see below), when there was a severe
maize shortage in Zambia, also due to a crop failure, and when Zambia was
persistently rumoured, in spite of official denials, to be secretly procuring
maize from Rhodesia, Zambia quickly concluded a trade agreement with
Malawi (*A.R.B.* (*Econ.*), 9171, 2037AC) which would enable it to buy more
easily a range of goods, including maize, from Malawi. However, Zambia had
to admit on 10 July 1971 that it was importing maize from Rhodesia, provoking the comment from the *Rhodesia Herald*: 'It is a measure of Zambia's
desperation and of the cost of under-the-counter deals that President Kaunda
has consented to negotiate this purchase openly.'
[36] *A.R.B.* (*Econ.*), 1971, 2067A. Had relations between Malawi and
Zambia been as bad as rather sharp-tongued speeches suggested, the Zambian
government might have been forced to 'lose face' earlier and perhaps not
only over maize. On the other hand, the Zambian government was faced with
these humiliations as a result of an attempt to *reduce* dependence upon, and
collaboration with, the white minority regimes.
[37] See *Monthly Bulletin of Key Economic Indicators*, December 1970.
[38] See section on Zambia, below.

have pursued a policy it could not sustain.[39] It was a vivid illustration of what South Africa, in concert with the white minority regimes and Malawi, could achieve in that part of Africa.

Within Malawi the increasing co-operation between Banda and the southern regimes was not without strains, some trivial but worth mentioning, others more serious. In the former category was the resentment apparently felt in Malawi that some expatriate companies preferred to employ South African women as clerical assistants in preference to Malawi women. Banda thought the practice should stop.[40] As far as South African women living in Malawi were concerned, they were welcome there, he said on a subsequent occasion, and provided that they were of good character and were really married to Malawians, they could register as citizens. Banda regaled his parliament with the remark 'You see, just now Malawi is very popular in South Africa, and every woman wants to pretend to marry a Malawian in order to come here.'[41] He was referring to Xhosa, Zulu and Sotho women, of whom he said there were 'many, many'. In fact at the 1966 census South Africans, mainly wives, were only 3 per cent of all foreign Africans in Malawi, a mere 9,000 in a population of 4 million.[42] The significance of Banda's remarks lay not so much in the attitude of condescension they showed as in the underlying fear of competition from South Africans among the semi-literate classes in Malawi. These apprehensions, expressed as early as 1966, would certainly militate against any chance of black South Africans benefiting from the success of the outward-looking policy in terms of work opportunities or the possibility of settling in Malawi.

Three years later unease about the South African connection manifested itself in a more ominous fashion. In 1968–70 there was a series of ritual axe murders, and in September 1969 political rioting in Mlanje. A series of confusing accounts of these episodes was given by Banda, who restricted reporting. Believing that the events were politically inspired, he expelled a Minister and some members of parliament from the Malawi Congress Party. The violence had a macabre aspect: a widespread belief among Malawians

[39] *A.R.B.* (*Econ.*), 1971, 2037AC, 2066C, 2067A.
[40] *Hansard,* 1956, p. 414.
[41] *Ibid.*, p. 583.
[42] There were then 520 non-Africans born in South Africa; see *Malawi Population Census*, Final Report, 1969, pp. vii–viii.

that the murders had been inspired by the government, which needed the blood to give to the South Africans in exchange for their aid. The Malawi police reported that the rumours 'produced particularly serious repercussions in the Palombe area of Mlanje and to a lesser extent in the contiguous district of Chiradzulu' in 1969.[43] In the minds of simple folk who were unable to understand the tortuous 'realities' of foreign policy, but who derived their image of white South Africans from migrant contract mine labourers, the friendship between their leader and the white South African government must have seemed a most unnatural thing, to be expiated with blood. Anthropologists might well conclude that the principles of 'legitimate exchange' had been breached.

Collaboration with the Portuguese also had its difficulties. Because of its contiguity with Mozambique, Malawi was early involved in the Portuguese colonial war there. In 1965 some 3,000 Mozambique refugees landed on Likoma Island in Lake Malawi; in 1966 about 20,000 Mozambicans sought refuge in the Southern Region, while 'Frelimo Freedom Fighters from PEA [Portuguese East Africa, i.e. Mozambique] . . . also on occasions fled into Malawi territory . . . [becoming] at times an embarrassment to Government'.[44] Frelimo were not the only problem, however, because the Portuguese themselves often made armed incursions into Malawi. These incursions became increasingly more serious, and it was officially recorded in 1968:

In a number of border areas, particularly in the Fort Johnston and Dedza areas, armed incursions occurred on a number of occasions by Portuguese military forces whilst on follow-up operations against insurgent groups of Frelimo. These follow-up operations by the Portuguese armed forces have brought repercussions upon the Malawians living in those areas adjacent to the border and a number of incidents, some involving the shooting of Malawians, have occurred.[45]

In 1971 there were further reports in the press of harrassment of Malawian villages by the Portuguese.

The long-term threat to Malawian security lay in Malawi being drawn into the Portuguese war, apparently with no choice but to

[43] *Annual Report of the Malawi Police Force*, 1969, p. 3. Rumours also circulated that Banda was selling able-bodied men to South Africa and that he disliked tribal groups such as the Ayao and the Alomwe: *Africa Contemporary Record*, pp. 813 ff.

[44] *Malawi Police Report*, 1965 and 1966, para. 16.

[45] *Ibid.*, 1969, p. 4.

accept the Portuguese 'right of hot pursuit'. As Malawians in the border areas are usually related to people across the frontier, the difficulty of mobilising the Malawians to assist a pro-Portuguese policy while their kin flee Portuguese protection must be enormous. Were the Malawian government to collaborate more actively in suppressing the Portuguese's enemy, Frelimo, then the conflict could spread deep into Malawi itself, threatening the already precarious internal situation in that country. Bad relations with neighbouring African States would add to the government's difficulties, making it all the more important for Banda to go on co-operating with South Africa.[46] Thus South African policy towards Malawi grew by its successes and even by the difficulties those successes created for Malawi: far from Banda's policy increasing Malawi's security, it created new security problems.[47]

Banda's relations with the Portuguese were not, however, without strains. He himself laid claim to some Mozambican territory and said he was opposed to Portuguese colonialism, the difference between him and other African leaders being thus only over methods of ending colonialism. Banda stated his view particularly lucidly when he related to his parliament his encounters during his visits to Mozambique in 1971:

[At a state banquet on the Island of Mozambique] I told the Governor General that they are colonialists and imperialists—I didn't beat about the bush. And when an African member of their Parliament gave dinner or lunch in my honour and he made a speech which implied that they were satisfied with things as they were . . . I told the Honourable MP there that if he and his people in Mozambique were satisfied with things as they were it was their business, but I wanted him to know that we in Malawi demanded our independence from the British and they gave it, and we like things as they are in Malawi now.[48]

[46] It has long been suspected, but, naturally, without confirmation, that there was a secret military pact between Banda's government and the government of South Africa, involving the construction of a South African air base at Lilongwe. See, for example, *Observer*, 17 May 1970; *Guardian*, 6 December 1971.

[47] *Observer*, 19 December 1971; *Guardian*, 6 December 1971. Intensification of the Mozambican guerrilla attempts to disrupt the construction of the Cabora Bassa dam threatened to affect the construction of the Nacala railway, and as a result Banda decided to ask the South African government for a consignment of arms. It was reported that South African instructors might be sent. See also *Guardian*, 19 August 1971.

[48] *Hansard, Debates of the Eighth Session, Second Meeting of Parliament,* 17 December 1971.

Regarding his attitude to the liberation movements Banda further explained graphically:

at Cabora Bassa itself newspapermen wanted to trap me, or they wanted me to say something against the nationalists. I said 'look, this is not a political platform, if you want to hear from me on political matters come to Blantyre'. I was not going to denounce the African nationalists there, why should I? After all, I feel as strongly as they do. The only difference between the African leaders and I [sic] . . . is their method of approach. That's all. That's all.

He went on to add that he was opposed to force because 'no one wins war. No one.' Although the latter remark was clearly humbug, there is every reason to believe that what was said before it was sincerely meant. Banda's speeches abound with references to his struggle against British imperialism. It is, indeed, his supreme claim to political legitimacy. To approve of Portuguese colonialism would not only set him against an entire continent, an entire age, absolutely, it would also by implication depreciate his own achievement. Even his own supporters would find it hard to swallow.

There were also prudential reasons why Banda did not wish to denounce the nationalists. Ever since independence and through the constitutional crisis Banda had sought to avoid a direct confrontation with the Mozambican liberation movements because of the dangers to his own internal security that this would involve. Consequently, although he forbade them to enter Malawi armed, imprisoning and deporting those who did, Banda did not, for example, harass Frelimo in Malawi. He allowed the movement to retain a political branch in Blantyre which had been set up before Malawian independence. Furthermore, so long as they were not armed they could make easy contact with Mozambican refugees in Malawi.[49] This was not different to the attitude adopted to other Mozambican organisations, as, for example, Coremo (a small group of Frelimo dissidents) and the obscure Portuguese-backed Union for the Independence of 'Rumbezia' (evidently the area between the Zambezi and the Rovuma rivers). The last group favoured peaceful negotiation with Portugal and intended to dissuade Frelimo members from using violence. It was possible for Frelimo to recruit, as the Portuguese

---

[49] The facts in this paragraph were derived from interviews with members of various liberation movements in Dar es Salaam in April 1973. I am particularly grateful to Mr J. Chisano of Frelimo.

claimed they did, among the refugees. Certainly, no difficulties were created for those who did leave to join the guerrillas.[50]

In the pre-independence period and before the constitutional crisis MCP Youth League also collaborated closely with Frelimo. Such remembered good relations had some effect. It is also doubtful whether the Malawian armed forces could be expected to be loyal to a thoroughgoing policy of support for Portugal. For one thing, they often found the conduct of the Portuguese troops provocative —it was subsequently to lead to armed clashes with Malawian forces in April 1973[51]—as successive Malawi police reports showed. In any case, with the country deeply divided, as it was during the period studied, armed conflicts with guerrillas would create political havoc in Malawi. Besides, the government did not have the means to engage the guerrillas in armed combat. Fortunately for the Malawi government, the guerillas did not force their way, although they did on occasion attack Mozambique targets which were of particular interest to Banda.[52] Fighting in the neighbouring Mozambican provinces sometimes spilled over and Malawi tended to find itself in the political cross-fire. It was indeed such incidents as well as the fairly cautious policy Banda adopted towards the Mozambican liberation movements which led to a feeling among Mozambican settlers and other whites in southern Africa[53] that Malawi supported 'terrorists', and which more than once severely tried Malawi–Portuguese relations, as when in November 1972, following incursions into Malawi by Portuguese troops pursuing guerrillas, the Portuguese ambassador to Malawi was withdrawn at his own request.

South African policy-makers also experienced difficulties in connection with their Africa policy. The accreditation of an ambassador from Malawi to South Africa provided an occasion for right-wing critics of the government to oppose the policy of admitting black diplomats to South Africa in the *verligte–verkampte* split. During the 1970 general election campaign the Malawian ambassador had

---

[50] *Ibid.*

[51] Officially denied by Portugal and Malawi.

[52] E.g. the Nacala railway under construction, and the road to Salisbury. I was told by a Frelimo representative in Dar es Salaam in 1973 that that organisation did not discriminate at all between Mozambican targets which were of interest to Malawi and those which were not. For his part, Banda has said the Cabora Bassa hydro-electric project will allow this country to exploit the bauxite on top of Mulanje, 'where work is going on at this time': *Hansard*, 13 December 1971.

[53] Cf. *Die Afrikaner*, 4 June 1971; *Dagbreek*, 14 June 1970.

to go on convenient leave for four months. By 1971 it seemed that the South African government had overcome its internal difficulties, for it managed to arrange a state visit by Banda to South Africa, which broke several of the customs and usages of *apartheid*.[54] But the visit did not inaugurate a season of relaxation in South Africa. On the contrary, prior to the National Party conferences—again it is impossible to say whether by design or by coincidence—the 'anti-terrorist' campaign was intensified.[55] Vorster also indicated that he was not favouring a liberal movement of South African policy when he sharply dismissed suggestions by Afrikaner intellectuals that the position of Coloureds, especially their political status, should be improved.[56] At the same time Vorster made his usual attacks on those bastions of 'liberalism', the English-language press and some English-speaking churchmen, but with more than the usual ferocity.[57] In

[54] S. Uys, 'Banda cracks the dogma', in *New Statesman*, 27 August 1971; see also *Guardian*, 14, 17, 19, 20, 21 August 1971, and *Times* for the same period. In Dr Banda's entourage were Miss C. T. Kadzamira, described as official hostess (*amptelike gasvrou*) and private secretary to the president, Miss M. Kadzamira, secretary of State House, Mr J. Z. U. Tembo, Governor General of the Reserve Bank, Mr A. K. Banda, Minister of Finance, Information and Tourism, Mr J. R. Ngwiri, Secretary of External Affairs, Mr Mkandawire, Senior Information Officer, and Captain R. Liabunya, *aide-de-camp* of the President, and the wives of some of these gentlemen. See *Die Burger*, 13 August 1971. Dr Banda made some of his more interesting remarks at the university of Stellenbosch, when, after telling an appreciative audience that he rejected violence, boycotts and isolation, he explained that he wanted, as he had always done, to build a bridge between black and white. If Arabs had become acceptable to Africans and vice-versa, why could the same not happen between white and black? 'You may now feel afraid [but] one does not know what the situation will be after a hundred or two hundred years. That is why I reject the idea of force, why I reject the idea of boycotts and isolation,' Banda said, and he obtained a standing ovation (for showing patience over the condition of black South Africans which he had not manifested either over Nyasaland or his own rise to power). See *Die Burger*, 18 August 1971.

[55] See, for example, the quarrel with Zambia over the Caprivi Strip, discussed below.

[56] See *Die Burger*, 5, 6, and 18 August 1971. Vorster rejected the suggestion (put forward by Gatsha Buthelezi of Zululand) that a national convention of all races should be called to discuss the future development of South Africa. See the report of his address to the Potchefstroom Centre for International Politics, *Die Burger*, 28 August 1971, thus showing that 'dialogue' with Banda was one thing and 'dialogue' within South Africa with black South Africans quite another.

[57] Cf. *Cape Times*, 7 October 1971, 8 October 1971; on war scares see *ibid.*, 13 October 1971. The *Cape Times* correspondent also made the point that the quarrel with Zambia and Vorster's contentious announcement that South African police had been instructed to chase 'terrorists' across the

these ways Vorster pre-empted a 'right-wing' attack over such 'liberalistic' policies as entertaining Banda.

After the state visit Banda renewed his attempts, which had been evident for some time, to lead a regrouping of African States by rallying round him all those leaders favouring 'dialogue' with South Africa.[58] He had tried to use visits to Malawi by President Khama of Botswana and by Chief Leabua Jonathan, Prime Minister of Lesotho, to this purpose.[59] Banda now sought to involve the leaders of the Bantustans in his African groupings, without apparently gaining the sympathy of some of the Bantustan leaders.[60]

In the period 1964–71 Banda, once associated with a militant nationalism, became the most forthright opponent of the anti-colonial and anti-*apartheid* movement in Africa. To comprehend this anomaly is a major task of any analysis of the Africa policy of South Africa and its impact on Malawi. The trite resolution of the anomaly was contained in Banda's own earlier explanations of his policy on grounds of 'realism'. The same view was uncritically adopted by J. G. Pike in his book on Malawi.[61] Malawi's foreign policy, according to Pike, was 'realistic' and was 'dictated largely by Malawi's geographic situation, its inherent poverty and the need to spur the economy'.[62] Dr Banda seemed to Pike to have been 'careful not to compromise [Malawi's] political independence, and [Malawi] probably [stood] to make considerable gains'.[63] Pike took little account of the fact that political realities, whatever they are, are mute and draw up no policies. Policies are conceived in the minds of men, and what 'reality demands' is, in political life, a *political* judgement, infused with moral and other evaluative preferences as well as objective observation. The appeal to realism is at best a statement of a problem—a description (often tendentious) of realities as apperceived—but it in no way entails injunctions to action in an

---

border overshadowed other political matters at the National Party congress. See also *Observer*, 21 November 1971.

[58] *Die Burger*, 20 August 1971; *Guardian*, 23 August 1971.

[59] Ministry of Information, 'Speeches made during the visit of Chief Leabua Jonathan, Prime Minister of Lesotho, 12–17 May 1967; also 'Speeches made during the first anniversary of the Republic of Malawi, 5–7 July 1967'.

[60] The most pro-government Bantustan leader, Chief Matanzima, explicitly declined an invitation to visit Malawi but gave no reason: *Guardian*, 31 August 1971.

[61] *Malawi: a Political and Economic History*, 1968.

[62] *Ibid.*, p. 163.　　　　　　　　[63] *Ibid.*, p. 192.

objective, logical sense. Nevertheless, the implicit argument that Malawi was so vulnerable to South African retaliatory measures, were it to collaborate in boycott plans against South Africa, that Banda could not help doing what he did, deserves consideration— if only because it has been repeated so often.

Malawi does not and did not at independence depend on South Africa either for aid or for trade. Its trade with South Africa was relatively small compared to its trade with Rhodesia—not to mention the UK.[64] Its outlets to the sea were the Portuguese ports and not South African ports. True, Malawi might expand its markets in South Africa,[65] attract South African investment, and obtain South African aid in exchange for an accommodating policy, but that would indicate future advantages and dependences rather than actual losses, or the 'suicide' which Banda said would follow from not co-operating with South Africa. Malawi might lose opportunities of future trade—but it would not perish—at least in this respect. In any case, Malawian poverty and lack of independence favoured a policy of compromise towards Rhodesia and Portugal which need not have encouraged the *intensification* of co-operation with South Africa. From the point of view of its exports (Malawi is a net importer *vis-à-vis* South Africa, by a large margin),[66] African markets, especially in Zambia and Tanzania, could, with goodwill all round, have been expanded. While Malawi's trade with South Africa (and Rhodesia) was substantially greater than its trade with Zambia over the period 1968–71, its exports to Zambia took a definite upward turn. Zambia took 4·25 per cent of Malawi's domestic exports on average, while South Africa and Rhodesia accounted for 4·00 per cent and 6·25 per cent respectively (the UK accounted for an average of 48·00 per cent). Imports revealed a similar pattern.[67] Table 7 shows the percentage shares of the main trading partners from 1968 to 1971. From the point of view of trade alone there was, therefore, no reason why Malawi should not have sought to conciliate Zambia as much as it did South Africa.

[64] See *Monthly Bulletin of Key Economic Indicators*, especially December 1970; also appendix 1.

[65] It is a market for primary produce only so far, and it is wholly unclear what would happen if Malawi were to start exporting manufactures. In any case, increased dependence on South African markets for agricultural produce would make the Malawian government even less able to oppose *apartheid* in deed as well as words.

[66] See appendix 1.

[67] See Malawi Government, *Economic Report*, 1972.

Malawi's dependence on South Africa has been argued for in another area—that of employment. Under colonial rule Malawi served as a reservoir of cheap migrant labour for the mines in South Africa (and in Zambia and Rhodesia). Workers were recruited for South African mines by the Witwatersrand Native Labour Association (WNLA; known in Malawi as Wenela), where they would work for periods of up to eighteen months on contract. There was also

TABLE 7 *Malawi's external trade: percentage shares of trade with main trading partners, 1968–71*

Country	1968	1969	1970	1971
(a) *Domestic exports*				
United Kingdom	51	46	52	43
Rhodesia	5	6	7	7
South Africa	5	3	4	4
United States	4	6	3	5
West Germany	3	3	3	2
Zambia	2	8	3	4
Other countries	30	28	28	35
Total	100	100	100	100
(b) *Imports*				
United Kingdom	31	30	26	28
Rhodesia	18	17	23	15
South Africa	11	15	13	11
United States	6	4	4	4
West Germany	4	4	3	4
Zambia	4	4	4	4
Others	26	26	27	34
Total	100	100	100	100

Source. Malawi government, *Economic Report, 1972.*

'free flow' migration—workers finding their own way into the republic—but increasingly this was frowned upon by the South African authorities.[68] In 1967 an agreement was entered into between Malawi and South Africa to regulate the system. Malawi undertook to curb 'free flow' migration, but nothing else was significantly changed, except that the new Employment Service Department in Malawi did some recruiting alongside Wenela.

[68] See *Ministry of Labour Report, 1963–67*, pp. 18 ff.; Pike, *op. cit., passim*; Chipembere, 'Malawi's growing links with South Africa', *passim*.

As before, provision was made for the employers to defer part of the monthly pay of the worker to be invested on his behalf in his individual account with the Malawi Post Office Savings Bank in the case of the Employment Service Department, or paid out in bulk to the worker on his return to Malawi in the case of Wenela workers. Thus through forced saving it was ensured that some revenue accrued to Malawi.

TABLE 8 *Malawian migratory labour: men issued with identity certificates, by country of destination, 1958–60 and 1963–67*

Country	1958–60	1963–67
All countries	210,744	279,841
South Africa	70,248	168,157
Rhodesia	121,539	97,708
Zambia	16,564	9,465
Other countries	2,393	4,511

Sources. Malawi *Ministry of Labour Report, 1963-67*, p. 27.

Men leaving for the foreign mines are issued with identity certificates, and the number of identity certificates issued is the basis of estimates of men working away from Malawi in the mines. It was estimated in 1967 that about 70,248 men worked in South Africa in 1958–60, a number which rose to 168,157 in 1963–67. Figures for Rhodesia and Zambia for the same period were 121,539 and 97,708 for Rhodesia and 16,564 and 9,465 for Zambia. Other countries (almost exclusively Tanzania) took 2,393 and 4,511 Malawians during the same periods. (See table 8.) The figures for the earlier period are probably understatements, since before the constitutional and political changes there were more 'free flow' migrants who are, of course, not covered by the number of identity certificates issued. Of these migrants it was estimated that there were about 34,000 in South Africa in 1969. The figures for Zambia and Tanzania are almost certainly grossly understated in both cases, because of the greater informality and ease with which Malawians could enter the labour markets of those countries.[69] Also the figures in table 7 do not include women; this would not make any difference to the South

[69] Since 1965 Malawians entering Zambia have been required to carry passports (not identity certificates). There are no data of passports issued to persons going to Zambia: see *Ministry of Labour Report*, p. 21, n. 4.

African figures because no Malawian women seek work there, but it would make a difference for the other countries. At the time of the 1966 census there were 18,000 Malawian women in Zambia.[70] A Zambian total of 43,000 would compare less favourably with the 70,000 and 160,000 estimated to be in South Africa and Rhodesia respectively at that time.[71]

The revenue accruing to Malawi from remittances was greatest in the case of South Africa, although it showed a downward trend after 1964, in comparison with revenue (much smaller in absolute value) from Rhodesia and Zambia. From table 9 it can be seen that

TABLE 9 *Malawian migratory labour: remittances by or on behalf of migrant workers, by source country, 1958–67 (£)*

Year	All countries	South Africa	Rhodesia	Zambia
1958–62	8,330,030	5,193,436	3,136,594	–
1963–67	9,020,993	6,469,434	1,489,335	1,862,224
1963	1,300,171	836,526	363,645	100,000
1964	1,578,742	1,163,733	282,808	132,201
1965	2,029,124	1,545,453	310,642	173,029
1966	2,127,664	1,522,613	271,503	333,548
1967	1,985,292	1,401,109	260,737	323,446

Source. Ministry of Labour Report, 1963–67, p. 39.

in 1958–62 South Africa accounted for over £5 million out of the total remittances of £8,330,030; and in 1963–67, about £6½ million out of a total of just over £9 million. The very low figure from Zambia is accounted for by the different labour system operated there. South Africa was able to contribute over the whole period about 72 per cent of all remittances, largely owing to the fact that most remittances from there were involuntary (deferred pay, workmen's compensation, deceased estates, etc.); the same is true for Rhodesia. Zambia, on the other hand, does not have a compulsory remittance system, payments being made to the worker directly.

[70] *Ministry of Labour Report*, p. 21; the figures for the period after 1965 are based on a statistical estimate assuming identical behaviour of Zambian figures as Rhodesian ones in 1965–67; but since Zambian recruits were increasing compared to Rhodesian recruits, who were decreasing on account of sanctions, the actual figures are probably understood by the *de jure* figures.
[71] *Ibid.*, p. 21.

The very low remittances from workers in Zambia is probably further accounted for by the fact that men are allowed to take wives with them or may marry in Zambia (which is not the case in South Africa) and are allowed to engage freely in the social life of Zambia, not being confined to male bachelors' compounds as in South Africa. A component of South African remittances accruing direct to the Malawi government were tax deductions.[72]

There were other indirect benefits from labour recruitment in the form of expenditure by the recruiting organisations in Malawi. Wenela expenditures in Malawi consisted in payments to the government (mainly contributions to the welfare fund), purchases from local suppliers and payments for services (salaries of staff, transport, etc.) and other unspecified payments. The totals for 1965, 1966 and 1967 were, respectively, £464,228, £401,413 and £385,560, which corresponded to net capital inflow of £359,936, £302,365 and £316,240 respectively.[73]

There seemed no doubt that, in financial terms, migrant labour, and especially an authoritarian labour regime of the sort operating between Malawi and South Africa, was beneficial. The Ministry of Labour calculated that:

The average yearly net inflow of £2·4 million in the years 1965–67 (from remittances and agency expenditures) represents some eleven per cent of total exports (visible and invisible), which amounted to an average of £22·7 million in these years. It represented the third item after tobacco, which averaged £4·6 million in 1956–67, and tea, which averaged 33·0 per cent of that trade deficit.[74]

Seventy-six per cent of these financial benefits came from South Africa.

It is very doubtful whether Malawi benefits all round—in sociological, political as well as economic terms—from the migratory labour system, or whether economic co-operation with South Africa will accelerate economic development of a kind that will be optimal

[72] In terms of the 1967 agreement, Malawi workers in South Africa (those officially recruited) are liable only for Malawian tax and not South African taxes.

[73] *Ministry of Labour Report*, table 2.4, p. 40.

[74] *Ibid.*, p. 22. It is evident from the report that the Ministry of Labour was at pains to show that the emigration to South Africa was more valuable than other emigration. Of course, the question (not answered) is, For whom? The migrant and his family, or the tax collector?

for the whole of Malawi society.[75] The matter has been argued out before,[76] and there is a view that, whatever development accrues from this co-operation, it will not be of an 'African socialist' kind. Whether this is to Malawi's benefit or not is a matter of opinion, depending on the ideological commitments of whomever it may concern to decide the question. At the very least, it is not a matter of 'objective reality' that Banda has helped to elaborate this particular pattern of co-operation. For, although he might in any case (whether he was a socialist or not) have maintained, as a temporary expedient at least, the migratory labour system, he has explicitly said that he favours capitalist development[77] and has not indicated any intention of changing the system.

It is evident from the figures we have given that from the point of view of employment opportunities for Malawians abroad the Zambian contribution (together with the Tanzanian or even alone) compares extremely favourably, for the periods given, with that of South Africa. From the point of view of the 'Malawian national interest', defined as the interests of Malawians rather than of the regime, this would on 'realistic' grounds have argued for a less hostile policy to Zambia as well as towards South Africa. It could, how-

[75] The gains from labour migration for example, in developmental terms are highly doubtful, especially seen in the perspective not only of the last five years but of the whole period of history in southern and central Africa during which it has been practised. There is a view that labour migration contributes to the underdevelopment of the sending countries. Economists are not agreed on the effects emigration has on economic growth and development. See, for example, C. Kindleberger, 'Emigration and economic growth', in *Banca Nazionale del Lavoro*, September 1965; R. A. Mundell, 'International trade and factor mobility', in *American Economic Review*, 1957; B. Thomas, International factor movements and unequal rates of growth', in *Manchester School*, 1961, which deal with the theoretical questions. The question of gains and losses cannot, however, be resolved without reference to a specific, chosen pattern of development. The very concepts 'gains' and 'losses' are misleadingly aggregative, since they imply the possibility of an unambiguous social welfare function; in fact gains and losses may accrue differentially to different social groups (classes, tribes, races, etc.), as is clearly the case in South Africa. These are some of the difficulties which have to be resolved before the rather pat view that Malawi benefits is taken literally and, worse, thought to hold in the long as well as the short run.

[76] Cf. R. Molteno, *South Africa and Africa*, 1970, and S. Gervasi, 'The nature and consequences of South Africa's economic expansion', unpublished seminar paper, Institute of Commonwealth Studies, University of London, 1971.

[77] This was in an elaborate comment on the Arusha declarations in 'Opening address to the National Convention of the Malawi Congress Party ... 1968', *Daily Bulletin*, 16 September 1968.

ever, be argued, wrongly in our view, that knowing that Zambia
would or could do little to retaliate where South Africa could do
much, Banda could disregard Zambian susceptibilities.[78] The truth
of the matter is that South Africa needed the labour from Malawi
because of the inability of the mining companies to recruit sufficient
labour at their levels of pay (and with the working conditions they
provide) within South Africa. Indeed, without Malawian and other
migrant labour the companies would be forced to raise wages or
improve working conditions for Africans. Because the labour costs
of the mining companies, on account of the high wages paid to
white workers, are high, such changes could not be absorbed without
the labour regime in South Africa being changed. Africans would
have to be admitted at lower rates of pay to occupations in the
industry previously reserved for white workers.[79] This would undoubtedly cause a commotion in South Africa; it might even lead to
attempts by white workers to collaborate with black workers to
ensure that the common job opportunities were not allowed to deteriorate, from the white point of view, any further. After all, this
was the experience on the Zambian Copperbelt when, in deference
to the needs of employers and the demands of African workers,
privileged white workers had to change their tactics also.[80] Job
reservation is a key feature of *apartheid*, and the consequent segregation of white and black workers with which it is associated were
considered by the South African government to be the guarantees
of 'industrial peace' in South Africa. In short, the migratory labour
system is not a form of aid to Malawi; in fact, Banda had enough

[78] Banda also knew that Zambia needed Malawian goodwill during the
period of sanctions against Rhodesia.

[79] Cf. J. B. Knight, 'A theory of income distribution in South Africa', in
Bulletin of the Oxford University Institute of Economis and Statistics, 1964.

[80] The response of European workers in Zambia to their failure to maintain job reservation had been to insist that Africans employed in categories
of jobs previously reserved for whites received 'equal pay for equal work' a
war-cry for which they gained the support of their South African counterparts (see above, p. 74), and although after self-government in Zambia
the mining companies were to impose a dual wage structure, the 'equal pay'
slogan had irreversibly affected Africans also (whom it had been intended it
would disadvantage by removing the incentive for the companies to employ
African labour in place of Europeans). The Brown Commission wrote in
1966, 'For twenty years the whole industry has been ringing with the battle-
cry of the European Union—"equal pay for equal work". It would have
been strange if this theme had not left its mark on African workers.' Republic
of Zambia, *Report of the Commission of Inquiry into the Mining Industry*
(the Brown Commission), 1966, p. 16.

bargaining power not to need to intensify his collusion with the South African government. A policy of silence, neutrality or even mild opposition would have served his purpose—of not provoking South Africa to the point of having to end the system—just as well. On the other hand, by voluntarily increasing his co-operation in this area, by accepting this labour regime as a permanent policy, rather than a temporary expedient, Banda, contrary to his opposition to interference in the internal affairs of other States, voluntarily collaborated in the repression of black labour in South Africa.[81] Nothing in all this supports the view that Banda's policy, *in its detailed particularity*, is explicable in terms of economic determination or geographical constraints. In essence, the policy reflected a deliberate ideological preference.

An alternative view to that of Pike is provided by Andrew Ross.[82] By this account, Banda's southern policy is to be seen as appropriate to a specific domestic political context, itself seen in the perspective of social location. Tribalism and class resentments were functional to a counter-revolution which Banda was launching and of which the southern Africa policy was a part:

Colonial rule was overthrown by the typical 'evolué' groups who were mildly left-wing by British political standards. They in turn have been overthrown by their chosen national figurehead, avowedly right-wing in economic and international affairs, who has utilised the frustration of the traditional leaders in society as well as that of older semi-educated men to channel all the latent antagonism of the cultural 'have nots' against the educated 'haves' of the new society.[83]

To this end Banda was said to have incited Chewa tribal feeling in an attempt to create a personal power base among them. Hence, among other things, his decision to build a new capital in Lilongwe, in Central Region, the tribal 'homeland' of the Achewa. There are features of Ross's analysis which are germane to the present work. If what he suggests concerning Lilongwe is true, then South Africa,

[81] An introductory study of labour repression in South Africa is that by S. Trapido, 'South Africa in a comparative study of industrialisation', University of London, SSA/70/1.

[82] Ross, 'White Africa's black ally'.

[83] *Ibid.*, pp. 93–4. Ross refers to tribal violence perpetrated by the secret societies, Zinyau and Atsalima, against non-Chewa civil servants and taxi drivers in Central Region. There was, Ross observes, little attempt by Banda to do anything about this violence.

by making possible the construction of the new capital, has directly involved itself in the internal politics of Malawi. Our own research confirms that Banda is avowedly and consistently right-wing, and that the Ministers who rebelled against him were part of the intellectual elite of Malawi and were left-wing. It is, however, unclear how much there has been replacement of 'haves' by 'have-nots' in the party and the government. There is also little concrete evidence that the 'have nots' have been mobilised systematically against the 'haves', or that there has been a change in the social distribution of power apart from the informal observations which Ross has made.[84]

As far as the benefits of collaboration with South Africa are concerned, there is no doubt that they accrue mainly to Central Region. The capital city which South Africa helped to finance would be built there, creating a dramatic increase in employment opportunities in construction work.[85] Also, most of the recruits for South African

---

[84] Achewa 'ascendancy' since 1964 is most clearly reflected in police recruitment in the 'other ranks' grade. It can be seen from the table below that their strength increased markedly in 1964–69. The same was true of the cousin tribe the Angoni. Whereas the total increase of other ranks was about 11·01 per cent, the Achewa increased by 41 per cent and the Angoni by 22·19 per cent. It is true, however, that the Atumbuka (Chipembere's tribe) also increased their strength, but in their case it was from an originally low figure. No conclusions can be drawn from such a short time series, but the figures do make out a case for further research:

Tribal composition of the police force, other ranks

Tribe	1964	1965	1968	1969
Anyanja	476	472	468	482
Alomwe	499	471	532	547
Ayao	297	288	287	273
Atumbuka	181	213	218	240
Achewa	342	472	484	484
Angeni	347	388	452	424
Akenga	15	18	25	21
Amanganja	66	69	97	99
Atonga	28	13	28	25
Ankhonde	29	26	53	50
Others	122	147	8	34
Total	2,402	2,577	2,652	2,679

Source. Malawi Police Report, various years.

[85] However, most private sector construction in 1968–70 took place in Southern Region (87, 87 and 76 per cent), Central Region accounting only for 12, 11 and 17 per cent of all construction work by value in the same period. See Monthly Bulletin of Key Economic Indicators, various issues.

mines (as distinct from Rhodesian and Zambian mines) came from Lilongwe.[86]

Proportionately most workers from Northern Region find their way to Zambia, while more Southerners migrate to Rhodesia. It is evident that this pattern was not new, although the 1963–67 figures show a definite confirmation of this pattern, as can be seen from table 10.

TABLE 10   *Malawian migratory labour: men issued with identity certificates, by district of origin and country of destination, 1958–60 and 1963–67*

	Destination		
Region of origin	*South Africa*	*Rhodesia*	*Zambia*
(a) *1958–60*			
Northern	3,464	5,752	9,920
Central	49,627	41,858	3,829
Southern	17,157	73,929	2,815
(b) *1963–67*			
Northern	13,367	3,656	3,640
Central	105,341	21,554	3,240
Southern	49,449	72,498	2,585

Source. Ministry of Labour Report, 1963–67.

The internal distribution in Malawi of the benefits of collaboration with South Africa suggests that Ross's argument deserves further research. If Banda were trying to create a power base in Central Region, then the migrant labour system would probably serve his purpose; but to endorse the conspiracy thesis implicit in Ross's analysis would be going further than the present research would sustain. The case is made, however, that Banda's southern policy should not be seen in isolation from the internal politics of Malawi. To these politics ethnic cleavages and competition between various status groups are naturally important, and Banda's reactions to those aspects of the internal situation bear directly on his external policies.

[86] Central Region accounts for a large proportion of the national labour force; with a manpower of 531,000 persons it is second after Southern Region, with 779,000 (Malawi population census, 1966). This must be borne in mind when the regional figures in table 10 are compared.

There is a final view of Banda's policy put forward by his former colleague, Chipembere, which, although it does not contradict what has been said, points to another direction of enquiry—the psychological, which is perhaps the most difficult to pursue successfully. Impressions of Banda's personal psychology, in so far as it is revealed in his public life, lend some plausibility to Chipembere's view:

> But if one who has known the president very well [writes Chipembere] and has worked closely with him for a long time may hazard a guess, the answer to the puzzle is this. President Banda, having found that Malawi cannot afford to fight South Africa, is unhappy to find that other countries can and that they are in fact backing armed internal revolution in South Africa. He is insulted that others can afford what he cannot afford. Because he cannot fight, everybody else should stop fighting![87]

Banda's vanity, Chipembere supposes, might well tell against South Africa in the end:

> he is the kind of man who could at any moment suddenly sever relatons with South Africa and even denounce it violently, if he felt personally insulted by some act of the South African government.[88]

The details of Banda's individual sensibility, are, however, far less important, given the political situation to which they may have helped to give rise, than the political and economic ideology to which they predisposed him in the first place, which with relentless logic draws him closer to South Africa with every passing year. It is to those forces that the outward-looking policy of South Africa owed its success in Malawi.

Zambia

Of the black States of southern Africa, Zambia has been the one most openly identified with militant opposition to the white regimes in that area, and at the level of public declarations, South Africa has been the most vociferous of the white regimes in reciprocating such hostility. Yet at the level of actual, as distinct from verbal, interactions, relations between the two regimes testify to a higher degree of mutual tolerance between Zambia and South Africa than might be expected. This is most clearly so in economic relations.

[87] H. B. Chipembere, 'Malawi's growing links with South Africa: a necessity or a virtue?', in *Africa Today*, 1971, p. 45.
[88] *Ibid.*, p. 44.

Similarly, for most of the period covered by this discussion hostility did not develop into open military confrontation. Relations between Zambia and South Africa in the seven years of Zambia's independence can therefore be seen as consisting in a balance of tendencies towards conflict and tendencies towards accommodation and co-operation. It is a major object of the ensuing discussion of the relations between Zambia and South Africa—at the bilateral, inter-governmental level[89]—to see how that balance has been maintained. In so doing, the discussion should reveal the internal and external limits of Zambia–South Africa relations.

Even before Zambia gained its independence in 1964 Kaunda and other nationalist leaders had expressed their hostility to minority rule in Southern Rhodesia, Portuguese colonial rule in Angola and Mozambique, and *apartheid* in South Africa. The leading nation-alist party in Zambia, the United National Independence Party (UNIP) identified itself with the pan-African movement through its participation in the Pan-African Freedom Movement for East and Central Africa (PAFMECA), and when PAFMECA was trans-formed into a wider movement including in its ranks southern African liberation movements and was renamed PAFMECSA Pan-African Movement for East, Central and Southern Africa)[90] Zambians continued to play an important part in its work, Kaunda serving as its president in its final years.[91] The Zambian leadership subscribed to the Afro-Asian policy of boycotting South Africa, although it was recognised that it would take time before Zambia could be expected to comply with that policy. After independence one of the preoccupations of the Zambian government was examin-ing means of implementing plans to reduce Zambia's dependence on the white-ruled States for its external communcations and for a wide range of goods and services.[92] The Zambian government focused on a plan to build a railway through the north to the Tanzanian port of Dar es Salaam, a plan which—after its rejection by the Western powers that had been approached—resulted in the

---

[89] As distinct from inter-country relations—social, cultural and economic —and as distinct from indirect relations through bloc memberships, or through participation in intergovernmental organisations.

[90] See Wallerstein: *Africa: the Politics of Unity,* chapter IX.

[91] *Ibid.*

[92] Cf. *A.R.B.* (*Econ.*), 1965, pp. 265B, 381C; Institute of Race Relations (London) *Newsletter,* June 1963, for an early statement of Kaunda's desire to forge a rail link with [then] Tanganyika.

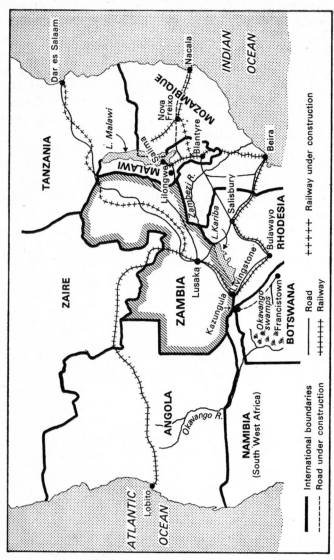

FIG. 4 *Zambia's outlets to the sea*

construction of the TanZam railway by the communist Chinese.[93]

Yet in spite of this hostility to South Africa (and the other white minority-ruled States), and despite the clear intention of the Zambian government to divert its country's trade away from South Africa, Zambia in 1964–65 showed every sign of continuing to be a dependent economic partner of the republic. There was an elaborate pattern of dependence inherited from the colonial period which could not be changed overnight. Although the Zambian government discontinued the practice of the former Northern Rhodesian administration of treating South Africa as a Commonwealth country for tariff purposes,[94] that in itself was unlikely to have any noticeable effect on the volume of trade between the two countries. South African manufactures were already entering at a higher tariff rate than competing UK and Rhodesian merchandise, South Africa being on the lowest preference column. Within Zambia, a South African company, Anglo-American Corporation of South Africa Ltd (later renamed Anglo-American Corporation of Zambia Ltd), dominated the all-important copper mining industry.[95] The mining industry itself consumed a considerable volume of South African produce, obtaining some essential goods, like dynamite and

TABLE 11 *Zambia's trade with South Africa, 1964–69* (K '000)

	Imports	Exports
1964	32,406	26,233
1965	41,379	24,856
1966	58,468	28,051
1967	72,172	25,444
1968	72,066	11,681
1969	69,946	7,671

Source. Republic of Zambia, *Monthly Digest of Statistics*, vol. VII, No. 4 (1971).

[93] *The Economist*, 29 June 1968; *Times of Zambia*, 28 August 1969, 19 September 1969; *The Zambia Rail*, 1 November 1969, 7 January 1970, 29 January 1970; *The Times*, 22 March 1971, 23 March 1971; 'Zambie: le point de non-retour' and 'Tanzam: un succès pour Pekin', in *Le Mois en Afrique: Revue française d'études politiques africains*, 1970.

[94] Northern Rhodesia: *Hansard No. 1, Official Verbatim Report of the Debates of the 1st Session of the Legislative Assembly, 10–20 March 1964*; A.R.B. (*Econ.*), 23 September 1965.

[95] Cf. Hall, *The High Price of Principles*, p. 87. In 1964 the then Minister of Commerce and Industry, Mr Mundia, said no further companies controlled from South Africa would be allowed to operate in Zambia.

gelignite, exclusively from South Africa. Table 11 gives the totals of
Zambian trade with South Africa in the years 1964–69. For skilled
manpower the industry relied on white expatriates from South
Africa (as well as from Britain and Rhodesia), and it would take
time before local Zambian manpower could be trained to take over
the jobs which had effectively been reserved for whites in colonial
Northern Rhodesia.[96] Table 12 shows the progress of Zambianisation
up to 1968. Some Zambians worked (until 1967) in South African
mines and it did not seem at independence that alternative jobs
would soon be found for them.[97]

TABLE 12   *The progress of Zambianisation, 1964–68*

	Total No. of expatriates	Total No. of Zambians in the field of expatriate employment
December 1964	7,621	704
March 1966	6,592	1,138
September 1966	6,358	1,884
October 1967	5,671	2,617
June 1968	5,024	3,691

The figures are not broken down by race and nationality; see, however,
Manpower Report, Lusaka, 1966, p. 11.

Zambian government policy seemed to defer to these apparent
realities. Kaunda even proposed, albeit in polemical tones, the
establishment of diplomatic relations between Zambia and South
Africa in 1964. His suggestion was not taken, in South Africa, to
have been made altogether in a spirit of controversy, for he drew
attention to the volume of business between the two countries.[98]
Within South Africa Kaunda's suggestion was supported by the
official opposition, by some English-language newspapers, and by
the chairman of Anglo-American, Oppenheimer.[99] Verwoerd was

[96] Cf. Republic of Zambia: *Report of the Commission of Inquiry into the
Mining Industry*, 1966, *passim*. Republic of Zambia, Ministry of Labour:
The Progress of Zambianisation in the Mining Industry, 1968, gave the
statistical summary of the progress of Zambianisation in table 12 above.

[97] See Hall, *op. cit.*, p. 90, and G. M. E. Leistner: 'Foreign Bantu workers
in South Africa: their present position in the economy', in *South African
Economic Journal*, 1967.

[98] *A.R.B. (Pol.)*, 1964, 15 January 1964; see also *Ass. Deb.*, vol. 10, col.
7369.

[99] *Natal Mercury*, 23 June 1966; *Sunday Times* (Johannesburg), 28 June
1966.

not at this stage willing to exchange diplomatic representatives and indicated as much, though not in a direct reply to the Zambian offer.[100] By fervently championing non-racialism within Zambia, Kaunda minimised conflict with the white minority in Zambia, some of whom were of South African origin or maintained close social links with white South Africans. By affirming that the Zambian government would not nationalise capitalist interests (in large part South African) and that it was eager to encourage foreign capitalists to invest in Zambia[101] the Zambian administration was able to present to some of the business classes in South Africa an image of 'reasonableness'. Thus Kaunda collected good opinions among some of the articulate whites in South Africa.[102]

The picture of a Zambia likely to continue collaborating with South Africa was, however, spoiled by the expressed intention of the Zambian government to continue supporting the pan-African movement, including the boycott policy against South Africa, to which end the Zambian government took measures from the beginning of 1965. Announcing the termination of the trade agreement between Zambia and South Africa,[103] the Minister of Commerce and Industry, Mr Mundia, declared on 30 December 1964 that the idea of a trade agreement with the South African regime was 'repugnant' to the government of Zambia.[104] In February Arthur Wina, the Minister of Finance, told the United Nations Economic Commission for Africa that the Zambian government was working out a trading policy aimed at ending trade with South Africa.[105] In March the Foreign Minister, Simon Kapwepwe, returning from the Organisation of African Unity's Council of Ministers' conference in Nairobi, announced that Zambia 'had been given an extension of time to ban South African goods but Zambia had been told to push ahead with plans for the boycott'.[106] In August President

[100] *Ass. Deb.*, vol. 10, cols. 4900–1.

[101] Cf. C. Legum (ed.), *Zambia: Independence and Beyond: the Speeches of Kenneth Kaunda*, 1966, p. 10.

[102] Cf. S. F. Waterson, MP, in *Ass. Deb.*, vol. 10, col. 7369.

[103] The agreement preserved the Commonwealth trading arrangements between South Africa and Northern Rhodesia after South Africa left the Commonwealth in 1961. See *A.R.B. (Econ.)*, 1964, 30 December and 2 November 1964.

[104] *A.R.B. (Pol.), ibid.*

[105] *Ibid.*, 10 February 1965.

[106] *Ibid.*, 8 March 1965. See also *Annual Report of the Ministry of Commerce and Industry, 1966, 1967, 1968, 1969, passim.*

Kaunda told a press conference that it would be 'impossible' for Zambia to exchange diplomatic representatives with South Africa 'under existing conditions'.

A long-drawn-out quarrel between the Zambian government and the British South Africa Company over royalties[107] indicated that the Zambian government would not adopt a passive attitude towards private companies; it may also have helped to qualify business optimism as to the likelihood of the lucrative colonial order continuing to be maintained for long.[108] So far as the ruling party in South Africa was concerned, the policies of non-racialism pursued by Kaunda were not at all helpful, since non-racialism was precisely what they objected to in South Africa. Kaunda himself believed that the South African government could not tolerate a non-racial Zambia and would seek its ruin.[109] The Zambian government expressed particular concern when South Africa began to construct an air base in the Caprivi Strip of Namibia, which is contiguous with Zambia. In June 1965 Kaunda accused the South African government of 'warmongering' and said the air base was a 'threat to our peace and order'.[110] When Kaunda said there would be no exchange of diplomatic representatives he cited the air base as one of the reasons why such an exchange was impossible.[111] Such Zambian allegations could could not have failed to cause concern in South Africa, since they tended to give weight to Afro-Asian arguments in the UN for action against South Africa on the grounds that its *apartheid* regime constituted a threat to the peace.[112]

The Rhodesian unilateral declaration of independence in 1965 created a new situation in which the boycott policy was for a time reversed and the problem of *apartheid* in South Africa was superseded by the Zambians' need to participate in efforts to bring the

[107] Hall, *The High Price of Principles*, pp. 71–92.

[108] *Times of Zambia*, 22 November 1965.

[109] *Ibid.*, 27 August 1965. Kaunda said that Zambia had concrete evidence that South Africa intended to spend £5 million to disrupt the Zambian economy. On 22 August 1967 he said, in response to Vorster's threat (see below), 'Zambia was being used as a scapegoat by people who wanted an excuse for shooting black Africans in Zambia and an excuse to destroy a country they envied. Zambia was making economic progress which challenged South Africa, and a non-racial, non-tribal State was being built which challenged Smith, Vorster and Salazar.'

[110] *A.R.B.* (*Pol.*), 319B.

[111] *Times of Zambia*, 27 August 1965.

[112] Cf. Austin, *Britain and South Africa*, chapter IV; P. Calvocoressi, *South Africa and World Opinion*, 1961.

rebellion to a speedy conclusion favourable to the interests of Rhodesia's black majority. Although the Zambian government was aware that the problem of Rhodesia could not be separated from that of Portuguese colonialism on the one hand, and that of *apartheid* on the other,[113] it could only hope, along with the United Kingdom government, that Rhodesia could be isolated from the other minority regimes in southern Africa. Kaunda had said at an Overseas Press Club luncheon in June 1963 that Northern Rhodesia (as it then was) and the United Kingdom could, if the latter co-operated, 'squeeze Southern Rhodesia economically until there was representative government there'. He added, 'Don't be deceived about possible aid from South Africa. South Africa has plenty to look after herself.'[114] Although it is unlikely that at the end of 1965 Kaunda still believed this to be the case, he hoped, *could only hope*, that South African support for Rhodesia would be limited. Much of his subsequent South African diplomacy can be seen as an attempt to realise that hope.

On New Year's Day of 1966 Verwoerd broke his silence on Rhodesia by proclaiming a policy of 'neutrality', which meant that South Africa would go on dealing with Rhodesia as if nothing had happened.[115] The racial solidarity with white Rhodesians was echoed by some members of the white community in Zambia.[116] White workers in the mines and the railways became restive when new exchange controls were introduced in March 1966, fearing that they might not be able to transfer as much of their earnings to their countries of origin as they had been used to doing; others feared that they might not be able to obtain employment in Rhodesia and South Africa when they returned if they extended their contracts to work in Zambia.[117] Industrial peace was restored within a short while, but race relations in Zambia remained strained. South African and Rhodesian external radio broadcasts did not hesitate to

[113] Cf. S. Kapwepwe, in *UNGAOR*, 1339th Plenary Meeting, 28 September 1965, A/PU 1339.

[114] Institute of Race Relations *Newsletter*, June 1963.

[115] See above, chapter IX.

[116] Cf. *BBC Summary*, Part IV, 1966, ME/2301/8/5; *A.R.B. (Pol.)*, 1966, 639B and 639C.

[117] *Times of Zambia*, 3 March, 1966 and 4 March 1966; cf. Ministry of Information press release 1243/66 for Kaunda's warning to companies which were not willing to collaborate in obtaining oil via the north—through Tanzania.

play up these feelings. Following the death of Mrs Myburgh,[118] and the deportation of twenty-five European families, a radio broadcast from South Africa quoted Rhodesian comment:

There are other countries where they [the whites] can live peacefully without fear for their lives, and in all probability the present 30,000-strong European population will rapidly dwindle to the mercenary few who are prepared to accept high wages in place of a home.[119]

For its part the Zambian government continued to condemn the South African regime, drawing particular attention to South African militarisation of the Caprivi Strip and its support of Rhodesia.[120]

Kaunda told a plenary meeting of the United Nations General Assembly:

Apartheid is on the offensive. The old commando spirit in South Africa is being implemented to extend the boundaries and the influence of *apartheid*. The Boer trek is on and is now instrumental to the wider concept of neo-colonialism.[121]

When the International Court of Justice refused to adjudicate in the South West Africa cases[122] Kaunda considered the World Court's decision 'sad news' and reflected that 'as long as colonialism remains in southern Africa, the problem of peace and stability will only continue to hang in the balance'.[123]

Zambia, however, did need some South African goodwill if it hoped to avoid the possibility of South Africa colluding with Rhodesia in retaliatory measures. Upon the death of Verwoerd, President Kaunda sent a personal telegram of condolence to Mrs Verwoerd, which could be interpreted as signifying that he was not in favour of violence against South Africa. The telegram read:

Your late husband and I were irrevocably opposed in public life, but I feel compelled as a Christian to offer you my personal sympathy at what must obviously be your and your family's most difficult time.[124]

[118] *A.R.B. (Pol.)*, 639B and 639C. Mrs Myburgh was stoned in a race riot.
[119] *BBC Summary*, 31 October 1966, ME/2307/8/10. Cf. broadcast of 25 October 1966, ME/2301/8/5, cf. also V. P. McKay, 'The propaganda battle for Zambia', in *Africa Today*, 1971.
[120] Mr Chivunga, in *UNGAOR, 21st Session, Special Political Committee: Report of the Special Committee on the Policies of Apartheid*, p. 217.
[121] President Kaunda, in *UNGAOR (1966) Plenary Meeting*, A/PV.1464.
[122] International Court of Justice, *The South West Africa Cases*, 1966, Rep. 6.
[123] *A.R.B. (Pol.)*, 1966, 615B, 10 August 1966.
[124] *Rhodesia Herald*, 10 September 1966.

At the death of Verwoerd, South Africa–Zambia relations were beginning to enter a new phase. In August 1966 South African police were engaged in counter-insurgency activity against Namibian freedom fighters who were said to have entered from Tanzania and Zambia.[125] Vorster, who succeeded Verwoerd, had warned South Africans at the beginning of July, while he was still Minister of Police, that about 5,000 South Africans were undergoing training in China, the Soviet Union and 'elsewhere'. South African police had arrested 'more than 150' trained saboteurs on their return to South Africa. He added that agents of Fidel Castro were organising subversion in South West Africa, Bechuanaland, Basutoland and Swaziland.[126] More warnings and statements about terrorism followed from Dr Hilgard Muller, the Foreign Minister, and from Lieutenant General Keevy, the commissioner of police. Vorster expected to take more vigorous measures to secure South African borders than Verwoerd had done, and thus impose strains on relations with Zambia, which was said to be implicated in the movement of 'terrorists'.

At the same time, in September 1966, the Zambian government had to contend with Portuguese displeasure at the activities of freedom fighters, who were said to be entering Angola from Zambia. The Portuguese Defence Minister, General Gomes de Arriaga, said that 'terrorists' who had failed to gain entrance through Cabinda in the North were now trying to cross on the south-eastern side of Zambia.[127] As Zambia was dependent on Portuguese good-will for the use of the Benguela Railway, which runs through Angola to the port of Lobito,[128] the Zambian government had to show some

---

[125] A.R.B. (Pol.), 1966, 598B.

[126] Mr Vorster, in an interview with Rhodesian radio on 3 July 1966; see BBC Summary, ME/2204/B/6; cf. also BBC Summary, ME/2252/B/4, for Johannesburg and Salisbury broadcasts of 29 August 1966.

[127] Johannesburg broadcast, BBC Summary, ME/2265/B/9, 14 September 1966. On 8 September 1966 President Kaunda told a press conference that the use of Zambia as a transit route for arms and ammunition destined for use against the 'colonialist' regimes had to stop immediately. See Times of Zambia, 10 September 1965, and Northern News, 5 June 1965, on previous difficulties arising from the transit of war materials. South African Railways and Portuguese East African Railways were unwilling to accept arms and ammunition deliveries destined for Zambia. On 9 September 1965 President Kaunda said that Portugal had agreed to lift its embargo on Zambian arms deliveries.

[128] See F. T. Ostrander, 'Zambia in the aftermath of Rhodesian UDI: logistical and economic problems', in African Forum, 1967, pp. 51–65.

gesture of opposition to terrorism. Vice-president Kamanga warned Angolan refugees in Zambia that his government would not tolerate the use of its territory as a base for military or para-military operations against the Portuguese government,[129] At the end of October the government of Botswana returned eleven infiltrators to Zambia. They had been captured by Botswana police near Kasane in northern Botswana. In a subsequent statement the Botswana government said it took 'the most serious view' of these 'incursions', affirmed that it would not allow its territory to be used as a base for violence against its neighbours, and warned that further violations would be dealt with 'more severely'.[130]

Within Zambia in the months of August, September and October there were several threats to internal security, clearly related to the relations between Zambia and the white regimes. There were acts of sabotage like the fire at Lusaka airport, when someone threw an incendiary bomb at the fuel tanks,[131] and there was racial rioting at Kitwe in October, which the President blamed on agents of either local racialists or local racialists inspired by foreign powers.[132] Towards the end of the year the Zambian government complained to the Security Council of Portuguese incursions into Zambian territory. Rejecting Portuguese allegations that Zambia was allowing 'illicit activities in its territory by individuals who commit acts of aggression against Portuguese territory', and rejecting Portuguese denials of the incursions, the Zambian delegation presented detailed accounts of Portuguese attacks on Zambian villagers in November and December of 1966.[133] There was a quarrel with South Africa also, when five members of the South African police illegally entered Zambian territory in the Victoria Falls bridge area. The Zambian government expressed indignation, although the South African Foreign Minister apologised, saying that the men had been on a private shopping expedition.[134]

[129] Lusaka, 4 October 1966: *BBC Summary*, ME/3201/8/5.

[130] Radio, Johannesburg and Salisbury, 26 October 1966: *BBC Summary*, ME/2302/8/1, and *A.R.B.* (*Pol.*), 1966, 633B.

[131] *BBC Summary* (Johannesburg broadcast), ME/2250/8/9, 26 August 1966; see also *Times of Zambia*, 20 October 1966.

[132] Lusaka, 31 October 1966: *BBC Summary*, ME/2307/8/10.

[133] UN, *Security Council Official Records, 22nd Year, Supplement for January–March 1967*, S/7664: letter dated 3 January 1967 from the representative of Zambia to the Secretary General (reference: Portuguese letter S/7632 of 12 December 1966 and Zambian statement LS/7612 dated 5 December 1966).　　　[134] *A.R.B.* (*Pol.*), 29 December 1967, 935B.

A new and dangerous situation was developing in southern Africa in general and in the relations between Zambia and South Africa. Sanctions had not brought down the Rhodesian regime, nor had it been possible to isolate Rhodesia from Portugal and South Africa. Zambia was very much at the mercy of the white regimes who were more sympathetic to Rhodesia than to Zambia. Nor was Zambia only isolated from Portugal, Rhodesia and South Africa; it was increasingly becoming isolated from the very architect of sanctions, the United Kingdom government. Zambians had long deplored the British government's unwillingness to use force against Rhodesia, which they believed would be speedier and more likely to succeed in bringing the rebellion to an end. Zambian–UK relations deteriorated considerably when, after indicating that it was unwilling to secure Zambian territory against Rhodesian retaliation by providing RAF support with striking power, the Wilson administration surreptitiously initiated 'talks about talks' with the Smith regime in April 1966.[135] When the British government engineered the postponement of the Commonwealth Prime Ministers' Conference from July to September, President Kaunda was even more indignant. He told a university audience:

While the British Government may have the ability to organise the calling of the Commonwealth Conference in September instead of July when in fact the pressing problem calls for it, they have no ability to organise me to remain within that organisation. What I have worked for is for my country to remain in a Commonwealth in which there lies sincerity and not cleverness of organisation.[136]

To Zambian threats of withdrawal from the Commonwealth the UK government replied with threats of cutting down its aid to Zambia.[137] It later transpired from Wilson that as British Prime

[135] Hall, *The High Price of Principles*, p. 149. Talks had clearly been intended much earlier. Harold Wilson writes that when he left Zambia in January 1966 after the Lagos Commonwealth conference 'I left the commonwealth Secretary, Arthur Bottomley, behind. I had sent a message through the Governor to Mr Smith saying that the Secretary of State would, at my request, visit Salisbury and stay with the Governor. He would be glad to meet Mr Smith, provided that this was not taken as implying recognition of the regime.' But Smith was not accommodating. According to Wilson, 'Mr Smith was playing it tough.' (Wilson, *The Labour Government, 1964–70*.

[136] Zambian Information Office press release No. 1267/66, 'Text of speech by President Kaunda on his installation as Chancellor of the University of Zambia on Tuesday, 12 July 1966'.

[137] Hall, *The High Price of Principles*, p. 151.

Minister he was concerned to protect British interests in Zambia and hoped indeed to take advantage of the UDI crisis to augment British exports to Zambia. Wilson wrote in his history of the Labour government:

Britain was utterly dependent on [Zambia's] copper supplies. Had they been cut off, either by the Rhodesians or by a Zambia made sullen by our refusal to use force, we would have had two million unemployed within a matter of months. This was not just speculation; it was more than a gesture when two Zambian Ministers were despatched to Moscow to discuss copper sales. True, had the Russians taken over Zambia's output, we might have hoped to buy from other suppliers whose production would no longer be used by the Russians. But suppose the USSR bought in order to stock-pile? It was an ugly situation which justified our sensitivity to Zambian demands for help.[138]

On Zambian trade Wilson wrote:

I was anxious that Zambia's requirements for consumer goods should be switched from Rhodesia to the Western world. I invited Sir Norman Kipping, retiring director-general of the Federation of British Industries, to spend some weeks in Zambia, working alongside the British economic team, identifying Zambian requirements and assisting British firms to meet them.[139]

If these were the prevailing attitudes in UK administration, it is not surprising that Zambian Ministers came to feel that they had been used as catspaws in the policy of sanctions (which they supported with extreme reservations), and that the UK government's estimate of the gravity of the ethical issues involved in the Rhodesian question was a good deal less than their own.[140]

With Zambia visibly becoming isolated from its main partner in sanctions against Rhodesia, the Zambian government became more vulnerable to pressures from the white regimes. In January 1967 President Kaunda complained of Rhodesian violations of Zambian air space and, apparently associating those violations with the incident of the South African policemen, warned that he was contemplating an east and central African alliance which would 'stand against any invasion from South Africa'.[141] The east and central

---

[138] Wilson, *The Labour Government*, pp. 182–3.
[139] Wilson, *op. cit.*, p. 182.
[140] Cf. Hall, *op. cit.*, pp. 49–151; cf. also Kapwepwe's remark after he left the Commonwealth conference (September 1966) that Mr Wilson was a racialist. See also H. Wilson's account of Kapwepwe and Arthur Wina (Zambian representatives at the conference) in his *The Labour Government*, pp. 279–80.   [141] *A.R.B.* (*Pol.*), 1967, 935B, 1 January 1967.

African alliance did not, however, materialise,[142] and it is in any case doubtful whether it would have secured Zambia from total destruction in the event of a conventional war with South Africa, Rhodesia and Portugal, or from economic ruin if South Africa and the two white regimes were to collude in retaliatory economic warfare against Zambia. In October 1967 Vorster warned that if Zambia, alone or in collaboration with other African States, were to attack South Africa, South Africa would 'hit it so hard' that it would not forget the beating in a short while.[143] The Zambian rejoinder was not immediate, and when President Kaunda replied he effectively denied that Zambia supported armed struggle against South Africa. He accused South Africa of seeking a conflict when Zambia had 'threatened nobody and provoked no one'. However, Zambia could rely on the willingness of its people to make sacrifices and would resist any aggressor.[144] For good measure, the OAU secretariat pledged the support of the OAU to Zambia.[145]

Throughout 1967 relations between Zambia and Portugal and Rhodesia particularly were difficult, while at the same time collaboration between South Africa and these regimes increased, especially on the common problem of increased guerrilla activity. South African police participated in counter-insurgency activity in Mozambique and Rhodesia, in the latter case in obvious defiance of the United Kingdom, which claimed that Rhodesia was its responsibility. The UK sent protests, which were disregarded, and no action followed to make good the claim to responsibility for Rhodesia of Her Majesty's government. It was made clear that the UK government 'did not want a confrontation with South Africa'.[146]

[142] Cf. however, Wallerstein, who wrote in 1967 that Nyerere and Kaunda, in recognition of Mobutu's denunciation of South Africa, met at Kinshasa. 'The three leaders have moved to consolidate the front against South Kinshasa, Zambia, Tanzania, Kenya, Uganda, Ethiopia, Sudan, Burundi, Congo–Brazzaville and the Central African Republic. This group, which has no name, has already signed a secret military pact.'—'Penetrating the continent', in *Africa Report*, February 1969 (reprinted from *The New Leader*, 25 September 1967). For attempts to revive this idea without success, see Institute of Strategic Studies, *Strategic Survey*, 1968, p. 43, and *Africa Confidential*, 15 March 1968.

[143] *Times of Zambia*, 16 October 1967.

[144] *Ibid.*, 23 October 1967, Kaunda's rejoinder was given at a rally in Luanshya.

[145] The OAU statement was made on 19 October 1967: *A.R.B. (Pol.)*, 1967, 891B.

[146] See Vorster, in *Ass. Deb.*, vol. 23, col. 4075; cf. Cockram, *Vorster's Foreign Policy*, p. 150.

In fact, it later transpired that the Wilson administration looked to South African support in bringing Ian Smith to a more accommodating attitude.[147] At the instance of the Governor of Rhodesia, the UK government protested to the Zambian government against the Zambians' support of 'terrorists'.

Direct action by South Africa against Zambia was at this stage minimal, and so by all accounts were South African violations of Zambian territorial integrity.[148] The fact that there was no direct inter-State dispute between Zambia and South Africa—apart, of course, from the mutual general hostility, the benevolent 'neutrality' of Zambia towards freedom fighters and the support of South Africa for Rhodesia and Portugal—may have helped to restrain the South African government from pursuing a more assertive policy against Zambia over the issue of terrorism at this time. The scale of guerrilla activity was, by all estimates, small within South African-controlled territory, and there was in any case little that South Africa could do with advantage against Zambia. Also, Zambia, in spite of its non-alignment, was co-operating more with the West than the East; it was also co-operating with South Africa economically; and as Wilson has pointed out, Zambian copper was important for the West. Any attack on Zambia would, therefore, have incurred not only widespread disfavour among the non-aligned and the communists, but also the displeasure of the white West to which South African governments have always been responsive. The hope that Zambians would, in any case, be forced by economic necessity to become 'realistic'[149] and collaborate with South Africa meant it

[147] Zambian documents suggest that Lord Goodman was sent to South Africa for a confidential exchange of views between South Africa and the UK. See Zambian High Commission, London: *Details of Exchanges between President Kaunda of Zambia and Prime Minister Vorster of South Africa* (hereafter *Details of Exchanges*), 1971, p. 20. Mr Wilson of the Goodman mission does not mention confidential exchanges with South Africa. Lord Goodman and Sir Max Aitken were, according to Mr Wilson, merely intended to try and see Smith: *The Labour Government,* pp. 565–6. However, Vorster's statement in parliament on 23 April 1969 implies that he had been approached—if not by the Goodman mission—by the UK government: 'I have made it very clear to Britain that I am neither prepared to twist Mr Smith's arm nor prepared to dictate to him.' Presumably what had been intended was some sort of economic ultimatum.

[148] *Africa Confidential*, 15 March 1968.

[149] Cf. E. M. Rhoodie, a South African diplomatist, who has argued along these lines in his *The Third Africa, passim*.

was better to be tolerant than risk inviting international opprobrium and spoiling the chances of a future *rapprochement*.

Reports in March 1968 that some 200 African nationalist fighters had crossed the Zambesi from Zambia to fight in Rhodesia[150] were a cue for the South African Defence Minister, Mr Botha, to reassure white South Africans. Speaking in the South African parliament on 3 April, he associated 'terrorism' with 'communism',[151] and warned that:

making a country available as a base for terrorists constitutes provocation of a nature which gradually becomes so serious that it turns to guerilla warfare. Such a situation recently arose for Israel. It then becomes necessary for a country to take stern action against those threats. I want to say this afternoon that it will be a good thing if the people who are inciting terrorism and guerrilla warfare against South Africa come to realise that provocation may eventually lead to severe retaliation for the sake of self-respect and peace.[152]

It is worth noting that the South African Defence Minister made no direct reference to Zambia. The Cape Nationalist daily *Die Burger*, however, did. In an editorial on the following day it dealt with the question of Zambia's support for 'terrorism'. What was of particular interest was that *Die Burger* tended to shift blame from the Zambian government, while not, of course, condoning the attitude of that government. This could be taken to justify a policy of relative forbearance towards Zambia to a militant party's rank and file. On the other hand, it is evidence that the image of 'reasonableness' to which allusion has already been made[153] may have had some effect on some members of the ruling party. *Die Burger* wrote:

Thinking people in South Africa are not without sympathy with Zambia's delicate position. The pressure which its government experiences from the

---

[150] Institute of Strategic Studies, *Strategic Survey*, 1968.

[151] Botha said terrorist attacks on South Africa were of a piece with Soviet activity in the Red Sea and elsewhere. The British withdrawal (from east of Suez) had created a large vacuum in the Indian Ocean, and as a result the threat against South Africa and southern Africa had increased: *Ass. Deb.*, vol. 23, col. 3328, Richard Gott (*Guardian*, 2 November 1971) quoted an interview with the then leader of the UPP, Simon Kapwepwe: 'Some people believe that South Africa is an independent country, but when it comes to Western world intrigues, South Africa is actually a Western colony. South Africa makes no statement without talking about communism and without saying to the West: 'I'm your watchdog. I'm your market, I'm your spy, I'm the guardian of your interests.'

[152] *Ass. Deb.*, vol. 23, col. 3328.

[153] See p. 218 above.

north to collaborate in plans of violence against its southern neighbours is strong and brutal. Too much reluctance [on Zambia's part] could be punished with more than [just] threats. Terrorists abound and are in a favourable position to strike against the leaders of a country which admitted them so freely. It could be that its pugnacious neighbours already have Zambia by the throat.

At the same time this is for South Africa, in the final analysis, a matter of its security and its life. Understanding Zambia's difficult position will not deter South Africa from [taking] steps to secure its existence.[154]

Rhodesian and South African prime ministers conferred, and contingents of the South African police continued to aid Rhodesian troops in anti-guerrilla operations in Rhodesia. The South African para-military intervention in Rhodesia (and in the Portuguese territories) was an assertion of South African power in the area, intended, no doubt, to indicate that this was an area which South Africa considered to be of vital importance for its own security[155] and, further, that the republic took a most serious view of the spread of revolutionary activity in southern Africa. A massive 'anti-terrorist' training exercise in August 1968—the much publicised 'Operation Sibasa'—was intended to demonstrate this.

Yet South African policy towards Zambia was relatively restrained —for the general reasons to which we have alluded. There were, however, particular African reasons, to which we now turn. The

154 *Die Burger*, 4 April 1968; cf. Rhoodie: 'At the beginning of 1967 President Kaunda stepped up his attacks on "racialism" in South Africa and following his visit to Red China in May 1967 these attacks assumed a more belligerent note. The most important question now is whether this is the real thing or chest-thumping to impress neighbouring Tanzania and the OAU. But certainly Kaunda's attitude towards South Africa in the economic sphere is becoming far more pragmatic.' Referring to racial rioting in Zambia, the South African diplomatist notes: 'Zambia's Kenneth Kaunda will undoubtedly have to put up with heavy pressure from other governments in black Africa to take a more active part in the "War of Liberation" against South Africa and Portugal' (*The Third Africa*, pp. 62 ff.). *Who* cultivated this image of Kaunda in National Party circles it is not possible to say. However, Zambian policy at the level of *actual* rather than *verbal* interactions was not self-evidently inconsistent with such an interpretation. South Africans for their part probably needed to believe that Kaunda was not lost, to confirm their view that it was only 'communists' or governments critical of the West, like the Tanzanian, who inspired hostility to South Africa; subsequent pro-South African studies have not, however, been as indulgent to Kaunda. Cf. Cockram *Vorster's Foreign Policy* and C. J. Maritz, 'Suid-Afrika en sy swart buurstate', in J. H. Coetzee, G. S. Labuschagne *et al.*, *Suid-Afrika en Suider-Afrika*, 1970.

155 Cf. Cockram, *op. cit.*, and Coetzee, Labuschagne *et. al.*, *Suid-Afrika en Suider-Afrika*.

South African government was pursuing its policy of trying, by patient persuasion rather than defiance, to win over African and Asian States to a new attitude towards South Africa. The so-called 'outward-looking' policy was being implemented.

The Zambian High Commission in London revealed in its publication of exchanges between Kaunda and Vorster that, after having rejected Zambia's offer of an exchange of diplomats in 1964, the Verwoerd government had started in 1965 'to send out feelers to Zambia with a view to establishing some kind of contact with the Zambian government'.[156] According to the High Commission, these feelers were ignored by the Zambian government. However, according to the same source:

In 1967 and early 1968, these feelers were intensified, with constant requests for co-operation. A list of subjects in which co-operation was possible was transmitted through a source. Among the main subjects proposed for consideration were:

(a) a possible meeting between Mr. Vorster and President Kaunda;
(b) Rhodesia. The question was asked, what compromise Zambia would prefer on the Rhodesian issue? It was suggested that the talks on the subject should include South Africa, Rhodesia and Zambia.

It was revealed that the South African authorities deplored what they called terrorism. This was the period when freedom fighters' operation in Rhodesia was at its highest intensity. Co-operation in many fields, including transport, airways, communications, commerce, industry and labour was among the subjects which would form a fruitful basis for the improvement of relations between Zambia and South Africa.[157]

The Zambian sources give no details as to who spoke to whom, what form the feelers took, or what were the detailed Zambian responses in the three-year period. It is highly improbable that the first 'feelers' in 1965, or the resumed 'feelers' in 1967, were rejected outright. For had they been it is unlikely that there would have been more such 'feelers' in 1968. At the very least, if South Africans sent messengers, those messengers received audience not once but evidently several times. If, on the other hand, the feelers were made by letter (not, intuitively, a likely course of action), then at least some of the letters must have been answered. The earliest letter published

---

[156] Zambian High Commissioner, *Details of Exchanges*, p. 2 (also published by Zambia Information Services, as *Dear Mr Vorster . . . , Details, etc.*).
[157] *Ibid.*

by the Zambian High Commission is dated 1 April 1968.[158] South African 'revelations' about the exchanges cast no light at all on the earlier period, so that any reconstruction of Zambian–South African diplomacy in this period must be speculative. It is significant, however, that the South African government did not deny the suggestions in the Zambian publication about 'feelers' having been sent. It seems, therefore, that it can be accepted that there was an exchange of views between the two governments which may have helped to restrain South African responses to Zambia.

The exchanges were, however, threatened by the persistence of Zambian attacks on South Africa, a speech on 21 May 1968 in Botswana by Kaunda leading, for example, to the cancellation of a meeting between President Kaunda and an emissary of Mr Vorster.[159] In Gaborone Kaunda talked of the political situation in South Africa as being 'potentially explosive'; he referred to the condition of Africans in South Africa, who remained without a voice. He reflected:

. . . no amount of force—arms, police, police-dogs, tear-gas, napalm bombs or any other suppressive measure—will stop their unquenchable thirst for freedom and individual liberty.

He later added:

Maybe the racist regime of South Africa, with its Nazi tendencies, wishes the extermination of Africans. The Nazis of Germany hated the Jews and slaughtered six million of them.

But we do not hate the white people of South Africa and we do not wish them to be dead, or to be exterminated. They deserve our love, but must

158 *Ibid.*, p. 6. Note that this was three days before Mr Botha's speech and *Die Burger's* (mouthpiece of the Cape Nationalist Party, to which Botha belongs) 'understanding' editorial.

159 See *The Times*, 22 April 1971: Vorster said, 'Dr Verwoerd felt from the time that Zambia became independent that it was in the interests of both countries, of South Africa as a whole and of all Africa, that some effort be made to arrive at an understanding.' See also *The Times* (Diary), 29 April 1971, which reported that Lord Walston, formerly parliamentary Under-Secretary at the UK Foreign Office, while on a lecture tour in South Africa during 1968 had three talks with Vorster, largely about Rhodesia, in which Vorster said he was anxious to solve the problem of southern Africa as a whole. Walston said that in that case relations between Pretoria and Lusaka would be of major importance. Walston suggested Vorster and Kaunda should meet or a trusted personal emissary should be sent. Walston did not call at Lusaka on his way home, but he did go to see the Zambian High Commissioner in London to pass on a message to the President. Kaunda's first reported reaction was to laugh—but there were contacts later which came to nothing.

reciprocate. They must realise that they are being misled by a small clique of racialists who wish that other races did not exist, except themselves.[160]

Kaunda also said that Africans in South Africa would not need to be agitated to achieve their objectives by independent African States; 'they [would] accomplish their objectives in the future completely on their own'.[161]

The cancellation of the meeting (planned for 24 May) between Kaunda and Vorster's emissary was not the end of contact. Another meeting was arranged with 'Vorster's men' and took place on 22 June 1968. Vorster says that, to his objections that in the light of the Botswana speech correspondence between himself and Kaunda was a waste of time, the latter answered that Vorster should not take any notice of the Gaborone speech, which had been intended for consumption by others.[162] Zambians reject this account, but give no alternative explanation of why the exchanges continued in spite of the 'hard-hitting speech', suggesting rather that South Africans were so eager for contact that they overcame their own objections.

It is common cause that the main topics of the subsequent exchanges—subsequent to Gaborone—were a meeting between the two correspondents, and the Rhodesian situation. Zambian sources say that the next letter to Vorster, replying to Vorster's of 2 May 1968,[163] was written on 15 August, and 'followed the reports emanating

[160] Times of Zambia, 22 May 1968; The Nationalist (Tanzania), 25 May 1968. [161] Ibid.

[162] Guardian, 22 April 1971; The Times, 22 April 1971.

[163] Kaunda's first letter (1 April 1968) had pointed out the difficulties of the Zambian government in the matter of collaborating with South Africa: 'The South African government has threatened to hit Zambia "so hard that they will not forget it". Economic and military assistance has openly been given by the South African government to the rebel regime in Rhodesia to sustain the latter in their bid to create conditions under which the minority will exercise unbridled control over the rights and well-being of the majority of human beings ... These factors, apart from the general attitude of the South African government towards the African people, have been the root causes of the growing distance between the people of South Africa and Zambia. Recent statements from South Africa have only confirmed the impressions about the offensive nature of the prejudices of the South African authorities against Africans, including African independent States.' Vorster had replied on 2 May 1968, and the spirit of his reply (with which Kaunda's of 15 August 1968 is to be contrasted) is contained in the following excerpts: '... your letter under reply strikes me as being as presumptuous as it is uninformed. Presumptuous in that you take it upon yourself to criticise the domestic policy as well as certain aspects of my government's foreign policy in terms like "offensive" and insinuating that our policy is unchristian. Furthermore your letter bristles with statements proving how uninformed you

from Mozambique that South Africa had thrown its military weight behind the Portuguese forces'. They draw attention to the military situation at this time:

During the first week of August 1968 the leader of the [South African] Opposition, Sir De Villiers Graaff, was reported to have made appeals for South African assistance to the Portuguese fighting forces in Mozambique and Angola.[164] At the same time, reports of miltary manoeuvres by South African forces in the Zambesi Valley in defence of rebel Rhodesia. This was the same period during which Zambian villages in the Western Province had been destroyed by Portuguese air raids.[165]

The letter of 15 August was undoubtedly conciliatory in tone. Kaunda stressed that he separated in his mind the problem of South Africa from those of Portugal and Rhodesia and that he did not, therefore, believe that 'the solutions which are being proposed for Rhodesia' were applicable to the situation in South Africa. He added, 'It is important to understand, therefore, that at no time have we considered that force is the answer in South Africa.' Kaunda's appreciations of the exchange of messages, and even of what South Africans were doing to 'solve' their problem, were also appeasing to the point of disingenuousness, and deserve to be quoted in full:

Since receiving your letter I have had opportunity to see some of your officials. I had an interesting meeting with them in June. I do hope that they derived a lot to learn from the exchange of views which the meeting afforded. Such contacts are useful, for ignorance is always the source of suspicion and fear, and both in turn breed conflict and all the attendant consequences. I know that we have been very misunderstood but all I can say is that we mean well and sincerely believe that politics of expediency do not provide a good foundation for lasting friendship. We believe that principles are for ages and expediencies only for the day.

It is in this spirit that, first, I accepted the visit of your officials to Lusaka and, secondly, I engaged in a frank exchange of views with them.

---

are about our real policy and objectives.' On Rhodesia: 'I am not aware that Rhodesia seeks to harm or to destroy Zambia. Nor has Rhodesia, like South Africa, to my knowledge, refused to co-operate with Zambia as an independent State on an equal footing. It might just, therefore, be worth your while to reconsider your own attitude' (pp. 12, 14).

[164] Sir de Villiers Graaff had, according to Cockram, proposed a motion to the United Party Cape Provincial Congress in September which called for 'non-military aid' from South Africa for the Portuguese in Angola. Cf. also Theo Gerdener, Natal Provincial Administrator, also quoted in Cockram's *Vorster's Foreign Policy*, pp. 168 and 169.

[165] *Details of Exchanges*, p. 16.

This meeting should be regarded as opening a possible channel of communication to ensure that our positions are clarified.

The discussions which we had with your government officials and the subsequent information which I have been able to receive have together confirmed our view held for a long time; viz, that the problem of South Africa is very different from that which obtains in Rhodesia or indeed in Angola or Mozambique. We are, therefore, interested to learn more of the evolutionary process of change which obviously is one of the most important phenomena in South Africa's future development. You have spoken in your letter, for example, of the fact that you are progressively leading 'the various black nations to self-determination and independence'. The final objectives of the South African Government in relation to these 'nations' and their relationship to the Government, for example, in Pretoria would be of interest to the critics of South African policy. This I certainly would be interested to know, although part of the story was explained by your officials. It would help provide a basis for future considerations.[166]

The Zambian High Commission publication says that the President's motive in the exchanges 'was to establish a line of investigation as to whether there was any fruitful purpose to be gained in preventing South Africa from strengthening the rebel regime in Rhodesia'.[167] The letter of 15 August can be seen as an earnest attempt to persuade Vorster against siding with Smith. Referring to the international obligations which made it imperative for Zambia to concern itself with South Africa (implied, rather than explicit), Kaunda wrote:

The problem would probably have been easier if it was not unfortunately accentuated by the involvement of your country in the current problems facing the rebels in Rhodesia. It is accepted that your government has every right to trade with anybody but I consider it is also the duty of friends to advise where dangers exist. We, for our part, have often been warned about communism and we have not ignored this advice. Similarly, it is imperative for us to point out that the Smith regime is not really helping South Africa nor is it helping the white people of Rhodesia.

. . . In conclusion, I feel bound once again to say that the rebel regime in Rhodesia may well be the key obstacle in the path towards better understanding. It is my hope and trust that you will consider your country's interests in this matter and, indeed, your whole position *vis-à-vis* the rebel regime.[168]

According to Zambian sources, Kaunda's letter was followed by a South African request for Kaunda to receive another emissary. It was intended that the emissary should learn Zambian views on a possible settlement in Rhodesia preliminary to a meeting between

---

[166] *Ibid.*, pp. 17–19.   [167] *Ibid.*, p. 24.   [168] *Ibid.*, p. 18.

the South African Prime Minister and Wilson's emissary to South Africa, Lord Goodman.[169] The emissary was received on 29 August 1968. In a letter of the same date Kaunda outlined his proposals for a referendum to test the reaction of the people of Rhodesia to the rebellion and to the form of government that would best serve their interests.

According to the Zambian sources the letter of 29 August was the last one to be written, but another emissary was received on 15 February 1969 'after persistent requests'.[170] The emissary presented suggestions about the intended meeting between Kaunda and Vorster. President Kaunda did not believe that such a meeting would be appropriate, with the result that the meeting never occurred. Vorster has said that the meeting was proposed by the Zambian President, but it is common ground between the two leaders that Kaunda was responsible for the failure of the meeting to be held.[171] Vorster has further alleged that Kaunda sent an envoy to him, in great haste, in March 1969, asking Vorster to restrain Portugal and Rhodesia, who, Kaunda believed, were about to attack Zambia. This account has been completely rejected by the Zambian government, which asserts that there were no contacts between 15 February 1969 and 3 May 1970.

It is not of great importance to the present discussion to establish which account is true or why the accounts differ. What is significant is that the contacts were proceeding during the critical months of 1968 and were not wholly abandoned until, so far as is known, March–April 1971, when South Africa was active in 'anti-terrorist' activity in Rhodesia and, it was feared, might support intensification of pressure on Zambia by Portuguese and Rhodesians. The continuance of the talks enabled both leaders to impress upon each other that, however opposed they were ideologically, they were not at daggers drawn. So long as the contacts were maintained the Zambian President could feel more secure in spite of the apparent militancy of the South African government and its supporters, while, conversely, in South Africa the scales were tipped in favour of a policy of relative forbearance in the face of militant Zambian public statements and the resultant suggestions for firm action against Zambian support of 'terrorists'.

[169] *Ibid.*, p. 20; see also n. 1, p. 178.   [170] *Ibid.*
[171] Cf. *Guardian* and *The Times*, 22, 23 and 24 April 1971; *Financial Times*, 25 April 1971.

Vorster referred to Kaunda as a 'double-dealer' and accused him of 'double-talk'. Certainly the hostility reflected in speeches like the one at Gaborone was discordant with the continuing diplomacy and the tone of at least one of the subsequent exchanges. But Vorster's abusive phrases are not exact, and they substitute invective for political understanding. It is the view of the present writer that Kaunda's policy is best understood as a deliberate and elaborate act of balancing the ambiguity of practical policy with his unambiguous hostility to the South African regime. His task was to avoid the 'logic of hostility', precipitating a physical—economic or military—confrontation at a time when the Zambian State could not, by any intelligent estimate, have survived it. Kaunda was particularly concerned to isolate Rhodesia, since his militant policy towards the Smith regime was possible (or even non-suicidal) so long as the confrontation with Rhodesia was substantially isolated from the wider conflict with the white regimes generally. It might have been hoped in Zambia that international action, particularly British action, would make this isolation possible, and therefore limit the burdens of insecurity that Zambians had to bear. British policy had however, been inadequate to achieve that, and Zambia was left with the choice of either following the British government in its slow but definite drift away from its earlier uncompromising position on Rhodesia, or face isolation in southern Africa. The second contingency could be delayed by ameliorating relations with South Africa, if only to the point of averting a final breakdown, although the consistent hostility, often and vigorously expressed, to South Africa necessitated that this could be only a very temporary interlude.

Zambia was all the more vulnerable because of its estrangement from the UK.[172] For so long as relations between Zambia and the UK were good, there were strong pressures on the white southern African regimes, which were responsive to the UK, with which they were on the same side of the Cold War fence, to tolerate Zambia also. After all, within South Africa itself South African policy was often justified as contributing to the security of the West,[173] with which white South Africans identified themselves and which successive South African governments have sought, directly or indirectly to implicate in the defence of white minority rule in South Africa. So long as Zambia was in the orbit of British influence

---

[172] See Hall, *The High Price of Principles*, pp. 114–77 and *passim*.
[173] See above, chapters II and III.

it could be expected not to give much support to any movement that would threaten the extensive interests of the UK in southern Africa. Such a movement, the South African government has long asserted, could only be communist-backed, since Western governments, however much they deplore the idea of *apartheid*, are, with the arguable exceptions of Sweden and Israel, manifestly friendly towards the *regime* in South Africa and are solicitous to maintain their existing lucrative interests there.[174] Responsiveness to the interests of the UK and the West might be expected to moderate South African reactions to a Zambia that was friendly to the West. Naturally, there would be quarrels and recriminations within southern Africa, but the Zambian position would be more secure mainly because of the associative 'principle'—the friend of a friend is not an enemy—as well as the diplomatic support that the UK could exert in circles influential on southern African governments.

Responsiveness is, however, a two-way process. South Africa will cosset UK and Western interests only if it believes that the UK and the West will do the same for South African interests, which can be summarised as the maintenance of white minority rule in South Africa. This assessment is consistent with conflicts within the two sides over southern African topics. The South African government was not responsive to UK policy in Rhodesia when it believed that policy would be ruinous for South Africa.[175] Similarly, the South African government was probably less responsive to UK interests when the UK under a Labour government was dilatory in its support for South Africa—especially on the question of arms. But above all, responsiveness explains the unwillingness of the Wilson government to 'risk a confrontation' and its decision to rely on the good offices of the South African government in its negotiations with Smith.[176]

If this assessment is correct, then the Zambian government seriously misunderstood the nature of its political situation in southern Africa. The rift in Zambia–UK relations came because the

[174] An analysis of UK interests in South Africa and 'how they might behave' is to be found in Austin, *Britain and South Africa, passim.* See also G. Arrighi and J. S. Saul 'Nationalism and revolution in sub-Saharan Africa', in *Socialist Register*, 1969.

[175] Cf. Vorster's statements in parliament, 1968 and 1969, *Ass. Deb.*, vol. 23, col. 4075, and vol. 26, col. 4580.

[176] On responsiveness, see D. G. Pruitt, 'An analysis of responsiveness between nations', in *Conflict Resolution*, vol. VI, No. 1, and references.

Zambian government expected the UK government to play a part wholly alien to British southern Africa policy, as manifest in tradition and as embodied in the concrete patterns of collaboration between the UK and the governments of the white-ruled territories. The tradition was to seek to influence the white governments rather than to coerce them, to accept that for all practical purposes those governments were valuable friends of British governments and should be treated as such, and, above all, to avoid being drawn into a major conflict with those regimes on behalf of Africans, and thus avoid upsetting the peace of 1909, which was achieved by British collusion, among other things, in the repression of black South Africans.[177] Conversely, Zambian–South African relations became dangerous when Zambia exceeded not only the limit of South African tolerance, but also of British collusion in the defence of African interests in Southern Rhodesia in particular, and in southern Africa generally.[178]

The Zambian position was dangerous. Zambia was not aligned to any important power and could most probably not interest any Western power in an alliance concordant with its hostility to the regimes of the south. Nor could it rely on a grand African alliance. An alliance with a communist power would probably carry with it severe consequences in the form of retaliation by the Western powers, notably the UK.[179] Zambians would probably have been apprehensive of such an alliance. Zambia was clearly not viable in

[177] This is very much a matter of subjective historical judgement. British writers like Lord Hailey, *The High Commission Territories*, and N. Mansergh, *The Price of Magnanimity*, prefer the view that in 1909 the UK was magnanimous to the Boers after its victory in the South African war and rather hoped that the Boers would one day become 'liberal' towards the natives. It is, however, difficult to reconcile such hope with representations made against 'magnanimity' by such outstanding South African liberals as Schreiner; it is also difficult to see what evidence could be produced that the Boers intended to become liberal. The unification conference had rather indicated the contrary. See, for example, Thompson, *The Unification of South Africa*; Hancock, *Smuts: the Sanguine Years*; H. J. and R. E. Simon, *Colour and Class in South Africa*, and N. Garson, *Louis Botha or J. X. Merriman: the Choice of South Africa's first Prime Minister*, 1969. Subsequently the UK government took a very conservative interpretation of its responsibilities in South Africa, as Malan argued so persuasively in *Wat ons het, hou ons*.

[178] I.e. in 1967–68.

[179] Through the cutting of aid for example, as had, according to Hall, already been suggested when Kaunda hinted in 1968 that he might leave the Commonwealth. *The High Price of Principles*, p. 151.

conventional inter-State war with South Africa.[180] The kind of war which might have enhanced its viability was guerrilla warfare, with the whole of Zambia transformed into a militant movement regime[181] rather than a conventional nation State. Such a situation would accord ill with what most influential Zambians wanted for themselves. The Zambian government was, for all these reasons, not averse to considering some gestures of goodwill towards South Africa.

In April 1969 Kaunda took the initiative at the fifth Summit of Heads of State and Government in East and Central Africa, in the drawing up of the Lusaka manifesto, which emphasised the preference of African States for non-violence and in measured terms urged the South African government to be more accommodating.[182] This was clearly a retreat from the more uncompromising denunciations of the white regimes which had become familiar. The manifesto affirmed commitment to the principles of human equality and self-determination as the only basis for peace and justice in the world. It accused the white minority of lacking that commitment:

It is on the basis of our commitment to human equality and human dignity, not on the basis of achieved perfection, that we take our stand of hostility towards the colonialism and racial discrimination which is being practised in Southern Africa. It is on the basis of their commitment to these universal principles that we appeal to other members of the human race for support.

If the commitment to these principles existed among the States holding power in southern Africa, any disagreements we might have about the rate of implementation, or about isolated acts of policy, would be matters affecting only our individual relationships with the States concerned. If these commitments existed, our States would not be justified in the expressed and active hostility towards the regimes of southern Africa such as we have proclaimed and continue to propagate.[183]

On the use of force against the 'southern African regimes' the manifesto stated:

[180] On viability in conflict, see K. E. Boulding, *Conflict and Defence: a General Theory*, chapter 4.

[181] On 'movement regimes' see, for example, R. C. Tucker: 'Towards a comparative politics of movement regimes', in *American Political Science Review*, 1961.

[182] Fifth Summit Conference of East and Central African States: *Manifesto on Southern Africa*, Lusaka, 14–16 April 1969. The manifesto is not, in fact, on southern Africa, since it does not deal with the High Commission Territories.

[183] *Ibid.*, p. 2.

We have always preferred, and we still prefer, to achieve it [the objective of liberation] without physical violence. We would prefer to negotiate rather than destroy, to talk rather than kill. We do not advocate violence; we advocate an end to the violence against human dignity which is now being perpetrated by the oppressors of Africa. If peaceful progress to emancipation were possible, or if changed circumstances were to make it possible in the future, we would urge our brothers in the resistance movements to use peaceful methods of struggle even at the cost of some compromise on the timing of change.[184]

Of particular interest was the manifesto's distinction between the three situations of Rhodesia, Portugal and South Africa in terms of what form of struggle—peaceful or armed—was appropriate. While the manifesto unequivocally condoned the recourse of liberation movements to armed struggle in Portuguese colonies and in Rhodesia, it made no reference to violent struggle in South Africa's case, but merely reaffirmed the signatories' adherence to the policy of boycotting South Africa.[185]

Within South Africa there were voices favouring a more militant policy towards Zambia. Only a week or so before the summit in Lusaka a Nationalist MP, Dr P. S. van der Merwe, had reflected in parliament that the time was 'opportune' for the Minister of Defence to issue once again a 'strong warning' to African countries which were 'accommodating, inciting and assisting terrorists'.[186] There was, however, no marked deterioration in the public diplomacy between Zambia and South Africa in the course of 1969—a balance presumably being maintained in South Africa between the attitudes favouring calling off the attempt to arrive at an understanding with Zambia (and being more punitive over 'terrorism') and those preferring a more patient policy.

To the South African government, trying to balance these dispositions, the announcement in November 1969 that China had signed the agreement with Tanzania and Zambia to construct the TanZam railway must have been difficult to ignore.[187] This agreement was by far the most dissociative (from the West and from the white south) that Zambia had ever undertaken. Quasi-socialistic measures like the Mulungushi reforms,[188] the partial nationalisation

---

[184] *Ibid.*, p. 3.
[185] Cf. paras. 13–15, 16–19 with 20–24; *Manifesto*, pp. 4–7.
[186] *Ass. Deb.* vol. 25, col. 5431.
[187] Institute of Strategic Studies, *Strategic Survey*, 1968.
[188] See Republic of Zambia: *Zambia's Guideline for the next decade: H.E. the President Addressing the National Council of UNIP at Mulungushi,*

of mining, and attempts at partial nationalisation of the financial sector of the economy did not have to be seen as a move away from the West—and therefore implicitly threatening to South Africa—since this kind of policy had come to be acceptable to some of the leading South African businessmen with interests in Africa.[189] They could in any case be attributed to nationalism rather than socialism. But after the initial boom in South Africa–Zambia trade after UDI, the Zambian government had tried with some success to reduce trade with South Africa,[190] and the reality of the TanZam project now made a substantial further diminution of Zambian dependence on the 'white south' more probable. Politically, the prospect of the communist Chinese gaining a toe-hold in southern Africa was of potent symbolical significance to politicians in whose political demonology Asians and communists had traditionally enjoyed pride of place.[191]

It was Kaunda's election to the chairmanship of the OAU in 1970 which provided the occasion for more disputes and for a further deterioration of relations. As chairman of the OAU Kaunda was placed in the forefront of the organisation's campaign to persuade governments in Africa and elsewhere not to collaborate with that regime. Yet precisely because of Kaunda's status as chairman of the OAU it would have been a famous victory for the South African government to win him over to the long-proposed meeting with Vorster. According to the Zambian government, more attempts were made in May 1970, when an emissary of Vorster 'suddenly appeared' in the hotel in which Kaunda was staying in Munich during his visit to West Germany. Once more the planned meeting with Vorster was discussed, the emissary suggesting November 1970. Kaunda said his programme was full and that 'at any rate, such a

---

9 *November 1968* and *Towards Complete Independence: Address by H.E. the President, etc., to the UNIP National Council at Matero Hall, Lusaka,* 11 August 1969.

[189] Cf. H. Oppenheimer, 'African development and the private investor', address to the Institute of Directors' annual conference in the Albert Hall, London, reproduced in *Kenya Weekly News*, 16 February 1968 (before Zambian nationalisation but after the Arusha declaration); A. Rupert: *Progress through Partnership*, 1969, comes quite close to the views expressed by Oppenheimer.

[190] This is truer of Zambian exports to South Africa than of Zambian imports from South Africa. See n. 5, p. 195.

[191] Cf. Malan's African Charter, discussed above, and G. D. Scholtz, *Die gevaar uit die Ooste, passim.*

meeting would have to be preceded by discussions between officials which had not yet taken place'.[192]

When the newly elected Conservative government in the UK announced in July that it would reopen the question of arms sales to South Africa,[193] a quarrel between Kaunda and the UK and South Africa became unavoidable—not least because of Kaunda's African role as chairman of OAU. There was an acrimonious exchange between Kaunda and Heath during Kaunda's visit to London as head of the delegation of non-aligned States which at their conference in Lusaka had condemned the resumption of arms sales to South Africa.[194] During the non-aligned conference South African aircraft had been observed to be particularly active along the Zambian border and had crossed into Zambian air space. This had evidently caused some agitation in Zambia.[195] Tension became even greater when, on 15 September, Vorster issued another warning against countries aiding 'terrorists' and said that in the event of large-scale guerrilla incursions South Africa would invoke 'the right of hot pursuit' into the territory harbouring terrorists. Vorster offered South African support to any country troubled by 'terrorists'.[196]

The quarrel with Heath and the indifferent reception of the non-aligned delegation in Washington[197] proved that the West was not very sympathetic to Kaunda's campaign, or so it must have seemed in Pretoria.[198] In October Botha, announcing that South Africa could manufacture napalm, told an election meeting:

Kaunda has chosen to side with the communists[199] and he is becoming more and more their lackey and slave. If Kaunda's terrorists try to attack South

[192] *Details of Exchanges*, p. 23.
[193] The Foreign Minister, Sir Alec Douglas-Home, announced on 20 July 1970 the willingness of HMG to consider South African orders for maritime equipment to defend the Cape sea route, but postponed a final decision. Institute of Strategic Studies, *Strategic Survey*, 1970.
[194] Cf. *Observer*, 13 September 1970; *Sunday Times*, 25 October 1970, See also *Lusaka Declaration on Peace, Independence Development and Democratisation of International Relations*, 1970.
[195] Personal communication from confidential Angolan source and eye-witness.
[196] *The Times*, 17 September 1970.
[197] Cf. *Sunday Times*, 25 October 1970, p. 6.
[198] *Sunday Times*, 25 October 1970, p. 6; Kaunda's opposition to the Cabora Bassa dam project (see above) must also have infuriated South Africa. *Ibid.*, p. 9; also *X-Ray*, July 1970.
[199] The UK and South African governments used the argument that arms shipments to South Africa were intended to help meet the USSR (communist) 'threat' in the Indian Ocean.

Africa, they will soon find out that it has ample means to destroy them completely.[200]

In December 1970 the view that Kaunda was on the side of the communists was endorsed by the Commissioner General for the Northern Territories in South West Africa (the only South African-controlled area in which guerilla fighters were operating) when he reflected that, unlike 'all our black neighbours and the former French territories in Africa', Kaunda was 'drifting away from the West towards communist China'.[201]

The arms issue showed the UK (and the US and France) either unwilling to choose between the forces against *apartheid* and the white south, or, if forced to choose, to choose the white south in preference to the forces represented by Kaunda in his advocacy of a boycott. On the other hand, they probably felt that they were not really called upon to choose—except by a very few Africans—since the regimes denouncing British policy towards South Africa would not consider British failure to comply sufficient reason to sever their ties with the UK, by which they evidently set much store.[202]

After the Singapore Commonwealth Prime Ministers' Conference, at which arms sales to South Africa were the dominant issue, Kaunda, Nyerere and Obote took the lead in denouncing British policy. Zambia's relations with South Africa took a further turn for the worse, i.e. from the point of view of accommodation. Vorster threatened to 'expose' Kaunda as a 'double-dealer' and a 'double-talker'.[203] It had already been revealed by the South African Foreign Minister, Dr Muller, that South Africa had 'contacts' with Zambia.[204] During March 1971 Kaunda received an emissary from South Africa, but it was unclear what the object of the visit was. Kaunda, according to the Zambian documents, advised the emissary that Vorster could go ahead with his revelations, since the Zambian President did not feel he had anything to hide.[205] According to the Zambians this meeting was in early March, but Vorster said in Cape Town on 23 April that South African and Zambian envoys

[200] *Sunday Times*, 25 October 1970.

[201] *Windhoek Advertiser*, 18 October 1970; see also the leader article.

[202] In going ahead with the deal the Tory government disregarded warnings voiced at the time that such an arms deal would wreck the Commonwealth.   [203] *Details of Exchanges*, p. 23.

[204] *Guardian*, 2 September 1970.

[205] *Details of Exchanges*, p. 23.

had met 'a few days ago' at Chipata, in Zambia, near the Malawi border, and the South African envoy was invited to Lusaka.[206]

During the early part of 1971 Zambia's relations with the Portuguese went through a very bad patch, with the Portuguese maintaining an unofficial blockade of Zambian merchandise in Mozambique following a dispute over Portuguese soldiers allegedly captured by Mozambican guerrillas operating from Zambia.[207] Zambia was forced into the invidious position of having to breach sanctions by obtaining maize from Rhodesia. When this was followed by the refoulement of some Rhodesian guerrillas—129, according to reports from Rhodesia—it appeared that Zambian policy towards Rhodesia was in disarray.[208]

At the time when revelations of the contacts with Vorster were made it had been speculated that Kaunda's political position in Zambia would in consequence be perilous. It had even been suggested that Vorster's object was exactly that, but it seems that there were also other motives probably more important. The South African government was scoring successes in the 'outward-looking' policy and Zambia under Kaunda had become a nuisance, especially as it incited opposition to those African leaders favouring a more conciliatory attitude to South Africa. Kaunda had to be discredited.

[206] *The Times*, 24 April 1971.

[207] See *Africa Digest*, June 1971, p. 44. Cf. also J. Hatch, 'The black man's burden', in the *Guardian*, 23 April 1971. According to Mr Hambaraci, Director of Zambian Information Services for Western Europe, the Portuguese had offered to establish a 'no man's land' along the borders of Mozambique if Zambia ceased to support liberation movements. At Kaunda's request, Hambaraci had gone to meet the Portuguese in Malawi to tell them that they should recognise the liberation movements and deal with them. *Financial Times*, 30 April 1971.

[208] *Guardian*, 23 August 1971, report from Peter Niesewand, Salisbury, 22 August 1971. Zambian sources put the figure at about sixty. It is unclear why they were handed over (by the Zambian army) to the Rhodesians. It was at the request of one faction of the Zimbabwe African People's Union (ZAPU) leadership, and the reason given is that the men were spies of the white regimes. It is, however, extraordinary that the Zambian government should have agreed to this, since it could have been a ploy of one ZAPU faction against another. It is not surprising, therefore, that the *bona fides* of the Zambian government have been called into question to the extent that it has been suggested that the men were delivered to the Rhodesians to ensure 'continued trade in both food and goods with Rhodesia and South Africa'. Confidential communications from academic and non-academic sources in London and Lusaka have confirmed this view. See, however, *Guardian*, 15 December 1971, for the *Zambia Daily Mail* account, which endorses the spy 'theory', with, naturally, not a shred of evidence nor a hint of explanation of the timing, or the large size of the 'catch'.

At the same time, the 'revelations' were timed to give maximum publicity to President Houphouet-Boigny's speech favouring 'dialogue' with South Africa, which followed shortly after the revelations and to which Vorster had specifically made reference in his own statements about Kaunda.[209]

If Kaunda did not fall as anticipated, the burden of external relations, together with the natural difficulties of new States— inefficient administration, corruption and shortages—did begin to tell on the internal life of Zambia. Throughout its seven-year history the Zambian polity had always been fissiparous, tribal or regional divisions being ever likely to bring about its complete dissolution. It has even transpired that in the Western Province, which consists largely of Barotseland, the South African government had encouraged secessionist feeling, and because Barotseland had traditionally supplied labour to the South African mines it was thought that Kaunda's policy of dissociating Zambia from the south would be most strongly opposed in Barotseland.[210] In 1971, however, discontent did not take the form of Barotse secessionism. Lozis and Tongas continued to maintain their disdain of Bembas and their opposition to a government constituted, in their view, of foreigners. But the revolt against the Kaunda administration which was led by the Bemba leader Simon Kapwepwe followed from a less clearly defined (in regional and tribal terms) dissatisfaction, which tended to take the form of a diminution of popular confidence in Kaunda (and his Ministers). It had become apparent in 1970 that some Ministers, including some who have remained loyal to Kaunda, were uneasy about his conduct of affairs, especially relations with the Cabinet.[211] But the first expression of lack of confidence in Kaunda came from much lower down, and, quite incongruously, from supporters of his policy of dissociation from and hostility to South Africa. The occasion was a demonstration against the French policy of selling arms to South Africa. Demonstrating students were roughly handled by the police and the President intervened ambiguously: refraining from publicly criticising the behaviour of the police, he told the students to leave the matter of French arms sales to him.

[209] *Guardian, The Times, Financial Times,* 29 April 1971; *Guardian,* 23 April 1971.

[210] G. L. Caplan, 'Zambia, Barotseland and the liberation of southern Africa', in *Africa Today,* 1969. See also *Africa Confidential,* 1965, No. 1.

[211] Personal communication from three confidential unofficial sources on separate occasions.

Ten students wrote him a letter in which they asked, rhetorically, why they should trust him when he had 'communicated with the enemy'. Enraged reactions by some of Kaunda's supporters to this insult to the President led to a series of incidents culminating in the closure of the university on 15 July 1971. Divisions were observed in the Cabinet over the issue of the closure of the university.[212]

Next there were rumours that a new party was being formed to contest the position of UNIP. After some weeks of rumour and speculation about the new party, Kapwepwe resigned from the government and announced the formation of the United Progressive Party (UPP). The UPP leadership consisted mostly of people who had recently been dismissed from ministerial positions by Kaunda. In their criticism of Kaunda and UNIP the UPP leadership proved one thing, that they were aware that there was widespread discontent on bread-and-butter issues and about the southern policies of the Kaunda administration, but no clear alternative policies were proclaimed. There was discontent on the 'left' and on the 'right', and it was evident from Kapwepwe's initial major speech that he hoped to appeal to both, and in regard to southern Africa he made ambiguous remarks, using a rhetorical style which might please the 'left' while completely reserving his position on relations with the white regimes. He declared, for example, 'We have even failed to grow maize . . . As a result, we have spent K32 million public funds to [obtain maize from] South Africa and Rhodesia.'[213] Criticising the moral quality of the leadership, he remarked enigmatically, 'We have fallen victims to flattery from imperialists . . .' Kapwepwe did not say who the 'imperialists' were. His party sought a merger —in the event, unsuccessfully—with the Zambian African National Congress (ANC) led by Harry Nkumbula, who favoured trade with South Africa, and whose party did not use the rhetoric of anti-imperialism. Kapwepwe subsequently said that UPP would oppose dialogue with South Africa, but admitted that it might be forced to change its stand when it finally merged with the ANC.[214]

Kaunda accused the UPP of being in league with foreign powers,

[212] Based on a detailed, written eye-witness account by a political scientist with journalistic training and experience and with thorough familiarity with African affairs. See also *Guardian*, 15 July 1971, and *Manchester Evening News*, 15 July 1971.

[213] *Zambia Daily Mail*, 23 August 1971; *Times of Zambia*, 23 August 1971;

[214] *Zambia Daily Mail*, 31 August 1971.

and of planning a violent overthrow of the State. About a hundred UPP supporters were imprisoned, while very little was done to re-strain UNIP supporters from intimidating supporters and suspected fellow travellers of the UPP.

UNIP was clearly faced with a crisis of considerable magnitude, and in the general state of discontent which prevailed a military *coup d'état* against the Kaunda administration was perhaps more likely than ever before. How far this fact influenced the UPP leader-ship to take the onerous step of challenging UNIP—onerous because having been key members of UNIP they knew how prone that party was to the use of political intimidation—we may never know. It is, of course, possible that they did not anticipate the mass detentions and hoped to be able to deal with UNIP thuggery on its own terms. But if there were a danger of the military forces seizing power, then Zambia's international position made the danger even greater. Soldiers very rarely seize power without making some judgement of likely external reactions. From that point of view Kaunda could hardly have been less vulnerable than Uganda's Obote, for the one country whose reactions to a *coup* were most likely to matter in the calculations of the Zambian army was the United Kingdom,[215] and Kaunda's relations with Britain had never been worse than they had then become. In the light of this it is of considerable interest that when Kaunda accused Kapwepwe of being an agent of foreign powers he scrupled to avoid any reference to the UK or the West[216] but named South Africa, Portugal and Rhodesia as the puppeteers. Then an extraordinary attack was made on East Germany, suggesting that it was implicated in Kapwepwe's dealings. Since politics makes strange bedfellows, it is not perhaps impossible that Kapwepwe was to be supported by both the GDR and the white south; but the severity of Kaunda's action against East Germany[217] was peculiar and, on past form, must have been gratifying to those in the UK and the West who may have thought that he was tending to lean towards the East. Kaunda did indeed

[215] The Zambian army was British-trained, and Britain has considerable social and cultural influence in Zambia because of the past colonial connec-tion.

[216] *Zambia Daily Mail*, 28 February 1971.

[217] *The Times,* 11 October 1971. A secret cold war had been going on for some time between East and West Germans in Zambia. The latter might have planted the story of East German involvement. The President tended to favour the West. (Based on confidential interviews, Zambia, May 1973.)

subsequently receive, for the first time in two years, a British Minister, while he said noticeably little on British discussion with Rhodesia. The eventual 'settlement' of the Rhodesian issue provoked severely critical Zambian comment, but even this was somewhat delayed.[218]

South Africans who supported Vorster exhibited the natural *Schadenfreude* in the circumstances of internal political division in Zambia. Vorster, dismissing Kaunda's allegation that his government was aiding Kapwepwe, recalled his correspondence with Kaunda in which he had written 'that South Africa wanted nothing from Zambia except that she was well run in the interests of southern Africa's stability'. He added, 'If President Kaunda had heeded my advice, he would still have been undisputed leader.[219] The Afrikaans newspapers *Die Vaderland*, *Die Burger* and *Rapport* stated their preference of Kapwepwe to Kaunda, *Die Burger* quoting a 'high official' of the Rhodesian security branch as having told its correspondent that 'Kapwepwe of Zambia [was] likely to be a man with whom southern Africa [would] be able to make a deal'.[220]

A month after these valuations were made, in the first week of October, Vorster told a National Party congress meeting that, following the death of a South African policeman and injuries to others after a 'terrorist' mine had exploded under them, the police had been instructed to pursue the 'terrorists' across the border (taken by virtually the whole South African press to mean the border with Zambia). Zambia took the matter to the Security Council of the UN, where the South African Foreign Minister denied that there had been violations by South Africa of 'the sovereignty, air space, and territorial integrity' of Zambia.[221] In South Africa the Prime Minister repudiated newspaper reports of his statement, and recriminations followed between Vorster and parts of the press.[222] In Zambia Vorster's speech enabled Kaunda to draw attention again to the external threats to the country, and provided the occasion for a military display in which the most newsworthy weapon was a British ground-to-air Rapier missile. There were no reports of weapons from the communist bloc.[223]

[218] BBC Radio 4, 29 November 1971.

[219] *Star*, 2 September 1971, and *Zambia Daily Mail*, 3 September 1971.

[220] *Die Burger, Die Vaderland* and *Rapport*, quoted in *Zambia Daily Mail*, 8 October 1971.

[221] *Cape Times*, 7 October 1971.   [222] *Ibid.*

[223] *Times of Zambia*, 9 October 1971.

It would be absurd to suggest that the internal problems faced by Kaunda and his party arose entirely from the burden of external relations, equally absurd to argue that they were of South African making, and even more absurd to suggest that if Kaunda had listened to Vorster he could sleep in spite of thunder. Zambia has always had intense divisive forces in its national political life, and it is just as plausible to suppose that external difficulties would maintain its precarious unity as to argue that they would exacerbate its divisions. To the extent, however, that difficult relations with the southern States may have contributed to the economic difficulties which have led to popular dissatisfaction, then it is correct to argue that external relations are not merely peripheral to the internal divisions. It would be hard to demonstrate that the difficulties experienced by Kaunda were part of the fall which it was predicted would follow from Vorster's revelations. Yet the 'revelations', whatever their objective worth, were a kind of failure of Kaunda's policy —after all, the exchanges *were* meant to be secret—and this may have contributed to the diminution of confidence in the President himself. At the same time the revelations, or, rather, the contacts and exchanges themselves, had pointed to a rift in the Zambian situation and indeed in the minds of Zambians, a rift between the desire for complete opposition to and dissociation from South Africa, and the surrender to the felt need for some contact in the interim between the commitment to dissociation and the achievement of complete dissociation.

This dramatisation of the element of necessity or *raison d'état* in Zambia's politics of principles,[224] together with the difficulties and divisions of 1971, may have had the effect of strengthening opinion within Zambia that favoured a review of the policy towards the south in the direction of normalisation. An opinion poll in November 1971 showed that over 40 per cent of Zambian university students were in favour of open trade with the white regimes.[225] At its conference in November the National Union of Students recommended that Zambia should have open trade links with South Africa.[226] On Rhodesia the *Times of Zambia*, while condemning the British 'settlement' with Rhodesia, considered that Zambia could

[224] 'Politics of principles' is a reference to the theme of R. Hall's book *The High Price of Principles*.
[225] *Sunday Times*, 24 October 1971.
[226] *Zambia Daily Mail*, 5 October 1971.

no longer 'consider herself in a firm position to continue along [the] path' of sanctions against Rhodesia. Zambia, it said, must 'look logic in the face' before retaliating against the British.[227] It was unclear how widespread these reservations had become or how far they would succeed in diverting the Kaunda administration from the policy it had until then, pursued. And if internal opposition did force Kaunda to revise his policy to the extent of allowing, even as a temporary measure, greater collaboration with South Africa, would the South African government be willing to provide a golden bridge for that retrograde movement? There is, however, a kind of logic in hostility which defies the ambiguities that necessity weaves into the concrete actions of States.

Certainly Zambia continued to give material support to the liberation movements. Its own population was also increasingly made aware of the conflict with the south—through the speeches of politicians, through the activities of the Ministry of National Guidance and through an effective government presence in the peripheral areas.[228] The sole political party, UNIP, had branches throughout the country; the policy of administrative decentralisation would, hopefully, bring the remote areas more closely in touch with government policy; and the posting of military and para-military forces to boundary areas which had been subjected to Portuguese or Rhodesian incursions would not only encourage those communities to feel more secure but would have an educational effect on the armed forces themselves in so far as it gave them an active role in the conflict with the south. All these policies were intended to secure that national integration and solidarity without which it was difficult to pursue any credible internal or external policy.

The most important policy decision in regard to the south was that of creating road and rail links with the north. This policy would probably have been adopted even if there were no political difficulties with the south. After all, there were clear long-term economic advantages to be derived from having access to diverse markets and sources of supply. There was every economic reason for reducing asymmetrical dependence on the south, and that could be achieved only by developing alternative economic relationships

[227] *The Times*, 26 November 1971.
[228] It was generally conceded that rather little of this political education was taking place, and that such as did occur was quite unsystematic.

with the north. However, the political situation in the south made the policy more urgent; provocations such as Rhodesia's closure of its borders with Zambia in 1973 gave weight to the Zambian government's pleas for popular support for this policy on the grounds that an overriding national interest was at stake;[229] at the same time the availability of links to the north would obviously increase Zambia's ability to support hostile actions against the southern regimes.

While, therefore, the Zambian government remained cautious in its actions—more so than in its words—the infrastructure, physical and political, was being laid for a more complete dissociation from the inherited links with the south and for greater freedom of action in support of the cause of African liberation.[230]

At the end of our period Malawi's relations with South Africa were much closer than had ever been thought possible between a black government and *apartheid* South Africa. There was every prospect that so long as Banda remained in power this friendship would grow. Zambia's relations with South Africa were bad, and deteriorating, during most of the period. Towards the end of the period, however, there were definite signs that powerful forces were at work in Zambia in favour of a policy of accommodation towards South Africa. After an initial deterioration, Zambia–Malawi relations also improved. It would be tempting to conclude that because of its greater wealth, thanks to its copper, Zambia had at first been

[229] In January 1973 Rhodesia closed its border with Zambia. Zambia did likewise, and did not reopen its border when on 3 March Smith reversed his decision. The encouragement thus given to Zambia's northward policy was probably the biggest blow ever delivered by a Rhodesian government to South Africa's long-term interests. This explains why Vorster, like Caetano, publicly dissociated himself from that step. See *K.C.A.*, 1973, 25797 and 25798.

[230] Despite the apparent moderation in statements on both sides, border incidents with the Portuguese and the Rhodesians (whom South Africa supports with men and materials) but not with South Africa itself have increased over the period since independence. The most spectacular developments that were said to have come to light in 1973 were raids by Rhodesian soldiers into border areas, laying land mines, and recruitment of fifth-columnists from Zambia for training in southern Africa for sabotage and possibly guerrilla activity against the Zambian government. At the time of going to press, legal trials involving some 100 men or more are proceeding, and the complete circumstances of recruitment have not yet become clear. Sources: *Zambia Daily Mail, Times of Zambia, Annual Police Reports* and my own investigations in Lusaka and in Southern Province, Zambia, in April–May 1973.

freer to defy South Africa, and that as soon as economic difficulties were experienced Zambian policy began to converge with the policy of Banda. This view is mistaken. Zambia, as we have seen, depends as much on South Africa as does Malawi—no less because its copper industry is South African-dominated. Sanctions against Rhodesia also made Zambia more dependent on South Africa for a wide range of goods and services previously supplied by Rhodesia. Zambia was therefore vulnerable to South African retaliatory measures throughout the period of sanctions. It was not because of its economic independence that the Zambian government adopted the attitude it did; it was in spite of its vulnerability. It is, of course, possible to argue that because of its greater poverty Malawi could ill afford to forego South African trade and aid, less still opt out of the migrant labour system. We have demonstrated, however, that if this was Banda's judgement, then his actions went further than was necessary to carry out that view. In the final analysis there is no way of making these comparisons objectively, since the matter depends on what is to be considered by each government a bearable privation. This involves value judgements, as does the correlative question as to whether the social functions in Zambia or Malawi of conflict with South Africa outweigh the dysfunctions of such conflict.

At the time of writing the *meaning* of Zambian policy is still very different from that of Banda's policy, quite apart from the obvious fact that there is friendship between Banda and Vorster. Banda chooses to collaborate with South Africa; Kaunda's government does not feel it has a choice for the while. Banda is friendly towards South Africa while Kaunda is still undoubtedly hostile. This would seem to indicate that the future development of Zambian policy— at both the verbal and the actual levels of interaction—need not be similar to that of Malawi. So long as Zambians feel they are constrained by necessity to collaborate, and so long as they consider themselves and the South African government to be reciprocally hostile, they may be expected to continue to seek ways of escaping the necessity to collaborate, on the one hand, and of contributing to the international opposition to the Pretoria regime, on the other.

At independence neither Malawi nor Zambia was viable in a major conflict with South Africa. Yet if they had acted together to maximise their alternative economic links with black Africa, for example, they might have been able to exercise more freedom of action relative to South Africa. To that extent their divergent responses to the common situation of weakness increased their vulnerability. South African successes in the area depended in no small measure upon that vulnerability.

XI *South Africa and the rest of Africa*

In 1965–66, when the important changes discussed in the previous chapters were occurring in southern and central Africa, it was generally accepted that African States were, as a group, implacably opposed to the South African regime and would continue to oppose any gradualist approach to the problem of *apartheid*. Indeed, the possibility of UN sanctions against South Africa was still a live issue in the early part of 1966, and the South African government took precautions against such a possibility.[1] Only three years previously, in 1963, African States had written into the charter of their Organisation of African Unity a commitment to the complete elimination of racialism and colonialism from the continent, and with the OAU had been created an African Liberation Council to execute that commitment. A number of African States had for some time been providing military training facilities to southern African nationalist organisations as well as supplying financial aid. The 'liberation of southern Africa' was so closely associated with the very idea of African unity that Austin could write at the end of 1965:

Pan-African sentiment is most easily generated in its anti-colonial setting and finds strongest expression in the common ground of the leaders' hostility to white supremacy. It is unlikely, therefore, that the African States will be prepared to abandon [southern African liberation], the tie that helps to keep them together.[2]

[1] See *UNGAOR, 22nd Session, Annexes*, Doc. A/6700/Rev. 1. There was, by this time, less optimism than had earlier been expressed by, for example, the International Conference on Economic Sanctions against South Africa (see R. Segal (ed.), *Sanctions against South Africa*, 1964); less than the optimism expressed in Legum, *South Africa: Crisis for the West*. Rather, the international Conference on South West Africa, meeting at Oxford between 23 and 26 March 1966, recommended that a campaign should be launched to persuade Western governments to withdraw their investments from South West Africa. See R. Segal and R. First, *South West Africa: Travesty of Trust*, 1967.

[2] Austin, *Britain and South Africa*, p. 34; cf. also M. E. Akpan, 'African goals and strategies toward southern Africa', in *African Studies Review*, 1971.

Opposition to South African *apartheid* thus gave African unity a definite, and among Africans an apparently uncontroversial, purpose which functioned both as the 'moral and mental basis' of unity and at the same time a pragmatic expedient to facilitate the organisation of inter-governmental co-operation in black Africa.

It had, however, long been obvious that the economic and military weakness and the political instability of African States was such that they could not for some time challenge South Africa militarily. When the OAU was being founded Eric Louw had observed that 'an American journal' had not been 'very far from the truth' when it described African States as 'bum and beggar countries'. He added contemptuously, 'These are the people who are threatening South Africa.'[3]

Louw had appreciated, nevertheless, that it was not enough to cry *Voilà la fange*, since African States could still create difficulties for South Africa: 'The newly independent States are in such a state of ecstasy that anything may happen.'[4] By 1965 it was clear that if African States could not resort to military intervention against South Africa, they could yet function as a well organised and resolute group against South Africa.[5]

South African Ministers continued to hope that African States would become 'mature', and J. J. Fouché, then Minister of Defence, thought that the 'danger of communism' might yet bring African States to co-operate with South Africa.[6] This was a view which Tshombe's co-operation with the South African government had encouraged.[7] As African unity continued to suffer setbacks, having taken a particularly severe battering in the succession of Congo crises, it remained to be seen in 1966 how strong pan-African sentiment would continue to be with regard to the white regimes of southern Africa.

The emergence as independent States in 1964–66 of Zambia, Malawi, Botswana and Lesotho, which are economically and geographically closely linked to South Africa, meant that not only would sanctions be breached by South Africa's most important black African trading partners, but that in the case of Malawi

---

[3] *Ass. Deb.*, vol. 7, col. 7312.   [4] *Ibid.*

[5] Cf. Austin, *op. cit.*, p. 35; 'It is precisely in these circumstances, out of a frustration born of the desire to act and the failure to act effectively, that the African States are likely to try and exert pressure on those powers which have substantial interests throughout the continent.'

[6] *Ass. Deb.*, 1963, vol. 7, col. 8622.   [7] See above, chapter III.

and Lesotho in particular a conservative influence was introduced into deliberations about boycotts. To a lesser extent it was also true of Botswana and Zambia. Rhodesian UDI, with its effect of making many of the States of southern and central Africa more dependent for their external trade on South Africa, also undermined to that extent the policy of isolation pursued by the OAU African leaders, urging strong action against Rhodesia at the OAU in 1965, could not but express the pious hope that South Africa would not come to the aid of Rhodesia in the military confrontation that was being advocated.[8]

Rhodesian UDI was a trial run for African States (and the rest of the world) in the business of liberating southern Africa from white minority rule. African governments failed to persuade the British government to act more forcibly and were themselves unable to intervene militarily, and when guerrilla activity drew the South African government actively into the fray, African States were still unable to intervene, or even to form a convincing defence alliance to meet reprisals which might follow the support some of these States gave to the guerrillas. In the first three months of UDI it emerged clearly that even on this question of white supremacy African unity was very imperfect as differences became manifest over measures to be adopted against the British government for its unwillingness to act decisively against the Ian Smith regime.[9] South African policy-makers could hardly have failed to take note of these divisions.

With regard to South Africa itself, the economic boycott had never been fully implemented by all the States that were in a

[8] M. Obote, after the meeting of heads of state of Kenya, Uganda, Tanzania and Zambia in Nairobi on 15 November 1965. See *A.R.B.* (*Pol.*), 1965, 408c.

[9] When 15 December passed without forceful action by Britain in Rhodesia, as had been demanded by the OAU summit, only Algeria, Congo–Brazzaville, Ghana, Guinea, Mali, Mauritania, Sudan, Tanzania and the United Arab Republic broke off relations with the UK. The Central African Republic, Chad, Ivory Coast, Madagascar, Togo, Tunisia and Nigeria opposed the idea of the ultimate end, the severance of relations. Zambia, on account of 'the difficult position in which Zambia would find itself in circumstances which would follow such action', did not sever relations with the UK. Congo (Democratic Republic), on grounds of Zambian and Rhodesian African interests, Ethiopia, and Kenya, on similar grounds, did not sever relations. Uganda, owing to requests from Zambia, Nigeria, Ethiopia and the UAR, decided to 'postpone' action on the OAU ultimatum and British defiance of it. See *A.R.B.* (*Pol.*), 1965, 423, *passim*.

position to do so.[10] Diplomatically, also, South Africa was less isolated than it seemed. There were numerous potential points of contact with African leaders, in the corridors of the UN and of other inter-governmental organisations, in the Chanceries of Western Europe and the Americas, and after the granting of political sovereignty to Botswana and Lesotho, and later Swaziland, in those countries also. In January 1967 Muller could report to parliament that since July 1966 'Ministers from Africa passed through Jan Smuts Airport on more than fifty occasions *en route* to South Africa or elsewhere'. That figure did not include guests attending independence celebrations in Botswana and Lesotho. Muller added, 'Such Ministers are regularly received and assisted by senior officials of my department. Personal contact is made and in that way a great deal of goodwill is created.'[11] In 1967 'observers' discovered the outward-looking policy. It was reported that in 1966 the director and editor-in-chief of the Kenya *Daily Nation*, once a personal secretary of Jomo Kenyatta, had visited South Africa to meet the tobacco industrialist Anton Rupert. Githii reportedly met South African Ministers as well. This visit was linked with the setting up by Rupert's company, Rothman's, of a subsidiary in Nairobi.[12] If the Kenya government was contemplating the normalisation of relations with South Africa, it would have to contend with some opposition in Kenya. In September 1966 a motion had been proposed in the Kenyan parliament urging the confiscation of all immovable property in Kenya which belonged to South African nationals. Ten members had voted for the motion, twenty-six had voted against it and there were ten abstentions which included four Assistant Ministers.[13] In September 1967, following the announcement of the opening of diplomatic relations between South Africa and Malawi, the opposition Kenya People's Union attacked the government for maintaining links with Malawi.[14] When, a year later, Banda received Dr Muller, the conservative *Kenya Weekly News* attacked Banda's attitude to his 'fellow Africans'.[15]

[10] Austin, *op. cit.*, chapter II; see also E. B. Kesselly, 'The organisation of unity as a functioning system', unpublished Ph.D. thesis, University of Manchester, 1971, appendix C.

[11] *Ass. Deb.*, vol. 19, col. 436.

[12] *Africa Confidential*, 6 January 1967; see also *Africa Contemporary Record*, 1968–69, p. 315.

[13] *A.R.B.*, vol. 2, No. 9, 363C.

[14] *Standard* (Tanzania), 15 September 1967.

[15] 11 October 1968.

Malawi's growing links with South Africa led to speculation that Ghana, now under a conservative military regime, might follow suit. Such rumours were vigorously dismissed by the Ghanaian High Commissioner in Dar-es-Salaam:

Ghana cannot under any circumstances consider the establishment of relations of any sort with *apartheid* South Africa. This is a position which Ghana cannot and will never compromise.

It is apparent that South Africa has launched a giant propaganda offensive to divide Africa, but to give credence to such vile propaganda is in fact to lend indirect support to the course of that inhuman regime.[16]

Indeed, at this time the National Liberation Council was eager to establish good relations with other African States; its chairman, General Ankrah, had promised in his New Year message that 'vigorous efforts' would be made 'against the white governments in Southern Africa'.[17] Throughout the period of military rule Ghana did not depart from the common African policy of boycotting South Africa. And when this policy towards South Africa was eventually challenged by the Busia regime the revision was, as will be seen, small and tentative. At this stage only one African government, apart from that of Lesotho, came out in favour of Banda's policy, and that was the Malagasy government under President Tsiranana.

In spite of the setbacks experienced over Rhodesia, the years 1967–68 did not see a 'de-radicalisation' of African feeling towards South Africa. Guerrilla activity in Mozambique was at its height, and in 1967 armed conflict began in Rhodesia also. South African participation in Portuguese and Rhodesian counter-insurgency activity merely served to increase hostility to South Africa at this time, although later on this form of white co-operation might have emphasised the weakness of African States and the vulnerability of States bordering on the 'white redoubt'. 1968 was a year for radicals everywhere. In America it was the *annus mirabilis* of the peace movement and, more pertinent to Africa, the soul movement, which probably exaggerated the revolutionary potential of black people everywhere, to which it drew attention. Elsewhere the left was in revolt, led mainly by students. The May revolt which contributed to the fall of General de Gaulle caused tremors in Senegal and Ivory Coast.[18] Such a climate of political opinion and feeling

[16] *Standard* (Tanzania), 12 September.
[17] *West Africa,* 14 January 1967, p. 59.
[18] *K.C.A.,* 23532A.

did not favour any substantial improvement of the fortunes of the white minority regimes.

These years were also the first two years of the Nigerian civil war, which had some effect on African orientations towards southern Africa. It divided Africans along unusual lines, Tanzania and Zambia collaborating with Ivory Coast and Gabon, for example, in championing the recognition of Biafra. Conservative–radical cleavages were thus temporarily suspended over a specific immediate problem, and differences were suppressed on other less immediate problems such as South Africa. On the other hand, precisely because African States were divided (with strong feeling on both sides) over Biafra, African unity became a rallying cry for both sides, and South Africa performed its usual function of providing the negative reference of the OAU. Indeed, protagonists on the Nigerian issue contended for the recognition of their militant pan-Africanism and opposition to neo-colonialism—Nigeria and Boumedienne's Algeria on the one side and Zambia on the other.[19] In March 1968 the OAU Council of Ministers, meeting at Addis Ababa, adopted the budget of the African Liberation Council without dissent for the first time.[20]

The South African government did not remain aloof from the Nigerian crisis. Towards the end of 1968 it sent medical supplies and food to Biafra.[21] There had been reports that South African mercenaries were aiding the Nigerian air force, but it transpired that the pilots concerned had been recruited in London and, apparently, to the embarrassment of the Nigerian government.[22] Nothing further was heard of these mercenaries after 1967. On the other hand Portugal, a close friend of the republic, supported Biafra, and reports circulated that South Africa, in league with Portugal and France (with which it was co-operating still more closely)[23] was supplying guns to Biafra. An account which appeared in the *Sunday Telegraph* in August 1969 claiming that the guns were flown via Botswana was denied by both the South African Defence Minister, Botha, and the President of Botswana, Sir Seretse Khama.[24] The reports were

[19] *West Africa*, 5 October 1968.   [20] *Ibid.*, 2 March 1968.
[21] *Ibid.*, 28 September 1968; *A.R.B.* (*Pol.*), 1969, 1500B.
[22] *Africa Confidential*, 22 December 1967; 3 November 1967.
[23] *Ibid.*, 20 January 1967; *Africa Contemporary Record*, 1968–69, 'France's year in Africa'. See also F. Chenu and M. Noel, 'La France et l'Afrique australe', in *Revue française d'études politiques africaines*, 1970.
[24] *A.R.B.* (*Pol.*), 1969, 1500B.

believed by the federal government in Nigeria[25] probably for their propaganda value but also because the Nigerian government was predisposed to believe them by its hostility to South Africa and Portugal.

If the South African government was seeking opportunities for its outward-looking policy, it could not find them on the federal side. The military regime under Gowon had early come under the influence of people who were by Nigerian standards left-wing. They included adherents of the Action Group which after 1959 had been opposed to the conservative policies of Sir Abubakar Tafawa Balewa, and whose opposition to Balewa had probably contributed to the latter's concessions to pan-African feeling.[26] They were Chief Awolowo, S. Ikoku, A. Enahoro, and J. S. Tarka. Already in 1967, then, the Nigerian federal regime had an orientation which would not have facilitated co-operation with South Africa.[27] Russian support for Lagos might also have made things difficult.

Although some officers on Biafra's side, especially Major Ifeajuna, had strong pan-Africanist feelings, the Biafran government, whatever its political preferences and ideological inclinations, was in a much weaker position from the point of view of support from the governments of the world. It readily collaborated with the Portuguese and could hardly have declined South African military assistance had it been offered. Indeed, a Biafran official of the ALC had even defected to the Portuguese, providing them with valued information on the liberation movements.[28] That, apart from humanitarian sentiment, would have been a good enough reason for support to be given to Biafra in the form of food and medical supplies. South Africa lost any goodwill it might have had—probably little indeed—in Nigeria as a result of its association with Biafra. It was immaterial whether the degree of collusion was as much as had been

[25] A. H. M. Kirk-Greene, *Crisis and Conflict in Nigeria*, 1971, vol. II, p. 122, n. 4.
[26] On Balewa's pan-Africanism see C. S. Phillips, Jnr, *The Development of Nigerian Foreign Policy*, 1964, pp. 89–107; on Awolowo's oppositional pan-Africanism, which came relatively late in the day, see pp. 62–7.
[27] Aminu Kano, Northern Region leader of the Northern Elements Progressive Union was another radical who became involved with the Gowon administration at an early date. I am grateful to conversations I had with Mr M. J. Dent of the University of Keele and my colleagues, W. Ajibola and F. O. Anifowose, on Nigerian politics in this period.
[28] Cf. Arrighi and Saul, 'Nationalism and revolution in sub-Saharan Africa', p. 171.

gossiped to be the case by journalists; what mattered was that Nigerian leaders believed the reports about gun-running and that South Africa's principal associates in African politics at the time, France and Portugal, were selling guns to Biafra.

By 1969, however, the southern African problem had long ceased to be the remote issue on which African States could always be expected passionately to agree and thereby paper over their deep disagreements. True, it could be superseded in immediacy by other problems on the continent, but the South African government for its part would not be distracted from establishing contacts, offering aid and trade, and trying to disengage individual leaders from the OAU anti-*apartheid* bloc. In southern Africa, and in Zambia particularly, diplomatic persuasion was given an aggressive thrust by the fact of South African military might (and that of its allies), which, like their economic power, was a daily observable fact. It may have been in deference to this power that the Lusaka manifesto was produced in April 1969, representing a more conciliatory mood on the part of its signatories towards South Africa.[29] The manifesto said that African leaders would talk rather than kill and considered that for so long as South Africa showed no sign of abandoning *apartheid* or of a commitment to human dignity it should continue to be boycotted and isolated.[30] The OAU adopted the manifesto in September 1969.

The South African Foreign Minister responded to the manifesto at a press conference in New York. South Africa would be willing to enter into a dialogue with African States, he said, but there was no prospect of such a dialogue because of the attitude of the latter:

By refusing to accept South Africa's repeated assurances that this commitment to human dignity exists in South Africa, Zambia, Kenya, Uganda and Tanzania are blocking a dialogue and are rendering the Lusaka manifesto devoid of the humanism and good faith which is essential to make it a document of genuine intent.[31]

Otherwise there was 'a lot' that he agreed with in the manifesto.

Muller was probably not very interested in multilateral exchanges with the OAU as such, not least because less formally South Africa

---

[29] See the section on Zambia, above. Cf. Shamuyarira, 'The Lusaka manifesto', in *The African Review*, 1971.
[30] See section on Zambia, above. Cf. Shamuyarira, *loc. cit.*
[31] *A.R.B.* (*Pol.*), 1969, 1543C.

was scoring successes in direct exchanges with single governments. Writing in 1969, the South African diplomatist E. M. Rhoodie noted that Ghana was surreptitiously increasing its trade with South Africa.[32] Saddled with debt and having difficulty in obtaining sufficient credit, the Ghanaian administration might well have been open to temptation. Figures of trade between South Africa and individual States not being published, it would, of course, be impossible to evaluate Rhoodie's assertion. But a change in Ghanaian foreign-policy thinking at the highest level was to emerge shortly after the October press conference of the South African Foreign Minister. Dr Busia, who assumed office as Prime Minister on 1 October 1969, was reported by Accra Radio on 7 November to have said that he did not believe the policy of 'non-communication' with South Africa would make for progress. In terms reminiscent of Banda he said he wanted to make Ghana a place where white South Africans could come and see for themselves that Africans were not as backward as they thought. He was opposed to *apartheid*, which he considered a danger to peace. Busia had evidently been speaking for himself only, for Victor Owusu, then Foreign Minister, hastened to point out that Ghanaian policy had not changed. Ghana would not deviate from UN and OAU policy and would not unilaterally enter into a 'dialogue' with South Africa. Rather, South African shipping and aircraft would still be debarred from Ghanaian ports and South African nationals would be admitted into Ghana only if they denounced the South African government.[33]

If the South African victory in Ghana was ambiguous, so also was the Nationalist Party's acceptance of the outward-looking policy. Responding to the taunts of the verkramptes, a deputy Minister of Agriculture who had had occasion to dine with black dignitaries from Lesotho expressed this ambiguity at a party congress when he said to his listeners, 'Do you think I enjoyed dining with blacks? But I had to do it as it was beneficial to my country.'[34]

A surer success was recorded in Madagascar, where a South African official delegation was received, amid protests from some members of the ruling party; the government, while condemning racial discrimination, considered that persuasion would be a more effective 'means of combat' than 'returning hate with hate'. M. Rabemananjara, the Foreign Minister, added that great economic

[32] Rhoodie, *The Third Africa*, p. 198.
[33] *A.R.B.* (Pol.), 1969, 1575C.   [34] *Ibid.*, 1576A.

advantages would follow from economic relations with South Africa, especially in tourism and by attracting 'a strong currency'.[35] The then Vice-president, André Resampa, would subsequently reveal that there was controversy over foreign policy in the government and that in relation to 'dialogue' financial considerations did indeed matter a good deal. Resampa recalled:

President Tsiranana had reproached me on several occasion for my attitude to a number of questions of foreign policy. In the case of South Africa, I made it clear from the beginning what I thought of *apartheid*. Moreover, I refused to receive the South African Foreign Minister, Dr Muller. It was not dialogue they were looking for but money.

In Gabon, too, a victory was achieved, although at the time it went unnoticed, for President Bongo later revealed that he had told a seminar of his party in September 1969 that he condemned the policy of passing motions denouncing South Africa, as these would not solve the problem. He did not believe in attempts to overthrow the South African government by violence, either.[36] It was later reported that in 1966 the South African Foreign Ministry, taking advantage of its flourishing relations with France, had started to pay particular attention to francophone States and to 'work on them'.[37] Gabon and Madagascar, then, were the first fruits.

It was not until late 1970, however, that the idea of a 'dialogue' with South Africa as an alternative approach to boycotts was launched vigorously into the sea of African diplomacy. The excitement generated by the election campaigns of 1970 would probably have deterred any African government from too precipitately advocating a change of policy towards South Africa, while on the South African side 'dialogue' was one of the bones of contention between the ruling party and the Herstigte Nasionale Party of Hertzog. After the South African general election in May there soon followed the British general election, which returned a Conservative government determined to resume the sale of arms to South Africa. That decision was to spark off a controversy in Africa which in turn encouraged both South Africa and the advocates of 'dialogue' to take the offensive.

At about the time that President Kaunda, on behalf of the Non-aligned Conference and the OAU, was touring the major western

---

[35] *Ibid.* See also *K.C.A.*, 1970, 23916B.
[36] *A.R.B.* (*Pol.*), 1971, 2099.
[37] Rudolph, Progrund and Clifton, in *Observer*, 29 November 1970.

capitals to dissuade governments from trading with South Africa in arms, M. Houphouet-Boigny, the President of Ivory Coast, addressing his party congress, called for a new approach to the South African question. Rejecting present African policies towards South Africa as unlikely to succeed, he called for a 'dialogue' with South Africa and an African conference to discuss such a dialogue.[38] Houphouet-Boigny's suggestion could not be lightly ignored because he had some influence among heads of state in francophone west Africa. There were organisational frameworks within which he could hope to advance his ideas and rally support before confronting the OAU. These organisations included the Conseil de l'Entente, a regional grouping in which Ivory Coast played a dominant role as a result of its greater wealth and because of the personal diplomatic style at which Houphouet-Boigny was adept and his high standing in French official circles, which were the common benefactors of the Conseil States. Less directly under the influence of Houphouet-Boigny, yet founded under his inspiration as a conservative, francophone alternative to the OAU, was the Organisation Commune Africaine et Malgache (OCAM). OCAM was the direct successor to the Union Africaine et Malgache (UAM), which in turn had been a successor to the earlier, conservative, Brazzaville group formed at the time of the Congo crisis of 1960.[39] In 1968 a journalist had remarked that Ivory Coast's Africa policy could best be described as 'a series of concentric circles of diminishing importance'.[40] The question in November 1970 was how the 'circles' would react. *Afrique Nouvelle*, reporting early reactions, speculated:

In the Conseil de l'Entent at least . . . two if not three States will not be in accord with the point of view of the Ivory Coast.[41]

Togo, the paper reflected, would accept the Ivoirien proposal on account of 'l'empiricisme qui preside actuellement aux destinées du pays et la démission d'une opinion publique apeurés par le cliquetis des armes'. Niger had more freedom of action within the Conseil, and Upper Volta generally followed the OAU, while Dahomey might reject the suggestion on account of the 'vigour of public opinion'.[42] In the event, Gabon and Dahomey agreed with Ivory

Coast; Niger, while not criticising Houphouet-Boigny, suggested that the matter should be discussed by all members of OAU, and if they decided against it it should be dropped; Togo hesitated, it being stressed that the Ivoirien lead would not automatically be followed.[43]

Three francophone governments immediately rejected the suggestion, Sékou Touré of Guinea considered that 'dialogue' would mean dishonour;[44] the Senegalese Minister of Culture and Information, denouncing *apartheid* as 'une infirmité de l'ame', said that it was a threat to peace.[45] President Ahidjo of Cameroon, who had been personally entrusted with the task of presenting the Lusaka manifesto to the UN, stressed the importance of faithfulness to the African resolutions passed at the UN and the OAU, and observed that the total liberation of the continent depended 'de notre fermeté a l'égard des oppresseurs des peuples africaines et . . . de notre unité et de notre solidarité'.[46] The government of Congo (Brazzaville) opposed the proposals.

The governments of Liberia, Nigeria, the Somali Republic, Uganda and Zambia spoke against the proposals, while the Kenyan Foreign Minister seemed to consider that Houphouet-Boigny's proposals were a legitimate interpretation of the Lusaka manifesto.[47] *Afrique Nouvelle* reported that although no formal invitation had been sent by Houphouet-Boigny to Siaka Stevens of Sierra Leone to attend the proposed 'dialogue' summit, Stevens was nevertheless having consultations with Houphouet-Boigny. A 'source close to the government' considered that if blacks were allowed to visit South Africa, that would be a diplomatic achievement against *apartheid*: 'Certainly,' declared the same source, 'a dialogue is preferable to an armed confrontation.'[48] Chief Jonathan of Lesotho supported the proposal.[49] Speaking in Ottawa on 10 November, Dr Busia defended the idea of a 'dialogue' with South Africa.[50] Once more, however, his Foreign Minister disagreed publicly, if not directly repudiating

[43] *Africa Contemporary Record*, 1970–71, c33.
[44] *Ibid.*
[45] *Afrique Nouvelle*, 19–25 November 1970.
[46] *Ibid.*
[47] *Ibid.*, and *Africa Contemporary Record*, c32–c33.
[48] 19–25 November 1970.
[49] *Africa Contemporary Record*, 1970–71, c33.
[50] *Ghana Today*, December 1970, January 1971; cf. *The Legon Observer*, 1–14 January 1971. Busia re-stated his view in parliament on 13 December 1970; see *Africa Contemporary Record*, 1970–71, c30–c31.

his leader.[51] Busia had visited Ivory Coast in May and it is most likely that 'dialogue' was discussed.

In Addis Ababa Diallo Telli, the Secretary General of the OAU, stated that he had heard from a number of heads of state who were solidly united in wanting to see the complete and unconditional overthrow of *apartheid*. In connection with that objective it was Telli's view that the proper place where differences of approach should be discussed was a conference of heads of state of the OAU.[52] There was much press comment, mostly hostile, on the Busia–Boigny proposal,[53] but there were relatively few official reactions, probably because Houphouet-Boigny addressed himself to his party rather than directly to other heads of state and government.

Before the dust had settled over the Ivoirien proposals Muller visited Madagascar at the head of a business delegation, and signed an economic agreement with the Malagasy government. South Africa would lend Madagascar R2·32 million at 4 per cent interest over twenty-five years to pay for a road system, the water supply and electricity improvements and extensions of the runway of Fascene airport at Nossi-Bè island, where a South African group would build a five-star hotel which they would run. President Tsiranana raised the possibility of South Africa building a large deep-water tanker port at Nerindra, and Muller agreed to raise the question with his colleagues in Pretoria. The South African government, according to Muller, considered it important to establish links with OCAM and promised 'most significant' developments at the OCAM summit scheduled for January 1971.[54]

The timing of Houphouet-Boigny's and Busia's speeches suggested that they were in response to the campaign to prevent the resumption of British arms sales to South Africa, which as the Commonwealth conference approached was gathering force. If they were meant to arrest the campaign, then the proponents of 'dialogue' misjudged the strength of feeling on the arms issue, which was such that at Singapore only Malawi spoke in defence of the British decision, when even Chief Jonathan spoke against the sale of arms.[55]

---

[51] *Africa Contemporary Record*, 1970–71, 8350–352; See also *K.C.A.*, 1970–71, 24555A.

[52] *Afrique Nouvelle*, 19–25 November 1970.

[53] *Ibid.*

[54] *A.R.B.* (*Econ.*), 1970, 1868.

[55] See chapter VI above; cf. Denis Healey's speech in South Africa, reported in *The Times*, 18 September 1970.

The failure of the campaign, and the failure of African leaders to retaliate against Britain for this defiance, probably encouraged the 'dialogue' party. The misadventures of Obote—overthrown in his absence by an avowedly conservative soldier—and the attacks on Kaunda's integrity by South African Ministers, who were angered by his conduct over arms sales, also threatened dissarray for the militant party. The wheels were once more set in motion for another round of the 'dialogue'.

The build-up to this round was elaborate. The matter was raised at the OCAM meeting in January 1971 by Madagascar, M. Rabemananjara submitted to the conference a 'communication' on 'International Economic Relations and Ideologies'. This justified Madagascar's co-operation with South Africa on grounds of 'realism'. There was no formal debate on 'dialogue', but it emerged from statements made by individual leaders that OCAM was divided on the issue. Thus the conference merely 'noted' the Malagasy 'communication'.[56] In South Africa, the Foreign Minister hinted that his government had contacts with Zambia. In a press conference on 19 March the Prime Minister 'unconditionally' accepted 'dialogue'—provided there was no interference in the internal affairs of South Africa. He accused Kaunda of 'double-talk' and at a subsequent press conference promised to reveal all in the debate on his vote in parliament in April.[57] When he did make his 'revelations' Vorster indicated that an African leader, in whom he was evidently well pleased, would soon make a major statement on 'dialogue'.[58]

Reaction to the March press conference came even before the 'revelation' and the promised major speech on 'dialogue'. The Ghanaian National Assembly debated on 22 March a motion attacking Busia's policy (the government won). The New Foreign Minister, William Ofori-Atta, considered that 'If it became possible for me to go to South Africa and enter hotels from which black men are banned, it will inspire them and I will enjoy it.'[59] On the same day Tsiranana reaffirmed his belief in 'dialogue'. Five days later the government of the Central African Republic confirmed that it

[56] K.C.A., 1970–71, 24555A.
[57] A.R.B. (Pol.), 1971, 2037B; Today's News, 2 April 1971.
[58] Guardian, 3 April 1971, 29 April 1971; The Times, 23 April 1971; Financial Times, 23 April 1971.
[59] A.R.B. (Pol.), 1971, 2037B.

favoured 'dialogue'. In anglophone Africa the Kenyan government, it was reported, was vacillating.[60]

A new and spectacular addition to the 'dialogue' party was General Idi Amin, who had overthrown Obote's militantly anti-*apartheid* government. However, in Uganda as in Ghana, there was considerable opposition to the idea of 'dialogue' within the ranks of the government's supporters. This was reflected in a major foreign policy statement issued by the Uganda government on 15 March. The Ugandan government pledged itself to continued support of the freedom fighters recognised by the OAU. It condemned the 'inhuman and abhorrent policy of *apartheid*', which, it considered, constituted a threat to international peace. It further condemned the British government's decision to sell arms to South Africa, and concluded that the solution of the problem of white minority rule in South Africa, Rhodesia and the Portuguese-controlled territories would, in the main, have to be a military one.[61] Amin's ready denunciation of Kaunda's 'double-talk' (which, incongruously, followed this policy statement) turned into the more wary offer to send a ten-man commission to investigate conditions in South Africa and report to the General (who would forward his report to the OAU.[62] Students in Uganda expressed their disapproval of 'dialogue' between Uganda and South Africa in strong but deferential terms.[63] The idea of a commission was politely rejected by Vorster, who indicated that if Amin, or one or two of his Ministers, wished to visit South Africa to meet members of the South African government they would be welcome. Amin, however, would brook no distraction. He published his replying telegram, which was in defiant mood:

Your refusal to receive my delegation, as I have no prior knowledge of the conditions of your country, would only imply to me that you may be having some problems with regard to the conditions of black Africans in South Africa.[64]

General Amin persisted in the view that 'a fact-finding mission, as previously proposed by me, would be more appropriate at this

[60] *Observer*, 29 November 1970; *Africa Contemporary Record*, 1970–71, C32–C33.
[61] *A.R.B.* (*Pol.*), 1971, 2251A.
[62] *Guardian*, 29 September 1971. In April Amin had said he would be ready to visit South Africa on condition the OAU favoured such a visit.
[63] *Guardian*, 2 October 1971.
[64] *Cape Times*, 14 October 1971.

stage'.[65] The idea of dialogue was laid to rest as far as Amin was concerned.[66]

On 28 April Houphouet-Boigny made his awaited speech to a large audience including a score of internationl journalists. The speech lasted five hours. He called for 'true neutrality' in place of non-alignment, and warned of the danger of communism in Africa. (Two days later he further explained that *apartheid* was a secondary problem to the divisions which the rejection of his 'true neutrality' would create. He warned that if anybody allowed himself to be drawn into a war with South Africa over *apartheid*, that would offer 'a new opportunity to communism to intervene with the well-known sad consequences'.[67] He repeated his call for an African summit to discuss the 'dialogue' proposal. Houphouet-Boigny raised the question of 'dialogue' at the meeting of heads of state of the Conseil de l'Entente a Ougadougou a few weeks later. No agreement was reached, and the final communique of the meeting did not even mention 'dialogue'.[68]

Following Houphouet-Boigny's second speech, more countries came out clearly against 'dialogue'. Siaka Stevens, addressing a rally on 20 May, condemned the proposal. At the end of Gowon's state visit to Kenya a statement was issued by the governments of Nigeria and Kenya condemning the Ivoirian proposal. The statement added that the Lusaka manifesto provided the only basis for a meaningful dialogue.[69] Kenya was no longer 'vacillating'. Despite the opposition to the Ivoirien proposal, Vorster felt emboldended to revive old hopes of South African leadership in Africa. He told a meeting in Port Elizabeth, 'If the positive signs of co-operation with the rest of Africa are interpreted correctly, South Africa may become the leading State of this continent.'[70] In other speeches made during the same period Vorster made it clear that he would

[65] *Ibid.*

[66] Uganda was not represented at the OAU summit, where it might have had an opportunity to elaborate its distinctive approach to the 'dialogue' question.

[67] *K.C.A.*, 1971–72, 24634B.

[68] *Ibid.* On further reactions to 'dialogue' see also *Afrique Nouvelle*, 6–12 May 1971.

[69] Dr Mungai, Kenya's Foreign Minister, had initially reacted to the Ivoirien proposal by saying that his government would be willing to discuss the Lusaka manifesto. It would seem that the later condemnation of 'dialogue' was due to the influence of Gowon—to some degree, at any rate. See *K.C.A.*, 1971–72, 246348B.

[70] *Ibid.*

accept 'dialogue' as an opportunity to get rid of some of the 'misconceptions' African leaders had concerning *apartheid*.[71] It was clear that the OAU conferences due to be held in June would be dominated by the 'dialogue' issue.

At the meeting of the Ministerial Council of the OAU (which precedes the Assembly of Heads of States and Governments) there was disagreement over the inscription of the 'dialogue' issue in the agenda of the council. The Ivory Coast did not wish the matter to be discussed by the Ministers but wanted it to be put directly to the Assembly of Heads of State. This was strenuously opposed by the Nigerian delegation. A compromise was proposed by Ethiopia, whereby specific reference to 'dialogue' would be omitted from the agenda inscription. This proposal was lost, fourteen states voting for it, seventeen voting against, and five abstaining. The Ivory Coast delegation walked out of the conference. The Upper Volta, Togo, Gabon and Dahomey delegations said that they would refrain from participating in the debates on 'dialogue' but that they would take part in the rest of the work of the conference. Only Malawi and Malagasy delegates spoke in favour of 'dialogue'. The council approved a declaration which rejected dialogue, affirming that any action on southern Africa should take place within the OAU framework and in consultation with the liberation movements. The declaration was approved by twenty-seven votes in favour, four against (Lesotho, Madagascar, Malawi and Swaziland) and two abstentions (Dahomey and Niger). Upper Volta did not participate in the vote, while Ivory Coast, Gabon and Togo did not take part in the debate at all.[72] Following this rebuff Houphouet-Boigny announced that he would not be attending the summit to defend

[71] *Ibid.*

[72] *K.C.A.*, 1971–72, 24737A; the Central African Republic, Congo–Kinshasa, Mauritius and Uganda were not represented at the OAU conference. The Central African Republic favoured dialogue, while the Congo–Kinshasa opposed it. Mauritius's attitude was quaint. Reacting to Houphouet-Boigny's April speech, Sir Seewoosagur Ramgoolan, the Mauritian Prime Minister, said on 18 May, 'No dialogue is possible between slaves and masters. Mauritius is a black and multi-racial country. It can conceive of dialogue only with countries ... where equality and fraternity are capital virtues and all discrimination is rejected.' His Foreign Minister, M. Duval, had said in Cape Town—he was there in a 'private' visit—that only spectacular concessions by South Africa in its racial policies could facilitate a dialogue with African States. His government would, however, continue to develop cordial trade relations with South Africa. See *K.C.A.*, 1971–72, 24634B.

his proposals but would send a ministerial delegation instead.[73] Tsiranana would also not attend.[74]

At the summit the Ivory Coast delegation produced a statement by Houphouet-Boigny embodying a request for a special meeting on 'dialogue'. The conference noted the statement but refused to vote on it. A resolution was passed rejecting 'any kind of dialogue with the racist minority regime of South Africa' and affirming that action concerning *apartheid* should be taken within the framework of the OAU, in close consultation with the liberation movements. The resolution further stated that the proposals for 'dialogue' were manoeuvres to divide African States and confuse public opinion in order to end the isolation of South Africa, and thus to maintain the *status quo* in South Africa.[75] Twenty-eight States voted for the resolution. There were six against and five abstentions, as follows:

Against	*Abstentions*
Gabon	Dahomey
Ivory Coast	Niger
Lesotho	Swaziland
Malagasy	Upper Volta
Malawi	Togo
Mauritius	

It can be seen from this list that the majority of negative votes and abstentions were francophone States. Only two francophone States voted with the leaders, Malagasy and Ivory Coast, while all Conseil States except Gabon and Ivory Coast obtained. It is, however, true that none of the Conseil de l'Entente States came out against the Ivoirien proposal. This was perhaps a measure more of the influence of Ivory Coast and of Entente solidarity than of real conviction on the part of the abstaining leaders. Indeed, abstention on a resolution which so sharply criticised a position which these heads of state had only shortly before either approved or sympathetically considered was odd. It could perhaps be explained only by the fact that while they rejected the view of 'dialogue' expressed by the resolution, they nonetheless accepted the view that all action concerning *apartheid* should take place within the framework of the OAU.

---

[73] *A.R.B.* (*Pol.*), 1971, 2123 ff.

[74] *Ibid.* Tsiranana was also protesting against the change of venue from Kampala to Addis Ababa.

[75] *Ibid.*; also *Cape Times*, 30 September 1971.

It is a measure of the difficulty of justifying 'dialogue' in an Africa accustomed to thinking of *apartheid* only in terms of militant rejection that the Ghanaian Foreign Minister voted with the majority and effectively, against the policy elaborated by Busia.[76] Swaziland, which at the ministerial conference voted for the resolution, voted against at the summit.

Houphouet-Boigny, in proposing 'dialogue', could claim that it was 'le dialogue honnête', since Ivory Coast, having hardly any economic relations with South Africa, could not be accused of having a material interest in 'dialogue'. Gabon was the only other State which voted against the OAU resolution which did not receive financial aid from, although it was increasing economic relations with, South Africa. The lucrative links between Malawi, Malagasy and Lesotho and South Africa have already been referred to. In 1970–71 South Africa, under a trade agreement, had bought up virtually the entire Mauritian tea crop, and under another agreement concluded in May 1971 undertook to buy even more in 1972.[77]

The OAU summit conference resolution was not the end of the affair. Malawi and Lesotho, as we have seen, took on the task of keeping alive the idea of a 'dialogue' outside the OAU. Houphouet-Boigny responded to the OAU decision by planning to send a dialogue delegation consisting of Ivory Coast and 'friendly countries' to South Africa.[78] *Le dialogue du mal partie* would now be pursued along the informal and factional lines to which the Ivoirien leader was fairly accustomed and which the South African government probably preferred. Apart, however, from the 'mini-OAU' into which the independence celebrations of Lesotho were converted, the informal summit did not occur in 1971. By contrast, the summit meeting of east and central African States, held at Mogadishu in mid-October, was converted into an anti-'dialogue' conference. It adopted the 'Mogadishu declaration', which contended that 'there is no way left for the liberation of southern Africa except armed struggle, to which we have already given and will increasingly continue to give our fullest support'. The declaration condemned African States which maintained diplomatic ties with South Africa and called for strict adherence to OAU policy. The conference also expressed its solidarity with Zambia in a 'Declaration on Aggression

[76] Cf. *Ghanaian Times*, 1 September 1971, 13 September 1971.
[77] *A.R.B.* (*Econ.*), 1971, 2037A. See also appendix III.
[78] In *Fraternité Matin*, quoted in *A.R.B.* (*Pol.*), 1971, 2250c.

against Zambia'. On a unilateral basis the Malagasy government despatched a delegation to South Africa whose negotiations with Pretoria resulted in the setting up of an Economic Commission to meet from time to time to discuss and arrange matters of common interest[79] (more or less along the lines of the earlier commission with France),[80] but the Malagasys, probably in deference to African opinion, demurred on the technical point of diplomatic relations. Similarly, M. Duval, the Mauritian Foreign Minister, led a delegation to South Africa, and M. Koffi Ndia of Ivory Coast also led a delegation to the republic.[81] M. Ndia denied that his trip was official. He had, he said, been invited by the South African government to make a short 'fact-finding stop-over', and in a 'personal capacity' he had made enquiries about 'dialogue' between Ivory Coast and South Africa. He had 'very favourable impressions' of South Africa.[82]

In the context of previous African attitudes towards South Africa the 'dialogue' campaign had the character of a right-wing revolt, and as such it requires explanation more than the adhesion of the majority to the usual multi-lateral African stand. Many of the explanations would probably lie in areas of African politics which cannot be examined here with economy and advantage. We shall therefore restrict ourselves to those aspects of African politics which bore immediately on South Africa. Further, we proceed from the assumption that the explanation required is other than the obvious, if facile, one that there was widespread disquiet in Africa over the effectiveness of methods previously adopted towards South Africa.[83] Such a general reason does not account for the form which the 'questioning' of previous methods took, in terms of who led the questioning, in what context, and the political processes (through or outside OAU, etc.) involved in the 'questioning'.

The first question which suggests itself is why the 'dialogue'

[79] *Die Burger*, 12 August 1971.

[80] The greatest pressure for close collaboration with South Africa comes from dependence of the economy on low-market-value agricultural commodities, but also evidently from French Mauritians, about 10,000 of whom live in South Africa—some 400 of them were said to have planned an invasion of the island after receiving training in South Africa. See *Africa Contemporary Record*, 1970–71, B151. On M. Duval's Tsiranana-esque views see B152. See also *Die Burger*, 12 August 1971.

[81] *A.R.B.* (*Pol.*), 1971, 2250C.

[82] *Ibid.*

[83] Cf. J. Mayall, *Africa: the Cold War and After*, 1971, p. 200.

campaign came to be led by Ivory Coast, which on the face of it had no immediate material interest in good bilateral relations with South Africa. President Tsiranana's personal friendship with Houphouet-Boigny, arising principally from their common conservatively pro-Western outlook on international and African issues, probably played no small part in exciting the interest of the Ivoirien President in the project. That the proposals were made by Houphouet-Boigny rather than by Tsiranana was probably a tactical point. For one thing, Ivory Coast could be seen to have no selfish material interest in making the proposals. Furthermore, Tsiranana had less influence in Africa and had already gone too far towards normalising relations with South Africa to be a credible or influential leader of a multi-lateral *démarche*. Busia, the earliest public advocate of 'dialogue' in west Africa, with a divided Cabinet and a hostile public opinion at home, and having less personal standing in Africa than either Houphouet-Boigny or Tsiranana, was easily eliminated from the leadership. Houphouet-Boigny readily accepted the anti-communist arguments for 'dialogue', and the idea of leading a conservative initiative in Africa was fully in character with the role he had played in African politics ever since Ivory Coast's independence.[84] In so far as he had a conception of African unity—and the campaign had implications for African unity because of the centrality of *apartheid* to OAU's rationale and because of the separate summit that was proposed for 'dialogue'—it meant no more than consolidating the right (moderates, if you prefer) in Africa, and thereby narrowing the influence of the left. The Ivory Coast President, having grave reservations about the OAU and pan-Africanism generally, had long seemed to see the OAU as just one of many African groupings with no special authority. In this regard he was at one with Tsiranana, whose government did not consider themselves Africans and placed no positive value on the idea of *African* unity.[85] Certainly, neither could be expected to scruple over much about any diminution of the authority of the OAU.

Yet if it was more tactful to confer leadership on Houphouet-Boigny rather than on Tsiranana,[86] that decision nevertheless had

[84] V. B. Thompson, *Africa and Unity*, 1964, pp. 257–63; *Africa Confidential*, 12 April 1968; Wallerstein, *Africa: the Politics of Unity, passim.*

[85] V. Thompson and R. Adloff, *The Malagasy Republic: Madagascar Today*, 1965, pp. 182–4.

[86] The leadership was probably not conspiratorially 'conferred'. It was the timing of Houphouet-Boigny's first speech and Vorster's advertisements of

its disadvantages. President Houphouet-Boigny was unpopular with a number of west African politicians. There was little 'dialogue' between Ivory Coast and Guinea, and Ivory Coast–Senegal relations were cool if correct. The Nigerian government could less easily forget the active support of Biafran secession by Ivory Coast than it could the recognition by remoter Tanzania and Zambia.[87] Nigeria's relations with Niger—which collaborates closely with Ivory Coast— were good, and co-operation had increased as a result of Niger's sympathetic stand over Biafra. This may have been an important reason for Niger not to identify itself with the Ivoirien proposals which Nigeria so firmly rejected. At the popular level Houphouet-Boigny's Ivory Coast was not much loved in Dahomey, Togo and Upper Volta,[88] although, principally for economic reasons, the leaders collaborated in the Conseil de l'Entente. The co-operation between Ghana and Ivory Coast was relatively superficial, for, as Ruth Schachter Morgenthau has observed, it did not extend to a matter that was more directly relevant—and vital—to both countries. Ivory Coast went ahead with the construction of its own hydro-electric dam on the Badama river when it could have imported electricity, to mutual advantage, from Ghana. In addition, with the exception of Tunisia and possibly Morocco, Arab governments, which had their reasons for wanting more leftism in Africa, could not easily follow the leadership of Ivory Coast. As for the rest of Africa, it could be argued that Ivory Coast under Houphouet-Boigny had never played an active part in the politics of liberation.[89]

---

his second speech which drew particular attention to Houphouet-Boigny's lucubrations. If there was any conferring of leadership, then the conferring would have been done between Tananarive, Pretoria—and Abidjan.

[87] Colonel Ojukwu was given asylum in Ivory Coast. Formal reconciliations between Nigeria and the various countries which had recognised Biafra took place in time for the September 1970 OAU conference. It was officially announced in Ivory Coast in October that Ojukwu would be expelled from Ivory Coast 'following an interview on British television', but as far as is known he was not in fact expelled. See *Africa Contemporary Record*, 1970–71, C3.

[88] The *Africa Confidential* article of 12 April 1968 is still an unrivalled review in this connection. See also *West Africa*, 1 July 1967, 14 October 1967, 7 October 1967, on some of the dramatic diplomacy between Guinea and Ivory Coast.

[89] The Tanzania *Standard*, responding to Houphouet-Boigny's first speech, noted that Houphouet-Boigny had not attended OAU summits since the founding of the organisation and that the Ivory Coast had never contributed to liberation funds; quoted in *Afrique Nouvelle*, 19–25 November 1970.

From the point of view of African 'revolutionaries' Côte d'Ivoire had long been *de l'autre côté de la barricade*. It should have been clear from the start, therefore, that on this as on most other issues Houphouet-Boigny would have little hope of extending his influence beyond his existing 'circles', and in particular the client States of the Conseil de l'Entente. These circles hardly extended to anglophone Africa but were restricted to the most francophile of French-speaking States, a factor which would have made Ivory Coast singularly suspect as a leader of a continent-wide revaluation of the dialectics of liberation.

The close collaboration between the countries of francophone Africa advocating 'dialogue' and France, which in turn was increasing its collaboration with South Africa, suggested that the governments of De Gaulle and Gaullist Pompidou would have exercised their influence on these States in favour of a more conciliatory attitude towards South Africa. France, which altogether disregarded the UN arms embargo against South Africa, was coming under increasing criticism in Africa for its policies. Might it not be expected that governments responsive to France would come to its aid? The francophile sentiments of the three who voted against the OAU resolution are well known. It is also known that they were linked to a desire for more aid from a France which was sluggish in this regard.[90] On this occasion in 1968 President Bongo of Gabon, while declaring a policy of 'Gabon first', admitted to being francophile—'we are French in heart and spirit'—and therefore Gabon had a right to ask France to do everything for it, and to give more aid.[91] Gaullist policy was to seek influence and good relations to French advantage with every country by the simple expedient of trying to secure the advantages of not being too closely identified with the US and the UK. This policy tended to blur the simplicities of the Cold War and often ran counter to the simpler pro-Western policies of the former colonies. The French, under de Gaulle, were quite happy to follow a policy of their own, sometimes aloof from or even in conflict with the policies of some of the most pro-French African States. On the project of more organised co-operation among *francophonie* advocated by Senghor and Bourguiba the

[90] *West Africa*, 19 October 1968 and 13 July 1968; also 11 May 1968.
[91] *West Africa*, 3 February 1968. According to C. and A. Darlington, the French government had intervened militarily to put Bongo's predecessor back into power, apparently to ensure that Gabon remained French economically as well as 'in heart and spirit'. See their *African Betrayal*, 1968.

French government had not been over-enthusiastic.[92] On relations with China French policy ran counter to the feelings of its most loyal African supporters.[93] Finally, on the more African question of the 1964 Congo crisis, over which Tsiranana and Houphouet-Boigny crossed swords with the OAU, absented themselves from the 1965 OAU summit and revived OCAM as a political counterweight to the OAU,[94] France differed, being the only Western European country to declare itself against the American–Belgian intervention in Congo.[95] It is arguable that the francophile States were so captive that France could ignore their susceptibilities. France was not a colony of its former colonies. On the other hand, France's independent action might be the strongest argument for francophile States to align themselves with France to increase sympathy in France with their condition, if they could not thereby increase their bargaining power.

If the maintenance of close relations with France was an important factor in the formation of attitudes towards South Africa, the relationship between the Quai d'Orsay and the 'dialogue' regimes was an aspect of wider conservatism of which it was not necessarily the cause. Conservatism in the post-colonial situation often expresses itself in the retention of the colonial order externally as well as internally.[96] This is most evidently the case with Malagasy, where the Tsiranana regime, having risen to power through the support of the Catholics and anti-communists of the coastal tribes who identified the communists with their former masters the Imerinas, had a vested interest in repressing communism. They saw in the Pax Gallica a check on a resurgence of Imerina power and therefore

[92] Cf. *West Africa*, 19 October 1968.
[93] Cf. de Lusignan, *French-speaking Africa since Independence*, the chapter on Madagascar; N. Heseltine, *Madagascar*, 1971, p. 200; and Adloff and Thompson, *The Malagasy Republic*, pp. 172–84. The Central African Republic, Chad, Dahomey, Gabon, Ivory Coast, Niger and Madagascar voted with South Africa; Lesotho, Swaziland, Malawi and Congo (Democratic Republic) against the admission of the People's Democratic Republic to the UN. See *The Times*, 27 October 1971.
[94] Ivory Coast actually wanted the OAU summit for 1966 postponed to spring 1967, Gabon to the end of 1967, in spite of the urgent question of Rhodesia, from the 1965 discussion of which they had been absent. See *A.R.B. (Pol.)*, 653c.
[95] Cf. P.-M. de la Gorce, 'De Gaulle et la decolonisation du continent noir', in *Revue française d'études politiques africaines*, 1970.
[96] Cf. Nettl and Robertson, 'The inheritance situation', in their *International Systems and the Modernisation of Societies*.

preferred the colonial order which suited the *côtiers* better. Ideological anti-communism combined with ethnic feelings in a definite
social structural setting to create an internal basis of conservatism.
The temptation must therefore be avoided of thinking that whenever
an African government pursues a conservative course it is merely
behaving as a more or less reluctant puppet of an imperialist. If
former colonial powers are able to 'puppeteer' African governments
it is often due as much to the predisposition of the particular governments to be 'puppeteered', which is in turn usually due to the nature
of the government's power base in the society and whether that
power base, described in class, ethnic or whatever terms, is apt to
derive advantage from conservative (or 'neo-colonial') policies at a
particular historical juncture. So, while France's inferred influence
on dialogue should not be discounted, it should not be allowed to
distract attention from the intra-African determinations of African
politics. Similarly, much of Houphouet-Boigny's preoccupation with
'communism' in Africa and the world as a whole derives from more
immediate threats to the internal security of his own regime.[97]

For the Malagasy government an external 'communist threat'
seemed to be represented by the much exaggerated growing presence
of Soviet naval power in the Indian Ocean. Tsiranana had always
been worried about the exposed position of Madagascar, which
occupies, for any naval power, an important strategic position in the
Indian Ocean.[98] What could be more natural for Tsiranana than
to redouble his attempts to secure Madagascar against the 'communist menace'? South Africa was the most powerful and most
anti-communist power in the area, having its own naval power
pretensions. What was more, there were excellent relations between
France and South Africa, so that co-operation with South Africa on
the part of the Malagasys would not antagonise the Quai d'Orsay.
On the contrary, the fact that South Africa was a relatively minor
power would have made such co-operation a lesser threat to French
interests than collaboration with either of the Anglo-Saxon powers.
A plan was, however, formulated in Britain, France, Portugal and
South Africa to collaborate on the development of Diego Suarez.[99]

When, following disturbances by students and workers, the

[97] One of the main objections of Houphouet-Boigny to Nkrumah's Ghana
and to Guinea was that they harboured his mortal political enemies.

[98] Thompson and Adloff, *The Malagasy Republic*, pp. 114 and 180–4.

[99] *Africa Contemporary Record*, 1970, reported that the South African
navy requested facilities at Diego Suarez; B133.

military ousted the Tsiranana government, policy towards South Africa, along with policy towards France and the world generally, changed. Official contacts with South Africa were severed and Muller announced towards the end of June 1972 that the South African government was suspending further dealings with Malagasy.[100] Diplomatic relations were subsequently (in November) established with communist China, ambassadors exchanged with the USSR, and progressively political relations including defence arrangements with France were 'decolonised'. This reform of foreign policy was emulated by Mauritius to the extent that diplomatic relations and visits were exchanged with Peking,[101] but in regard to South Africa Mauritian policy did not change. In the case of Malagasy national unity required, as national reconciliation in Lesotho also required, among other things a more radical posture in relation to South Africa. Lieutenant Commander Didier Ratsiraka, the Malagasy Foreign Minister, noted that while policy towards South Africa had not produced the desired results, it was 'a bone of contention' among the Malagasy people. Although neither Malagasy nor Mauritius discontinued trade with South Africa or forbade private investment from that source, South African policy in Africa had suffered a severe setback, and so also had its naval power pretensions in the Indian Ocean.

What of *anglophonie*—or rather, the pro-dialogue anglophone States? If the States already separately discussed (Lesotho and Malawi) are left out, it is Ghana and Uganda's 'dialogue' policy which needs to be accounted for. Dr Busia and his supporters were always opposed to communism, although how close a relationship with the West was desirable to the majority of these supporters was far from clear.[102] Anti-communism was relevant to Ghana after the overthrow of Nkrumah because of the more immediate danger for

[100] See *A.R.B.* (*Pol.*), 1972, 2502A, 2630A.

[101] *Peking Review*, 1 June 1973.

[102] This was evident from the cautious definition of Ghana's international political orientation when Busia, while professing non-alignment, indicated in measured terms his preference for the West. See *A.R.B.* (*Pol.*), 1969, 1575C. In September 1971, after the Finance Minister, H. Mensah, had said in July that Britain had exacted harsh terms from Ghana, Busia stated that he was impressed by 'the friendliness and undoubted evidence of goodwill and sincere determination' of Heath and his colleagues to help Ghana. See *West Africa*, 10 September 1971. Consider also the 'Abbot affair', which showed, among other things, evidence of unease over too great a deference towards 'expatriate' interests in the final year of the NLC. Cf. *Africa Contemporary Record*, 1968–69, p. 495.

the new rulers from a revival of 'Nkrumahism'. This reinforced a conservative tendency in the ruling party. Under civilian rule, with more scope for political activity, the fear of 'Nkrumahism' was greater, and the conservative orientation of post-Nkrumah Ghana became more marked, expressing itself in such measures as the expulsion of 'aliens' in favour of indigenous vendors.[103] Moreover, Busia sought to solve Ghana's economic problems through increased aid from the West, and especially the United Kingdom, to which purpose it would help to be responsive to British objectives in southern Africa. Yet Ghanaian conservatism under Busia was inward-looking, rather than preoccupied with external African affairs, and it is unlikely that Busia and his Ministers would have lost much sleep over the Chinese or the Russians gaining influence in remote parts of Africa and the Indian Ocean. It was via the domestic situation of inflation and the external debt problem that 'dialogue' affected Ghana. South Africa could be a useful trading partner. Indeed, if we are to believe Rhoodie,[104] the first 'dialogue' speech in 1969 might have been intended to legitimate an already existing pattern of co-operation with South Africa. Also, a more conciliatory policy towards South Africa would be welcomed in the West, and Busia might hope that such appreciation would be reflected in negotiations about debt repayment and import credits. Championing 'dialogue' and sabotaging the anti-arms sales campaign would secure much needed British official goodwill. Yet the 'British factor' in Busia's policy can be overstated. It should be borne in mind that the first 'dialogue' speech was made in 1969, long before the arms issue erupted; consultations with Houphouet-Boigny took place before the Conservatives gained power in England. Also, 'dialogue' was very much a personal interest of the Prime Minister rather than an agreed policy of the whole government. There is a case for the view that Busia was determined to uproot every flower of the Nkrumahist wilderness for the good of Ghana, as he would have thought, although possibly to indulge as well a desire for private revenge. Here again, external pressures (Western connections), would have operated only because of the internal social bases of conservatism which predisposed the government to see external 'communist threats' as well as internal dangers. A military coup, led by Lieutenant Colonel Acheampong, removed Busia, and with him

[103] *Africa Contemporary Record*, 1969–70, 8473–4.
[104] Rhoodie, *The Third Africa*, p. 198.

his policy of 'dialogue'. As with so many coups—e.g. the Malagasy one of the same year—a notably pro-Western leader, conservative in political style, was replaced by an avowedly populist military regime, which although still within the orbit of Western influence, was more assertive of national interest: depreciating, for example, the submission to foreign pressure implied in the previous Ministry's devaluation of the Ghanaian currency by 45 per cent. Certainly, right-wing positions were tenable in Africa, as so many military and civilian regimes had shown, but a non-populist, rather aloof species of African toryism was vulnerable to all manner of nationalist challengers from the right as well as the left.

. General Amin's position on 'dialogue' can also be seen to have been related more to Uganda's internal political situation and the bearing of external alignments with powers other than South Africa upon that situation. Amin, who had private discontents, overthrew the Obote government while Obote was still in Singapore, where he had strongly condemned British policy on arms sales to South Africa. Amin knew, as everyone did, that there was much dissatisfaction with the Obote government. The fact that the head of state was away made it easier to seize power—after the example of the first Ghanaian *coup d'état*. Thus when a friend intercepted a telephone message from Obote in Singapore ordering the arrest of Amin, already suspected of seditious inclinations, the General pre-emptively seized the State. He thereupon immediately indicated that he would collaborate closely with the United Kingdom, and, at the same time, he reversed the militant condemnation of British arms sales to South Africa. It was later reported that on his visit to Britain Amin was advised to seek 'dialogue' with South Africa.[105] It is incontrovertible that Amin's attitude to South Africa was residual to this attitude to Britain, whose support for his *coup d'état* he hoped to gain. It was also of a piece with his rejection of what Obote had done and his determination to create a new order. Indeed, once British–Ugandan relations were on a sure footing Amin lost interest in the 'dialogue' business, partly in deference to feeling in Uganda and in the OAU but partly also because, the arms controversy having died down, 'dialogue' was no longer immediately important for the collaboration with Britain which Amin needed to secure the domestic political situation in Uganda. Relations with Britain would sub-

[105] *Cape Times*, 30 September 1971.

sequently deteriorate as a result of Amin's foreign policy ambitions, which Britain refused to support, and in consequence of the general's attempting to shore up his tottering State by launching an 'economic war' involving the expulsion of British Asians. In the African context, too close identification with the controversial advocacy of 'dialogue' would lose Amin's regime friends—and not only among militants like Zambia and Tanzania—without any tangible advantage. Thus Amin identified his regime with the cause of colonial and racial liberation in Africa. Incongruously, however, his Foreign Minister announced in August 1971 that Uganda was suspending contributions to liberation movements until it was satisfied that their activities were directed solely to freeing Africa's non-independent territories. He did not explain why he was not satisfied that they were doing so. In general, Ugandan foreign policy pronouncements lacked coherence and were often contradictory.[106] Nevertheless, Amin, like so many other African leaders before and after him, saw that while the material advantages to be gained from conciliating the white south were small, it was virtually impossible to mobilise popular opinion behind such a policy while within the mind of the very elite that supported him collaboration with the white powers created a grave division.

Although Amin frequently pledged his support to the liberation struggle, even offering Uganda as base for the African High Command he believed to be desirable for the successful conclusion of that struggle, the real facts of his foreign policy belied that public position. His conflicts with Tanzania, which refused to recognise his government, honoured the deposed president, and provided training facilities for anti-Amin Ugandan guerrillas, made the General prepare to launch an attack on Tanzania with the support of Portugal, itself the object of a liberation struggle based in Tanzania. The idea was that he would thereby not only rid himself of a subversive menace from the south but would also be able to annex to Uganda a corridor to the sea, including the port of Tanga. The actual military onslaught, Amin and his advisors reasoned,[107] would

---

[106] Although his foreign policy seemed arbitrary and impulsive, Amin also seemed to have a sure instinct for political survival in international affairs, for example, limiting his confrontations in east Africa to Tanzania. More important, there was a deal of mental lucidity in his assuming an anti-South African rhetorical position during a period when he was conspiring to invade Tanzania with the assistance of Portugal.

[107] These reportedly included a retired British major.

be three-pronged, involving a simultaneous attack by the Portuguese from the south, the Ugandan air and land invasion, and an internal rising which could be led by the former Vice-president of Tanzania, Oscar Kambona.[108] Amin tried to obtain support of this project first from the Israelis, then from the British. When he failed he turned against both powers. Thus while diplomatic prudence encouraged his affirmations of support for the cause of liberation, the inexorable logic of reaction and its inevitable conflict with revolutionary forces led him to seek belligerent alliance with imperial Portugal. The eventual detente between Tanzania and Uganda still had in the middle of 1973 a decidedly hollow ring, while the liberation movements regarded Amin's policies as a menace to their cause.

Among the countries which did not go over to the 'dialogue' side there were some which were decidedly unhappy about the militant policy towards white-controlled southern Africa. Kenya was one of these countries, and it is of particular interest, for, while the general ideological tendency of its government was profoundly anti-revolutionary,[109] its material interests went against a policy of conciliating the white south. By the mid-1960s there were reports of Kenyan contacts with South Africa and even rumours of an important 'deal' between the two countries. In 1968 Rothman's, the South African tobacco company, was allowed to float a share issue in Nairobi, where it was to establish a subsidiary. In a short while, however, Rothman's sold out to the British American Tobacco Company for reasons believed not to have been entirely economic. Enterprises like the Old Mutual Insurance Company with South African origins and connections were allowed to continue operating in Kenya.[110] On the issue of 'dialogue', Kenya at first vacillated, it studiously refrained from officially criticising Banda's policy towards South

[108] It has been reported in East Africa that Kambona has on more than one occasion visited Mozambique and Portugal (see *Drum*, April 1973 E.A.). I am also grateful to David Martin for an extensive and informative interview (April 1973) on this subject.

[109] For a good, if oblique, conceptual discussion of the considerable de-radicalisation of Kenyan politics since independence see G. C. Mutiso, 'The structure of inter-ethnic and inter-racial interaction', in National Christian Council of Kenya, *Community Relations Workshop Report*, 1972. Also full of insights, and referring to some of the linkages between domestic and external politics: E. M. Godfrey and G. C. Mutiso, 'The political economy of self-help: Kenya's Harambee Institutes of Technology', I.D.S. University of Nairobi, 1973.

[110] See N.C.C.K.'s *Who Controls Industry in Kenya*.

Africa, and, on one occasion, its Foreign Minister, Dr Mungai, stated that his government was in favour of the OAU giving an audience to the Bantustan chiefs.[111] Its attitude towards the liberation movements was distant. On the other hand, Kenya's relations with those powers often criticised by radicals for collaborating with Portugal and South Africa—namely Britain, France and the US— were very close—the RAF, for example, having staging rights in Kenya.

In material terms Kenya might hope to benefit from 'normal relations' with South Africa. In addition to the normal gains from trade (South Africa had, before independence, been an important market for its pyrethrum and soda ash) tourism, which is a politically and socially dominant industry in Kenya, would benefit to some degree. Moreover, South African investment would help to relieve the shortage of capital from which it suffers. However, none of these gains (which were, in any case, highly speculative) would outweigh the certain losses which would follow the break-up of the East African Common Market, upon which Tanzania would insist if Kenya befriended Pretoria. Thus however much ideological inclination (and the advice of friendly non-African powers) might suggest on the issue of the south, the government of Kenya had to proceed with counted steps.

The unity between the policy position adopted towards the UK, towards South Africa and towards domestic issues was clearly recognised by critics of the government, as one incident will serve to illustrate.[112] In March 1973 a demonstration was held in Nairobi to commemorate the Sharpeville massacre. The speeches given at the rally in Jeevanjee Gardens (over which an old branch of Barclays Bank DCO looms obliquely) dealt at length with foreign domination of Africa generally, which they deplored, and even contained illusions to general Black Power sentiments. With great feeling 'neocolonialism', 'exploitation' and undemocratic tendencies in Africa were condemned, and South African *apartheid* itself seemed to be regarded as only the worst symptom of a more general malaise.

[111] Dr Mungai later explained to South African exiled organisations that he hoped to familiarise the Bantustan chiefs with the thinking of independent Africa. The policy suggested by Dr Mungai had been strongly commended (by the US particularly) to a number of African governments, and might well be the next phase of the 'dialogue' controversy.

[112] See 'A view from the left: the lessons of Malagasy', *University Platform*, 27 July 1972 (subsequently banned).

It was only one target in a wider struggle for continental liberation.[113]

What 'communist danger' did the militant policy on South Africa
involve, and how? Houphouet-Boigny, in advocating 'dialogue',
had repeatedly drawn attention to such a 'danger'. He could have
meant a lot of things, but he probably meant that the militant
position on South Africa, favouring, as it did, revolutionary activity
which the West was unwilling to support, provided an entry point
for communist influence in Africa. In this regard he could have
pointed to the Chinese involvement in the TanZam railway (which
was the direct outcome of the policy of African isolation of the white
south and the West's unwillingness to encourage or support that
project). Moreover, unable to gain support from most Western
governments, liberation movements received military aid—instruc-
tion and equipment—from communist countries (and 'leftist' African
and European countries). African States eager for revolutionary
activity against South Africa could not logically reject the friendship
of communist powers. At the same time, African collaboration with
the West was being called into question as Western governments
showed themselves unresponsive to African appeals for the isolation
of South Africa. Clearly, revolutionary orientations towards South
Africa had a potentially radicalising effect in Africa, especially with
regard to extra-African alignments. This assessment is not based on
any direct evidence of the thinking of all the 'anti-communists' yet it
is not mere conjecture: it is an exfoliation of the logic of the conservative position, which in the absence of direct evidence is the only
means of relating 'dialogue' to the characteristic concerns of such
governments as that of Ivory Coast in the field of international
relations.

To summarise, under the general concept of a communist menace
are included threats to the existing extra-African alignments of
African powers. In the field of domestic politics the fear of 'communism' may amount to no more than fear of one's left-wing
opponents. External and internal political issues are closely linked,
and to both the policies of the former colonial powers are with

[113] Personal observation, Sharpeville day, 1973. The tendency of protests
over southern Africa to spill over into protests about domestic problems,
always coupled with allegations of continuing imperialist control, is one
reason why even governments hostile to South Africa are not keen on anti-
South African activity by their citizens.

varying degrees of directness important. It was, after all, no mere coincidence that the States most favouring 'dialogue' were also those least critical of their formed metropoles. Austin reflected in 1966 that anglophone African States were unlikely to press a quarrel with Britain over South Africa to the point of disrupting the Commonwealth pattern of post-colonial relations.[114] And, true enough, in the period under discussion, even radical States were readier to sever relations with Britain than take the more decisive step of leaving the Commonwealth.[115] To the extent that these post-colonial relations were important, it can be seen that just as the earlier pan-African policy of South Africa was conceived in a colonial context which it presupposed, so now the residual power of the former colonial powers remains important for the Africa policies of the governments of South Africa.

It would be a mistake to suppose that States which opposed 'dialogue' were not apprehensive of the possibility of the Cold War being intensified in Africa in consequence of the revolutionary struggles in southern Africa, or that they were indifferent to the effect their support for a militant stand on South Africa might have on their relations with the former metropolitan powers and indeed other powers. Rather, it is more likely the case that many did not feel that they were called upon to choose between the order which prevailed and the alternative future which Houphouet-Boigny and others seemed to have in mind. In a way, also, commitment to the Organisation of African Unity, with which the miltant stand on *apartheid* is closely connected, was a means of avoiding precisely the polar division of the continent which the Ivory Coast leader said he feared. It could be argued from this point of view that southern African liberation provided an alternative focus for the collective diplomacy of Africans to the more divisive questions of East–West conflict, and that on pragmatic grounds it was better for the peaceful among Africans to concentrate attention and energies on

[114] *Britain and South Africa*, p. 56. Others have argued that precisely because of their post-colonial orientation, economically as well as politically, towards the UK, France and the US, the contribution of African States to the African revolution is likely at the present juncture to be small or even, in some cases, negative. Cf. Arrighi and Saul, 'Nationalism and revolution in sub-Saharan Africa'.

[115] Nothing came of President Kaunda's threat to leave the Commonwealth over Rhodesia; and no African State left the Commonwealth over the British decision to sell arms to South Africa.

southern Africa. Also, like nationalism, southern African liberation was an issue that both the centre and the left could champion as a less divisive form of radicalism within their own polities. Such and similar functional arguments could be used in favour of militancy, in addition to the merits of the southern African liberation cause itself. The States opposing 'dialogue' were, of course, not all like-minded. There were those who would champion the southern African revolution even if, and perhaps all the more if, it led to the radicalisation of the politics of the continent in the direction of more or less revolutionary populist or socialist values and away from the Western values which are part of the colonial heritage. There were others still who, while not subscribing to these views, still felt that the influence of the West (Western Europe especially) in Africa was disproportionate and that the gaining of some influence by communists in Africa was no more than redressing the balance, favouring non-alignment and the democratisation of international relations. Some might argue that if non-communist regimes in Africa did not support the revolutionaries, who would in any case revolt, that would be the greatest boon to communists, as their influence on the liberation movements and their supporters in Africa would be enhanced. But perhaps most important of all, many States did not believe that the revolutionary struggles in southern Africa had made the danger of communism—if it was a danger—any greater than it would otherwise have been. As the conflict in southern Africa develops the situation might change. If it called for more sacrifices on the part of African States, especially those near the affected territories, and if it forced on those regimes drastic realignments with far-reaching implications in their domestic politics, then differences on the issues discussed might become more important; then the solidarity of African States, even now much qualified, might become a lot more difficult to take for granted. This is to say no more than that the southern African revolution is a major part of the African revolution. Yet many African leaders might feel that there is no reason to anticipate the future by taking up rigid ideological stands at the present stage, or that it is not the business of good government to do so.

The 'dialogue' controversy affected, and was affected by, a wide range of matters which had little direct bearing on *apartheid*. Intra-African alignments and rivalries—especially in west Africa—and attitudes to extra-African alignments featured importantly. In East

Africa too there is reason to suppose that Uganda's changing attitudes were influenced in no small way by the relations between Amin and the two heads of state who opposed his coup, namely Kaunda and Nyerere. So long as these leaders were at loggerheads with him, Amin was not disposed to support the project with which they and his predecessor were closely identified, namely, militant oposition to the white south. Yet, Uganda, like most African States, was not in favour of creating difficulties for itself in Africa generally on behalf of South Africa. Even the governments advocating 'dialogue' hedged their proposals with qualifications—they mainly favoured a multilateral *démarche* and they all claimed that 'dialogue' was a weapon against *apartheid*. Many identified themselves with the OAU Lusaka manifesto, which South Africa rejected. On account of all these qualifications, and because of the remoteness of the factors influencing African postures on 'dialogue', it must be inferred that with respect to South Africa's position in Africa the 'dialogue' movement was a very inconclusive development.

There is, indeed, nothing quite conclusive in the art of temporal government. The developments over 'dialogue' indicated a thaw in African attitudes towards South Africa and set the scene for other unusual happenings in the relations of African States with white South Africa. A kind of dialogue with white South Africa began soon after the OAU summit, when a number of African heads of government received the leaders of the loyal oposition—Progressive Party—Mr Eglin and Mrs Suzman MP. They met heads of government in Kenya, Ghana, Gambia, Tanzania, Zambia, Malawi, Senegal and Botswana, with whom they discussed the question of normalising relations with South Africa or a dialogue with the South African government in that connection. Most of the African leaders insisted that 'dialogue' with the South African government could take place only on the basis of the Lusaka manifesto. Mrs Suzman, after their meeting with President Nyerere of Tanzania, remarked:

As we naturally expected, President Nyerere [was] as firmly opposed to any kind of dialogue as ever but he did hold out a slight hope if there were a commitment by South Africa towards racial change.[116]

Eglin added that Nyerere was 'pleased to meet us as representing at least a small breakthrough against *apartheid*'. The Progressive Party leaders concluded that:

[116] *Cape Times,* 14 October 1971.

If the Nationalist government were to move even perceptibly from its present stance on *apartheid* towards the provision of gradual non-white franchise envisaged in the Lusaka manifesto it would win more friends among the leaders of black Africa than it would ever have thought possible.[117]

There were probably mixed motives in the acceptance of Eglin and Mrs Suzman by the African leaders: a desire to know more about the white South Africans whom they discussed so often, a desire not to seem too intractable, a desire perhaps to acknowledge Mrs Suzman's work in exposing and questioning the government's treatment of political prisoners and of Africans generally, and probably also a desire to have the view of the heads of state better represented within South Africa. In the case of the Ghanaian government the reception of the Progressive Party leaders was consistent with its policy of 'dialogue', and the same holds for Malawi. But whatever the motives of the African hosts, there can be no doubt that the Eglin–Suzman tour was of a piece with the outward-looking policy and that their reception was in character with the overall decline in African militancy signified by the Lusaka manifesto. The Progressive Party did not go on tours of African capitals before the outward-looking policy or before the 'dialogue' campaign. True, the party had always been less critical of, and more conciliatory towards, African States. In South Africa it favoured a qualified franchise which went further than the UP and the NP were prepared to go in the direction of a multi-racial polity. Yet the PP was loyal and favoured the normalisation of relations with South Africa, it was opposed to boycotts and even more to revolutions. The qualified franchise proposals of the PP had long been rejected by South African African nationalist organisations.

The visit thus raised questions as to whether it was the State and the whole establishment, or merely the government in power, which were affected by the isolation policies still upheld in the Lusaka manifesto and reaffirmed in the 'no dialogue' resolution of the OAU. Surely it must have been considerations of this kind which motivated the Nigerian government to refuse the PP delegation an audience? As for Houphouet-Boigny of Ivory Coast, he refused the PP delegation an audience for different reasons: he was at the time engaged in discussions with the South African government over the proposed delegation of Ivory Coast and friendly countries to be

[117] *Ibid.*, 15 October 1971.

sent to South Africa, and, it was presumed, did not wish to offend the South African government by receiving a delegation from a minority party.[118] The PP leaders were welcome to meet other members of the Ivory Coast government, but they declined to do so.

From the point of view of South African foreign policy, the 'dialogue' campaign was a success which could not be measured only in terms of its acceptance or rejection as a continent-wide policy. First, it can be seen as the attempt of governments who had already dissociated themselves from OAU policies towards South Africa to legitimate publicly courses of action on which they had already decided (and in some cases acted upon unilaterally). They were thus able to take the offensive against the militants rather than have to justify defensively their breach of the common stand. Secondly, once these countries had publicly established their revisionist positions on South Africa, it would be easier for South Africa to increase its economic interaction with them and, through them, with the rest of the continent without the restrictive effects of secret dealing. Finally, if the South African government could be seen to have broken the uniform opposition—militant opposition— by African governments in a position so to oppose, then it would be easier to undermine the growing pressures outside Africa against the republic; for the resolute and apparently united stand of Africans on South Africa had always provided the strongest self-interest arguments for Western governments solicitous over their economic interests in Africa to diminish their co-operation with South Africa. Finally, South African policy-makers had at last succeeded in convincing a fair number of African governments that they and South Africa had at least one common interest which was a greater threat to the continent than *apartheid*, namely 'communism'. The question of southern African liberation would never again be divorced from the ideological divisions which advocates of African unity could never quite subdue, and for that reason African solidarity over *apartheid* could never again be taken for granted.

[118] *Ibid.*, 5 October 1971.

The Africa policies
of the governments of South Africa
1945-73

In the period covered by this work major transformations occurred in the external environment of South Africa. Of these the most drastic were the changes brought about by decolonisation in Africa. For South Africa's white community, which is itself a product of colonialism, decolonisation was a disturbing development, and it was to be expected that it would feature as a central preoccupation in South African foreign policy. Indeed, the republic's policy towards Africa in the post-war period was little more than a reaction to the passing of colonial Africa and to the uncertainties and dangers which that seemed to entail. The 'pan-African' policies of the earlier period were a reaction to decolonisation in Africa; the 'outward-looking' policy of the later period was a response to the situation created by the emergence of black African States.

The main aims of the pan-African policies of South Africa were, however, conceived before the substantive changes brought about by the transfer of power from the imperial capitals to local African governments. They therefore presupposed the continuation of the imperial political order in Africa more or less as it had been in 1945–1946. When it became apparent that the imperial powers were in fact decolonising, South African policy sought to arrest or to delay such change. Even when independence came, the residual influence of the former colonial powers remained important for subsequent Africa policies, such as the outward-looking policy of the South African government. Underdevelopment, defined as a general situation, accounts both for the persistence of these patterns of influence and the successes of the South African government after independence. In retrospect, therefore, it is clear that there is considerable continuity in the relationship between South Africa and the rest of the continent, a continuity further underlined by the fact that South Africa maintained its distinctive political character throughout these years. The basic aim of the Africa policies of South Africa thus remained the same during the whole period, namely, to establish an African political context which was ideologically and organisationally favourable to white minority rule in South Africa. Whether this objective was stated as 'preserving Africa for white Christian civilisation', as Malan had put it, or countering 'communism' and 'terrorism', merely reflected South African acknowledgement of the fact that the world and Africa, after as before independence, continued to change faster than South Africa. It is in this fact that most of the difficulties of South African foreign policy are to be found. Despite all the adjustments which they made in their foreign policy, successive South African governments continued to pursue the same domestic policies which gave rise to external opposition to South Africa.

In the introduction to this study we indicated that the history of the Africa policies pursued by South Africa could be expressed in terms of the internal contradictions of these policies on the one hand and of the contradictions between South Africa and the rest of the continent on the other. The intensification of these contradictions resulted in the earlier policies being superseded by later ones, which in time sustained a similar fate. In the foregoing chapters this element of contradiction has been followed in some detail, and it now remains to summarise our arguments. In doing so, we shall also expatiate on the view that South Africa's policy towards the rest of Africa was a fundamental failure despite its apparent successes. It failed equally during the first period *vis-à-vis* the colonial powers and during the later period of African assertion: Africa was not made safe for *apartheid*.

South African pretensions to leadership in Africa, in partnership with the colonial powers, failed principally because the 'African' powers—with the exception of Portugal—were decolonising, while the main aim of South Africa was to arrest or to delay decolonisation. They also failed because what South Africa intended for the continent—indefinite white supremacy unqualified by any concessions to the multi-racialism of the post-war period—was inconsistent with the means by which the imperial powers hoped to exercise their control in the final phase of their 'stewardship'. Such a policy of white supremacy would have created tensions in the colonies calling for costly interventions by the metropolitan powers, which were increasingly reluctant to use force in their colonies after the second world war.

In addition the discrepancy in power in Africa between South Africa and the imperial powers would have made the idea of partnership unreal. There was a surface plausibility in South Africa's pretensions, owing to its higher economic and technological development compared with other African countries, to the part it had hitherto played in international organisations, and because of its membership of the Commonwealth and its identification with the West. Yet it was South African policy which in the end minimised this potential for 'African' leadership. Firstly, when South Africa came under pressure in the United Nations as a result of India's questioning the treatment of Indians in South Africa, the Union government was not disposed to make any important concessions, thus encouraging India at a later date to broaden its complaint into an attack on the policies of *apartheid* generally. Secondly, soon after Smuts' departure from office official South African enthusiasm for the British Commonwealth declined, owing to the ascendancy of Afrikaner republicanism. Republicanism tended to undermine that unity of 'British South Africa' around which Smuts had built his imperial dreams. For their part, British policy-makers decided to limit as far as possible the growth of South African influence in their southern African territories by encouraging 'racial partnership'. The pro-Western posture also proved to be of limited effect at the working level, as distinct from the level of verbal affirmation. South Africans were involved militarily only in Korea and in the 'gateway to Africa' in the early 1950s; for the rest, the South African government showed itself reluctant to be drawn outside Africa. Yet a regional African role in the defence of the West was difficult to define, and from the point of view of the major 'African' powers Africa was not sufficiently a problem area to encourage concerted action involving South Africa. Consequently, little was achieved apart from the conversational conferences in Nairobi and Dakar. If the African empires were not considered to be faced with external threats, no 'African' power was likely to call on South Africa to police its empire. South Africa thus lacked an effective entry point into the defence politics of the continent. The UK valued South African naval co-operation over Simonstown, especially after 1956; but by the 1960s the UK was withdrawing from south, as well as east, of Suez. Even in the mid-1950s the Simonstown agreements were not extended into the African Defence Organisation which South African politicians wanted. South Africa's importance to the West lay mainly in the economic field; it was an important trading partner for Britain and, as a gold-producing country, it was important to an international monetary system, in which gold played a large part. This, however, had little to do with African roles.

South African technological and economic achievements had greater relevance. In the early post-war years South Africa collaborated with other 'African' powers in the CCTA and the CSA and associated bodies. Yet tensions over race meant that South Africa had reservations about the expansion of technical and scientific co-operation if it meant involving the UN. In this respect it was in agreement with the colonial powers, which preferred to keep the hostile, anti-colonial influence of the UN at bay. The tendency of empires towards exclusiveness, however, entailed a further contradiction for South African policy: Britain dominated the trade of its African colonies, to the annoyance of some of the supporters of the South African government, and it does not appear that the latter even as much as tried to influence French imperial trade policies. This exclusiveness was not, however, much of an issue in the late 1940s and early 1950s, since South African trade and investment in Africa were small and concentrated in the neighbouring Rhodesias. There was little likelihood, despite official wishes to the contrary, that South African economic power would provide in the near future a bridgehead for political influence. Besides, the powers that counted in Africa were located in Europe, and the relative calm ensured by the continuance of empires meant that there was no immediate imperative for South African governments to exert themselves conscientiously in a politically directed economic diplomacy.

As decolonisation proceeded, *pari passu* with the deterioration of South Africa's standing in the world, the earlier hopes of leadership began to recede: the grander schemes of Smuts and Malan were clearly obsolete. In South Africa itself opposition to *apartheid* was gathering head, reaching a peak in 1959–60. Commensurately, international and African pressure for the isolation of South Africa increased. The emergent Africa was clearly not going to be safe for *apartheid*. South African policy towards Africa became more defensive, and foreign policy makers were reluctantly obliged to accept the irreversibility of the changes which had occurred. In the behaviour of the Foreign Office there was a change also. The Foreign Minister established social contacts with some black leaders, while the government offered co-operation and technical aid to willing black governments. Internally, the doctrines of 'white supremacy' yielded to the more defensive slogans of 'white survival' and 'separate development', which, although they meant the same thing, were concessions—intellectually at least—to the growing opposition to *apartheid*. Yet *apartheid* was actually intensified in South Africa, and the security laws were made more effective. Externally, South Africa became more closely identified with other white minority regimes in Africa and with their resistance to decolonisation, thus making a nonsense of its avowed acceptance of the changes which had occurred and of its offers of friendship and co-operation with black African States.

The perilous situation created in Africa encouraged ideological revisions in South Africa. The ruling elite focused its attention on the material conditions for 'white survival', namely, the threatened markets abroad, the maintenance of State security, and the reduction of tensions among whites within South Africa and of avoidable friction (within the framework of inequality) with blacks. South Africa was increasing its economic and technological power, and the years of crisis were also years of growing material strength. Imperceptibly the structure of white society changed, owing to higher social mobility, especially among Afrikaners. Increased white immigration also helped to accelerate that change. These social transformations were of a piece with the conversion of white society to a more materialist orientation; indeed, they contributed to it. Tensions ensued within the white polity, but strong opposition to the government was limited and ineffective in its attempts to reverse the materialistic trend. This was to be expected now that the government had become virtually identified with the State, whose power as patron and regulator had grown over the years. All these developments tended to instil the element of *raison d'état* into the ruling party's official ideology.

This was evident too in the infractions of racial segregation begun by Louw and culminating in Banda's visit to South Africa. *Realpolitik*, which is the operational correlative of State interest, was particularly evident in South Africa's diplomacy over the Rhodesian UDI. Although South Africa aided Rhodesia, it stopped short of embroiling itself in major difficulties with Britain, or of formally recognizing Rhodesia as an independent State. Nor did it forego the opportunities of lucrative trade at the expense of Rhodesia in central Africa. Yet increasing acceptance of these classical principles of statecraft did not alter the essential character of the South

African political system. Instead, the principles were harnessed to the task of strengthening the existing political order.

With these adjustments at the cognitive and affective levels of foreign policy orientation, it became possible to exert South African economic and military power to evident advantage. Opportunities to do so were provided by such external events as UDI, the World Court judgement on South West Africa in 1966, the granting of independence of the former High Commission Territories, and the insecurities of more distant African States, such as Malawi, Madagascar and Ghana. Towards the end of the 1960s and in the early 1970s South Africa achieved victories as a number of black States accepted its aid, and as more argued for a revision of the policy of isolating South Africa. Its influence in southern Africa was greater than it had ever been and was now extending to remote parts of former French Africa. To this extent the withdrawal of European imperial hegemony from Africa (leaving behind the condition of underdevelopment, dependence, and the related associative tendencies referred to in chapter 1), favoured South African penetration of parts, at any rate, of Africa. We have also argued in the last chapter that the post-independence role of the former and existing imperial powers in Africa has tended to be supportive of South African policy, either by manifest collusion (as in the case of Portugal) or by the indirect exercise of conservative influence (by British and French governments). Yet South Africa continued to occupy only a secondary position relative to the former metropolitan powers, and it was unclear how the relationship between South Africa and these powers would develop in the increasingly common spheres of influence. Would it be competitive or would it be collaborative, with South Africa as a junior partner? Such questions remained important, for the Africa policy was only a part of a wider foreign policy with which it had to be harmonised and to which, if it were successful, it might be expected to contribute. The definition of roles might be more important in the near future in such areas as Mozambique and Angola, where economically South Africa seemed to be occupying a 'sub-imperial' position. If South Africa should wish to extend its influence it might have to do so at the expense of the 'host' benefactors, and this might result in tensions between South Africa and those other powers. In our period there was no accessible evidence that this had occurred, but its likelihood for the future remained very real.

Against the successes of South African policy must be set the
new difficulties which were arising—no less from such successes than
from old problems. First, by the time the 'outward-looking' policy
was contrived a qualitative change in the politics of southern Africa
had taken place. Guerrilla activity had been introduced into the
area and had a double significance: it meant the importation of
hostile external influences, and it confirmed that shift of southern
African politics towards violence which had begun at the end of the
1950s. Second, as South Africa became drawn into para-military
activity in Angola, Mozambique and Rhodesia it widened its battlefields and reduced the chances held out by the Lusaka manifesto of
a separate peace with the rest of Africa. Similarly, as South African
political and economic involvement in such countries as Malawi
increased, South Africa seemed likely to be drawn into their domestic
politics. Such 'imperial' relationships are essentially conflictful even
if it might (for a while) be possible for South Africa to keep the
conflict within acceptable limits.

The experience of Malawi illustrates the special difficulties of the
post-colonial situation in at least one important respect. While the
insecurity of Banda's regime and its reactions to the situation of
underdevelopment provided South Africa with an entry point into
Malawi, the latter's collaboration with South Africa and the kindred
regimes of Portugal and Rhodesia increased the problems of internal
security. New States are notoriously unstable, and no diplomatic
success is quite conclusive.

With respect to countries farther to the north, this inconclusiveness
was underlined by the fact that southern Africa is remote from their
day-to-day concerns. We have argued that those governments which
pursued an actively revisionist policy towards South Africa—the
policy of 'dialogue'—had only an indirect *practical*, as distinct from
an emotive and intellectual, interest in South Africa. Their interest
arose from their wider external alignments, an internal insecurity,
and their general attitude to inter-State relations in Africa as they
took place within the framework of the OAU. The fear among
them that 'communist influence' might spread in Africa as a result
of guerilla activity in southern Africa was more a 'generalised
anxiety' than a specific—and therefore predictable—policy preoccupation. In this regard it is worth noting that even the foremost
advocates of 'dialogue' affirmed their opposition to *apartheid*,
asserting that 'dialogue' would hasten its overthrow. They might be

expected at the very least to insist on some token concession by South Africa—if only to prove that 'dialogue' worked—and if South Africa yielded they might be encouraged to press for more concessions. If South Africa remained intransigent the traditional African view that the republic should be isolated might recover some of the support it appeared to be losing to the 'dialogue' movement. It should also be borne in mind that the policies of 'dialogue' were mostly attributable to particular governments and even to individual leaders, so that there was no guarantee that they would be continued after the departure of those leaders. Finally, some of the governments which collaborated with South Africa and which, therefore, tempered their hostility to *apartheid*, such as Zambia and Botswana, felt they were doing so under the force of circumstances. For that reason their future collaboration with South Africa, especially if they gain more freedom of action in the economic and communications fields, might be even more qualified. After all, these governments have opposed 'dialogue' outside the framework of the OAU. And, as we saw with Malagasy and Ghana, internal upheavals undid what had been achieved.

Given all these qualifications of South Africa's diplomatic victories in post-colonial Africa, it can hardly be said that, taken all round, South African policy was a success. Judged by its principal aim —to make Africa safe for *apartheid*—it must be considered to have failed. If Africa was less dangerous for South Africa than its governments had once feared it would become, it was due much more to the physical and organisational weakness of African States than to the success of South Africa's policies towards the rest of the continent.

It has been a major aim of this book to show that during the period under review there were ineliminable and fundamental contradictions in South Africa's situation in Africa. There was conflict between the South African desire to maintain an essentially colonial order within South Africa and the need to accept fully the implications of the decolonisation of Africa. Ideological conflict wove irreconcilable contradictions into the structure of South African policy, and, as we have demonstrated, these contradictions were the main obstacle to the success of the Africa policies of the governments of South Africa.

Appendixes

Summary of Malawi's external trade, 1965–69 (£)

	1965	1966	1967	1968	1969
(a) *Imports*					
Country of origin:					
Rhodesia	7,430	6,167	5,323	5,245	5,164
UK	5,169	8,420	7,233	8,949	9,124
South Africa	11,266	1,964	1,960	3,207	4,563
Japan	1,369	1,345	2,138	1,407	1,607
Zambia	361	2,615	1,766	1,156	1,318
USA	546	857	704	1,636	1,169
West Germany	587	648	709	1,073	1,084
Australia	531	461	395	420	529
India	371	475	412	342	317
Hong Kong	386	596	734	480	415
Pakistan	182	357	424	338	341
All others	2,345	2,241	3,628	4,837	5,108
(b) *Exports (excluding re-exports)*					
Country of destination:					
UK	6,417	6,669	9,107	8,498	8,345
Rhodesia	1,383	780	635	782	1,203
South Africa	564	477	457	772	606
USA	362	405	536	805	1,143
Netherlands	600	693	834	705	715
Sierra Leone	316	342	317	296	399
Hong Kong	171	45	182	133	30
Canary Is.	265	271	267	205	397
France	368	326	148	256	150
Kenya	325	157	227	91	24
W. Germany	181	420	351	529	513
Italy	134	94	442	104	50
Ireland	435	536	466	763	576
Zambia	107	224	388	393	1,538
All others	1,914	2,396	2,195	2,448	2,598

Source. Economic Report, 1969.

APPENDIX II   *Summary of Zambia's external trade, 1966–69* (K)

	1966	1967	1968	1969
(a) *Imports*				
Country of origin:				
South Africa	58,468,432	72,172,550	76,065,596	69,902,860
South West Africa	170,168	314,570	506,614	1,493,359
Botswana	998,262	782,510	1,650,604	1,668,829
Swaziland	317,312	1,332,474	2,474,543	1,518,930
Rhodesia	46,360,160	32,235,394	22,573,006	21,771,008
Mozambiqur	603,410	745,068	698,106	916,349
Malawi	483,018	800,940	741,237	2,769,900
Congo (Kinshasa)	2,198,402	235,690	879,091	772,995
Egypt	80	6,260	137,629	98,574
Tanzania	843,012	9,003,300	3,073,810	4,800,910
Kenya	1,309,228	2,910,914	4,297,101	6,328,306
Uganda	26,902	10,038	128,081	110,697
(b) *Exports (including re-exports)*				
Country of destination:				
South Africa	28,050,896	96,486,134	11,680,824	7,581,010
South West Africa	6,698	3,234	1,987	27,807
Botswana	55,142	88,164	136,230	457,261
Swaziland	–	58,040	1,543	92
Rhodesia	5,012,986	2,035,764	951,000	411,016
Mozambique	411,578	121,050	326,307	1,223,098
Malawi	4,368,854	3,619,998	2,362,694	2,690,836
Congo (Kinshasa)	2,437,920	4,057,036	2,436,437	1,129,673
Egypt	67,668	–	654	115,629
Tanzania	405,540	439,986	199,434	1,384,436
Kenya	654,362	459,982	504,119	843,590
Uganda	134,388	104,050	67,511	141,359

Source. Ministry of Trade Report, 1969.

APPENDIX III   *Additional notes on trade*

1. South African official publications do not reveal the republic's trade with individual African States from the 1960s on, but merely give the total for the whole of Africa. Several countries thought to be trading with South Africa, moreover, do not publicise this traffic. Consequently it is difficult to substantiate speculation about openings for trade having been a major consideration of the countries most closely involved in the 'dialogue' controversy. Data for pre-1960s trade, as well as the general pattern of all these countries' trade, suggest that the trade with South Africa could be only very small.

2. The United Nations *Yearbook of International Trade Statistics* gives no information to indicate whether Dahomey, Ivory Coast, Niger, Togo and Ghana traded with South Africa from the mid-1960s. Some data exist of Ivory Coast's trade with Angola, which was, expectedly, very small. Malagasy has information only up to 1965. In 1964 and 1965 imports from South Africa were worth $550,530 and $118,690, while exports amounted to $478,020 and $153,130 in value respectively. Gabon and Mauritius have full and frank figures (see tables 1 and 2).

3. Among the countries opposing 'dialogue' were some which did not observe the boycott of trade with South Africa. Of these, Congo and Zaire have published figures for the years of the outward-looking policy (see tables 3 and 4).

4. Although South African trade with African countries would obviously have been greater without the general boycott—and the restrictive effects of 'under the counter' deals—there is nevertheless no clear relationship between levels of trade with South Africa and support for the 'dialogue' movement.

1. *Gabon: trade with South African Customs Union* and Portugal compared with world total* (US $ 000)

	South African Customs Union	Portugal	World total
Imports			
1966	0	1	65,662
1967	31	51	67,185
1968	153	90	64,308
1969	114	64	77,910
1970	136	102	79,831
Exports			
1966	18		99,935
1967	63		119,571
1968	85		124,423
1969	2	111	142,043
1970	18		121,184

* Trade is not given as specifically with the Republic of South Africa, though that is a reasonable inference.

2(a). *Mauritius: trade with South Africa, 'Portuguese East Africa' and Southern Rhodesia* (us $ 000)

	South Africa	Portuguese East Africa	Southern Rhodesia
Imports			
1964	6,775	193	276
1965	7,258	145	243
1966	5,727	24	8
1967	6,417	48	–
1968	5,652	–	–
1969	5,629	–	–
1970	6,811	–	–
1971	6,513	–	–
Exports			
1964	477	71	8
1965	2,476	129	7
1966	275	39	0·4
1967	706	105	–
1968	1,244	–	–
1969	1,712	–	–
1970	2,186	–	–
1971	2,849	–	–

Note. Figures up to 1968 converted from rupees. Conversion factors: up to 1967, us $1 = 4·762 rupees; in 1968, us $1 = 5·556 rupees.
Source. UN *Yearbook of International Trade Statistics*, various issues.

2(b). *Trade with South Africa as a percentage of Mauritius's world trade*

	Imports	Exports
1964	8·3	0·6
1965	9·4	3·8
1966	8·2	0·4
1967	8·2	1·1
1968	7·5	1·9
1969	8·3	2·6
1970	9·0	3·2
1971	7·8	4·4

3. *People's Republic of the Congo: value of imports from and exports to the South African Customs Union, 1966–70* (US $ 000)

	Imports	Exports
1966	187	1,202
1967	196	1,536
1968	235	2,396
1969	204	2,705
1970	181	2,804

4. *Zaire: value of imports from and exports to South Africa and Rhodesia, 1966–70* (US $ 000)

	South Africa	Rhodesia
Imports		
1966	12,678	7,452
1967	7,822	4,446
1968	7,592	6,924
1969	–	
1970	104	7,123
Exports		
1966	13,714	58
1967	3,890	10
1968	1,396	–
1969	–	
1970	0	22

Selective bibliography

STATE PAPERS

South Africa, Government Printer, Pretoria:

Parliamentary Debates, House of Assembly, 1945–71.
Estimates of Revenue and Expenditure, 1945–71.
Annual Statement of Trade and Shipping, 1945–71.
Statistical Yearbook, 1968, 1969.
Quarterly Report of the South African Reserve Bank, various years.
Exchange of Correspondence between the Governments of India, Pakistan and the Union of South Africa, in regard to a Round Table Conference to discuss a solution to the Indian Question, July 1949 to June 1950.
African Markets for Union Manufacturers, Cape Town, 1942.
Report of the Commission of Enquiry into the Socio-economic Development of the Bantu Areas (summary), 1955.
Report of the Commission of Enquiry into White Occupancy of the Rural Areas, 1960.
Report of the Commission of Enquiry into Occurrences in the Windhoek Location on the Night of the 10th December 1959 and into the direct causes which led to the occurrences, 1960.
Report of the Commission of Enquiry into Policy relating to the Protection of Industries, 1958.

Malawi, Government Printer, Zomba:

Hansard, Official verbatim report of the debates of the Malawi parliament, various years.
National Accounts and Balance of Payments, various years.
Annual Report of the Malawi Police Force, various years.
Ministry of Labour Report, 1963–67.
Malawi Population Census.

Zambia, Government Printer, Lusaka:

Northern Rhodesia Hansard: Official verbatim report of the debates of the 1st session of the Legislative Assembly, 10–20 March, 1964.
Hansard: Official verbatim report of the debates of the Zambian National Assembly, various years.
Monthly Digest of Statistics, various numbers.
Manpower Report, Lusaka, 1966.

The Progress of Zambianisation in the Mining Industry, 1968.
Report of the Commission of Enquiry into the Mining Industry (the Brown Commission Report), 1965.
Zambia's Guidelines for the Next Decade: H. E. The President Addressing the National Council of UNIP at Mulungushi, 9th November 1968.
Towards Complete Independence (Address of H.E. the President etc., to the UNIP National Council at Matero Hall, Lusaka, 11 August, 1969).
Details of Exchanges Between President Kaunda of Zambia and Prime Minister Vorster of South Africa (High Commission, London).

United Nations Organisation, New York:

United Nations General Assembly Official Records, various years.
Security Council Official Records, various years.
Yearbook of International Trade Statistics.

BOOKS

Biographical works

Amery, L. S., *My Political Life,* III: *The Unforgiving Years,* London, 1953.
Benson, M., *Tshekedi Khama,* London, 1960.
Gann, L. H., and Gelfand, M., *Huggins of Rhodesia,* London, 1964.
Hancock, W. K., *Smuts,* I: *The Sanguine Years,* Cambridge, 1962; II: *The Fields of Force,* Cambridge, 1968.
Hancock, W. K., and Van Der Poel, J., *The Smuts Papers,* II.
Kruger, J., *President C. R. Swart.*
Lyttleton, O. (Viscount Chandos), *The Memoirs of Lord Chandos,* London, 1962.
Malan, D. F., *Afrikaner Volkseenheid en My Ervarings op die Pad Daarheen,* Cape Town, 1959.
Mandela, N. R. (ed. R. First), *No Easy Walk to Freedom,* London, 1965.
Welensky, Sir Roy, *Welensky's 4000 days: the Life and Death of the Federation of Rhodesia and Nyasaland,* London, 1964.
Wilson, H., *The Labour Government, 1964–1970: a Personal Record,* London, 1970.

Area studies

Abshire, D. M., and Samuels, M. A., *Portuguese Africa: a Handbook,* London, 1969.
Adam, H., *Modernising Racial Domination: the Dynamics of South African Politics,* London, 1971.
Austin, D., *Britain and South Africa,* London, 1966.
Austin, D., and Weiler, H. (ed.), *Interstate Politics in Africa,* I, 1965.
Ballinger, M., *From Union to Apartheid: the Trek into Isolation,* 1969.
Benson, M., *South Africa: the Struggle for a Birthright,* London, 1969.
Biermann, H. H., *The Case for South Africa,* New York, 1963.
Brookes, E. H., and Macaulay, J. B., *Civil Liberty in South Africa,* London, 1960.

Bunting, B., *The Rise of the South African Reich*, Harmondsworth, 1964.

Cabral, A., 'A brief report on the situation of the struggle, January–August 1971' (mimeo).

Calpin, G. H., *Indians in South Africa*, Pietermaritzburg, 1949.

Calvocoressi, P., *South Africa and World Opinion*, London, 1961.

Carter, G. M., *The Politics of Inequality: South Africa since 1948*, London, 1958.

Cervenk, Z., *The Organisation of African Unity and its Charter*, London, 1958.

Coetzee, J. A., *Nasieskap en politieke groepering in Suid Afrika*, Pretoria, 1969.

Cockram, G., *Vorster's Foreign Policy*, Cape Town, 1970.

Darlington, C. and A., *African Betrayal*, New York, 1968.

Davidson, B., *The Liberation of Guinea: Aspects of an African Revolution*, Harmondsworth, 1969.

Doro, M. E., and Stultz, N. M., *Governing in Black Africa: Perspectives on New States*, New Jersey, 1970.

Feit, E., *African Opposition in South Africa: Dynamics of the African National Congress*, Oxford, 1962.

Franck, T. M., *Race and Nationalism: the Struggle for Power in Rhodesia–Nyasaland*, London, 1960.

Franklin, H., *Unholy Wedlock: the failure of the Central African Federation*, London, 1963.

Gann, L. H., and Duignan, P., *Colonisation in Africa, 1870–1960*, Cambridge, 1969.

Garson, N., *Louis Botha or J. X. Merriman: the Choice of South Africa's First Prime Minister*, London, 1969.

Gray, B., *The Two Nations: Aspects of the Development of Race Relations in the Rhodesias and Nyasaland*, London, 1964.

Hailey, Lord, *The High Commission Territories*, London, 1963.

Hall, R., *The High Price of Principles: Kaunda and the White South*, London, 1969.

Halpern, J., *South Africa's Hostages: Basutoland, Bechuanaland, and Swaziland*, Harmondsworth, 1965.

Hepple, A., *South Africa: a Political and Economic History*, London, 1966.

Heseltine, N., *Madagascar*, London, 1971.

Horrel, M., *South Africa's Workers: their Organisation and Patterns of Employment*, Johannesburg, 1969.

Keatley, P., *The Politics of Partnership*, Harmondsworth, 1963.

Kirk-Greene, A. H. M., *Crisis and Conflict in Nigeria*, Oxford, 1971.

Kruger, D. W., *South African Political Parties and Policies, 1910–60*, London, 1960.

Labuschagne, G. S., *Suid-Afrika en Afrika: die staatkundige verhouing in die tydperk, 1945–66*, Potchefstroom, 1969.

Legum, C., *South Africa: Crisis for the West*, London, 1964.

— *Zambia—Independence and Beyond: the Speeches of Kenneth Kaunda*, London, 1966.

Lee, J. M., *Colonial Development and Good Government: a Study of the*

Ideas expressed by the British Official Classes in Planning Decolonisation, *1939–64*, Oxford, 1967.

Leys, C., *A New Deal in Central Africa*, London, 1960.

Lombard, J. A., Stadler, J. J., and Van der Merwe, P. J., *The Concept of Economic Co-operation in Southern Africa*, Pretoria, 1968.

Lusignan, G. de, *French-speaking Africa since Independence*, London, 1969.

Mackay, V. P., *Africa in World Politics*, New York, 1963.

Malan, D. F., *Wat ons het, dit hou ons*, Stellenbosch, 1924.

Mansergh, N., *Documents and Speeches on British Commonwealth Affairs*, *1931–52*, ii, London, 1963.

— *The Price of Magnanimity: South Africa, 1906–61*, London, 1963.

Marcum, J., *The Angolan Revolution, i: The Anatomy of an Explosion*, Cambridge, Mass., 1969.

Marquard, L., *The Peoples and Policies of South Africa*, London, 1960.

Mayall, J., *Africa: the Cold War and After*, London, 1971.

Mathews, F., *Law, Oorder and Liberty in South Africa*, Cape Town, 1970.

Molteno, R., *South Africa and Africa*, London, 1971.

Mondlane, E., *The Struggle fof Mozambique*, Hardmondsworth, 1968.

Mortimer, E., *France and the Africans, 1944–60: a Political History*, London, 1969.

Murray, G., *The Governmental System of Southern Rhodesia*, Oxford, 1970.

O'Brien, C. C., *To Katanga and Back: a UN Case History*, London, 1962.

Palley, C., *The Constitutional History of Southern Rhodesia*, Oxford, 1966.

Pike, J. G., *Malawi: a Political and Economic History*, London, 1968.

Phillips, C. S., Jnr., *The Development of Nigerian Foreign Policy*, Evanston, Ill., 1964.

Rhoodie, E. M., *The Third Africa*, Cape Town, 1969.

Roberts, M., and Trollop, A. E., *The South African Opposition, 1939–45*, London, 1947.

Rupert, A., *Progress through Partnership*, Cape Town, 1969.

Sampson, A., *The Treason Cage: the Opposition on Trial in South Africa*, London, 1958.

Scholtz, G. D., *Die gevaar uit die Ooste*, Johannesburg, 1960.

Segal, R., *Sanctions against South Africa*, Harmondsworth, 1964.

Segal, R., and First, R. (eds.), *South West Africa: Travesty of Trust*, London, 1967.

Simons, H. J., and R. E., *Class and Colour in South Africa: 1850–1950*, Harmondsworth, 1969.

South African Federated Chamber of Industries, *Report of the African Export Goodwill Trade Mission, 1946*, Johannesburg, 1946.

Spence, J. E., *The Republic Under Pressure*, London, 1965.

— *The Strategic Significance of Southern Africa*, London, 1971.

— *Lesotho: the Politics of Dependence*, London, 1968.

Thompson, M., *The Unification of South Africa*, Oxford, 1960.

Thompson, V. B., *Africa and Unity*, London, 1964.

Thompson, V. B., and Adloff, R., *The Malagasy Republic: Madagascar Today*, Stanford, Cal., 1965.

Vandenbosch, A., *South Africa and the World*, Kentucky, 1970.
Van Wyk, S., *Die Afrikaner in die Beroepslewe van die Stad*, Pretoria, 1968.
Walker, R. A., *A History of Southern Africa*, Cambridge, 1957.
Wallerstein, I., *Africa: the Politics of Unity—an Analysis of a Contemporary Social Movement*, New York, 1967.
University of Zambia, Faculty of Humanities and Social Studies, *Zambia and the World: Essays on Problems relating to Zambia's Foreign Policy*, Lusaka, 1970.
Wellington, J. H., *South West Africa and its Human Issues*, Oxford, 1967.
Wilson, F., *Labour in the South African Gold Mines*, Cambridge, 1971.
Wilson, M., and Thompson, L. M., *Oxford History of South Africa*, II, Oxford, 1971.

ARTICLES

Adam, H., 'The South African power elite', in Adam (ed.), *South Africa: Sociological Perspectives*.
Alavi, H., 'Imperialism, old and new', *Socialist Register*, 1964.
Arrighi, G., and Saul, J. S., 'Nationalism and revolution in sub-Saharan Africa', *Socialist Register*, 1969.
Austin, D., 'Pan-Africanism, 1957–63', in Austin, D., and Weiler, H. W., *Inter-State Relations in Africa*, II.
— 'White Power', *Journal of Commonwealth Political Studies*, 1969.
Balandier, G., 'La Situation coloniale: approche théorique', *Cahiers Internationaux de Sociologie*, 1951.
Brand, S. S., and Tomlinson, F. R., 'Die plek van die Landbou in die Suid-Afrikaanse volkshuishouding', *South African Journal of Economics*, 1966.
Caplan, G. L., 'Zambia, Barotseland and the liberation of southern Africa', *Africa Today*, 1969.
Chenu, F., and Noel, M., 'La France et l'Afrique Australe', *Le Mois en Afrique*, 1970.
Chipembere, H. B. M., 'Malawi's growing links with South Africa: a necessity or a virtue?', *Africa Today*, 1971.
Craig, J., 'Zambia–Botswana road link: some border problems', in University of Zambia etc., *Zambia and the World*.
De la Gorce, P. M., 'De Gaulle et la décolonisation du continent noir', *Le Mois en Afrique*, 1970.
Delavignette, R. L., 'French colonial policy in black Africa, 1945–60', in Gann and Duignan, *Colonialism in Africa*.
Dore, R. P., 'Function and cause', in Demerath and Peterson, *System, Conflict and Change*.
Eisenstadt, S. N., 'Social change, differentiation and evolution,' in Demerath and Peterson, *System, Conflict and Change*.
Galbraith, J. S., 'The turbulent frontier as a factor in British expansion', in *Comparative Studies of Society and History*, 1960.
Galtung, J., 'A structural theory of imperialism', *Peace Research*, 1970.

Geertz, C., 'Ideology as a cultural system', in Apter (ed.), *Ideology and Discontent*.

— 'Ritual and social change: a Javanese example', in Demerath and Peterson, *System, Change and Conflict*.

Gervasi, S., 'The nature and consequences of South Africa's economic expansion', unpublished seminar paper, London University Institute of Commonwealth Studies, 1971.

Hoskyns, C., 'Congo, crisis, July 1960–December 1961), in Austin and Weiler (ed.), *Interstate Relations in Africa*.

Kindleberger, C., *Emigration and economic growth*, Banca Nazionale del Lavoro, 1965.

Knight, B. J., 'A theory of income distribution in South Africa', *Bulletin of the Oxford University Institute of Economics and Statistics*, 1964.

Kooy, M., and Robertson, H. M., 'The South African Board of Trade and Industries; the South African customs tariff and the development of South African industries', *South African Journal of Economics*, 1966.

Kuper, L., 'African nationalism in South Africa', in Wilson and Thompson (ed.), *Oxford History of South Africa*.

Landes, D. S., 'Some thoughts on the nature of economic imperialism', *Journal of Economic History*, 1961.

Leistner, G. M. E., 'Foreign Bantu workers in South Africa: their present position and future prospects', *South African Journal of Economics*, 1967.

Morgenthau, R. S., 'Old cleavages among new West African States: the heritage of French rule', *Africa Today*, 1971.

Nolutshungu, S. C., 'Issues of the Afrikaner "enlightenment"' *African Affairs*, 1971.

— 'Party system, cleavage structure and electoral performance', *African Review*, 1973.

Ostrander, F. T., 'Zambia in the aftermath of Rhodesian UDI: logistical and economic problems', *African Forum*, 1967.

Person, Y., 'La France et l'Afrique noire: histoire d'une aliénation', *Le Mois en Afrique*, 1971.

Spacensky, A., 'Dix ans de rapports franco-malgaches', *Le Mois en Afrique*, 1970.

Spence, J., 'South Africa in the modern world', Wilson and Thompson (eds.), *Oxford History of South Africa*, III.

Sutcliffe, R. B., 'Stagnation and inequality in Rhodesia, 1946–68' unpublished seminar paper, R.I.I.A., 1971.

Zartman, W., 'Africa as a subordinate State system in international relations', in Doro and Stultz (eds.), *Governing in Black Africa*.

PERIODICAL PUBLICATIONS

Today's News (South Africa House, London).
Keesing's Contemporary Archives.
Africa Research Bulletin.
Africa Digest.

Africa Confidential.
Africa Contemporary Record.
Strategic Survey (Institute of Strategic Studies, London).
Newsletter of the Institute of Race Relations, London.
Survey of Race Relations (South African Institute of Race Relations).
Africa Report.
Press Digest (South African Information Department).
BBC Summary of World Broadcasts.
Thought (South African Institute of Race Relations).
Botswana Daily News.
Malawi News Agency Daily Bulletin.
Report from South Africa (South African Information Department).
FCI News: Official Journal of the South African Federation Chamber of Industries, later as *The Manufacturer.*
Press releases of various governments.

NEWSPAPERS

South Africa:

Die Burger.
Cape Times.
Pretoria News.
Star.
Die Transvaler.
Windhoek Advertiser.
Natal Mercury.
Daily Dispatch.
Die Vaderland.
Dagbreek en Sondagnuus.
Hoofstadnuus.
Rand Daily Mail.
Rapport.

Others:

Rhodesia Herald.
Northern News (Zambia).
Times of Zambia.
Zambia Daily Mail.
Standard (Tanzania).
Kenya Weekly News.
Daily Graphic (Ghana).
Afrique Nouvelle (Guinea).
Guardian (London).
The Times (London).
Observer (London).
Sunday Times (London).
Financial Times (London).

Index

Abbot affair, 284n
Abyssinia, 85, 155, 157, 261n, 275; *see also* Ethiopia
Accra conference, 78, 81
Acheampong, I. K., 285
Achewa, 216n
Action Group, 265
Addis Ababa, 81, 94, 264, 271
Africa Institute, 72, 99
African Charter, 45–8, 57; after Malan, 61; effects of political change on, 73, 88, 96
African Defence Organisation, 49, 61, 64, 68, 299
African Liberation Council, 81, 94, 265
African National Congress of South Africa, 81, 100, 106–7, 179, 182, 197
African National Congress of Zambia, 251
African Resistance Movement, 109
Afro-Asian group, 76, 82, 219
Ahidjo, A., 270
Air bases, 203, 204
Airmen, 65
Air space, violations of, 247, 253
Aitken, Sir Max, 182
Algeria, 19, 20, 261n, 264
American Pacific, 168
Amin, I. D., on 'dialogue', 273, 286; on domestic politics, 286; political relations, 286–8; thoughts of, 293
Anglo-American Corporation, 143, 167, 221, 222
Anglo-Transvaal, subsidiaries of, 143
Angola, assistance to, 7; relations of with Katanga, 88; investment projects in, 124; refugees from, 145; Afrikaners in, 165; trade with South Africa, 164–5; dam project in, 166; Brazilian trade mission to, 170n; political developments in, 170–3; South African role in, 173, 302; oil production in, 175; views

of Graaff on, 238; South African paramilitary activity in, 303
Argentina, 170n
Armies, 'native', 33, 68
Arms sales, Botswana's views on, 144; views of Lesotho on, 148–9; British, 183; Kaunda's mission against, 247–8, 271; French, 250
Arriaga, K. de, 227
Association of Chambers of Commerce of South Africa, 104
Atlantic, south, 70, 81, 169, 170
Atlantic Charter, 47
Atlantic Richfield, 265
Awolowo, Chief Obafemi, 265

Balewa, Sir Abubakar Tafawa, 265
Bamangwato, 29, 55, 139
Banco de Estado de São Paulo, 170n
Banda, H. K., visit of, to South Africa, 125, 148, 206–7, 206n; in Cairo, 192; in Cabinet crisis, 193, 215; rail links projected by, 193–194, 194n; UN policy of, 195; external political relations of, with liberation movements, 197; development projects, 197; criticism of OAU, 199; on 'dialogue', 199, 206n; on Portuguese colonialism, 203; on projected Cabora Bassa dam, 204; on liberation movements, 204–5; political motivation of, 215–17; psychological motivation of, 218; ideology of, 218; on visit of Muller, 262; insecurity of, 303
Bandung, 76, 84
Bank of Lisbon and South Africa, 166
Bantu Laws Amendment Act, 98
Bantustans, 116–19, 121, 143, 180, 207
Baring, Sir Evelyn, 28n
Barotseland, 250
Basterraad, 160